JAPHETH IN THE TENTS OF SHEM

STUDIES ON JEWISH HELLENISM IN ANTIQUITY

PIETER W. VAN DER HORST

JAPHETH IN THE TENTS OF SHEM

Studies on Jewish Hellenism in Antiquity

PEETERS

LEUVEN – PARIS – STERLING, VIRGINIA

2002

Library of Congress Cataloging-in-Publication Data
Horst, Pieter Willem van der.
Japheth in the tents of Shem: studies on Jewish Hellenism in antiquity/by
Pieter W. van der Horst.
p. cm. – (Contributions to biblical exegesis and theology; 32)
Includes bibliographical references (p.).
ISBN 9042911379 (alk. paper)
L. Judaism – History – Post-exilic period, 586 B.C.-210 A.D. 2.
Jews – Civilization – Greek influences. 3. Hellenism. I. Title. II. Series.

BM176 H575 2002
296 09 015-dc21

2002022972

© 2002 — Peeters, Bondgenotenlaan 153, B-3000 Leuven

ISBN 90-429-1137-9
D. 2002/0602/58

Abbreviations of reference works, series, and periodicals are those that are in
use in the *Journal of Biblical Literature*.

CONTENTS

PREFACE

In 1994 I published a volume of essays entitled *Hellenism – Judaism – Christianity: Essays on Their Interaction.* A second and much expanded edition appeared in 1998 (Leuven: Peeters). Since then my interest in the topics treated in that book, especially in the interaction between Jewish and Hellenistic culture, has intensified, and this has resulted in the research presented here. The present volume contains 15 essays, most of which have been previously published (and have been updated here), while some are new. All of the essays were written within the framework of the research programme, "The Cultural Milieu of Early Christianity" at Utrecht University's Faculty of Theology, of which I have been the director for the last decade of the 20th century. It is this 'cultural milieu of early Christianity' in the broader sense that constitutes the unifying factor in this volume, as in the previous. Collecting and interpreting evidence for the study of religion, philosophy, languages and literature in the near-millennium between Alexander the Great and Muhammad has been, and still is, the focus of the Utrecht research programme.

Inevitably, when essays are written on related subjects for different occasions, there tends to be some overlap, as is the case in this volume between the chapters 5 and 6, and 14 and 15. I have not tried to eliminate this overlapping in the final version because this would have damaged the internal structure of some of the contributions making it difficult, or even impossible, to read them as self-contained studies. The author trusts that the disadvantage of some overlap is outweighed by the advantage of having readable essays.

The title motif of this volume is taken from Gen. 9:27 where Noah says that "Japheth will dwell in the tents of Shem." In early rabbinic tradition this was believed to mean that in the tents of Shem, *i.e.*, among the Jewish people, the words of the Torah may be read in the language of Japheth, *i.e.*, Greek (see *Genesis Rabba* XXXVI 8 and b. *Megillah* 9b). This interpretation was put forward in the context of a discussion on the validity of the Septuagint, the first Greek translation of the Torah. Later this expression became a metaphor for the development of a Judaeo-Greek culture.

I am grateful to Peeters for their willingness to again publish a volume of my essays. I would like to thank the other publishing houses mentioned in the ackowledgements for their permission to reprint the articles. I owe a special debt of thanks to my friend Dr. James N. Pankhurst for being so kind to correct the English of almost all the articles in this volume. I hope that the readers will experience as much pleasure reading these contributions as I did writing them.

Utrecht, December 2001

ACKNOWLEDGEMENTS

1. 'Greek in Jewish Palestine in the Light of Jewish Epigraphy,' in J.J. Collins & G.E. Sterling (eds.), *Hellenism in the Land of Israel*, Notre Dame: University of Notre Dame Press, 2001, 154-174
2. 'The Last Jewish Patriarch(s) and Graeco-Roman Medicine' (unpublished)
3. 'Neglected Greek Evidence for Early Jewish Liturgical Prayer,' *Journal for the Study of Judaism* 29 (1998) 278-296
4. 'Was the Synagogue a Place of Sabbath Worship Before 70 CE?,' in S. Fine (ed.), *Jews, Christians, and Polytheists in the Ancient Synagogue. Cultural Interaction during the Graeco-Roman Period*, London-New York: Routledge, 1999, 18-43
5. 'The Greek Synagogue Prayers in the *Apostolic Constitutions* book VII,' in J. Tabory (ed.), *From Qumran to Cairo. Studies in the History of Prayer*, Jerusalem: Orchot, 1999, 19-46
6. 'Jews and Christians in Antioch at the End of the Fourth Century,' in S.E. Porter & B.W.R. Pearson (edd.), *Christian-Jewish Relations Through the Centuries*, Sheffield: Sheffield Academic Press, 2000, 228-238
7. 'The Tombs of the Prophets in Early Judaism,' English version of *Die Prophetengräber im antiken Judentum* (Franz-Delitzsch-Vorlesung 2000), Münster: Institutum Judaicum Delitzschianum, 2001
8. 'Antediluvian Knowledge: Graeco-Roman and Jewish Speculations About Wisdom From Before the Flood,' expanded version of 'Wisdom From Time Immemorial: Ancient Speculations About Antediluvian Knowledge,' in: C. Kroon & D. den Hengst (eds.), *Ultima Aetas: Time, Tense and Transience in the Ancient World. Studies in Honour of Jan den Boeft*, Amsterdam: VU University Press, 2000, 95-106
9. '*Sortes*: Sacred Books as Instant Oracles in Late Antiquity,' in L.V. Rutgers, P.W. van der Horst, H.W. Havelaar, L. Teugels (eds.), *The Use of Sacred Books in the Ancient World* (Contributions to Biblical Exegesis and Theology 22), Leuven: Peeters, 1998, 143-174
10. 'Celibacy in Early Judaism,' English version of 'Celibaat in het vroege jodendom,' *Kerk & Theologie* 52 (2001) 22-32
11. 'Maria Alchemista, the First Female Jewish Author,' *Zutot* 1 (2001)
12. 'Who Was Apion?' (unpublished)
13. 'The Distinctive Vocabulary of Josephus' *Contra Apionem*,' in L.H. Feldman & J.R. Levison (edd.), *Josephus'* Contra Apionem: *Studies in its Character and Context* (AGAJU 34), Leiden: Brill, 1996, 83-93
14. 'The Samaritan Languages in the Pre-Islamic Period,' *Journal for the Study of Judaism* 32 (2001) 178-192
15. 'Samaritans at Rome?' (unpublished)

ABBREVIATIONS

ABD	Anchor Bible Dictionary
ANRW	Aufstieg und Niedergang der Römischen Welt
ARW	Archiv für Religionswissenschaft
BAR	Biblical Archaeology Review
BASOR	Bulletin of the American School of Oriental Research
BICS	Bulletin of the Institute for Classical Studies
BKAT	Biblischer Kommentar zum Alten Testament
BPhW	Berliner Philologische Wochenschrift
CIJ	Corpus Inscriptionum Judaicarum
CPh	Classical Philology
CPJ	Corpus Papyrorum Judaicarum
CRINT	Compendia Rerum Iudaicarum ad Novum Testamentum
DDD	Dictionary of Deity and Demons in the Bible
EKK	Evangelisch-Katholischer Kommentar
Enc. Jud.	Encyclopaedia Judaica
ERE	Encyclopedia of Religion and Ethics
FGH	Fragmente der griechischen Historiker
GLAJJ	Greek and Latin Authors on Jews and Judaism
HTR	Harvard Theological Review
HUCA	Hebrew Union College Annual
ICS	Illinois Classical Studies
IEJ	Israel Exploration Journal
JBL	Journal of Biblical Literature
JHS	Journal of Hellenic Studies
JQR	Jewish Quarterly Review
JSHRZ	Jüdische Schriften aus hellenistisch-römischer Zeit
JTS	Journal of Theological Studies
KP	Der Kleine Pauly
LCL	Loeb Classical Library
NP	Der Neue Pauly
NTS	New Testament Studies
OCD	Oxford Classical Dictionary
PG	Patrologia Graeca (ed. Migne)
PLRE	Prosopography of the Later Roman Empire
RAC	Reallexikon für Antike und Christentum
RE	Paulys Realencyclopädie der Classischen Altertumswissenschaft
REJ	Revue des Études Juives
Rev. Bibl.	Revue Biblique
RGG	Religion in Geschichte und Gegenwart
RHPhR	Revue d'histoire et de philosophie religieuses
RHR	Revue de l'histoire des religions
SEG	Supplementum Epigraphicum Graecum

TRE	Theologische Realenzyklopädie
TWNT	Theologisches Wörterbuch zum Neuen Testament
VC	Vigiliae Christianae
WBC	Word Biblical Commentary
ZDMG	Zeitschrift der deutschen morgenländischen Gesellschaft
ZNW	Zeitschrift für neutestamentliche Wissenschaft
ZPE	Zeitschrift für Papyrologie und Epigraphik

1. GREEK IN JEWISH PALESTINE IN THE LIGHT OF JEWISH EPIGRAPHY

I, Justus, the son of Leontius and of Sappho, lie (here) dead,
(I) who, after having plucked the fruit of all (kinds of) wisdom,
left the light, (and left also) my poor parents in endless mourning,
and my brothers too, alas, in my Beth She'arim.
And having gone to Hades, I, Justus, lie here now
with many of my own kindred, since mighty Fate so willed.
– Be of good courage, Justus, (for) no one is immortal.[1] *–*

This epitaph of a boy with a Latin name, the son of a father with a Greek name and a mother with a Greek name (that of the best-known Greek poetess at that), is written in Homeric hexameters; it follows a number of well-known Greek conventions in the composition of epitaphs; it mentions Hades and Moira (the Greek goddess of Fate). Yet it is Jewish! It was written by a Jew in the first half of the third century CE and it was found in the impressive catacombs of the rabbinic city of Beth She'arim where famous rabbis were also buried since the beginning of the third century. And Justus – or at least his family – apparently felt at home there: the stone speaks, with "evident pleasure,"[2] of "*my* Beth She'arim" (line 4). Here we see our topic in a nutshell. But it is a topic that bristles with problems.

The study of the Hellenization of Palestine in the light of epigraphical sources is hampered right from the start by a very serious handicap. This handicap is that there is no comprehensive corpus of all the epigraphic material from the Land of Israel covering the period between Alexander the Great and Muhammad. If we want to base our argument on a comprehensive survey of inscriptions for this near-millennium, we

---

[1] Κεῖμαι Λεοντεῖδης νέκυς Σαφοῦς υἱὸς Ἰοῦστος
ὃς πάσης σοφίης δρεψάμενος καρπὸν
λεῖψα φάος, δειλοὺς γονέας ἀκαχημένους αἰεί,
αὐτοκασιγνήτους τε, οἴμοι, ἐν οἷς Βεσάροις
καί γ᾽ ἐλθὼν εἰς Ἅδην Ἰοῦστος (...) αὐτόθι κεῖμαι,
σὺν πόλλοισιν ἑοῖς, ἐπὶ ἤθελε Μοῖρα κραταίη.
– Θάρσει, Ἰοῦστε, οὐδεὶς ἀθάνατος. –

[2] Thus the editors, M. Schwabe and B. Lifshitz, *Beth She'arim II: The Greek Inscriptions*, New Brunswick: Rutgers University Press, 1974, 107. The inscription is no. 127 in their collection.

are completely at a loss, since one would have to consult many hundreds of books, periodicals and museum catalogues in order to get an overview of the evidence. Collecting and publishing all this material would be a mammoth task far beyond the capabilities of one scholar; only a team would be able to do so. Most fortunately there is such a team now, but the project is still in its infancy (alas for me). The *Corpus Inscriptionum Iudaeae/Palestinae* (CIIP) will be a new corpus of all inscriptions, in all languages, arranged topographically, found in Israel (including the West Bank, Gaza, and the Golan Heights) and dating from the 4th century BCE to the 7th century CE. I owe this description to Professor Jonathan Price from Tel Aviv University who initiated the whole enterprise. The corpus will include a full re-editing of every text, a drawing or photograph, textual apparatus, English translation, and commentary. The estimate is that there will be between 6000 and 7000 texts in the corpus.[3] This is exactly the tool we need if we want to carry out the type of investigation that is the topic of this paper. But we simply do not have it now, so we will just have to make do. But what *do* we have?

As to the Jewish material, we have first of all the old Frey.[4] In the much maligned second volume of his *Corpus Inscriptionum Iudaicarum* (henceforth: *CIJ*), he collected some 530 Jewish inscriptions from Palestine. This is still, in spite of all its shortcomings,[5] a very valuable collection, but when we compare the number of 530 texts to the estimated 1800 texts in the provisional database of Jonathan Price (which admittedly is still incomplete), we can gauge how great the progress in this field has been in the past six decades or so. To mention only the most important partial collections that have appeared after 1952 and pertain to ancient Palestine, we have the group of epitaphs edited by B. Bagatti and J. T. Milik in their book *Gli scavi del Dominus Flevit (Monte Oliveto –*

---

[3] Other scholars involved in the project include Benjamin Isaac, Hannah Cotton, Leah di Segni, Ada Yardeni, Werner Eck, Alla Stein, and Israel Roll.

[4] J.-B. Frey, *Corpus Inscriptionum Judaicarum*, vol. 2, Vatican City: Pontificio istituto di archelogia cristiana, 1952. Vol. 2 covers Asia and Africa. Vol. 1, which was published in 1936 but was reprinted with an extensive Prolegomenon by Baruch Lifshitz in 1975 (published by Ktav), covers Europe. I leave out of account here the still older and more outdated collections by J. Oehler, "Epigraphische Beiträge zur Geschichte des Judentums," *Monatsschrift für Geschichte und Wissenschaft des Judentums* 53 (1909) 292-302, 443-452, 525-538; S. Klein, *Jüdisch-Palästinisches Corpus Inscriptionum* of 1920; and P. Thomsen, *Die lateinischen und griechischen Inschriften der Stadt Jerusalem* of 1922.

[5] See L. Robert, *Bulletin Epigraphique III (1952-1958)*, Paris: Les Belles Lettres, 1974, no. 24 (pp. 101-104).

Gerusalemme). Parte I: La necropoli del periodo romano (Jerusalem: Franciscan Publishing House, 1958). We also have the fine volumes with the epitaphs from Beth She'arim by B. Mazar, *Beth She'arim I: Report on the Excavations 1936-1940* (Jerusalem: Massada, 1973), by M. Schwabe and B. Lifshitz, *Beth She'arim II: The Greek Inscriptions* (New Brunswick: Rutgers University Press, 1974), and by N. Avigad, *Beth She'arim III: Report on the Excavations during 1953-1958* (Jerusalem: Massada, 1976). There are further two important books in modern Hebrew: J. Naveh, *On Stone and Mosaic. The Aramaic and Hebrew Inscriptions from Ancient Synagogues* (Jerusalem: Sifriyat Ma'ariv, 1978) and its Greek counterpart by L. Roth-Gerson, *The Greek Inscriptions from the Synagogues in Eretz-Israel* (Jerusalem: Yad Yitzhak ben Zvi, 1987). An important new collection is also to be found in the publication by R. Hachlili of the epitaphs of the so-called Goliath family in Jericho ("The Goliath Family in Jericho: Funerary Inscriptions from a First-Century A.D. Jewish Monumental Tomb," *BASOR* 235 [1979] 31-65). And finally there is the recent collection of ossuaries and their inscriptions by L.Y. Rahmani, *A Catalogue of Jewish Ossuaries in the Collections of the State of Israel* (Jerusalem: Israel Academy, 1994).[6] For the rest of the material one has to consult a very wide variety of scholarly journals over which most of the new finds are scattered (but especially in the *Israel Exploration Journal* and the *Revue Biblique*), and the annual instalments of the 'Bulletin Epigraphique' in the *Revue des études grecques* (since 1938) for the Greek material. The best way to keep track of new Jewish inscriptions in Greek, however, is to consult the section "Palaestina" in the annual *Supplementum Epigraphicum Graecum* (= SEG), even though, inevitably, it is always lagging years behind.[7] For tracing new inscriptions in Hebrew and Aramaic the *Bulletin d'épigraphie sémitique (BES)*, published in the periodical *Syria* (since 1967), is the best tool.[8]

There is a considerable overlap between some of the above-mentioned collections that has to be taken into account. When we add up what we

---

[6] One might add recent publications such as the book by R.C. Gregg & D. Urman, *Jews, Pagans, and Christians in the Golan Heights. Greek and Other Inscriptions of the Roman and Byzantine Eras* (Atlanta: Scholars Press, 1997), but that is a collection of not only Jewish, but also pagan and Christian epigraphical material; it will be left out of account here also because for too many of these 240 inscriptions the religious affiliation cannot be established at all.

[7] Very useful also is the *Guide de l'épigraphiste*, edd. F. Bérard *et al.*, Paris: Ecole Normale Supérieure, 1989; 3rd ed., completely revised, Editions Rue d'Ulm, 2000.

[8] It is also useful to check the Hebrew journal *Hadashot Arkheologiot*. See further my *Ancient Jewish Epitaphs*, Kampen: Kok Pharos, 1991, 13-15.

have in the volumes mentioned here and subtract the overlapping items, we arrive at a total of some 900 inscriptions, which is still a very far cry from the 1800 in the CIIP database. The situation is still worse as far as Christian and Pagan material is concerned, and that is a good reason to limit ourselves here to the Jewish evidence in order not to complicate things further, although it is important to keep in mind that, if we leave the Jewish material aside, "from the third century BCE we find almost exclusively Greek inscriptions in Palestine."[9] And these run into the thousands (possibly some 6.000).

When we now try to establish the percentage of Greek inscriptions in the Jewish evidence, we find that of Frey's 530 inscriptions 315 are in Greek (several of them in fact being bilingual);[10] which is 60%. Of the 43 inscriptions from the cemetery of Dominus Flevit 12 are in Greek; which is 29%. In Beth She'arim, however, of the 246 epitaphs no less than 218 are in Greek; which is 88%. Of the 32 tomb inscriptions of the Goliath family 17 are in Greek, which is 53%. And of Rahmani's 240 inscribed ossuaries 87 are in Greek (16 of which are bilingual); which is 37%.[11] These percentages vary widely, from 29 to 88% (and we will have to come back to that), but anyway the overall average of Greek inscriptions is slightly more than 53%.[12]

How does this compare to the average in the provisional database of the CIIP? The percentage of Greek inscriptions in this comprehensive collection has not yet been established, but Professor Price was so kind to let me know that his provisional estimate is that "of the Jewish inscriptions well over half, I would say even 70% have some Greek writing on them."[13] He adds the important observation that this includes not only the inscriptions which are exclusively Greek but also

---

[9] M. Hengel, *Judaism and Hellenism*, London: SCM Press, 1974, vol. 1, 58.

[10] In 1974 Mussies counted 440 Jewish inscriptions in Greek in Palestine on the basis of CIJ and SEG; see G. Mussies, "Greek in Palestine and the Diaspora," in S. Safrai & M. Stern (edd.), *The Jewish People in the First Century 2* (CRINT I 2), Assen: Van Gorcum, 1976, 1042.

[11] Roth-Gerson's book is left out of account here since it contains purposefully only Greek inscriptions.

[12] I do not know on the basis of what data Lee Levine can state that "the overall percentage of Greek inscriptions in Roman-Byzantine Palestine jumps to over 55 percent" (L. I. Levine, *Judaism and Hellenism in Antiquity: Conflict or Confluence*, Seattle – London: University of Washington Press, 1998, 180), but he is certainly very close to the truth. For if we would add to these statistics the fact that in the still unpublished collection of 30 ossuaries from Scythopolis all of them contain only Greek inscriptions, the average percentage indeed "jumps to over 55 percent"!

[13] E-mail communication of 18 Dec. 1998. Price cautiously adds, "but don't hold me to this!"

the considerable number which are bilingual, containing both Greek and Hebrew or Aramaic. Interestingly enough, Latin makes no appearance in the Jewish inscriptions from Palestine.[14] If for safety's sake we round off Price's impression that the Greek material is well over half, maybe even 70%, to – say – 60%, we see something very significant. This is not only rather close to the average of 53% that we have just arrived at, but it is also exactly the percentage of Greek inscriptions in the old collection of Frey. So even though in the past 65 years[15] the material has more than tripled, the numerical ratio of Greek and non-Greek material has not changed at all![16] And that is a striking and very important observation.

If more than half of the Jewish epigraphic material from the period between Alexander and Muhammad is in Greek, what does that tell us? Can we readily draw the conclusion that for more than half of the Jewish people in their homeland their native language was Greek, not Aramaic?[17] That would be overhasty, for we first have to address the question of the representativeness of this material. Can we say, for instance, with Lee Levine, on the basis of the fact that some 37% of the Jerusalem ossuaries are in Greek, that "we can *safely* [italics added] set this number as the minimum percentage of those inhabitants in the city who preferred Greek"?[18] Can we follow Martin Hengel who, on the basis of some 40% Greek ossuary inscriptions in Jerusalem concludes

---

[14] Cf. the remark by H.B. Rosén: "Das Lateinische konnte sich den palästinischen Sprachen nicht als Prestigesprache gegenüberstellen, nicht nur weil es in Palästina auf ein bereits fest verankertes und eingewurzeltes Griechisch gestoßen ist, sondern wohl eher deshalb, weil dieses Griechisch Träger einer spezifischen Landes- und Nationalkultur war, die man heute jüdischen Hellenismus nennt, und weil die Sprachen Palästinas Ausdrucksmittel einer mehr als tausendjährigen Literatur waren, welche der lateinischen weder an geistigem Prestige noch an Verwurzelung im Volke in irgendeiner Weise nachstand" (in "Die Sprachsituation im römischen Palästina," in his *East and West: Selected Writings in Linguistics,* vol. I, München: Wilhelm Fink, 1982, 489; cf. *ibid.* 493-494).

[15] Even though *CIJ* II was published only in 1952, Frey's volume reflects the 'Stand der Forschung' of the early thirties of our century.

[16] The percentage of Greek inscriptions in the Jewish Diaspora is ca. 85%. See my *Het Nieuwe Testament en de joodse grafinscripties uit de Hellenistisch-Romeinse tijd,* Utrecht: Faculteit der Godgeleerdheid, 1991.

[17] On Aramaic as the principal spoken language of Palestine see E. Schürer, *The History of the Jewish People in the Age of Jesus Christ,* vol. II, Edinburgh: Clark, 1979, 20-28 (with bibliography). For a similar discussion about the choice of language for Jewish epitaphs in Italy see D. Noy, "Writing in Tongues: The Use of Greek, Latin and Hebrew in Jewish Inscriptions from Roman Italy," *Journal of Jewish Studies* 48 (1997) 300-311; and cf. L. V. Rutgers, *The Jews in Late Ancient Rome. Evidence of Cultural Interaction in the Roman Diaspora,* Leiden: Brill, 1995, 176-209.

[18] Levine, *Judaism and Hellenism in Antiquity* 76.

as follows: "Auch wenn man davon ausgeht, daß Ossuarinschriften überwiegend von Gliedern der Mittel- und Oberschicht stammen, so darf man doch annehmen, daß ca. 10-15% der damaligen Bewohner Jerusalems als Muttersprache Griechisch sprachen"?[19] Should we agree with Baruch Lifshitz, who confidently states: "La proportion des textes épigraphiques grecs par rapport à la quantité des inscriptions découvertes à Jérusalem témoigne de l'emploi de la langue grecque par une partie assez considérable de la population de la ville"?[20] These are very difficult questions, the more so if we take seriously Josephus' somewhat enigmatic remark, "Our people do not favour those who have mastered the languages of many nations" (*Ant.* XX 264).[21]

Demographers of the ancient world constantly have to struggle with the problem of the scarcity and the questionable representativeness of the sources. To give an example: Of the various classes into which ancient Greek and Latin inscriptions fall, by far the largest numerically is that of epitaphs. In many tens of thousands of these inscriptions the age at death is mentioned. But, as a specialist in the epigraphy and demography of the Roman Empire has calculated,[22] even so we only know the age at death of ca. 0,015% of all people in the first 5 centuries of the Empire. (He made the calculation on the basis of the assumption that in 500 years there are approximately 16 generations, each of which on average counted some 20 million people; this total of some 320 million divided by the total number of inscriptions with age indication yields 0,015%). Even if these numbers needed to be substantially corrected, the overall picture would hardly change. We will always remain far below 1% of the total population. This fact raises the serious problem of how representative this less than 1% is for the population of the Empire as a whole.[23] As a matter of fact that completely depends upon whether or not we can

---

[19] Hengel, "Der vorchristliche Paulus" in M. Hengel & U. Heckel (edd.), *Paulus und das antike Judentum*, Tübingen: Mohr, 1991, 257-258. In "Jerusalem als jüdische und hellenistische Stadt," in his *Judaica, hellenistica et christiana: Kleine Schriften II*, Tübingen: Mohr, 1999, 147, Hengel speaks of 10-20%.

[20] Lifshitz in "Jérusalem sous la domination romaine," *Aufstieg und Niedergang der Römischen Welt* II 8, New York – Berlin: W. de Gruyter, 1977, 459. Cf. also M. Hadas, *Hellenistic Culture: Fusion and Diffusion*, New York – London: Columbia University Press, 1959, 36: "The most forceful evidence that Greek had become the vernacular comes from epigraphy."

[21] See T. Rajak, *Josephus: The Historian and His Society*, London: Duckworth, 1983, 46-50.

[22] M. Clauss, "Probleme der Lebensalterstatistiken aufgrund römischer Grabinschriften," *Chiron* 3 (1973) 395-417, here 411.

[23] See, e.g., R. MacMullen, "The Epigraphic Habit in the Roman Empire," *American Journal of Philology* 103 (1982) 233-246.

clearly get into the picture the possibly distorting factors in the data at our disposal. There are distorting factors, although to what extent they really distort our picture is a matter of ongoing debate. Let us review here only the most important of them and try to find out how these factors may have influenced our Jewish material from Palestine.

Although it is certainly true that the only area in which the influence of Hellenistic culture upon the Jewish people can be more or less quantified is the realm of epigraphy,[24] we have to ask what is the statistical status of our data. To begin with the number of inscriptions as compared to the number of Jews in our period, we have to concede that it is indeed only an extremely tiny minority of whom we have their epitaphs or honorary inscriptions. If we take our period, spanning almost a thousand years, to have comprised about 33 generations (30 years for one generation, for the sake of convenience), and if we take a generation as averaging 1 million Jews (in Palestine only, that is),[25] then we have 900 inscriptions for 33 million Jews: that is to say, one inscription for every 37.000 Jews. Even if the average number of Jews per generation would have to be further reduced or if we would take the ca. 1800 inscriptions of the CIIP project as our basis, we would not even reach 0,025%. From a statistical point of view that is a hopeless situation, for what can we say about the 99,975% other Jews whose tombstones or honorary inscriptions have not been preserved, if ever they had one? To put it another way: Is it possible that the Greek inscriptions belong only to a very tiny upper class of less than 1% of the Jews whereas the vast majority of the people would never phrase their inscriptions in Greek? This is an extremely improbable suggestion, it would seem to me, for the following reasons.

Many Jews were definitely too poor to erect tombstones inscribed with epitaphs, but that does not necessarily imply that the inscribed stones we do have all derive from the upper classes. There is ample evidence that the epitaphs in Greek represent a wide stratum of the population.[26] There

---

[24] Thus Levine, *Judaism and Hellenism* 180.

[25] To be sure, this number is an estimate and also 2 million or half a million could be a reasonable estimate, but for the present purposes that hardly makes a difference. In the scholarly literature on the subject the estimates vary from half a million to 5 million; see the surveys in A. Byatt, "Josephus and Population Numbers in First Century Palestine," *Palestine Exploration Quarterly* 105 (1973) 51-60, and G. Stemberger, "Juden," *Reallexikon für Antike und Christentum* 19 (Lieferung 147, 1998) 172. By assuming a Jewish population of 1 million we keep on the safe side; so does R. H. Pfeiffer, *History of New Testament Times*, New York: Harper, 1949, 189.

[26] See J. Barr, "Hebrew, Aramaic and Greek," in *The Cambridge History of Judaism*, ed. W. D. Davies & L. Finkelstein, vol. II, Cambridge University Press 1989, 102 with n. 4. The same applies to the Jewish epitaphs of Rome; see H.J. Leon, *The Jews of*

is a great difference between a metrical epitaph in Homeric hexameters engraved upon luxurious and expensive sarcophagi with elaborate decorations on the one hand and poorly scratched names on potsherds or wall-plaster that marked the graves of deceased on the other (and we have many of the latter sort). The former is a manifestation of wealth and status; the latter is usually the contrary (though not necessarily so). To be sure, "the desire to emulate Graeco-Roman mores (and the means to do so) was far more pronounced among the upper than the lower social strata,"[27] but there are numerous very simple and poorly executed tombstones with inscriptions in poor Greek that undeniably stem from these lower strata of Jewish society. The persons who had their tombstones in Beth She'arim inscribed with Greek epitaphs include not only rabbis and public officers but also merchants and craftsmen.[28] Lieberman already wrote that "the very poverty and vulgarity of the language of these inscriptions shows that it was spoken by the people and not written by learned men only."[29] As to the many synagogue inscriptions in Greek collected by Lea Roth-Gerson,[30] there can be little doubt that most of them were meant to be read by the regular visitors of these buildings, that is, the common people who were members of the local community, who were supposed to be able to make sense of them. And no doubt they were. As Goodenough remarked: "The Jews who went to the synagogues (...) admired the Aramaic or Hebrew but read the Greek."[31]

Ancient Rome, Peabody: Hendrickson, 1995 (= repr. of the 1960 ed.), 75-92, and Rutgers, *Jews of Late Ancient Rome*, passim. Feldman's theory that so many ossuaries have inscriptions in Greek only to prevent non-Jews from molesting the graves is absolutely not convincing; see L. H. Feldman, *Jew and Gentile in the Ancient World: Attitudes and Interaction from Alexander to Justinian*, Princeton: Princeton University Press, 1993, 14 and 22 (the whole first chapter of this book, pp. 3-44, is directed against Martin Hengel c.s.).

[27] Levine, *Judaism and Hellenism in Antiquity* 24.

[28] See R. Hachlili, *Ancient Jewish Art and Archaeology in the Land of Israel*, Leiden: Brill, 1988, 103.

[29] S. Lieberman, *Greek in Jewish Palestine*, New York: Feldheim, 1965, 30. See also the conclusion of J.N. Sevenster, *Do You Know Greek? How Much Greek Could the First Jewish Christians Have Known?*, Leiden: Brill, 1968, 183. A comparable instance of that category is the motley mixture of graffiti in the necropolis of Maresha/Marissa, which were definitely scratched there by common people, for the Greek is vulgar and has many orthographic errors, but it is Greek these people (partly Idumaeans, partly Phoenicians) wrote. See SEG VIII 247-261 and SEG XLII 1439-1454, with Rosén, "Sprachsituation" 504, and Sevenster, *Do You Know Greek?* 112-113.

[30] See her book mentioned above in the text. More than one third of the synagogue inscriptions from Israel are in Greek.

[31] E. R. Goodenough, *Jewish Symbols in the Greco-Roman Period* II, New York: Pantheon Books (Bollen Foundation), 1954, 123.

In this connection it is important to notice that it is not only in Jewish, but also in Samaritan synagogues that dedicatory or honorary inscriptions were in Greek. The seven inscriptions uncovered in the recently excavated Samaritan synagogue in El-Khirbe are all in Greek.[32] And that is not an isolated case. In Ramat Aviv, to the north of Tel Aviv, an excavation of an ancient Samaritan synagogue has yielded three inscriptions: one in Samaritan Aramaic, two in Greek, the only complete one reading "Blessing and peace be upon Israel and upon this place, Amen". And also in another Samaritan synagogue in ancient Palestine, in Beth She'an-Skythopolis, three of the four inscriptions found there are in Greek, only one in Samaritan Aramaic.[33] This evidence corroborates the impression we get on the basis of the Jewish material.[34] It may be an exaggeration to say with A. W. Argyle, "To suggest that a Jewish boy growing up in Galilee would not know Greek would be rather like suggesting that a Welsh boy brought up in Cardiff would not know English,"[35] but it is certainly not as far from the truth as many of his critics would claim.[36]

Moreover, the epigraphic material itself should not be considered in isolation. Papyri,[37] the legends of coins,[38] and the literary sources[39] also

---

[32] SEG XLII 1423-1429.

[33] See G. Reeg, *Die antiken Synagogen in Israel, II: Die samaritanischen Synagogen,* Wiesbaden: Reichert, 1977, 572-3, 631. See now also SEG XLII 1474 for another new Greek inscription from a Samaritan synagogue in Israel.

[34] For a wider survey of Samaritan evidence for Hellenistic influence see my essay "Samaritans and Hellenism" in my *Hellenism – Judaism – Christianity: Essays on Their Interaction,* Leuven: Peeters, 1998 (2nd ed.), 49-58.

[35] A. W. Argyle, "Greek Among the Jews of Palestine in New Testament Times," *New Testament Studies* 20 (1973/74) 88.

[36] The whole debate is summarized by G.H.R. Horsley, *New Documents Illustrating Early Christianity,* vol. 5, Macquarie University: The Ancient History Documentary Research Centre, 1989, 21.

[37] See S.E. Porter, "The Greek Papyri of the Judaean Desert and the World of the Roman East," in S.E. Porter & C.E. Evans (edd.), *The Scrolls and the Scriptures. Qumran Fifty Years After,* Sheffield: Sheffield Academic Press, 1997, 293-316, and H.M. Cotton, W.E.H. Cockle & F.G.B. Millar, "The Papyrology of the Roman Near East: A Survey," *Journal of Roman Studies* 85 (1995) 214-235.

[38] Though they are hard to use for the present purpose because coins were instruments of propaganda. See Y. Meshorer, *Jewish Coins of the Second Temple Period,* Tel Aviv: Am Hasefer, 1967; Y. Meshorer, *City Coins of Eretz Israel and the Decapolis,* Jerusalem: Israel Museum, 1985. Cf. the remarks by J. C. Greenfield, "The Languages of Palestine, 200 BCE – 200 CE," in H. H. Paper (ed.), *Jewish Languages. Theme and Variations,* Cambridge, MA: Association for Jewish Studies, 1978, 147, and by F. E. Peters in his response, *ibid.* 161.

[39] For a short survey of Palestinian Jewish writings in Greek see S. E. Porter, "Jesus and the Use of Greek in Galilee," in B. Chilton & C. A. Evans (edd.), *Studying the Historical Jesus,* Leiden: Brill, 1994, 139-142. Also Hengel, *Judaism and Hellenism* 88-102.

suggest strongly that many Jews in Judaea and the Galilee were able to speak or understand Greek, even if they did not belong to the upper classes. There is, for instance, the much debated and very significant Greek papyrus letter by Soumaios from the Bar Kochba archive (one of the three that are in Greek, P. Yadin 52 = SB VIII 9843).[40] However great its problems of interpretation may be,[41] it almost certainly does imply that the author (perhaps Bar Kochba himself or at least one of his fellow soldiers) was not able to write Hebrew or Aramaic and for that reason wrote the letter in Greek (ἐγράφη δὲ Ἑληνιστὶ διὰ τ[ὸ ...]μαν μὴ εὑρηθῆναι Ἑβραεστὶ γράψασθαι). Even though of the some thirty documents in this archive the vast majority (90%) are deliberately in Hebrew and Aramaic,[42] which is quite understandable in a religiously motivated and nationalist revolt, there are three documents in Greek. And there can be little doubt that this was due to the fact that for many (but how many?) Palestinian Jews Greek, the *lingua franca* of the Near East in the Roman period, had become the language of their daily life, even for the followers of the Jewish leader of the second revolt against Rome who used the archaic Hebrew script on his coins.[43] This letter from the Bar Kochba archive demonstrates that this did not apply to the cultural elite only, for the letter was written in a sloppy hand and bristles with spelling errors. Moreover, Soumaios expected his Jewish addressees to be able to read the Greek letter, besides the other ones addressed to them in Hebrew and Aramaic.[44] Similar observations could

---

[40] *Editio princeps* by B. Lifshitz, "Papyrus grecs du désert de Juda," *Aegyptus* 42 (1962) 240-256. Re-editions include J. T. Fitzmyer in "The Languages of Palestine in the First Century A.D." in his *A Wandering Aramean. Collected Aramaic Essays*, Missoula: Scholars Press, 1979, 29-56, here p. 36 (now conveniently reprinted in S. E. Porter, *The Language of the New Testament: Classic Essays*, Sheffield: Sheffield Academic Press, 1991, 126-162, here p. 142).

[41] Good recent surveys of the debate and assessments of the problems are B. Rochette, "Le SB VIII 9843 et la position du grec en Palestine aux deux premiers siècles après J.-C.," *Archiv für Papyrusforschung* 44 (1998) 42-46, and L. Devillers, "Le lettre de Soumaïos et les Ioudaioi johanniques," *Revue Biblique* 105 (1998) 556-581.

[42] See F. Millar, *The Roman Near East, 37 BC – AD 337*, Cambridge MA – London: Harvard University Press, 1993, 545-552, for a useful survey of all the documents, with the update by Cotton, Cockle & Millar, "The Papyrology of the Roman Near East" 229-231.

[43] L. Mildenberg, "Der Bar-Kochba-Krieg im Lichte der Münzprägungen," in H. P. Kuhnen, *Palästina in griechisch-römischer Zeit* (Handbuch der Archäologie II 2), München: Beck, 1990, 357-366; idem, *The Coinage of the Bar Kochba War*, Aarau – Frankfurt: Verlag Sauerländer, 1984.

[44] In view of this data it is hard to understand how the great papyrologist Herbert Youtie can state, "Greek never became a vital linguistic factor in Palestine comparable to Hebrew or Aramaic"; see his response to Jonas Greenfield in Paper (ed.), *Jewish Languages* 157.

be made, *mutatis mutandis*, on the Murabba'at papyri and the documents from the Babatha archive, the majority of which are in Greek.[45] In this connection it is telling that of the 609 papyri from the Roman Near East in general found outside Egypt – the *vast* majority of which are from Roman and Byzantine Palestine – some 325 are in Greek: that is almost 55%![46]

The important observation in rabbinic literature to the effect that in Caesarea Maritima (and certainly also elsewhere) synagogue services were conducted in Greek leads to the same conclusion,[47] which in its turn is confirmed by the famous Justinian *Novella* 146 (of the year 553 CE).[48] Also, the fact that so many inscriptions are bilingual, containing Hebrew or Aramaic with Greek translation, may be an indication that for many Greek was more readily understandable than the other two languages. Telling, too, are the finds of Greek documents in Qumran, Massada, and other sites of the Judaean desert, and the thousands of Greek loanwords in rabbinic literature (and several even in the Copper Scroll from Qumran).[49] But all this has already been so eloquently and elaborately argued by Martin Hengel that it is superfluous to go into the matter again.[50] It is

[45] See P. Benoit, J. T. Milik & R. de Vaux (edd.), *Les grottes de Murabba'at*, 2 vols., Oxford: Oxford University Press, 1961, and N. Lewis, *The Documents From the Bar Kokhba Period in the Cave of Letters: Greek Papyri,* Jerusalem: Israel Exploration Society, 1989. Of the 36 documents in the Babatha archive 26 are in Greek.

[46] Based on Cotton, Cockle & Millar, "The Papyrology of the Roman Near East."

[47] j. *Sotah* VII 1, 21b and other references in S. C. Reif, *Judaism and Hebrew Prayer*, Cambridge: Cambridge University Press, 1993, 350 n. 47; W. F. Smelik, *The Targum of Judges*, Leiden: Brill, 1995, 6-7; and Levine, *Judaism and Hellenism* 160-161. On Caesarea and the dominant position of Greek there, also among Jews, see B. Lifshitz, "Césarée de Palestine, son histoire et ses institutions," *Aufstieg und Niedergang der Römischen Welt* II, 8, Berlin: W. de Gruyter, 1977, 490-518. Also K. G. Holum, *King Herod's Dream: Caesarea on the Sea*, New York & London: Norton, 1988. On "the Greek of the synagogue" see the chapter with this title in Lieberman's *Greek in Jewish Palestine* 29-67.

[48] On this *Novella* see A. Linder, *The Jews in Roman Imperial Legislation*, Detroit: Wayne State University Press, 1987, 402-411, who conveniently presents the text with translation and commentary.

[49] For the Greek loanwords in the Copper Scroll see Schürer, *History* II 78. For the rabbinic traditions about the young men of the House of the Patriarch who studied the Greek language and Greek 'wisdom' see S. Lieberman, *Hellenism in Jewish Palestine*, New York: The Jewish Theological Seminary of America, 1962, 100-114. Cf. in general on the Patriarchs' knowledge of the Greek language and Greek 'wisdom' my essay "The Last Jewish Patriarch(s) and Graeco-Roman Medicine" (elsewhere in this volume).

[50] See his *Judaism and Hellenism*, and more recently his *The 'Hellenization' of Judea in the First Century after Christ*, London: SCM Press, 1989, passim (now in expanded German version in his *Judaica et hellenistica: Kleine Schriften I*, Tübingen: Mohr, 1996, 1-90); also his "Der vorchristliche Paulus" in M. Hengel & U. Heckel (edd.),

not unimportant to observe that none of our sources ever mention the presence of interpreters in situations where Palestinian Jews had to talk with Greeks.[51] "There is no sign that the acquisition of Greek was felt as very difficult,"[52] though many may never have arrived at a level higher than what was necessary to keep up simple conversations with Greek fellow townsmen without being able to write Greek. Here the general question of literacy comes in, but in view of a lack of a comprehensive study of literacy in ancient Judaism – a real desideratum![53] – we have to leave that matter aside. Let me only remark that it was not only literate people with knowledge of Greek who erected inscribed tombstones. As a matter of fact anyone could do that since the texts on the stones were most of the time incised by professional stone-cutters who had a large number of stock phrases to provide their clients with examples. Here it is important to keep in mind the distinction between bilingual speakers and literate bilinguals: *i.e.*, inability to write does not necessarily imply inability to speak a language.[54]

Another factor that may distort our picture is the fact that a majority of the inscriptions were found in urban centres, not in the countryside, so that the figures we have may yield averages that do not accurately reflect either cities or countryside, although they certainly do reflect cities more accurately than the countryside.[55] What was true for major cities such as Jerusalem, Caesarea, Jaffa, Sepphoris, let alone Scythopolis (which belonged to the Decapolis)[56] and other Hellenistic cities,[57] need not necessarily apply to the many small towns and villages in Judea and the

---

Paulus und das antike Judentum, Tübingen: Mohr, 1991, 177-294, esp. 256-265; finally his "Jerusalem als jüdische und hellenistische Stadt," in his *Judaica, hellenistica et christiana: Kleine Schriften II*, Tübingen: Mohr, 1999, 115-156. For a good summary of criticisms of Hengel's position (with bibliography) see L. L. Grabbe, *Judaism from Cyrus to Hadrian*, 2 vols., Minneapolis: Fortress Press, 1992, I 150-153.

[51] Thus Mussies, "Greek" 1056.

[52] Barr, "Hebrew" 103.

[53] See, e.g., B. Spolsky, "Triglossia and Literacy in Jewish Palestine of the First Century," *International Journal of the Sociology of Language* 42 (1983) 95-109. After the completion of my article Catherine Hezser published her full-scale study of the problem: *Jewish Literacy in Roman Palestine*, Tübingen: Mohr, 2001.

[54] Cf. Horsley, *New Documents V*, 24. Grabbe overlooks this when he concludes overhastily that the use of Greek was "confined to a particular segment of the population, namely, the educated upper class" (*Judaism* I 158). Cf. also the same minimalist position in Schürer, *History* II 74.

[55] On this also Rosén, "Sprachsituation" 490.

[56] Thirty ossuaries of Jews found in Scythopolis have only inscriptions in Greek!; see G. Fuks, "The Jews of Hellenistic and Roman Scythopolis," *Journal of Jewish Studies* 33 (1982) 409-410.

[57] See the chapter on the Hellenistic cities in Schürer, *History* II 85-183.

Galilee.[58] "It is quite possible to interpret the paucity of Greek inscriptional data in Upper Galilee as reflecting a genuine linguistic conservatism, if not a conscious attempt to preserve a dominant Semitic ambience."[59] Unfortunately we have hardly any means to establish with any precision how great the differences in this respect between city and countryside were. We do know, however, that the Roman administration passed on imperial decrees in inscribed form to the local population (not in Latin but) in Greek, assuming that these edicts could be read not only by inhabitants of the greater urban centres. The famous *Diatagma Kaisaros* from the village of Nazareth is a clear case in point.[60] Here at least a good many of the local Galileans were expected to be able to read it.[61]

A further distinction that has to be made is of a chronological nature. There can be little doubt that the process of Hellenization was, in general, a progressive one. To quote Lee Levine, "The degree of Hellenization was clearly of a different order in the first to fourth centuries CE than in the third to first centuries BCE."[62] Even though the production of Jewish literature in Greek seems to have decreased after 70, the proportion of Greek inscriptions as compared to Hebrew and Aramaic ones increases (except in Jerusalem, where there is a drop-off of epitaphs in general after 70). It would seem that what once was limited to certain circles or strata of society gradually permeated into other societal areas as well.

One could also wonder whether perhaps the preponderance of Greek in the epitaphs has to do with the genre. It is a well known fact that the genre of *carmina sepulcralia* was a Greek creation, and Greek genres had fixed rules as to form, language, and style. So maybe this fact also

---

[58] It has to be added, however, that there do not seem to exist significant regional variations in the sense that there is more Hebrew material in Jerusalem or more Greek in the coastal areas, as Prof. J. Price reminds me in a private communication. For a similar distinction between urban areas and countryside in neighbouring Phoenicia see J.D. Grainger, *Hellenistic Phoenicia*, Oxford: Clarendon Press, 1991, 77-83, 108-111 *et aliter*. Cf. also F. Millar, "The Problem of Hellenistic Syria," in A. Kuhrt & S. Sherwin-White, *Hellenism in the East*, London: Duckworth, 1987, 110-133.

[59] E. M. Meyers & J. F. Strange, *Archaeology, the Rabbis and Early Christianity*, London: SCM Press, 1981, 91.

[60] See my *Ancient Jewish Epitaphs* 159-161, and the detailed study by B. M. Metzger, "The Nazareth Inscription Once Again," in his *New Testament Studies: Philological, Versional, and Patristic*, Leiden: Brill, 1980, 75-92. The recent study by E. Grzybek & M. Sordi, "L'*Edit de Nazareth* et la politique de Néron à l'égard des chrétiens," *Zeitschrift für Papyrologie und Epigraphik* 120 (1998) 279-291, is unconvincing.

[61] See Meyer & Strange, *Archaeology* 84; Sevenster, *Do You Know Greek?* 117-121.

[62] Levine, *Judaism and Hellenism in Antiquity* 26.

caused Greek to predominate as the language of tomb inscriptions? That is very implausible, however, for although that certainly applied to tomb inscriptions with metrical poetry – of which we have only two instances in Jewish Palestine[63] – it did not apply to the other forms, for example, the many instances of only the name of the deceased, whether or not followed by the age at death, a form that, moreover, also had its predecessors in Hebrew and Aramaic as early as biblical times.[64] So the constraints of genre did not play a role as distorting factor as far as the knowledge and use of Greek in inscriptions by Jewish inhabitants of ancient Palestine is concerned. We can therefore assume that people recorded the names of their deceased in Greek because Greek was their first language (or at least because they were fully bilingual).[65]

A special case is the disproportionally great number of Greek epitaphs from the catacombs of Beth She'arim. A percentage of almost 90% is all the more striking since the city was a rabbinic centre of great renown and several famous rabbis were buried there. It is tempting to see this high percentage in the light of the fact that precisely on account of the fame of the city as a prestigious centre of rabbinic learning, many Jews from the diaspora wanted to be buried there. And indeed, there are quite a number of Greek inscriptions from Beth She'arim that clearly indicate that the deceased did not originate from Palestine. We find ten epitaphs of men and women from Palmyra, Byblos, Tyre, Sidon, Beirut, and Antioch, (BS II nos. 92, 100, 137, 141, 147, 148, 164, 172, 199, 221), all of them from Syria.[66] It is clear that we have to do here with immigrants

---

[63] These and the other metrical inscriptions by Jews were collected by me in "Jewish Tomb Inscriptions in Verse," in my *Hellenism – Judaism – Christianity* 27-47 (reprinted from J. W. van Henten & P. W. van der Horst (edd.), *Studies in Early Jewish Epigraphy*, Leiden: Brill, 1994, 129-147). There is one other metrical inscription from Palestine, in Marissa, but it is not Jewish (see SEG VIII 244).

[64] See for instance K.A.D. Smelik, *Writings from Ancient Israel. A Handbook of Historical and Religious Documents*, Edinburgh: T.& T. Clark, 1991, 152-155; and in general G. I. Davies, *Ancient Hebrew Inscriptions,* Cambridge: Cambridge University Press, 1991.

[65] See also the verdict by Joseph Fitzmyer in "The Languages of Palestine" 35: "It is unlikely that the language chosen for most of these crudely incised identifications was merely the *lingua franca* of the day. Rather, they bear witness to the widespread and living use of Greek among first-century Palestinian Jews." Cf., however, Rajak, *Josephus* 57: "Now those who put Greek on their tomb need not be Greek speakers, just as Latin on English gravestones was not put there by Latin speakers, but adopted because it was associated with worship and study." *Ibid.*: "Greek was the language of some Jews in Jerusalem."

[66] S. Safrai, "Relations Between the Diaspora and the Land of Israel," in S. Safrai & M. Stern (eds.), *The Jewish People in the First Century* (CRINT I 1), Assen 1974, 194, and J. J. Price, "The Jewish Diaspora of the Graeco-Roman Period," *Scripta Classica*

from the neighboring country, although it must remain uncertain for what reason they left Syria and settled in Beth She'arim. Was it in order to be buried in the neighborhood of the great rabbis, or was it for a more down to earth reason such as trade interests, or for other reasons? Be that as it may, it is not a matter of surprise that these inscriptions from diaspora Jews are in Greek. But it should immediately be added that this accounts only for 10 out of 218 inscriptions, that is less than 5%. From a theoretical point of view it cannot be ruled out that many of the remaining 208 Greek epitaphs also derive from diaspora Jews who do not identify themselves as such, but that seems extremely unlikely. As a matter of fact many of the deceased are explicitly said to have originated from other places in Roman Palestine, and for the rest of the inscriptions the most natural assumption is that the deceased were locals.[67] And most of these also used Greek as the language of their inscriptions, which was very probably also their daily language. This seems to be corroborated by the metrical epitaph with which I started this paper (BS II 127). Let us briefly have a closer look at it.

As I already indicated above, the most striking thing about this exceptional epitaph is that the deceased indicates that he is a native from Beth She'arim ('my Beth She'arim') and at the same time he presents us with the most thoroughly Greek epitaph in ancient Palestine one could imagine. To be sure, it is exceptional, but there it is. It is Greek not only in its Homeric language, but also in its form and contents, although it should be conceded that from a metrical point of view the poem is far from faultless. From a morphological point of view, however, the poem is remarkably free from errors, apart from one instance of iotacism (line 6). This poetic inscription is a clear demonstration that (at least some) Palestinian Jews were not only quite familiar with the Greek language but also with Greek literature, for the poem is full of Homeric phraseology and diction. This is one of the two poetic inscriptions from Beth She'arim (for the other one see BS II 183).[68] It is written in alternating dactylic hexameters and pentameters (disticha), as is usual in epigrams. The deceased speaks in the first person, which occurs very often in

---

Israelica 13 (1994) 173. In other Greek funerary inscriptions from Israel we also find Jews from abroad, especially from Alexandria (e.g. CIJ 918, 928, 934; but cf. also 882, 889, 910, 925, 931, 954 [?], 991; Dominus Flevit no. 9).

[67] See Z. Weiss, "Social Aspects of Burial in Beth She'arim: Archeological Finds and Talmudic Sources," in L. I. Levine (ed.), *The Galilee in Late Antiquity*, New York and Jerusalem: The Jewish Theological Seminary of America, 1992, 357-371.

[68] Also, the other Homeric poem (BS II 183) does not give any indication that the deceased or his family derived from elsewhere than Beth She'arim.

pagan Greek funerary epigrams. In line 1 Λεοντεΐδης for 'son of Leontios' is already an imitation of Homeric patronymics (cf. 'Ατρεΐδης for 'son of Atreus'). In line 2 the intentionally emphatical **πάσης** σοφίης ('all wisdom' or 'every sort of wisdom' or 'all kinds of wisdom') is important, since it seems to indicate that it was not only Jewish wisdom (*i.e.* Torah study, which flourished at Beth She'arim) but also secular Greek learning that Justus had been educated in. In Greek epigrams *sophia* is often used for 'excellence in one of the arts or in learning' – it was used, for instance, of poets, orators, and jurists – whereas in Jewish tradition, wisdom (*chokhma*) had a wide range of religious overtones.[69] It is therefore not accidental that it is in the concept of *sophia* that we see the two worlds of Judaism and Hellenism reaching out to each other here. "The man described in this epigram was educated both in Greek and Jewish learning. (…) The Jew Justus, a citizen of that town which was for many decades a center of Jewish scholarship, and apparently also the author of the inscription, used this expression in the sense accepted in his Hellenized environment."[70] In line 3 λιπεῖν φάος ('leaving the light' for 'dying') is a Homeric expression (*Od.* XI 93), as is ἀκαχημένους, 'mourning' (*Od.* IX 62, 105, 565, etc.). Αὐτοκασίγνητος for 'brother' in line 4 is very common in Homer. Βέσαρα (line 4) for Beth She'arim occurs also in Josephus (in the form Βήσαρα, *Vita* 118-119). With the expression 'in my Beth She'arim,' the author would seem to express the Jewish idea of being laid to rest among one's own people.[71] 'To go to Hades' in line 5 in the sense of 'to die' is common both in Homer and in Greek funerary epigraphy. In Jewish writings 'Hades' had lost its religious-mythological meaning (God of the underworld); hence the LXX translators used it to render *she'ol,* and it occurs 10 times in the New Testament. Μοῖρα κραταίη in line 6 (a typically Homeric verse ending) would at first sight seem to be more difficult to reconcile with Jewish ideas. Moira was since Homer the Greek goddess of fate, but apparently Justus sees no problem in using the term, in the tradition of Greek epigrams, to say that it was his destiny to die young.

---

[69] See, *inter multos alios*, R. E. Murphy, "Wisdom," *Anchor Bible Dictionary* 6 (1992) 920-931, and E. E. Urbach, *The Sages: Their Concepts and Beliefs*, Jerusalem: Magnes Press, 1975, Index *s.v.* 'wisdom.' Schwabe-Lifshitz, *Beth She'arim II* 100, mention several Jewish parallels to the expression *pasa sophia*.

[70] Schwabe-Lifshitz, *Beth She'arim II* 99-100; on p. 101 they rightly emphasize that "in this one hexameter [read: pentameter!] concepts from two different worlds meet and are combined."

[71] Thus Schwabe-Lifshitz, *Beth She'arim II* 107. The use of ὅς (or ἑός, as in line 6) for ἐμός is a late-epic feature.

The θάρσει formula in line 7 – which is from a different speaker – is a too much debated and too extensive matter to deal with here in any detail.[72]

Now it should be noted that this is not the first time we come across Homeric poetry in the land of Israel. From several centuries earlier, probably from the second century BCE, we have the epic poems of Philo and Theodotus, both of them probably of Palestinian provenance.[73] The fact that we do not have any other traces of this kind of literary activity from the centuries between these two poets from the second century BCE and the third century CE in which the two metrical epitaphs in Beth She'arim were written may be striking to the uninitiated, but to anyone familiar with the vicissitudes of the tradition history of ancient literature and epigraphy in general and Jewish literature and epigraphy in Greek in particular this is not as telling as one might be inclined to think. There may, or may not, have been a much greater production of Homeric poetry (Sosates is a case in point: we know only his name, all his works are lost),[74] or of Greek literature in general, or of Greek epitaphs, or even of just Greek words on tombstones, in Hellenistic-Roman Palestine than we will ever be able to know, but these two key points – Greek Homeric poetry in both the second century BCE and the third century CE – should make us aware of the potential there was in principle.

How far have we come? Not much further than our predecessors, I am afraid. Can we still subscribe to the verdict of one of the greatest experts in the linguistic situation of Roman Palestine, Chayim Rosén, "daß die κοινή [Griechisch] in weitestem Ausmaß unter den Juden Palästinas verbreitet war" and that "bis in die einfachsten Volksschichten hinab der Gebrauch des Griechischen zu beobachten [ist]"?[75] It is hard to say yes or no, but our evidence does not fully warrant such far-reaching conclusions. Yet I am inclined to put it this way: The burden of the proof is on the shoulders of those scholars who want to maintain that Greek was not the *lingua franca* of many Palestinian Jews in the Hellenistic-Roman-Byzantine period in view of the fact that more than 50%,

---

[72] See my *Ancient Jewish Epitaphs* 121-122.

[73] C. R. Holladay, *Fragments from Hellenistic Jewish Authors II: Poets*, Atlanta: Scholars Press, 1989, 70-72 and 208-210. Now also E. R. Gruen, *Heritage and Hellenism: The Reinvention of Jewish Tradition*, Berkeley – Los Angeles, 1998, 120-127.

[74] See S. J. D. Cohen, "Sosates, the Jewish Homer," *Harvard Theological Review* 74 (1981) 391-396.

[75] Rosén, "Sprachsituation" 510.

maybe even some 65% of the public inscriptions is in 'the language of Japheth.' The minimalist interpretations that have been put forward by several scholars (Feldman, Rajak, Grabbe, the new Schürer) have turned out to be unconvincing. It is on the basis of the sketched evidence that as early as 1965 the great Jewish epigrapher Baruch Lifshitz was able to conclude: "The Greek language and Greek culture had penetrated all the Jewish communities of the Greek east."[76] Rosén and Lifshitz are probably by and large right, but their statements should be qualified by adding that this does not imply that a majority, or even a large minority, of Jews were monolingual Greek-speakers. For most, or at least many, of the Jews in Palestine, Greek most probably remained a second language, certainly outside the urban areas.[77] We may tentatively conclude that Roman Palestine was a largely bilingual, or even trilingual, society[78] – alongside the vernacular Aramaic (and, to a much lesser extent, Hebrew) Greek was widely used and understood – but we have to add that the degree of use and understanding of the Greek language probably varied strongly according to locality and period, social status and educational background, occasion and mobility.[79] As far as we can see, however, opinions will remain divided over this issue.[80]

---

[76] "L'hellénisation des Juifs en Palestine," *Revue Biblique* 72 (1965) 520-538, quote at 538. Cf. also his "Du nouveau sur l'hellénisation des Juifs de Palestine," *Euphrosyne* n.s. 3 (1970) 113-133. Cf. Lieberman, *Greek in Jewish Palestine* 39: "We have seen how deeply Greek penetrated into all the classes of Jewish society of Palestine."

[77] Thus also Mussies, "Greek" 1058. Cf. Fitzmyer, "Languages of Palestine" 46.

[78] See B. Spolsky, "Jewish Multilingualism in the First Century: An Essay in Historical Sociolinguistics," J.A. Fishman (ed.), *Readings in the Sociology of Jewish Languages*, Leiden: Brill, 1985, 35-51, esp. 40-41 where trilingualism ('triglossia') is stressed. See also Ch. Rabin, "Hebrew and Aramaic in the First Century," in S. Safrai & M. Stern (edd.), *The Jewish People in the First Century 2* (CRINT I 2), Assen: Van Gorcum, 1976, 1007-1039. But cf. R. Schmitt, "Die Sprachverhältnisse in den östlichen Provinzen des Römischen Reiches," *Aufstieg und Niedergang der Römischen Welt* II 29, 2, Berlin – New York: W. de Gruyter, 1983, 554-586, here 576: "Man wird die Sprachgemeinschaft dieses Landes mit gutem Recht als bilingual bezeichnen dürfen."

[79] See G.H.R. Horsley, *New Documents V*, 19, though he says that this consensus view is 'an uneasy one.'

[80] I owe special thanks to Professor Jonathan Price of Tel Aviv University, who was so kind not only to send me information about the CIIP project but also to read the first draft of this paper and to send me his valuable critical remarks. Also my colleagues Dr. Gerard Mussies and Dr. Leonard V. Rutgers cheerfully volunteered to comment upon the first draft of this paper.

2. THE LAST JEWISH PATRIARCH(S) AND GRAECO-ROMAN MEDICINE

About the last Jewish patriarch, Gamaliel VI, who lived in the closing decades of the fourth and the first decades of the fifth century, very little is known from Jewish sources. Almost all we know about him derives from Pagan and Christian writings.[1] One of the most fascinating details in our information is that a Christian medical author writes that he received from Gamaliel the patriarch a recipe for the medical treatment of spleen diseases. Further information comes from the famous pagan orator Libanius of Antioch, who had a lively correspondence with the patriarch, among other things about Gamaliel's son who seems to have studied under this orator. These and other data to be discussed evoke an image of a wealthy, learned, openminded and powerful patriarch who was well versed in Greek culture, also in its medical aspects.

Let us begin with the curious report by a Christian doctor, Marcellus Empiricus of Bordeaux (Burdigala in Gaul), about Gamaliel's recipe. In his *De medicamentis*, written about 410, he tells us the following:

> "For the spleen there is a special remedy which was recently demonstrated by the patriarch Gamaliel on the basis of approved experiments."[2]

This short quotation raises at least two intriguing questions: How could a Christian Latin author from Gaul know a recipe or form of treatment developed by the *nasi'* in Palestine, and why did this Jewish patriarch occupy himself with medical affairs? These are difficult questions that we can only try to answer in a tentative way.

---

[1] The same applies to the other patriarchs of the fourth and early fifth centuries; see G. Stemberger, *Juden und Christen im Heiligen Land. Palästina unter Konstantin und Theodosius*, München 1987, 184. By contrast, for the patriarchate in the second and third centuries it is only rabbinic sources that we are dependant on. The best modern studies of the Jewish patriarchate in late antiquity to date are D. Goodblatt, *The Monarchic Principle. Studies in Jewish Self-Government in Antiquity*, Tübingen 1994, 131-231, and the comprehensive monography by M. Jacobs, *Die Institution des jüdischen Patriarchen*, Tübingen 1995.

[2] *De medicamentis* XXIII, 77 *ad splenum remedium singulare quod de experimentis probatis Gamalielus patriarchas proxime ostendit* (p. 408 in the edition by M. Niedermann & E. Liechtenhan, Berlin 1968 [Corpus medicorum latinorum, vol. 5]).

One of the few important things we know about Marcellus Empiricus is that he was a Christian and had a high position at the court of the emperor Theodosius I (379-395) in Constantinople, although he probably wrote his work only during the reign of his grandson, Theodosius II (408-450).[3] Now it is known from various sources that Theodosius I had a very good relationship with the Jewish patriarch of Palestine, as did his successors, the emperors Arcadius and Honorius.[4] Several imperial edicts from the Codex Theodosianus, most of which were published in the nineties of the fourth century, take the patriarch under the emperor's protection, emphasize his rights, and explicitly prohibit any public insult of the patriarch.[5] That, nonetheless, Theodosius II degraded and demoted the patriarch in 415, deprived him of his honorary titles and severely restricted his authority and power, had to do with the fact that Gamaliel VI, as Codex Theodosianus formulates it, "supposed that he could transgress the law with impunity" (XVI 8, 22 *Gamalielus existimavit se posse inpune delinquere*). From what follows, it becomes clear that Gamaliel was charged with having had new synagogues built, which was against the imperial laws; with having acted as judge in lawsuits between Jews and Christians; with possessing Christian slaves whom, moreover, he had converted to the Jewish faith.[6] It is not so that the patriarchate was abolished by the emperor, but from a later decree (Cod. Theod. XVI 8, 29 from 429) it becomes clear that the patriarchate no longer existed, apparently because the patriarch's dynasty lacked (legitimate or suitable?) heirs.[7]

The main issue for us here is, however, that these and other witnesses make clear that the Jewish patriarch was a highly regarded person at the imperial court and for a long time enjoyed respect and even protection

---

[3] N. Kind, Marcellus (58), *Pauly-Wissowa's Realencyclopädie der classischen Altertumswissenschaft* 14 (1930) 1498-1503. It cannot be excluded that Marcellus remained in function at the imperial court after the death of Theodosius I.

[4] See, e.g., Goodblatt, *The Monarchic Principle* 133-139.

[5] See for these texts A. Linder, *The Jews in Roman Imperial Legislation*, Detroit-Jerusalem 1987, Index s.v. patriarch, and the discussions by Stemberger, *Juden und Christen im Heiligen Land* 184-213, and by B. S. Bachrach, 'The Jewish Community of the Later Roman Empire as Seen in the *Codex Theodosianus*,' in J. Neusner & E.S. Frerichs (eds.), *"To See Ourselves as Others See Us." Christians, Jews, Others in Late Antiquity*, Chico 1985, 399-421.

[6] H. Graetz, *History of the Jews* II, Philadelphia 1956, 618 speculates that it was because of his elevated position at the court that Gamaliel considered himself privileged to be lax in his observance of the emperor's laws against the Jews, even though, as Graetz had earlier said, "the Middle Ages really begin for Judaism with Theodosius II."

[7] See Stemberger, *Juden und Christen* 208-211 (207 on the unsuitability for the office of sons of the later patriarchs); also Linder, *The Jews* 320.

by the emperor. This enabled him to strengthen his position of power over Jewry and to increase his influence and wealth. In the light of these data it is no wonder that our sources sometimes reflect great tensions and even conflicts between the patriarch(s) on the one hand and the rabbis on the other.[8] Along with the patriarch the rabbis themselves gradually "became a force, individually and collectively, in official communal affairs, *provided* they were willing to cooperate with the Patriarch and the latter wanted or needed them. This was the *sine qua non* for such advancement."[9]

In the centuries after the destruction of the Jerusalem temple in 70, the position of the patriarchs – possibly created by the Romans in the post-war period[10] – developed slowly but gradually into one of considerable political power.[11] It is no exaggeration to say that they were in fact nothing less than heads of state of Roman Palestine, responsible only to the emperors. Fergus Millar speaks in this connection of "members of what became a sort of rabbinic dynasty" and of "an almost royal court."[12] In order to provide an ideological foundation for the hereditary patriarchal regime, the members of the House of Gamaliel began to make (unhistorical) claims to Davidic descent.[13] Quite often they were immensely rich patrons,[14] or rather aristocratic rulers, surrounded by bodyguards, and wielding extensive power accorded them

[8] For data see L. I. Levine, *The Rabbinic Class of Roman Palestine in Late Antiquity*, Jerusalem-New York 1989, 134-139, 186-191 (135: "... many rabbis of the late third and fourth centuries had little sympathy or concern for this office"); G. Alon, *Jews, Judaism and the Classical World*, Jerusalem 1977, 374-435, esp. 424-432; Stemberger, *Juden und Christen* 190-191. A. I. Baumgarten, 'Rabbi Judah I and His Opponents,' *Journal for the Study of Judaism* 12 (1981) 135-172. Much of the opposition to the patriarchs was probably caused by the patriarchal tax (*apostolê* or *aurum coronarium*) imposed upon the Jewish communities; see Stemberger, *ibid.* 195-199; Goodblatt, *Monarchic Principle* 136-139; Levine, *Rabbinic Class* 170.

[9] Levine, *Rabbinic Class* 139 (first italics added).

[10] Goodblatt, *Monarchic Principle* 219-231.

[11] For criticism of the traditional presentation of the patriarch as the head of the Sanhedrin, see K. Strobel, 'Jüdisches Patriarchat, Rabbinentum und Priesterdynastie von Emesa: Historische Phänomene innerhalb des Imperium Romanum der Kaiserzeit,' *Ktema* 14 (1989) 39-77, esp. 45, and Levine, *Rabbinic Class* 76-83.

[12] *The Roman Near East (31 BC – AD 337)*, Cambridge MA – London 1993, 383.

[13] On these claims see Goodblatt, *Monarchic Principle* 143-175. Note that towards the middle of the third century Origen writes about "how great is the power wielded by the ethnarch [= patriarch], granted by Caesar. We who have experienced it know that he differs in no way from a king of the nation" (*Epistula ad Julium Africanum* 14 [20], from ca. 240 CE). Cf. j.*Sanh.* II 8, 20c (*in fine*) and other passages mentioned by Goodblatt, *Monarchic Principle* 142.

[14] On their great wealth see M. Avi-Yonah, *Geschichte der Juden im Zeitalter des Talmud* II, Berlin 1962, 229; Stemberger, *Juden und Christen* 197-198.

by the Roman emperors.[15] It is for that reason that the emperors finally endowed them with the highest honorary titulature (*viri clarissimi et illustres*).[16] It should be emphasized, however, that this very high public status of the Jewish patriarchs, with power over Jews probably even outside Palestine,[17] was a relatively late development which took place partly only in the course of the third century (since Judah ha-Nasi) but especially and politically most forcefully in the second half of the fourth and the first decade of the fifth century CE.[18] This is ironic enough, for, as Lee Levine has said, "it was with the advent of Christian Rome that the office reached a peak of prominence and influence. With the backing of Christian emperors, extensive political leverage was once again added to religious authority. From all indications, the last century of the Patriarchate, which coincided with the advent of Byzantine rule, was one of the most flourising in the history of the office."[19]

---

[15] For a list of areas of communal life dominated by the patriarch in Palestine see Levine, *Rabbinic Class* 137.

[16] This title originally belonged only to members of the highest senatorial class, e.g. a *praefectus praetorio*. See, e.g., S. W. Baron, *A Social and Religious History of the Jews* II, New York-Philadelphia 1952, 192-3. Baron speaks of the "extraordinarily benevolent treatment" accorded to the patriarchs by the emperors, but he soberly adds that it was mainly political and fiscal reasons that accounted for this treatment.

[17] See *Cod. Theod.* XVI 8.8 (392 CE), XVI 8.13 (397 CE), XVI 8.15 (404 CE), and the discussion by Linder, *Jews* 186-189, 201-204, 220-222, and by Goodblatt, *Monarchic Principle* 134. Cf. also Epiphanius, *Panarion* XXX 11.

[18] Strobel, 'Jüdisches Patriarchat' 60-68. M. Goodman, *Mission and Conversion. Proselytizing in the Religious History of the Roman Empire,* Oxford 1994, 110-111, speculates that this development probably marked "an important stage in the process by which rabbinic Judaism became normative." See also his essay 'The Roman State and the Jewish Patriarch in the Third Century,' in L. I. Levine (ed.), *The Galilee in Late Antiquity,* New York – Jerusalem 1992, 127-139. Stemberger, *Juden und Christen* 184 remarks: "Von einer innerjüdischen Führungsinstitution, die im Lauf der Zeit auch vom Staat anerkannt wurde, entwickelte sich das Patriarchat immer mehr zu einem nach außen gerichteten Amt, dessen Einfluß auf die innerrabbinische religiöse Diskussion entsprechend abnahm;" and *ibid.* 188: "Gerade in der Zeit, da das Christentum sich schon als Staatsreligion durchgesetzt hat, ist demnach die offizielle Anerkennung der jüdischen Führung am höchsten, eine fürwahr auffällige Tatsache." Unfortunately, most of the details of this process of the development of the patriarch's power remain unknown, but it may be added that this process coincided with the slow but gradual development of the rabbinic class from a very small, separated, self-contained and closely knit ingroup of elitists without influence into an authoritative body that became more integrated with Jewish society at large by trying to overcome the long-standing antagonism between the rabbis and the common people; see Levine, *Rabbinic Class* 23-42, 112-133.

[19] L. I. Levine, 'The Jewish Patriarch (Nasi) in Third Century Palestine,' *Aufstieg und Niedergang der Römischen Welt* II 19, 2, Berlin-New York 1979, 685.

The Church Father Jerome reports in the nineties of the fourth century that the emperor Theodosius I even had a very high ranking Roman official executed at the request of Gamaliel since the man had illegally appropriated documents of the patriarch.[20] Even though there is no hard evidence for it, it is highly probable, yes even almost certain, that at least some of the later patriarchs knew the emperors personally and visited them in their courts in Rome or Constantinople.[21] And that could fully explain how the Gallic doctor and author Marcellus Empiricus, who had been working at the court of Theodosius I in Constantinople, could have met the Jewish patriarch Gamaliel and learned a new method of medical treatment from him.

But that still leaves us with the second question: is it realistic to regard Gamaliel VI as a physician or at least as a person with medical interest and knowledge? Let us begin by saying that we can establish that we know of the existence of a considerable number of Jewish physicians in the Roman empire.[22] It seems that, exactly as in our own days, many educated Jews in antiquity were deeply interested in medical science and knowledge (which – by the way – is rather striking in view of the fact that the Hebrew Bible does not exhibit any such interest[23]). Rabbinic literature itself is a telling example of this interest: in this literature, which was definitely not written by medical doctors, one is confronted with an amazingly large quantity of Greek medical knowledge. A striking example of this is the amount of scientific gynecological, sexological and embryological information in the treatise *Nidda* in both Talmuds. For instance, as I have demonstrated elsewhere, rabbinic discussions in this tractate (and elsewhere as well) clearly demonstrate that several rabbis had extensive knowledge of Greek theories about the viability of seven months' children, about the way an embryo comes into being, about the much debated existence of female semen as a contribution to embryogenesis, and they were even able to develop their own

[20] *Epistula* 57, 2-3.
[21] If the rabbinic stories about the dialogues between Rabbi Judah ha-Nasi and Antoninus (whoever this emperor may have been) contain any historical kernel, it would seem that a similar situation existed as early as the beginning of the third century CE. Note that Caracalla visited Palestine in 215/6 CE. According to *Gen. Rabbah* LXIII 8, the patriarch Judah III met the emperor Diocletian when the latter was visiting Caesarea Philippi (ca. 300 CE).
[22] A very good survey is to be found in F. Kudlien, 'Jüdische Ärzte im Römischen Reich,' *Medizinhistorisches Journal* 20 (1985) 36-57.
[23] See for instance L. P. Hogan, *Healing in the Second Temple Period,* Fribourg-Göttingen 1992, 3-26; J. Barr, *Biblical Faith and Natural Theology*, Oxford 1993, 178-179.

interesting variants of these Greek theories. Also the medical vocabulary of the Talmudic literature betrays the influence of Greek terminology.[24] From the closing period of the Talmud, the second half of the sixth century CE, we have the first medical handbook in Hebrew, written by Asaph ha-Rophe, whose work continuously sings the praises of the great Greek physicians, especially Hippocrates, Dioscorides and Galen (the book even includes a Hebrew translation of Hippocrates' *Aphorisms*).[25] But even a much earlier writer such as Josephus exhibits a more than ordinary interest in medical matters.[26] And we know that in the first centuries after the beginning of the Common Era there were also Jewish medical authors who wrote their works in Greek or Latin. Pagan authors confirm this. For instance, in the first half of the first cent. CE, Cornelius Celsus writes in his *De medicina* (V 19,11 and V 22,4) about two recipes composed by a certain *auctor Iudaeus*; and in the first half of the sixth cent. CE, the Neoplatonist Damascius writes in his *Vita Isidori* (Fr. 335) about a Jewish doctor Domnus, who is also known as a commentator on Hippocrates.[27] We may therefore draw the conclusion that there was a strong post-biblical tradition of interest in medical knowledge among the Jewish cultural elite, not only among doctors but also among other intellectuals, including the rabbis.

It is easy, then, to imagine that someone with a high cultural level such as the patriarch could indeed have appropriated medical knowledge (or perhaps could even have been a doctor). And of the high cultural level of Gamaliel we have proofs. These are not only his good con-

---

[24] See in general F. Rosner, *Medicine in the Bible and the Talmud*, New York 1977; J. Preuss, *Biblical and Talmudic Medicine*, New York 1978; S. Krauss, *Talmudische Archäologie* I, Leipzig 1910, 252-267. On embryological knowledge in early rabbinic Judaism see P. W. van der Horst, 'Seven Months' Children in Jewish and Christian Literature from Antiquity,' in my *Essays on the Jewish World of Early Christianity*, Fribourg – Göttingen 1990, 233-248, and idem, 'Sarah's Seminal Emission: Hebrews 11:11 in the Light of Ancient Embryology,' in my *Hellenism – Judaism – Christianity: Essays on Their Interaction*, Kampen 1994, 203-223. It is striking that in the series of recipes in Bavli *Gittin* 69b comparatively much attention is paid to problems of the spleen with which Gamaliel VI too had occupied himself.

[25] See L. Venetianer, *Asaf Judaeus, der älteste medizinische Schriftsteller in hebräischer Sprache* (3 vols.), Budapest 1915-1917; S. Muntner, Asaph ha-Rofe, *Enc. Jud.* 3 (1972) 673-676; the best recent survey (with bibliography) is S. Newmyer, 'Asaph the Jew and Greco-Roman Pharmaceutics,' in I. Jacob & W. Jacob (eds.), *The Healing Past. Pharmaceuticals in the Biblical and Rabbinic World*, Leiden 1993, 107-120.

[26] See S. S. Kottek, *Medicine and Hygiene in the Works of Flavius Josephus*, Leiden 1994.

[27] See M. Stern, *Greek and Latin Authors on Jews and Judaism* I-II, Jerusalem 1974-1980, I 368-9 and II 679 (cf.672 n.3), and especially the above mentioned article by Kudlien, 'Jüdische Ärzte.'

tacts with the imperial court or his capability to find a new sort of medical treatment for the spleen; it is especially his very friendly contact with one of the most well-known and influential pagan orators of his days, namely Libanius of Antioch, as it is apparent from the correspondence between the two (dating from 388-393). Unfortunately, of this correspondence only Libanius' part, his letters *to* the patriarch, has been preserved, not those *from* the patriarch.[28] Nonetheless, from Libanius' letters we can draw a number of important conclusions. The patriarch wrote to him in Greek; Libanius wrote to the patriarch in elegant classical Greek, assuming as a matter-of-course that Gamaliel could read this; more than that, Libanius' letters to the patriarch contain a variety of subtle allusions to persons and stories in Greek literature and mythology which were obviously child's play for Gamaliel; Libanius and the patriarch had many friends and acquaintances in common; they wrote to each other about all sorts of political and cultural matters; time and again Libanius shows his awareness of the very great political influence of the patriarch; possibly even a son of Gamaliel studied rhetoric under Libanius.[29] In sum: Libanius writes to a highly-developed and cultured man of the world, not to a person who lives in a self-chosen isolation; far from that. His Jewish patriarch knew Greek literature, Greek science, Greek mythology, and he was very much *au courant* with the political affairs of the empire.[30] It is, therefore, not strange at all to find that such a highly civilised and learned person also had medical knowledge and that he took pleasure, when paying a visit to the imperial

---

[28] All letters can be found in M. Stern, *Greek and Latin Authors on Jews...* II 580-599; in R. Foerster's Teubner edition these letters are nos. 914, 917, 973, 974, 1084, 1097, 1098, 1105 (on the possible inclusion of no. 1251 see Stemberger, *Juden und Christen* 193-194).

[29] This is not absolutely certain, however; see the discussion of the problem of the addressee of *Ep.* 1098 by Stern, *Greek and Latin Authors* II 596.

[30] See Stemberger's paragraph 'Patriarchat und hellenistische Kultur', in his *Juden und Christen* 205-208; on p. 208 he rightly speaks of "ein gemeinsames Bildungsniveau" of Libanius and Gamaliel (cf. the remark by Avi-Yonah, *Geschichte der Juden* 228: "Der Patriarch konnte mit den griechischen Rhetoren verkehren, da er die Bildung seiner Zeit beherrschte"). See also the illuminating remarks in P. Brown, *Authority and the Sacred. Aspects of the Christianisation of the Roman World*, Cambridge 1995, 48. For the possible implications of the Hammat Tiberias mosaic and inscriptions for 'patriarchal Hellenism' see M. Dothan, *Hammath Tiberias. Early Synagogues and the Hellenistic and Roman Remains*, Jerusalem 1983, 33-70 (with too much speculation, however); K. Strobel, 'Jüdisches Patriarchat' 48; Levine, *Rabbinic Class* 178-181. It is also important to notice that of the many epitaphs in the patriarchal burial site of Beth She'arim the vast majority are in Greek; see my *Ancient Jewish Epitaphs*, Kampen 1991, 23, 130.

court in Constantinople, in telling his latest medical discovery to his
Christian colleague, the court physician Marcellus Empiricus. Or perhaps even more: that – maybe – he wrote a treatise on the treatment of
spleen diseases of which he handed a copy to Marcellus (or sent it to
him). This fully belongs to the historical possibilities.[31]

The two questions I raised at the beginning of this contribution have
now received more or less an answer, however tentative it may be. There
is, however, one serious complication in all this that I have left unmen-
tioned so far but that has to be dealt with, albeit briefly. That Gamaliel
VI lived at the end of the fourth and the first decades of the fifth century
is beyond any reasonable doubt. That there has also existed a Gamaliel
V is obvious as well. The problem is now that some scholars place
Gamaliel V chronologically at the beginning of the fourth century, others, however, in the final three decades of that century.[32] If the latter dating is correct, then it is quite possible that all data I have assembled as
pertaining to Gamaliel VI would have to be divided over two Gamaliels:
The correspondence of Libanius,[33] Jerome's information and the early
decrees from the Codex Theodosianus would have to be related to
Gamaliel V, the remarks of doctor Marcellus and the later Theodosian
decrees to Gamaliel VI.[34] Or, to make it even more complicated, the data
might even have to be divided over three persons, since there is a
medieval Jewish chronicle, Seder Tannaim we-Amoraim, that inserts a
certain Jehuda IV between Gamaliel V and Gamaliel VI, and there are
indeed some scholars who traditionally situate this Jehuda chronologically between ca. 385 and 400,[35] without any other evidence to prove
such a dating, however. Now it has to be stated that the existence of a

---

[31] When W. Bacher, 'Gamaliel VI,' Jew. Enc. 5 (1903) 563, writes: "Gamaliel VI
appears to have been a physician," he too easily overlooks other possibilities. H.
Graetz, History of the Jews II, Philadelphia 1956, 618 writes in the same vein: "He
was a physician..."

[32] See for instance L. I. Levine, 'The Jewish Patriarch (Nasi) in Third Century Palestine'
688; Stemberger, Juden und Christen 212-213; Stern, Greek and Latin Authors II 582-
583; Chr. Burchard, 'Gamaliel,' Der kleine Pauly II, München 1975, 688.

[33] Stern, GLAJJ II 582: "It is not easy to identify the patriarch with whom Libanius cor-
responded."

[34] This is in fact the solution adopted by W. Bacher in his entries on Gamaliel V and
Gamaliel VI in the Jewish Encyclopedia 5 (1903) 562-3, and by Stern, GLAJJ II 583.

[35] E.g., S. Safrai, 'Amoraim,' Encyclopaedia Judaica II, Jerusalem 1972, 871, and G.
Alon, The Jews in Their Land in the Talmudic Age, Jerusalem 1980-84, 739 n.1, and
several others. See now the convenient chart of the traditional reconstruction of the
Gamalielian line in Goodblatt, Monarchic Principle 143, and M. Jacobs, Die Institution des jüdischen Patriarchen, Tübingen 1995, 205-211, who also points out that the
text of STA is corrupt in the place where the patriarchal dynasty is enumerated (§3).

Jehuda IV is by no means certain, on the contrary: the only data about him is the mention of his name in a historically very unreliable and late chronicle. So it would seem that we can safely ignore this patriarch.[36] But even if this is not the case, we do have to reckon with two Gamaliels. The great problem is that Jewish sources tell us next to nothing about these two patriarchs. What we know about them comes largely from pagan and Christian sources. These state clearly and unambiguously that in the first two decades of the fifth century Gamaliel VI was at first highly esteemed by the emperor(s) and later fell into disgrace, but about Gamaliel V we do not get to know anything that is chronologically unambiguous. He did live in the fourth century, but when exactly, nobody knows.[37] He could be the immediate predecessor of Gamaliel VI, but he could equally well have lived much earlier in the fourth century.[38] Again, we do not know. It still remains a distinct possibility, however, that all data pertain to one and the same patriarch, Gamaliel VI, who in that case would have remained in office from ca. 385 till sometime between 415 and 425, a not impossible range.[39] But let us state quite clearly and unambiguously: about the chronology and dates of the last five or six Jewish patriarchs we have no means whatsoever to attain any certainty.

In a sense this uncertainty is not as regrettable for the subject under consideration as it might seem. For even if it were necessary to assume that the data from Marcellus Empiricus, the Codex Theodosianus, and Libanius must be divided over two (or even three) persons, the picture would not drastically change. On the contrary, for in that case we would have data about more than one patriarch to the effect that in the final half century of the history of the Jewish patriarchate we have to do with strongly hellenized personalities with a secular cultural training who

---

[36] The unhistorical hodgepodge which is M. Aberbach's article 'Judah IV' in *Enc. Jud.* 10 (1972) 334 can be dismissed. Jacobs, *Institution* 210, remarks: "Schon der zeitliche Abstand des STA zu den erwähnten Personen ist zu groß, als daß das Werk als verläßliche Quelle gelten könnte."

[37] In spite of Levine, 'The Jewish Patriarch' 685-688, Goodblatt, *Monarchic Principle* 143, and the editor's survey in *Enc. Jud.* 7 (1972) 298.

[38] In that case, it is not unimaginable that we might situate a 'Judah IV' somewhere between Gamaliel V and Gamaliel VI, but that must remain sheer specualtion.

[39] That is the position of, e.g., O. Seeck, 'Gamaliel VI,' *Realencyklopädie der classischen Altertumswissenschaft* VII (1912) 690, and it is taken for granted in the *PLRE*. See now also Jacobs, *Institution* 333: "Die Aufteilung dieser Belege auf einen sog. Gamaliel V. und einen Gamaliel VI. hat keine hinreichende Grundlage in den Quellen. Vielmehr dürfte es sich in all diesen Fällen um dieselbe Person, nämlich den letzten bekannten *nasi*, handeln."

combined their political power with hellenistic learning. It is, therefore, not so unexpected that we hardly find any data about these persons in rabbinic literature,[40] whereas we do find them in pagan and Christian sources of late antiquity. It is very remarkable that, even as late as a century after the conversion of Constantine, the Jewish patriarch could still engage in an open-minded and free exchange of thoughts with pagan and Christian scholars and authorities of his days.[41]

[40] Cf. Stemberger, *Juden und Christen* 208: "Weitgehende kulturelle Anpassung an die hellenistische Umwelt, höchstes Ansehen und gewaltiger politischer Einfluß, gleichzeitig ein gewisser Abstand gegenüber rabbinischen Kreisen bestimmen also das Bild des Patriarchats, wie es sich aus den Angaben der nichtjüdischen Texte ebenso wie aus dem Schweigen der rabbinischen Literatur ergibt."

[41] It is one of the great merits of Stemberger's book *Juden und Christen im Heiligen Land* that it corrects quite a number of clichés on the period after Constantine on the basis of a careful scrutiny of the sources. But it was already Salo W. Baron who remarked (*Social and Religious History* II 192: "For more than a century the Christian empire continued to recognize the Palestinian patriarchate as both the supreme office of imperial Jewry and a high office of the state." See also B. S. Bachrach, 'The Jewish Community of the Later Roman Empire as Seen in the *Codex Theodosianus*' 421.

3. NEGLECTED GREEK EVIDENCE FOR EARLY JEWISH LITURGICAL PRAYER

In 1935 the British papyrologists H.I. Bell and T.C. Skeat published their well-known work *Fragments of an Unknown Gospel*.[1] It was the publication of Papyrus Egerton 2, which contained large fragments with fascinating portions of a hitherto unknown early Christian Gospel text that drew a great deal of attention from the scholarly world. The concentration of the ensuing debate on Pap. Egerton 2 diverted attention from the other, smaller Greek texts published in the same volume, Papyri Egerton 3-5, all three of them being regarded by their editors as early Christian texts, as the subtitle of their book clearly indicated. It is the purpose of this paper to draw attention to one of these neglected texts, Pap. Egerton 5, described by Bell and Skeat as a "Leaf from a Liturgical Book." It is a single leaf from a codex, measuring 19x17 cm., with 17 lines of text on both sides, to be dated to the end of the fourth or the beginning of the fifth century CE. Where in Egypt it was found is unknown; the papyrus is now in the British Library.[2] The editors say it is from a Christian liturgical book, even though they admit that its text is "if anything, more difficult than most of the earlier finds to identify" (56). The claim that it is from a *Christian* liturgical book that this papyrus leaf derives is, as we shall presently see, debatable. The papyrus contains a prayer, the text of which in the translation by the first editors runs as follows:[3]

> (1) *A [=verso]*
> "(2) sanctify, sustain, gather, govern, (3) establish, glorify, confirm, pasture, (4) raise up (?), enlighten, pacify, (5) administer, perfect – the people (6) which Thou hast established, the peculiar people, (7) the people which Thou hast ransomed, the people which (8) Thou hast called, Thy people, the sheep of (9) Thy pasture. Thou art the only physician (10) of our ailing souls, keep us in Thy joy (?), heal us (11) in sickness, cast us not away (12)

---

[1] *Fragments of an Unknown Gospel and Other Early Christian Papyri*, London 1935.
[2] For a description of its physical features see also E. G. Turner, *The Typology of the Early Codex*, Philadelphia 1977, 142, and J. Van Haelst, *Catalogue des papyrus littéraires juifs et chrétiens*, Paris 1976, 300, no. 921 (here the papyrus is called P. Lond. Christ. 4).
[3] *Fragments* 59. For corrections to their translation see further below.

as unfit to receive Thy healing. The word (13) of Thy mouth is the giver of health.

B. (14). These things we beg of Thee, Master; remit (15) whatever we have done amiss, check (?) whatever leads (?) us (16) to sin, neither record against us all that we (17) have done unlawfully. Forgiveness of sin (18) *B [=recto]*

(19) is the expression of Thy long-suffering; it is a fair thing, (20) o Immortal, not to be wrath with mortals, doomed to destruction, (21) short-lived, inhabiting a toilsome world. (22) Never dost Thou cease to do good, for Thou art bountiful, (23) Thou givest all, taking nought, for (24) Thou lackest nothing; every righteous thing is Thine, unrighteousness (25) alone is not Thine. Evil is that which Thou wouldst (26) not, the child of our imaginations. (27) Receive from us these psalmodies, (28) these hymnodies, these prayers, these supplications, (29) these entreaties, these requests, these (30) confessions, these petitions, these thanksgivings, (31) this readiness, this earnestness, these vigils, (32) these [...], these couchings upon the earth, these (33) prayerful utterances. Having a kindly (34) master in Thee, the eternal King, (35) we beseech Thee [to behold?] our pitiful state...

Here, unfortunately, the text breaks off, in the middle of the prayer. The letters A and B in the upper margins of verso and recto respectively might be taken to be page numbers, but the occurrence of the letter B at the end of line 13 seems to point in another direction. If the prayer in the middle of which the first page (verso) begins is prayer A, the header may have been added to indicate that fact, just as B may well have been added as a header to the second page (recto) to indicate that this page continues the text of prayer B which had started at line 14 of the previous page. So it would seem that we have here the last 13 lines of prayer A and the first 21 lines of prayer B. However, the abrupt ending of text A and the equally abrupt beginning of text B seem to militate against the assumption that we have to do here with the complete text of liturgical prayers, the editors say. They compare for this numbering of prayers the Byzantine *Prayers of the Faithful* (Εὐχαὶ πιστῶν α', β') and suggest that "the papyrus contains some part of the Mass of the Faithful" (56). At the same time they have to admit that the text of the prayers does not show the slightest resemblance to any of the *Prayers of the Faithful* in Byzantine liturgies. Phraseology and vocabulary are entirely different and there is no reference whatever to the Oblation. Also comparison with the Egyptian Rite or other extant liturgies turns out to be of little help for there is no trace of similarity to be found in the prayers of these documents. The prayers of the papyrus do use for the most part a biblical vocabulary but the composer made no use of quotations from the biblical text,[4] much unlike "the centos of Biblical phrases which make up so large a part of extant liturgies" (57). After having noted the composer's preference for epic diction,[5] the editors leave it at that.

This is not a very satisfactory situation and one might have expected that other scholars would try to find solutions to the enigma this prayer text poses before us. As we will see, in the 65 years since its publication only two scholars have paid attention to this text, both of them regarding it as an early Jewish prayer text.

The first one was Joseph Wahrhaftig.[6] In the *Journal of Theological Studies* of 1939 he published a short article to the effect that the papyrus contains a Jewish prayer.[7] Wahrhaftig points out that the editors' thesis that the prayer is Christian involves great difficulties. "For instance, the text lacks any allusions to anything specifically Christian and cannot be related to any known liturgy."[8] Even though the text cannot be identified with any extant Jewish prayer either, there are nevertheless several points of connexion between the fragment and Jewish liturgy. Wahrhaftig says that not only does the text not contain anything characteristically Christian, it also contains passages which cannot possibly be Christian at all. Moreover, many of the expressions in the text can be directly and completely translated back into Hebrew, which suggests that the author thought in Hebrew or followed a Hebrew model. Using Biblical language and allusions without direct quotations is characteristic of many ancient Jewish prayers, as for instance Ben Sira ch. 51 and the Eighteen Benedictions. Also the litany-like repetitions have their parallels in Jewish prayers. Resemblances of these repetitions with passages in the apostle Paul's epistles are not to be explained by assuming knowledge and use of Paul's letters by the composer – as Bell and Skeat did – but by the fact that "in such passages Paul uses the Jewish prayer-style" (377). Wahrhaftig discovers five complete sections in our text: lines 2-8 ask God to sanctify, protect etc. his people; lines 9-13 contain a petition for the healing of the soul; the third section, lines 14-21, is a prayer for protection from and forgiveness of sins; lines 22-26 praise God's great goodness; section five, in lines 27-33, contains a petition to accept the

---

[4] With the possible exception of Ps. 78:13 in line 8.
[5] They point to words such as ἄδεκτος, ἄφθιτος, κοτέειν, ἐπικήριος, τέκος, εὐκτήριος.
[6] So far I have not been able to trace any biographical data of this scholar.
[7] "A Jewish Prayer in a Greek Papyrus," *JTS* 40 (1939) 376-381. The article was translated from the German by J. N. Sanders, who occasionally inserted some critical notes of his own.
[8] Ibid. 376.

prayers. The concluding lines, 33-35, are the beginning of a new prayer, most of which is now lost. Seemingly Christian vocabulary, as for instance the use of φωτίζειν in line 4, can be completely explained in Jewish terms; giving it its Christian connotations – here 'to baptize' – would make nonsense of the text. Seeing an allusion to Jesus Christ in the petition for healing is unnecessary since similar petitions occur in Jewish prayers as well. Whereas the word εὐχαριστία in the singular is used in Christian literature of the period always in the sense of 'eucharist,' its use in the plural here undoubtedly is the equivalent of *berakhoth*. The emphasis on 'the people,' that God has "sanctified, sustained, gathered, governed, established, glorified, confirmed, pastured, raised up, enlightened, pacified, administered, and perfected" (2-5) is too typical of Jewish prayers as to be able to receive a Christian interpretation. Lines 14-16 and 28-32 have striking parallels in the liturgy for the Day of Atonement. And the expression αἰώνιος βασιλεύς (34) is a rendering of *melekh ha'olam*. It is not a perfect rendering, but the composer sometimes made minor mistakes in translating Hebrew terms. So, for instance, in line 6 he speaks of the people ὃν ἔκτισω, 'which Thou hast created,' whereas it should probably have been 'which Thou hast acquired,' *'am zu qanita*.[9] Wahrhaftig concludes that our text is most probably a paraphrase of the Shemoneh 'Esreh. Section 1 (sanctification, sustenance, etc.) parallels the first benediction of the Shemoneh 'Esreh, section 2 (healing) the fourth benediction, section 3 (forgiveness) the second benediction, section 4 (mercy) the third benediction, section 5 (the acceptance of prayer) the fifth benediction, and the final lines echo the sixth benediction of the Shemoneh 'Esreh. The order is almost identical, and in view of some echoes of the liturgy for Yom Kippur (fasting, vigils) it would seem that the papyrus contains a paraphrase of the Amidah for the Day of Atonement of which the form was not yet fixed in those early days. Wahrhaftig concludes: "Thus the intention of the author of the text preserved in this fragment was to put before a congregation of Egyptian Jews who spoke Greek and had very little command of Hebrew – or before one such Jew – the heart of the daily prayer – perhaps of that for the Day of Atonement – namely, the Shemoneh 'Esreh."

Some four years later, the famous Arthur Marmorstein published an article in the *Jewish Quarterly Review* on what he called the oldest form of the Eighteen Benedictions.[10] In this important study Marmorstein tries

---

[9] Wahrhaftig is right here but for the wrong reasons; see below the footnote on line 6.
[10] "The Oldest Form of the Eighteen Benedictions," *JQR* 34 (1943/44) 137-159.

to demonstrate that this new Greek fragment is a new source in the never ending search for the oldest form of the Amidah. He agrees in many respects with Wahrhaftig, but at the same time he is of the opinion that it was not the Shemoneh 'Esreh for the Day of Atonement that was the source of the Greek prayer. "The text is a translation of the daily *Sh(emoneh) E(sreh)*" (138). Marmorstein sees in the papyrus "a leaf from the oldest Jewish prayerbook extant" (138), in use among the Greek speaking Jews from Egypt, and possibly in other parts of the Diaspora as well. He conjectures that the text is probably contemporaneous with the Hebrew Ben Sira and hence welcomes the find, "although presented in Greek" (! 138), as of major importance in rediscovering the earliest form of the Amidah.

How much Marmorstein differs from Wahrhaftig in the details of interpretation may be clear from the following. The thirteen requests for God's people in the form of imperatives, which form the opening lines of the prayer, are not just the equivalent of the first benediction of the Amidah but can be identified with several *berakhoth* in the Shemoneh 'Esreh, some of them easily, others with some difficulty. The easy instances are the following: 'sanctify' (1) is the *Qedusha* (3), 'sustain' (2) is the *Birkat ha-Shanim* (9), 'gather' (3) is the *Qibbuts Geluyoth* (10), and 'govern' (4) is *Hashavat ha-Mishpat* (11). Marmorstein says that it cannot be pure accident that the numbers 2, 3, and 4 of the fragment are in the same order as 9, 10, and 11 in the Amidah. The remaining imperatives are to be divided into two groups, one of which can still relatively easily be identified, the other however less easily. Probably nr. 10, 'enlighten,' is *Da'at* (4), and nr. 11, 'pacify,' is the *Birkat Shalom* (19). Maybe nr. 12, 'administer,' could refer to *Avodah* (17), and nr. 7, 'pasture,' could have arisen from a misreading of *Ge'ula* (7) in which the initial word *r'h* (*re'eh*) was read as *r'h* (*ro'eh*). But from here onwards the identifications begin to become more and more uncertain. In the end Marmorstein is left with five items for which he cannot find an equivalent in the Amidah.

Then he turns to the four longer prayers of the papyrus and remarks that the 13 one-verb-petitions plus the 4 longer prayers add up to 17, which "is the actual number of the original *Sh.E.*" (141). The four fuller prayers (on health, forgiveness, thanksgiving, acceptance) show their originally Hebrew character in vocabulary, style, and thought from beginning to end, says Marmorstein. The prayer for health turns out to be the equivalent of *Refu'a* (8), the one for forgiveness is *Selichah* (6), thanksgiving is *Hoda'a* (18), and the one for the acceptance of prayers is *Shomea' Tefillah* (16). Marmorstein then indulges in speculations about the Hebrew 'Urform' of these prayers and about the mistakes which the translator made in producing the Greek version, but that can be left aside for the moment. He further points out a remarkable coincidence: the fourth of the longer prayers contains 15 different expressions for liturgical forms and gestures (lines 27-33), but three other liturgical texts from the Siddur, namely the *Kaddish*, the *Yishtabach*, and the *Emet we-yatziv*, also contain 15 expressions of praise and glory, and there are to be found 15 expressions of praise in the *Barukh she-amar* as well, as had already been remarked in the Middle Ages.[11] Marmorstein then summarizes the provisional results of his search: the Greek prayer contains 17 benedictions, as did the original Shemoneh Esreh, 10 of which can be regarded with certainty as corresponding to one another, and 2 hypothetically; five are lacking a clear counterpart. These five are in the Greek text 'establish' (5), 'glorify' (6), 'confirm' (7), 'raise up' (9), and 'perfect' (13); and in the Shemoneh 'Esreh *Avoth* (1), *Gevuroth* (2), *Teshuva* (5), *Al ha-tzadiqim* (13), and *Binyan Yerushalayim* (14), the latter combined with *Mashiach ben David* (15) according to the old Palestinian version. The *Birkat ha-minim* (12) had not yet been made part of the Amidah in the early date Marmorstein adopts for it. He now identifies 'glorify' (6) with *Avoth*, since "the keynote of the benediction is the *glorification of God*" (151). The glorification *of the people* that the Greek text speaks of is to be understood as God's glory *through* his people. 'Confirm' (7) is probably to be identified with *Gevuroth* since that benediction confirms the people's trust in God as *mechayyeh ha-metim* and "the similarity of גבר or חזק (as used in the old text of the Palestinian rite) may be considered as a connecting link between the present *Sh.E.* and the original Hebrew prayer used by the Greek translator" (152). The request 'perfect' (13) can now be seen to be the equivalent of *Teshuva* since true repentance means perfection. 'Raise up' (9) must remain doubtful if only because the Greek text is only partly readable here and uncertain, but as well as 'establish' (5) it "may have been the forerunner of the benediction for Jerusalem" (153). But these cannot but remain guesses. Finally Marmorstein demonstrates that the five relative clauses all of which begin with "the people which..." (lines 5-8) contain thoroughly biblical and Jewish conceptions. He concludes his study with a curious piece of uncritical Talmud exegesis to the effect that the Amidah with 17 benedictions is a very ancient institution that existed long before the destruction of the Second Temple. The Greek

---

[11] Ibid. 147.

fragment may reflect that prayer in one of its earliest stages of development. In this shape the prayer survived till after the destruction of the
Temple. The final ordering and arrangement of the benedictions as well as
the elaboration of their contents were undertaken in Javne, but our
papyrus demonstrates that in many cases the 17 benedictions grew out of
only one word (one verb) or very brief formulae. "The development of
the *Sh.E.* proved that the oldest form was actually very brief. As late as
the middle of the third century such short *Sh.E.* have been current, e.g. the
prayer called הביינו (see b. Ber. 29a, pal. Ber. 2.4)" (158-9). Marmorstein
also suggests that the shortened forms of the Shemoneh 'Esreh actually
reflected the older forms and that these enable us to see that the earliest
form of the Amidah was very different from the final composition of the
Amoraic period. Thanks to the papyrus find, "we may have recovered the
oldest form of Jewish prayer used in the last century of the Temple. We
recover further a clear and eloquent testimony for the high religious standard of the ordinary Jew in the time of Jesus" (159). Thus Marmorstein.

It is a remarkable fact that one cannot but say that, after the thorough
treatment by Marmorstein, our papyrus fragment has fallen victim to
complete neglect. As far as I am able to see, there are no publications
whatever on our text from the last 55 years. In the comprehensive *Encyclopedia Judaica* not a single word is devoted to our document, as far as
one can judge on the basis of the Index volume. Neither does David
Flusser mention the papyrus in his exhaustive overview of prayer materials from the period between 200 BCE and 200 CE.[12] Victor
Tcherikover and Alexander Fuks nowhere even refer to it in their *Corpus Papyrorum Judaicarum*,[13] even though they do include other material of which the Jewish origin is a matter of debate. The volumes of the
Berichtigungsliste der griechischen Papyrusurkunden aus Ägypten do
not mention any publications on our papyrus either.[14] Elias Bickerman

---

[12] D. Flusser, "Psalms, Hymns and Prayers," in: M.E. Stone (ed.), *Jewish Writings of the Second Temple Period*, Assen-Philadelphia 1984, 551-577.

[13] 3 vols., Cambridge MA 1957-1964.

[14] M. Lattke, *Hymnus. Materialien zu einer Geschichte der antiken Hymnologie*, Freiburg-Göttingen 1991, 265, still lists Pap. Egerton 5 under Christian Papyri and does not give any bibliography after 1935. C. H. Roberts, *Manuscript, Society and Belief in Early Christian Egypt*, London 1979, 78, just mentions the papyrus (here called 'P. Lond. Christ. 5') as one that has "been thought to be Jewish." H. Leclercq, in the lengthy lemma "Papyrus" in the *Dictionnaire d'archéologie chrétienne et de liturgie* XIII (Paris 1937) 1370-1520, quotes all of the papyrus (in both Greek and French) as a Christian "fragment liturgique" (1474).

mentions the papyrus, albeit only in a footnote, to the effect that the great historian of Hellenistic religions, Arthur Darby Nock, had told him that there is no reason to suppose that the prayer is Jewish, his argument being as follows: "Since both Jewish and Christian prayers used the Old Testament phraseology, there are necessarily some parallels to the Amidah in P. Egerton 5,"[15] a remarkably superficial observation on the part of such a famous scholar. It is hard to say what are the reasons for this more than half a century of neglect of such a fascinating and potentially important document. Is it due to the fact that most papyrologists are not Judaic scholars and that most Judaic scholars are not papyrologists? I do not know, but I do know that this papyrus text deserves to be saved from oblivion. A fresh look at the material is long overdue, and in the following paragraphs I will make a modest beginning of this badly needed investigation.

Let me begin by raising the most obvious question: is the prayer text Christian or Jewish? The case of the two Jewish scholars is strong here. Of course, the fact that there is not to be found anything specifically Christian in the prayer text does not in itself constitute a compelling proof that the prayer is non-Christian. There are some other instances of ancient prayers that we know to be Christian on other grounds but whose contents are completely devoid of Christian characteristics. A striking example is Pap. Berlin 9794, a document from the second half of the third century containing five Christian prayers for various occasions, four of which are explicitly Christian but one of which is only implicitly so; it lacks anything characteristically Christian, being in fact no more than a free rendering of the concluding prayer of the Hermetic treatise *Poimandres* (ch. 31-32).[16] So the lack of Christian specifica is not conclusive of itself. However, (1) it is only a very tiny minority of the hundreds of early Christian prayer texts that are extant to which this applies;[17] (2) this kind of non-explicitly Christian prayers are always very short texts. In longer Christian prayer texts sooner or later either Jesus Christ is mentioned or there is an otherwise undeniable reference to some Christian idea or a New Testament passage. The fact that in our two full pages of prayer text there is nothing of the sort militates

---

[15] E.J. Bickerman, "The Civic Prayer for Jerusalem," *HTR* 55 (1962) 169 n. 28; repr. in his *Studies in Jewish and Christian History*, vol. 2, Leiden 1980, 296 n. 27 (290-312).

[16] For text and translation see P. W. van der Horst & G. E. Sterling, *Prayers from the Ancient World*, Notre Dame 2002 (forthcoming).

[17] As will be confirmed by a glance at the almost 250 papyri with Christian prayer texts listed by J. van Haelst, *Catalogue* 263-330.

strongly against a Christian origin, the more so since the emphatic passage on forgiveness (14-19) has no reference whatever to Christ's mediatorship in regard to God's forgiveness.[18] Moreover, in this case this negative argument is reinforced by positive ones, the most important of them being the following. Firstly, many elements in the papyrus text have their closest parallels in Jewish prayer texts. Now Jewish prayer texts could have been adopted and used by Christians, as is clearly proven by the collection of Jewish liturgical documents in the seventh book of the *Apostolic Constitutions*.[19] In such known cases, however, the originally Jewish documents were always christianized to a greater or lesser degree. Not the slightest christianization is discernible, however, in Pap. Egerton 5. Secondly, not only are the closest parallels those in Jewish prayer texts, but these parallels derive for the most part from one specific Jewish prayer, namely the Amidah, as both Wahrhaftig and Marmorstein have abundantly demonstrated. It would seem, therefore, that we can safely follow them in their assumption that the prayer is Jewish.[20] Does that imply that we also have to swallow their suggestion that we have here a very early Greek form of the Amidah? That brings us to our second question: how convincing are Wahrhaftig's and especially Marmorstein's hypotheses to the effect that the papyrus represents one of the oldest stages of the Amidah?

Here the ground becomes more slippery. Even though Marmorstein had a very fine intuition, that does not mean that this great scholar was always right. Wahrhaftig, who knew the Shemoneh 'Esreh very well, could find parallels to only 6 benedictions of this prayer, whereas Marmorstein found parallels to no less than 16 *berakhoth* of the Amidah. This should make us wary of overhasty conclusions. Marmorstein may have suffered from a certain degree of 'Entdeckerfreude' which always makes one see more than there really is. Also the enormous differences between what he sees as the oldest form of the Amidah on the one hand and the reconstruction of such an early form by Louis Finkelstein on the other cannot fail to make us very cautious.[21] We should also bear in

---

[18] The claim by Bell and Skeat (60) that the enumeration in lines 31-32 is based upon 2 Cor. 11:23.27 can be dismissed; see below.

[19] See D. A. Fiensy, *Prayers Alleged to be Jewish. An Examination of the Constitutiones Apostolorum*, Chico CA 1985.

[20] That the leaf is from a codex is no argument to the contrary. Even though the codex was probably an early Christian invention, after the third century Jews started to use the codex instead of the scroll; see Roberts, *Manuscript, Society and Belief* 75-76.

[21] See L. Finkelstein, "The Development of the Amidah," *JQR* n.s. 16 (1925/26) 1-43 and 127-170.

mind that comparison of our papyrus text with the Amidah is much complicated by the fact that there has *never* been a time in which there was a fixed text of all the *berakhot* that was accepted as authoritative by all Jewish communities. All we have is a wide variety of versions, so a comparison should focus on motifs and meanings rather than on words and phrases.

Let us begin with the very different evaluations of the 13 opening imperatives by Wahrhaftig and Marmorstein. Of course, they most probably were not the opening lines of the prayer, since they lack any form of address, but we have no way of knowing what preceded these lines; perhaps only "Oh Lord" or a section of praise before the requests. Now Wahrhaftig regards these as a rendering of or the equivalent of the first *berakhah* of the Amidah (*Avoth*), without giving any arguments for this view, whereas Marmorstein sees in them short versions of no less than 13 *berakhoth* of the Amidah, only δόξασον ('glorify,' line 3) corresponding to *Avoth*. Is either of these suggestions very probable and, if so, which is the more probable one? To me it seems almost absurd to see these 13 imperatives, followed – to be sure – by 'the people which you have made your own' etc., as in any way equivalent to the first Benediction, whichever version of that *berakhah* one takes. But it is hardly easier to believe that the imperatival statement 'glorify your people' could render the gist of the benediction in *Avoth*. So both scholars have presented a very weak case as far as *Avoth* is concerned.

What about Marmorstein's other identifications of the list of imperatives? It has to be admitted that here he sometimes makes a stronger case. That 'sanctify' (ἁγίασον) reminds one of the *Qedusha*, even though there it is God himself not his people who is sanctified, cannot be denied. And that the second, third, and fourth of the imperatives ('sustain, gather, govern') show a strong similarity in subject and order to the ninth, tenth, and eleventh of the *berakhoth* in the Amidah (*Birkat ha-Shanim, Qibbuts Geluyoth*, and *Hashavat ha-Mishpat*) is clear to any reader. So here Marmorstein seems to move towards firmer ground. That there is a thematic affinity between the imperative 'enlighten' (sc. your people) and the fourth *berakhah*, i.e. *Da'at*, and between 'give peace' and the *Birkat Shalom* (19), also stands to reason. But the other identifications as far as the 13 imperatives are concerned are much too speculative. I for one cannot see, for instance, how 'administer' (οἰκονόμησον) could possible be a form of the benediction *Avodah*, and that 'perfect' (τελείωσον) is to be identified with *Teshuva* since repentance leads to perfection is ingenious but hardly constitutes a convincing proof. On the other hand I would suggest one further identification: 'raise up' (ἀνάστησον) with *Gevuroth* (2) because of that *berakhah*'s emphasis on the resurrection of the dead (*techiyyat ha-metim*).

But we are still left with the four longer prayers in lines 9-33. It is a fascinating observation that on Marmorstein's count the papyrus' text contains 17 prayers, the number of *berakhot* the Amidah is supposed to have originally had. But it is hard to say what value we may attribute to that fact. It may after all be sheer coincidence. The same applies to his observation that the fourth of the longer prayers contains 15 terms for liturgical acts, a number that is identical to that of the expressions of praise in other prayers of the Siddur. I will leave this aside for the moment in order to first examine whether Marmorstein's identifications of these four prayers with *berakhoth* in the Amidah can stand up to criticism.

I would submit that here Marmorstein has his strongest case. It can hardly be coincidental that these four prayers on healing, forgiveness, thanksgiving, and acceptance of prayers have their precise counterparts in the benedictions *Refu'a*, *Selichah*, *Hoda'a*, and *Shomea' Tefillah*. One might of course object here that themes such as healing, forgiveness, thanksgiving and acceptance of prayers are so commonplace in ancient prayers that nothing can be built on such an observation. But I think Marmorstein's observations cannot be dismissed that easily. When we take a closer look at the materials we see, for instance, that both prayers for health or healing contain three imperatives and an expression of praise, that the prayers on forgiveness of sins show a remarkable similarity in wording ('forgive us for we have sinned' — 'forgive us what we have sinned'), that both thanksgiving prayers stress God's never ending goodness and beneficence, and that both prayers for acceptance are repetitive in that they stress the theme of God's acceptance of the prayers by means of various ways of phrasing it.[22] I suggest that all this cannot be sheer coincidence. There must at least be some connection between these Greek prayer texts and the Hebrew Amidah. Let us face the facts: Here is a prayer text that bristles with biblical language and motifs; it cannot possibly be Christian (and definitely is not pagan), so it must be Jewish; at least 10 of the 17 petitions (6 in the series of 13 short imperatives, 4 in the longer prayers) show an undeniable thematic affinity with *berakhoth* in the most central one of Jewish prayers, the Amidah. And this counting is based only on those

---

[22] This becomes even clearer if comparison is made with the expanded versions (compare *qolenu, tefillatenu, tachanunim* with *euchai, deêseis, aitêseis, axiôseis*).

of Marmorstein's identifications which are likely to be right. We could add two equations of our own: the already mentioned 'raise up' with *Gevuroth*, and that of the final line, "We beseech Thee to act (?) according to our pitiful state" (35), with *Ge'ula*, the seventh *berakhah*, which begins with "Look upon our affliction." In that case we could make at least 12 equations between the papyrus and the Amidah. What are we to make of that?

Marmorstein says we have here the oldest form (or one of the oldest forms) of the Amidah, dating back to the Second Temple Period, but this dating is unacceptable. The papyrus is to be dated to the final decades of the fourth or the opening decades of the fifth century, and even though the text can reasonably be assumed to be older than that, there is no proof whatever that it derives from the period before 70, let alone the beginning of the second century BCE, as he would have us believe. In my opinion there are from a theoretical point of view four possibilities.

The first one is that we have to do here with a Jewish prayer but that the thematic similarities with *berakhoth* in the Shemoneh Esreh are pure coincidence and due to the fact that these are quite common requests for any Jewish prayer. This possibility cannot be ruled out, but I do not think it is the most likely one. The second one is that we have here an early form of the Amidah that demonstrates that many if not all of the *berakhoth* developed out of a single imperative. This is Marmorstein's position, but the problem here is that it is very hard to envisage a stage in which only a small number of these imperatives had begun to develop into more elaborated prayers whereas the others remained in their rudimental form. Moreover, why would this very early form remain in use in Egypt some 400 to 500 years after its composition? The third possibility is that we have here an abbreviated Amidah, a *tefilah qetsarah*, in which the Amidah (or part of it) is reduced to its essentials. We know that this kind of shortened Shemoneh 'Esreh existed in Tannaitic and Amoraic times and the Talmud even presents us with the full text of a beautiful example of such a condensed version of the Amidah (the so-called *Havinenu*).[23] So this suggestion by Marmorstein

[23] See m. *Ber*. IV 3 with b. *Ber*. 29a (also t. *Ber*. III 7 and j.*Ber*. IV 3, 8a). Samuel's well-known version of an abbreviated Shemoneh 'Esreh (מעין י"ח) in the Bavli runs as follows: "Give us discernment (*havinenu*), o Lord, to know Thy ways, and circumcise our heart to fear Thee, and forgive us so that we may be redeemed, and keep us far from our sufferings, and fatten us in the pastures of Thy land, and gather our dispersions from the four corners of the earth, and let them who err from Thy prescriptions be punished, and

should be seriously considered, even though one need not accept his corollary thesis that this shortened form reflected the oldest form of the Amidah. One has to explain, however, why in the Greek papyrus some of the *berakhoth* were so drastically shortened that nothing more than one word (an imperative) was left and that in this way 13 benedictions were compressed into one, whereas 4 (or 5) others were left unaltered. Here, however, the fact that the manuscript indicates by means of an A and a B that there is a distinction between the section with the string of imperatives on the one hand and the longer prayers on the other may be of some use. The Bavli's example of a shortened Shemoneh 'Esreh in *Berakhoth* 29a makes clear that according to the rabbis (or some rabbis) not all *berakhoth* lent themselves to abbreviation. According to Talmud Bavli Mar Samuel (third cent. CE) includes the much abbreviated contents of only the thirteen (or twelve) middle benedictions into one; the first three and the last three he leaves intact. Now unfortunately neither can the 13 imperatives from the Greek prayer's opening lines be said to coincide with the thirteen (or twelve) middle benedictions of the Amidah nor can the 4 longer prayers be said to coincide with the first and last three benedictions, even though there is some overlap. The important thing, however, is the principle of distinction: some prayers (13 in both cases!) may be shortened, others may not. In this respect one could reasonably suggest that Samuel's example was just one of many possibilities of which we now see another one in our papyrus.[24] If the verso side of the papyrus would contain the opening line of the prayer – which is not certain, as we have seen – its abruptness is nicely paralleled by what Joseph Heinemann has called "the aggressive manner of address" of several forms of *tefillah qetsarah*.[25] What remains problematic in this solution, however, is that exactly in the abbreviated part we find a drastic expansion: lines 5-9, with their five times repeated 'the people,' cannot exactly be said to contribute to the shortening of the prayers. Therefore, a somewhat more sophisticated solution is to be offered, and that brings us to the fourth possibility.

This fourth option is no more than a revision or adaptation of the third. I envisage the following process. The Shemoneh 'Esreh gradually

---

lift up Thy hand against the wicked, and let the righteous rejoice in the building of Thy city and the establishment of the Temple and in the exalting of the horn of David Thy servant and the preparation of a light for the son of Jesse the Messiah; before we call mayest Thou answer; blessed art Thou, o Lord, who hearkenest to prayer."

[24] For abbreviated versions of the Seven Benedictions of the Amida see J. Heinemann, "One Benediction Comprising Seven," *REJ* 125 (1966) 101-111.

[25] J. Heinemann, *Prayer in the Talmud*, Berlin 1977, 188.

evolved in the period from the first through the fourth centuries. If ever there was an 'Urtext' – which is very doubtful[26] – we will never be able to reconstruct it because the materials at our disposal simply do not enable us to do so. Our Greek papyrus does not contain the 'oldest form,' let alone the 'Urtext,' of the Amidah either. As soon as the Amidah, with a not yet fixed number of *berakhoth* in a not yet fixed order[27] and a not yet fixed textual form,[28] began to spread outside Palestine, various Diaspora communities developed their own variants of this prayer in Greek, suited to their own needs and, in a predominantly Greek environment, sometimes with originally Greek elements added.[29] Especially in areas of the Diaspora where the rabbis had not yet gained influence or dominance, the communities felt free to develop their own brand of Amidah. Maybe one should not even speak about the Amidah here, but about a generally recognized model or pattern of prayer that was adopted by both Palestinian and Diaspora Jews and adapted differently in different communities, and that contained the building blocks of what in the hands of the later rabbis was to become the Amidah. In Egypt, the small Jewish communities left after the devastating war of 115-117 CE developed their own forms of prayer in the period from the middle of the second to the middle of the fourth century. The community (-ies) from which our papyrus derives possibly knew a tradition about a shortened Amidah, or perhaps even knew only a shortened Amidah, but a different one from Samuel's instance mentioned in the Bavli (which is by and large section A of the papyrus). They also had traditions about other prayers connected to the shortened Amidah but of a more elaborated nature, which in their community had taken on a somewhat different shape than in rabbinic circles (which is by and large section B of the papyrus, though I do realize that I have to assume then that the copyist erred in putting the B four lines too late, in 13 instead of in 9). Different

---

[26] Elias Bickerman remarks about the Amidah: "It would be absurd to try to fix the 'original' wording of a traditional text. What we can hope to attain is the original meaning of a benediction" ('Civic Prayer' 164). Cf. also K. Kohler, "The Origin and Composition of the Eighteen Benedictions with a Translation of the Corresponding Essene Prayers in the Apostolic Constitutions," *HUCA* 1 (1924) 392 (387-425): the Amidah is "the product of a gradual growth and development." But see now especially the treatment by S. C. Reif, *Judaism and Hebrew Prayer*, Cambridge 1993, chs. 3-4.

[27] Cf. b. *Ber.* 34a: "The intermediate benedictions have no fixed order."

[28] See e.g. I. Elbogen, *Jewish Liturgy*, Philadelphia – New York – Jerusalem 1993, 28; and Heinemann, *Prayer*, passim.

[29] See, for instance, below the note on line 24. For references to synagogal liturgies in Greek see Reif, *Judaism and Hebrew Prayer*, 350 n. 47.

berakhoth than in rabbinic circles were abbreviated, different ones were kept in a longer form, but nonetheless, due to the fact that they worked with traditional material, their text is still recognizable for us as a form of the Amidah. The objection that the rabbinic rule is that an abbreviated Amidah was only meant to be used in a situation of emergency or pressing need[30] is not valid, for, as Elbogen already remarks, there is evidence that "even in public worship these abridged forms were in use."[31] Apart from that, rabbinic rules were quite often ignored by the common people.

If there is truth in the hypothesis that we have here an early form of what was to become the Amidah, one of its striking aspects is that the text is totally devoid of references to the Patriarchs, to the people of Israel, to Jerusalem, and to the Messiah. In other words, national elements which would have made the prayer immediately recognizable as Jewish are absent. How is that to be explained? It cannot be excluded that in an early phase of its development the Amidah did lack these elements. It is also possible that, if some or all of these elements *were* present in one version in circulation, they were lacking in another. And one should not rule out the possibility that in an abridged version these elements simply dropped out. After all, the Bavli text of the *Havinenu* lacks the names of the Patriarchs, of Israel, and of Jerusalem; only the reference to the Messiah is retained. Be that as it may, the absence of these references should not be taken to imply that the prayer is not Jewish. However, I have to concede honestly that a very different explanation cannot altogether be ruled out. As I have indicated before, we know that in some early Christian communities Jewish communal prayers were taken over and slightly christianized by adding references to Jesus Christ and the New Testament. Do we here perhaps have a case of a Jewish prayer, an abridged Amidah, taken over by Christians and 'christianized' only by deleting the explicitly Jewish references? It does not seem to me a very viable hypothesis, but nothing is impossible in the world of late antiquity.

By way of conclusion I now present the text once more in translation, this time my own. It differs from the one by Bell and Skeat in that I will render it into a more modern idiom than they did and in that my understanding of the text is in some places slightly different from theirs.

[30] See, e.g., M. Nulman, *The Encyclopedia of Jewish Prayer,* Northvale NJ 1993, 171, who states on the basis of rabbinic sources that this is the rule.
[31] *Jewish Liturgy* 54.

(1) A [Verso]
(2) Make holy,[32] nourish,[33] gather,[34] govern,[35] (3) support,[36] glorify,[37] establish,[38] herd,[39] (4) raise up,[40] enlighten,[41] bring peace[42] (to), (5) administer,[43] make perfect[44] -[45] the people (6) that you have made your own,[46] your special people,[47] (7) the people that you have redeemed,[48] the people that (8) you have called,[49] your people, the sheep which (9) you graze.[50] Of our sick soul you (10) are the only doctor,[51] keep those who are sick in your joy (?),[52] (11) heal us, do not throw us away (12) as not capable of receiving your healing.[53] The word (13) that goes out from your mouth[54] is the giver of health.

[B] (14) These things we ask you, Master,[55] forgive us (15) all the sins we did,[56] keep in check (?)[57] what may lead us (16) to sin, and do not write down against us[58] all the (17) unlawful acts we committed. Forgiveness of sin

---

[32] Cf. Ez. 20:12 etc. References in the following notes are to the LXX.

[33] Cf. Gen. 50:20-21 etc.

[34] Ps. 105(106):47; 146(147):2; Is. 11:12; 27:13; 56:8.

[35] Sap. Sal. 8:40.

[36] 1 Macc. 14:14.

[37] 1 Esdras 9:52.

[38] Ps. 118(119):28.

[39] 2 Kings 7:7.

[40] Amos 7:2.5

[41] Micha 7:8. Cf. 1 Kings 3:9-12; 2 Chron. 1:10.

[42] Job 5:24. 'Give peace to your people' would seem to me to be a more adequate translation of εἰρήνευσον than 'pacify' as Bell and Skeat have it.

[43] Cf. Ps. 111(112):15

[44] Mt. 5:48; in a prayer context, Didache 10:5.

[45] Between the lists of imperatives and 'the people' the papyrus has a blank space with a stroke in the centre of the line. It may be tentatively suggested that it is the space where the Tetragrammaton should have been written in Hebrew characters but the scribe did not know how to write it. For other examples see Roberts, Manuscript 76-77.

[46] Here one has to read ἐκτήσω instead of ἐκτίσω – an evident case of itacism – in view of the fact that κτίζω is never used in medial forms and that Ex. 15:16 reads ὁ λαός σου ὃν ἐκτήσω, in a passage that has more echoes in lines 5-9. Note that in Deut. 32:6 it is said that God both ἔκτισεν and ἐκτήσατο His people Israel.

[47] Cf. Ex. 19:5; 23:22 etc.

[48] Cf. Ex. 6:6; 15:13.

[49] Is. 45:3 etc.

[50] Ps. 78(79):13; Cf. Ps. 22(23):1; 94(95):7; 99(100):3 etc.

[51] Jer. 17:14; 40:6. Here the idea of health is spiritualized, whereas in the benediction Rephu'a the accent is more on healing of the physically ill. However, the Palestinian version reads: "Heal us... from the sickness of our heart"!

[52] This translation is a mere guess since the reading of the Greek is very uncertain. The papyrus has ση αγαλλ[..........]ρει which the editors tentatively restore to σῇ ἀγαλλ[ιάσει τῇ]ρει, which is strange Greek, however.

[53] Cf. b. Shab. 12a: God as rophe' choley 'ammo Yisra'el.

[54] Is. 55:11; Jos. 6:10; Esth. 7:8; Ps. 19:15; 36:4; 78:1; Prov. 5:7; 18:4; Eccles. 10:12.

[55] Though by far not as frequently as κύριος, as a form of address for God δεσπότης is often found in the LXX.

[56] Cf. Ps. 50[51]:3-4.

[57] The reading is uncertain: κάτ[εχε].

[58] Here the idea is that of a heavenly book in which men's good and bad deeds are recorded. For καταγράφειν see Ex. 17:14 etc.

(18) B [Recto]
(19) is the work of your forbearance. It is fitting, (20) o imperishable one, not to act in wrath against mortals who are doomed to die, (21) who have only a short life, who live on a toilsome earth. (22) You do well[59] without interruption, for you are free from envy,[60] (23) you give everything whereas you take nothing, for (24) you are in need of nothing,[61] every good thing is yours, evil (25) alone is not yours,[62] wicked is what you do (26) not want, a product of our thoughts. (27) Accept[63] from us these psalmodies, (28) these hymnodies, these prayers, these invocations, (29) these entreaties, these petitions, these (30) expressions of gratitude, these requests, these blessings, (31) this zeal, this earnestness, these vigils, (32) these [fasts?],[64] this lying on the ground,[65] (33) these prayerful sounds. Since we have in you a Master (34) that loves mankind, King of the ages,[66] (35) we beseech you to act in agreement with your compassion[67] for our present circumstances.[68]

Appendix: The Greek text of Papyrus Egerton 5.[69]

(A)
2   ἁγίασον, διάθρεψον, ἐπισύναξον, διοίκησον,
     στήρισον, δόξασον, βεβαίωσον, ποίμανον,

---

[59] God as welldoer: Ps. 12(13):6; 56(57):2 etc.
[60] The motif of God's ἀφθονία does not occur in the LXX, but it is also not specifically Christian since it occurs also in pagan Greek literature. See W.C. van Unnik, *De ἀφθονία van God in de oudchristelijke letterkunde*, Amsterdam-London 1973.
[61] Here it is emphasized that God does not lack anything, which is an idea derived from the later Platonic *theologia negativa*. Line 23 is almost literally identical to *Corpus Hermeticum* 5:10: πάντα δίδως καὶ οὐδὲν λαμβάνεις.
[62] That God is far removed from any evil is a commonplace in the Hellenistic and Roman period among Greeks, Jews and Christians.
[63] Note that in almost all versions of the Amidah the 17th benediction (Avodah) begins with "Accept...".
[64] 'Fasts' is a conjecture that was apparently made by Wahrhaftig (see *JTS* 40 [1939] 377 n.4) and that formed part of the basis for his contention that we have here the Amidah for Yom Kippur. If only the vigils are left, this basis is very weak since Yom Kippur apparently was not the only occasion for vigils. See Philo, *De vita contemplativa* 83, for vigils held by the Therapeutae (in Egypt!).
[65] The combination of vigils, fasts and lying on the ground is also to be found in Athanasius' *Vita Antonii* 4:1:... ἀγρυπνοῦντι ... ἐν νηστείαις καὶ χαμευνίαις. This parallel does not constitute proof in any way that the prayer is Christian!
[66] One has to read here either τὸν αἰώνιον βασιλέα (Eternal King) or τῶν αἰώνων βασιλέα (King of the Ages), the latter of course being strikingly similar to, if not identical with, *melekh ha-'olam(im)*.
[67] Litt. 'things worthy of (your) compassion.'
[68] The translation of this final line is far from being certain.
[69] The text presented here is not an edition of the papyrus, but a corrected and restored text. At the end it will be indicated where the papyrus has a different reading. For an edition with photographs of the papyrus see my article 'Papyrus Egerton 5: Christian or Jewish?', *Zeitschrift für Papyrologie und Epigraphik* 121 (1998) 173-182.

4	ἀνάστησον, φώτισον, εἰρήνευσον, οἰκο-
	νόμησον, τελείωσον ------- τ[ὸν] λαὸ[ν]
6	ὃν ἐκτήσω, τὸν λαὸν τὸν [π]εριούσιον,
	τὸν λαὸν ὃν ἐλ[υ]τρώσω, [τ]ὸν λαὸν ὃν
8	ἐκάλεσας, τὸν λαόν σου, [τὰ] πρόβατα τῆς
	νομῆς [σου. ψ]υχῆς ἡμῶν ν[ο]σούσης ἰατρὸς
10	μόνος εἶ σύ, σῇ ἀγαλλ[ιάσει τή]ρει νοσέοντας,
	ἡμᾶς θεράπευσον, μὴ ἡμᾶς ἀπ[ο]ρίψῃς
12	ὡς ἀδέκτ[ο]υς σῆς θεραπ[εί]ας. σοῦ ἀπὸ
	στόματος λόγ[ο]ς ὑγιείας [ἐ]στὶν δοτήρ. Β.
14	ταῦτ᾽ αἰτούμεθα παρ[ὰ σοῦ], δέσποτα, παρὲς
	ὅσα ἡμάρτομεν, κάτ[εχε] εἴ τι ἁμαρτάνειν
16	[φ]έρει, καὶ μὴ [ἡ]μῶν κ[ατα]γράψῃς ὅσα πα-
	ρανόμως ἐπράξαμεν. [σ]ῆς ἀνεξικακίας
18	(Β)
	ἔργον ἄφεσις ἁμαρτιῶν. εὐπρεπές ἐστιν,
20	ἄφθιτε, θνητοῖς μὴ κοτέειν ἐπικήροις,
	ὀλιγοβίοις, ἐπίμοχθον [γ]ῆν ἔχουσιν. εὐ-
22	[ερ]γετῶν οὐ διαλείπεις, [ἄφ]θονος γὰρ εἶ σύ,
	πᾶν δίδως οὐθὲν λαμβάνων, ἀνεν-
24	δεὴς γὰρ εἶ, πᾶν ἀγαθόν [ἐσ]τιν σόν, κακὸν
	δὲ μόνον οὐ σόν, φαῦλόν ἐστιν ὃ μὴ
26	θέλεις, τέκος ἐννοιῶν ἡμετερῶν. -------
	προσδέξαι παρ᾽ ἡμῶν τὰς ψαλμῳδίας,
28	τὰς ὑμνῳδίας, τὰς εὐχάς, τὰς παρακλή-
	σεις, τὰς δεήσεις, τὰς ἀξιώσεις, τὰς
30	ἐξομολογήσεις, τὰς αἰτήσεις, τὰς εὐχαριστίας,
	[τὴν] προθυμίαν, τὴν σπουδήν, τὰς ἀγρυπνί-
32	ας, τὰς [..........], τὰς χαμευνίας, τὰς
	εὐκτηρίους φωνᾶς. φιλάνθρωπον ἔχ[ον-]
34	τες δεσπότην σέ, τὸν αἰώνων βασιλέα,
	ἱκετεύομεν τὰ καθ᾽ ἡμᾶς οἴκτου ἄξια

The papyrus reads in line 5 τελιωσον, in line 6 εκτισω, in line 16 φερι, in line 19 ευπρεπον, in line 20 κιτεειν, at the end of line 29 τας τας, and in line 34 αιωνιων.[70]

[70] I owe thanks to the Institute for Advanced Studies at the Hebrew University for having offered me the opportunity to write this contribution in the framework of the project "The Early History of Jewish Prayer and Liturgy" and to the following colleagues in the Jerusalem research group for useful hints and other forms of support: Gerald Blidstein, Esther Chazon, Stefan Reif, and Joseph Tabory. Also Lee Levine kindly provided me with several valuable comments on the first draft of this paper.

4. WAS THE SYNAGOGUE A PLACE OF SABBATH WORSHIP BEFORE 70 CE?

Before 70 CE there were no separate synagogal buildings and, if there were, they did not serve as places of worship on the Sabbath. These, put briefly, are two propositions which have been increasingly argued in recent years. The first theory, that there were no synagogues in the sense of buildings (at least not in Palestine), was launched by Howard Kee (in 1990). I will deal with it only summarily because it has already been competently and sufficiently refuted by other scholars. The fullest case for the second proposition, that synagogues were not places of Sabbath worship, was recently presented by Heather McKay (in 1994), and I will discuss her theory in more detail.

Kee has the following arguments for his theory.[1] In Jewish sources up till the third century CE the word *synagôgê* is used only in the sense of 'assembly' or 'congregation,' in accordance with the original meaning of the word and with normal Greek usage, and not for a place of assembly, let alone for a building. For the place of assembly the early sources always use *proseuchê*, literally (place of) prayer (*beth tefillah*), but this need not have been a building at all, let alone a separate building for this special purpose, and in fact it was not. And even if it was, a *proseuchê* is still not a synagogue. Only after the fall of the Temple, in order to strengthen a sense of solidarity essential to the preservation of the Jewish identity, does *synagôgê* (*beth knesset*) become the term for the house of assembly for worship. "It was only after 70 CE that the synagogue began to emerge as a distinctive institution with its own characteristic structure" (7). The famous Theodotus inscription, which seems to imply the existence of a synagogue in or near the Temple in Jerusalem, is always, but without any foundation, dated before 70, whereas a date in the second half of the second century CE or even later is much more likely. The so-called synagogues of Masada and Herodium have been wrongly identified as synagogues; they were no more than public places. There is not a single building from the first century or earlier

---

[1] See H.C. Kee, "The Transformation of the Synagogue after 70 C.E.," *New Testament Studies* 36 (1990) 1-24.

which has been indisputably identified as a synagogue. Places of prayer were merely parts of private houses or rooms in other buildings which had been set apart (or were rented) for worship. Buildings which can be rightly regarded as synagogues are not found before the third century (in this he follows Joseph Gutmann). This applies equally to Palestine and to the Diaspora. Places of prayer from before the third century which have been found in the Diaspora are without exception rooms in private houses or rented rooms in other buildings; identifications of buildings as synagogues before the third or fourth century are almost always due to wishful thinking on the part of archeologists. The New Testament passages in the Gospels and the book of Acts which talk about synagogues refer either to the Jewish congregations or to informal meetings of Jewish believers; and if they do clearly mean a building, we are dealing with an unhistorical retrojection into an earlier period of a situation which only developed at the end of the first century (this is mainly the case in the work of Luke and Matthew). Thus far Kee.

In a first, short reaction written in the same year Ed Sanders calls Kee's article "remarkably ill-informed."[2] He starts with Kee's attempt to discount the Theodotus inscription.[3] This Greek inscription from Jerusalem will recur later in this contribution and I therefore quote the text in full:

> Theodotus, son of Vettenus, priest and head of the synagogue, son of a head of the synagogue, grandson of a head of a synagogue, had this synagogue built for reading (5) of the Law and instruction in the commandments, and also the guest lodgings and the rooms and the water systems for the accommodation of those who come from abroad and need (accommodation). (This synagogue) was founded by his ancestors, the (10) elders, and Simonides.[4]

Sanders points out that Kee's late dating is improbable if only because such a text must have been written in a period when there were still wealthy priestly families in Jerusalem who thought it was worthwhile to build guest rooms and bathing facilities (*miqva'oth*) near the Temple for Greek-speaking pilgrims. This requires a date before 70. (Five years later Rainer Riesner adduced other and more compelling arguments showing that this inscription cannot possibly date after 70.)[5] Sanders

---

[2] E.P. Sanders, *Jewish Law from Jesus to the Mishnah*, London: SCM Press, 1990, 341 n. 29.

[3] Sanders, *Jewish Law* 341 n. 28.

[4] *Corpus Inscriptionum Judaicarum* [= CIJ] no. 1404.

[5] R. Riesner, "Synagogues in Jerusalem," in R. Bauckham (ed.), *The Book of Acts in its Palestinian Setting* (The Book of Acts in its First Century Setting 4), Grand Rapids: Eerdmans, 1995, 194-200.

also notes that Kee consistently ignores or misinterprets our main witnesses to Judaism before 70, namely Josephus and Philo. E.g. the fact that the places where the Jewish authors talk about a *proseuchê* as a building are barred from the debate on the synagogue is indicative of Kee's special pleading. I want to quote some of these places mentioned by Sanders to show how far Kee is wide of the mark.

In his *Life* 277 Josephus describes an event in the mid-sixties of the first century which took place in Tiberias. He says: "The next day [a Sabbath!] all the people assembled in the synagogue (*proseuchê*), a very large building which could contain a large crowd." The fact that Josephus uses the term *proseuchê* here instead of *synagôgê* is reason enough for Kee to disregard this place, even though Josephus is clearly talking about a building of very large dimensions (not a living-room or small meeting-place) in which people assembled on the Sabbath. Another incident involving the synagogue in Caesarea occurs in the same period and is described by Josephus in *War* II 285-290. The Jews, says Josephus, had a *synagôgê* there next to a piece of land owned by a Greek. They wanted to buy this piece of land for a large sum of money (evidently to enlarge the synagogue), but the owner rejected their offer and filled up the area with small businesses and workshops, so that the Jews were confined to a very narrow alley. The aim, then, was pure harassment. When the Roman governor Florus left the city on a Friday to go to Samaria, the Greeks saw their opportunity. "On the following day, a Sabbath, when the Jews assembled in the synagogue, they discovered that a Caesarean mischief-maker was sacrificing birds beside the entrance on a pot turned upside down" (289).[6] The Jews were outraged by this grave insult to their laws and desecration of their place. After some commotion they took their Torah scroll and left in search of the governor. Sanders rightly remarks here that this synagogue, too, was clearly not a living-room or multipurpose space. It was a sacred place to them which had been profaned (*memiasmenon*) by this heathen act, so that they had to remove the Torah scroll. The fact that the sacrilege took place on Saturday morning suggests that this especially was the time

---

[6] O. Michel & O. Bauernfeind, *Flavius Josephus. De bello judaico* I, Darmstadt: Wissenschaftliche Buchgesellschaft, 1959, 445 n. 156, point out that, though this event may have only involved a general mockery of the Jewish cult, there was possibly a more vicious dimension to this Greek action: in Lev. 14 the sacrifice of birds is a purificatory offering after leprosy, and in the anti-Jewish literature of the Greeks and Romans the Jews are often depicted as lepers originally driven out of Egypt; see M. Stern, *Greek and Latin Authors on Jews and Judaism*, 3 vols., Jerusalem: The Israel Academy of Sciences and Humanities, 1974-1984, Index *s.v.* leprosy.

when the Jews visited this building.[7] Finally, Philo in *Quod omnis probus liber sit* 81 talks about the *hieroi topoi hoi kalountai synagôgai*, 'the holy places which are called synagogues,' where the Jews assemble on the seventh day and sit down in rows for reading and explanation of the Torah. This, too, seems at least to suggest holy places which are particularly designed for worship on the Sabbath.

Sanders also points out that Kee interprets archeological data to suit his own purposes. Thus he makes the synagogues in Gamla and Magdala "nothing more than private houses in which the pious gathered for prayer" (8). Sanders says that, besides the fact that Kee's pronouncements on Magdala are irrelevant because this synagogue post-dates 70, the whole remark cuts no ice:

> The pre-70 synagogue at Gamla is nothing like a private house. I do not mean that it had a Gothic spire: all that is left is the floor and part of the wall. It is one large room, with rows of benches around the sides. Connected to it, with a window looking into the main room, is a very small room which might hold eight or ten people at a pinch. Private houses look quite different. Nor is the building an enormous public edifice within which some space was set aside as 'the synagogue;' there is just one room, with a few rows of seats, and very small additional room (342).

This tendentious interpretation of archeological data by Kee is also in evidence when he insists that, according to archeologists, these supposed synagogues have '*no* distinctive features.' When archeologists say this kind of thing, Sanders notes, they are referring to such elements as a niche for the Torah scroll, a special orientation of the building (e.g. towards Jerusalem), etc. They really do not mean that the floor plans of such buildings look like private houses, and no one who sees such a floor plan would ever think so.[8]

Another American theologian, Richard Oster, challenges Kee on the supposed anachronisms in Luke's two-part work.[9] Against Kee's theory of a complete Lucan retrojection of post-70 forms of synagogal worship into the period of 50 years before, Oster puts forward the following. It is quite right to point out that scholars all too often projected back onto the pre-70 period the situation which arose once the rabbinic rules were accepted by most Jews. So scepticism is a healthy corrective in this matter. But there

---

[7] *Not* the *only* time, as Sanders says (*Jewish Law* 342 n. 29).
[8] See also Riesner's remarks, "Synagogues in Jerusalem" 184-187.
[9] R.E. Oster, "Supposed Anachronism in Luke-Acts' Use of συναγωγή: A Rejoinder to Howard Kee," *NTS* 39 (1993) 178-208. He quotes e.g. Kee's conclusion (*NTS* 1990, 18): "Thus we apparently have in Luke-Acts the later forms of synagogal worship read back into the time of Jesus."

is enough literary and archeological material from before 70 to enable us to judge whether Luke writes about the synagogue in an anachronistic way. In sources from the Second Temple period *proseuchê* is the most common word used to designate a synagogue building, whereas the *synagôgê* may indicate a congregation, an assembly, as well as a building or a place of assembly. It is not clear why authors prefer one word to the other or use the two words alternately,[10] but the fact that Luke mainly has *synagôgê* cannot possibly, at least on the basis of the available sources, be explained by assuming that he is adjusting to the changed situation after 70, in which increasingly, according to Kee, *synagôgê* also refers to the place of assembly. Moreover, Kee tries to prove his case by means of a highly simplistic dichotomy between the two words *proseuchê* and *synagôgê*, though this far from reflects the actual linguistic situation. Pre-70 sources display a large variety of terms for the place where Jews assemble: *didaskaleion, hieros peribolos, amphitheatron, oikêma, proseuktêrion, sabbateion, hieron, (hieros) topos, proseuchê,* and *synagôgê*.[11]

Oster also points out that Kee ignores material which refutes his thesis, e.g. an inscription from the mid-fifties of the first century, from Berenike in the Cyrenaica (= Benghazi in Libya), which talks about a decision taken by the *synagôgê* (in the sense of congregation) of the local Jews to honour those who helped repair the *synagôgê* (in the sense of place of assembly).[12] Moreover, Kee suppresses material from Josephus which fits

---

[10] Hengel, not altogether implausibly, has suggested a geographical explanation, in the sense that *proseuchê* is more the word which was used in the Diaspora, whereas *synagôgê* was more current in Palestine (see his essay "Proseuche and Synagogue: Jüdische Gemeinde, Gotteshaus und Gottesdienst in der Diaspora und in Palästina," in G. Jeremias *et al.* (eds.), *Tradition und Glaube. Das frühe Christentum in seiner Umwelt* (FS K.G. Kuhn), Göttingen: Vandenhoeck & Ruprecht, 1976, 157-184, repr. in J. Gutmann (ed.), *The Synagogue. Studies in Origins, Archeology and Architecture*, New York: Ktav, 1975, 27-54).

[11] See the survey in Oster, "Anachronism" 186. All in all these words occur some 60 times in pre-70 Jewish sources; half of these (30) are *proseuchê*. The word *oikos* (house) does not occur! For a discussion of the terms, see the still valuable overview in S. Krauss, *Synagogale Altertümer*, Hildesheim: Olms, 1966 (= Berlin-Wien 1922) 11-17, 24-27. For another refutation of the theory that the terminological variation indicates a substantial difference in function, see now also F. Hüttenmeister, "'Synagoge' und 'Proseuche' bei Josephus und in anderen antiken Quellen," in D.A. Koch & H. Lichtenberger (eds.), *Begegnungen zwischen Christentum und Judentum in Antike und Mittelalter* (FS H. Schreckenberg), Göttingen: Vandenhoeck, 1993, 163-181. I. Levinskaya, "A Jewish or Gentile Prayer House? The Meaning of Προσευχή," *Tyndale Bulletin* 41 (1990) 155-159, argues that the term *proseuchê* never refers to a Gentile house of prayer but always to a Jewish one.

[12] See G. Lüderitz, *Corpus jüdischer Zeugnisse aus der Cyrenaika*, Wiesbaden: Reichert, 1983, no. 72, and B. Lifshitz, *Donateurs et fondateurs dans les synagogues juives*, Paris: Gabalda, 1967, no. 100.

ill with his theory, namely thee passages in which this author undoubtedly uses *synagôgê* for a building in the pre-70 period. We already saw
one of these (the episode in Caesarea); a second passage (*Wars* VII 43-4)
mentions that the successors of Antiochus IV Epiphanes gave back to the
Jews in Antioch the bronze votive offerings stolen by him from the Temple of Jerusalem, so that they could keep them in their synagogues (*tas
synagôgas autôn*). Finally, Josephus (*Antiquities* XIX 299-305) relates
that in the fourth decade of the first century the non-Jewish inhabitants of
Dor (next to the present-day kibbutz Nachsholim), to taunt the Jews, had
placed a statue of emperor Claudius in their synagogue (*eis tên tôn
Ioudaiôn synagôgên*). The Roman governor Petronius subsequently wrote
a letter to the residents of Dor saying that a statue of the emperor belongs
in his own temple (*naos*) rather than in that of another, and certainly not
in a *synagôgê*. All these are unmistakable cases of the word *synagôgê*
being used for a building that served as a holy place before 70. Similar
remarks could be made about material from Philo, but I leave this aside
here.[13]

According to Kee, Luke commits the following anachronisms: (a) he
wrongly presents the Jews as assembling in special (synagogal) places
before 70; (b) he suggests that these religious services had a special organization and liturgical formulas or patterns; and (c) he claims that Jews
regularly attended the synagogue on the Sabbath. But, Oster says, these
are not anachronisms at all. On the contrary, this is precisely the state of
affairs which we find reflected in his contemporary Josephus, who had no
reason to indulge in this form of anachronism. As for (a), Oster, like
Sanders, points to Kee's misleading presentation of the information on
the pre-70 synagogue in Gamla. No archeologist has ever suggested that
this building was merely a 'private home' in which the faithful came to
pray. Precisely in this case, there is much to be said for the view that we
are dealing with a first-century synagogue from the period before the fall
of the Temple, probably in fact the earliest known example from the land
of Israel.[14] As for (b), Luke's presentation of religious services according
to a pattern (standing up, Torah reading, sitting down, Torah interpretation, the presence of a *hypêretês* [= *shammash*?]; see Luke 4:16-20), in
the light of what we know about other Hellenistic religious communities

[13] See Oster, "Anachronisms" 190-1.
[14] See esp. S. Gutman, "The Synagogue at Gamla," in L.I. Levine (ed.), *Ancient Synagogues Revealed*, Jerusalem: Israel Exploration Society, 1981, 30-34; and Z. Maoz,
"The Synagogue of Gamla and the Typology of Second-Temple Synagogues," *ibid.*
35-41.

it would be very strange if the meetings were not somehow structured and formalized (consider e.g. the strict Greek-influenced organization of the Essenes and how this is reflected in their assemblies).[15] Later information on the organization of synagogues in the Roman Diaspora clearly shows the influence of Greek forms of organization. Similarly, the Jewish manumission inscriptions from the middle of the first century which were found on the northern coast of the Black Sea and in which the owner gives back the slave his or her freedom in the synagogue (*proseuchê*) are patterned on Hellenistic models where, in a temple, the slave receives a conditional release, specified here as "a measure of religious devotion to the *proseuchê* and its religious services."[16] This involves a formal ceremony in a synagogue in which the community assumes a formal role of supervision. The collection of annual donations to the Temple in Jerusalem also presupposes a form of organization, like the communal meals. In other words, to blame Luke for attributing a certain form of organization to the pre-70 synagogue and a structure to its religious services is merely naive, for it is just what one would expect. Organized Torah reading and interpretation is in fact precisely what Philo and Josephus present as characteristics of the Sabbath assemblies in the synagogue.[17] As regards (c), regular attendance of the synagogue on the Sabbath (see e.g. Acts 15:21), here, too, authors like Philo and Josephus provide a clear testimony. To quote just one text, Philo writes:

> Every seventh day the Jews occupy themselves with the philosophy of their ancestors by dedicating their time to (the acquisition of) knowledge and contemplation of the things of nature [= theology[18]]. For what are the houses of prayer (*proseuktêria*) in every city but schools of insight, courage, good sense, justice, piety, holiness and every other quality by which duties to man and God are discerned and performed? (*Vita Mosis* II 216).

---

[15] On Greek influence on the organizational form of the Essenes, see M. Weinfeld, *The Organizational Pattern and the Penal Code of the Qumran Sect*, Fribourg: Editions Universitaires – Göttingen: Vandenhoeck & Ruprecht, 1986. Orphic mystery communities also held structured meetings in which both reading from their holy books and singing of hymns played a role; see R. Baumgarten, *Heiliges Wort und Heilige Schrift bei den Griechen*, Tübingen: Gunter Narr, 1998, 70-121. For possible Orphic influence on Judaism, see M. Hengel, *Judentum und Hellenismus*, Tübingen: Mohr, 1969, 171, 367-8, 478.

[16] Oster, "Anachronism" 199. Oster is aware of the somewhat uncertain nature of this interpretation of the obscure formulation *chôris es tên proseuchên thôpeias te kai proskarterêseôs* in *CIJ* 683 (= *Corpus Inscriptionum Regni Bosporani* [= *CIRB*] 70).

[17] Standing and sitting in the synagogue is described in the same way by Philo in *Spec. leg.* II 62. On p. 202 Oster shows that the *hypêretês* mentioned in Luk. 4:20 also occurs in pre-70 Jewish sources (*Corpus Papyrorum Judaicarum* [= *CPJ*] 138).

[18] See F.H. Colson's note on *Abr.* 99 (LCL ed. VI, p. 52).

Oster rightly ends his refutation of Kee with the words: "Nothing was discovered from literary or archaeological sources which supports the accusation that Luke's narrative is characterized by anachronisms about the synagogue."[19]

Of course, it is not my concern to 'save' Luke from the hands of his critics.[20] The important thing is to see that this fierce attack on the traditional view of the synagogue in the period around the beginning of the Christian era has been convincingly repelled because almost no sound arguments were used.[21] But we are not yet home and dry. It may again or still seem certain that there were synagogues in the pre-70 period – no one knows exactly how long – not just in the sense of Jewish congregations but also in the sense of buildings where these congregations met. And it may seem certain that these places were regularly attended on the Sabbath, and that the Torah was read and explained there. But one more question has not been conclusively answered: was the synagogue a place of worship on the Sabbath?

This brings us to the second element in the title of this contribution: the first was *place*, the second *worship*. In her book *Sabbath and Synagogue: The Question of Sabbath Worship in Ancient Judaism*,[22] Heather McKay recently set out the following theory. (She was not the first to present it, but has done so more fully and incisively than any other scholar.) In Judaism there was no communal worship on the Sabbath before the year 200 CE. Not until the third century does this become a rule in the life of the Jews in antiquity. She rightly distinguishes between 'Sabbath observance' and 'Sabbath worship.' To refrain from work is not in itself a form of worship. She defines worship as follows:

> rites and rituals which pay homage, with adoration and awe, to a particular god or gods. Worship could include sacrificing plants and animals, dancing, playing music, singing hymns or psalms, reading or reciting sacred texts, prayers and blessings. (...) Prayer to the deity and singing of psalms to or about the deity, exhortations to follow the commands of the deity as understood by the believing community – all these count for me as worship.

---

[19] Oster, "Anachronism" 208.
[20] Another scholar who launched a devastating attack on Kee is R. Riesner, "Synagogues in Jerusalem" 179-210.
[21] In "A Changing Meaning of Synagogue: A Response to Richard Oster," *NTS* 40 (1994) 281-283, Kee fails to advance new arguments.
[22] Leiden: Brill, 1994.

But "reading, studying and explaining texts I do not necessarily regard as worship, *unless* given a place in a planned session of worship" (3), which means that "the group's understanding of the god as *addressee* of the worship is vital to my definition" (4). At first sight this definition seems fair enough, but we will find that it fails to do justice to certain facets of the material. Furthermore, she stipulates that Sabbath worship must be distinct from other, daily forms of worship. If the same prayers are offered or the same songs sung on the Sabbath as on all other days, even communally, this is not a form of Sabbath worship.[23]

In the first chapter McKay shows that, with regard to the Sabbath, the Hebrew Bible only requires that the Israelites do not work, but never that they praise God or pray to him on this day. This seems to me indisputable and does not call for further investigation. In particular her discussion of the many passages in which the Sabbath and the new moon occur in parallel word pairs demonstrates that both occasions are days on which only officials in the temple cult are expected to perform special religious acts or rituals, but not the ordinary Israelite.[24]

In the remaining seven chapters McKay deals with all the relevant material from the five centuries between 300 BCE and 200 CE. It is impossible here to repeat her detailed account of all these data. I will therefore confine myself to the broad outlines of her argument, discussing details only when it is necessary to show where her explanation or argument fails to do justice to the sources.

In the apocryphal and pseudepigraphic literature she notes an increased interest in and emphasis on the observance of the Sabbath as a day of rest, but there is no evidence that ordinary Jews were expected to go beyond the injunction not to work. No trace of a communal cult on the Sabbath is to be found. 2 Macc. 8:27 says that Judas Maccabaeus, after his first victory, extolled God on the next Sabbath with his soldiers and that together they thanked the Lord who brought them safely to that day (*tôi diasôsanti eis tên hêmeran tautên*). This is explained by McKay as follows: "It seems to be prompted by the victory rather than by the sabbath" (48). I think this is right, though the almost literal agreement with the well-known berakhah *shehecheyanu*

[23] McKay had already expressed her ideas more briefly in her essay "From Evidence to Edifice: Four Fallacies about the Sabbath," in R. Carroll (ed.), *Text as Pretext* (FS R. Davidson), JSOTSSS 138, Sheffield: Sheffield Academic Press, 1992, 179-199.
[24] McKay does not mention that in Neh. 8-9 Torah reading and explanation are followed by praise and penitential prayer.

lizman hazeh is remarkably reminiscent of the (later?) synagogal liturgy.[25]

We are on more dangerous ground when McKay tries to discount material from Qumran. There, according to McKay, we find clear references to cultic celebration of the Sabbath by the community of Qumran Essenes.[26] Thus the *Shirot 'Olat ha-Shabbath* distinctly mention a heavenly or 'angelic' Sabbath liturgy in which the congregation takes part;[27] and *11Q5*, where David's compositions are listed, says that he not only wrote 3,600 psalms, and 364 songs for each day of the year to accompany the daily burnt offering, but also 52 songs for the Sabbath offerings.[28] And there is more. McKay is thus forced to conclude on the one hand "that the group worshipped together – as a community – on the sabbath in ways that included the singing of special songs" (54), but on the other hand she raises the question "whether the members of the community sang their special sabbath songs as a community of priests giving a sacrifice of song to God, or whether they can truly be described as non-priestly Jews gathering for worship on the sabbath" (56). We should not forget, she adds, "that this community was far removed from mainstream Judaism, both geographically and theologically. Thus any practices celebrated there may have been quite alien to the activities of city- or country-dwelling Jews" (59). But we will see that, in this respect, the Qumranites may prove less 'far removed from mainstream Judaism' (whatever that may be!) than McKay would have us believe.

In addition to that, McKay does not mention a passage in the pseudo-Philonic *Liber Antiquitatum Biblicarum* (XI 8) where, in a free rendering of the Decalogue, the author has God say about the Sabbath: "You shall not do any work on it (...) except to praise the Lord in the congregation of the elders and to glorify the Mighty One in the assembly of the

---

[25] See J.A. Goldstein, *II Maccabees*, Garden City: Doubleday, 1983, 336.

[26] P. 53: "The weekly sabbath was a day both of observance and worship for the community members."

[27] See F. García Martínez, *The Dead Sea Scrolls Translated*, Leiden: Brill, 1994, 419-431.

[28] See F. García Martínez, *The Dead Sea Scrolls Translated* 309. McKay overlooked the relevant material from *4QDibHam* (= *Divre ha-Me'orot*, 'The Words of the Luminaries'), a document that comprises prayers for each day of the week and that "exhibits a clear distinction between the Sabbath hymns and the petitionary prayers assigned to the six regular weekdays," thus E. Glickler Chazon, "On the Special Character of Sabbath Prayer: New Data from Qumran," *Journal of Jewish Music and Liturgy* 15 (1992/93) 2 (1-21). I owe thanks to Esther Chazon for drawing my attention to this important article, that is all the more relevant in that she demonstrates the non-sectarian character of this document.

aged" (with an allusion to Ps. 107:32). It is clear that the author presupposes here a form of communal Sabbath worship.[29]

Philo and Josephus are extremely important witnesses in this matter (as we saw) and therefore deserve extra attention. According to McKay, there is no evidence in either of worship on the Sabbath. Though on various occasions Philo talks about regular meetings of Jews on the Sabbath, he never calls the places of assembly synagogues (he calls them *proseuchai*, *proseuktêria*, and even *synagôgia*, but not *synagôgai*) and he never talks about cultic activities in this context, but about reading, instruction, and study of the Torah. Thus Philo mentions a senior Egyptian official who tries to dissuade the Jews from observing the Sabbath by saying: If a great disaster took place on the Sabbath, "will you sit in your *synagôgia*, while you assemble the congregation and safely read your holy books, explaining any obscure point, and thus in peace and quiet discuss at length your ancestral philosophy?" (*Somn.* II 127). And in another passage: "On every seventh day countless schools (*didaskaleia*) are open in every city, schools of wisdom, temperance, courage, justice, and other virtues, schools in which the scholars sit in order and quietly, with their ears alert" (*Spec. leg.* II 62). Finally, the passage quoted at greater length above: "To this very day the Jews every seventh day occupy themselves with the philosophy of their ancestors (...). For what are the houses of prayer (*proseuktêria*) in every city but schools of wisdom...?" (*Vit. Mos.* II 216).[30] McKay calls these passages descriptions of "educational gatherings (...) where religious, social and moral topics are discussed, (...) a teacher-student ambience" (66). Philo never calls these places of assembly 'synagogues,' so that there is no question of synagogal Sabbath services, but rather of educational Sabbath meetings in houses of prayer. In the anti-Jewish riots of the year 38 many of these houses of prayer in Alexandria, where Philo lived, were destroyed by non-Jews (a kind of 'Kristallnacht' *avant la date*). Apparently these buildings were regarded by non-Jews as the community centres of the Jews, and moreover as holy buildings,[31] for at

---

[29] In his commentary on this passage, Howard Jacobson also points to Jub. 2:21 as a parallel; see his *A Commentary to Pseudo-Philo's* Liber Antiquitatum Biblicarum, Leiden: Brill, 1996, vol. 1: 468.

[30] Cf. *Legatio* 156: "He [the emperor Tiberius] knew that they [the Jews of Rome] had houses of prayer in which they gathered, especially on the holy seventh day, to receive collective instruction in the ancestral philosophy."

[31] See A. Kasher, "Synagogues as 'Houses of Prayer' and 'Holy Places' in the Jewish Communities of Hellenistic and Roman Egypt," in D. Urman & P.V.M. Flesher (eds.), *Ancient Synagogues*, vol. 1, Leiden: Brill, 1995, 218-220.

the start of the conflict they tried to desecrate these by placing statues of emperor Caligula in them (*Flacc.* 41-50). But, again, there is no talk about songs of praise or prayer, and these buildings are not called 'synagogues.' This is confirmed by Philo's description of a Sabbath meeting in his apologetic work *Hypothetica*:

> He (God) asked them to assemble in the same place on all these seventh days, to sit together there in a modest and orderly manner, and to listen to these laws, so that no one would remain ignorant of them. (13) And indeed they always assemble to sit together, most of them in silence, except when it is the practice to express approval of what is read.[32] One of the priests or elders present reads the holy laws to them and explains them one by one till about the late afternoon. Then they go home, not only filled with expert knowledge of their holy laws, but also considerably advanced in piety (*Hyp.* VII 12-13).

Philo's description of the Sabbath observance of the monastic and ascetic Jewish group of the Therapeutae, in his *De vita contemplativa*, is also worth quoting in its entirety:

> (30) Six days per week they study philosophy, entirely alone and by themselves, locked up in the closets mentioned above, without ever passing the outside door or even looking at it from a distance. But on the seventh day they always meet together, as if for a general assembly; they sit in order according to their age, in an appropriate attitude, that is to say, with their hands inside their robes, the right hand between the breast and the chin, the left hand down the side. (31). Then the eldest who also has the fullest knowledge of their doctrines comes forward and speaks to them, with a quiet demeanour, a quiet voice, reasoned and full of insight. He does not make an exhibition of rhetoric, like the orators and sophists of today do, but examines and interprets the exact meaning of the thoughts, and this does not go in at one ear and out at the other, no, it passes through the ear to the soul and stays there for good. All the others listen in silence, expressing their approval only by their looks or nods. (32) This common sanctuary, where they always meet on the seventh day, is a double enclosure, one part reserved for men, the other for women. For it is customary that women also form part of the audience and listen with the same ardour and dedication. The wall between the two rooms is some three to four cubits high from the ground[33] and is built in the form of a breastwork, but the section above up to the roof is left open. This is done for two purposes: first, to preserve the modesty becoming the female sex, and second, so that the women sitting within earshot can also listen, for there is nothing to obstruct the voice of the speaker.

---

[32] E.g. by saying 'Amen.'

[33] Between 1.50 and 1.80 meters. That is to say: high enough to prevent men and women from seeing each other.

Though this strongly resembles the description of a synagogal Sabbath service (in a 'sanctuary'), the essentials, prayer and praise, are lacking, and this is all the more striking, says McKay, because in his description of the everyday life of the Therapeutae, Philo explicitly mentions prayer and praise as daily elements of their monastic life (§29: "So they do not confine themselves to contemplation, they also compose songs and hymns to God in all kinds of metres and melodies and they write these down in rhythms which are necessarily most solemn"). In other words: the weekday assemblies are religious and cultic, i.e. religious services, whereas the Sabbath assemblies are reserved for study only! And the fact is that "study and contemplation are by no means the same as worship," says McKay (73).

The only place where Philo talks about *synagôgai* is the passage in *Omnis probus* 81-82 mentioned above, where he says about the Sabbath meetings of the Essenes:

> The seventh day is regarded as holy; on it they abstain from work and go to holy places called synagogues. There they sit in order according to their age, the younger below the elder, to listen with appropriate decorum. Then someone takes the books and reads from them, and another, who is among the most expert, comes forward to explain what is not understood.

Though this passage speaks of 'holy places' which are called 'synagogues,' where this Jewish group meets 'on the Sabbath,' there is no mention of worship and praise, and so, as with the Therapeutae and other Jews, there is no worship here on the Sabbath. "When Jews assemble on sabbath, it is not to worship, but to read, study and discuss Torah" (77).

The same picture is found in Josephus. He also describes Sabbath assemblies, but these are devoted to political discussions and to study of the Torah. Total abstinence from all forms of work is and remains the most important and the most emphasized trait of the Sabbath in Josephus. Very important is a long passage in his *Vita* (272-303), where Josephus describes a scene which takes place on a Sabbath in the *proseuchê* of Tiberias in the sixth decade of the first century. A delegation from Jerusalem had come to Tiberias with the intention of conveying Josephus to Jerusalem or otherwise killing him. On the morning of the Sabbath the people assembled in the very large building which is called *proseuchê* to debate the issue with the delegation. Controversy arose and Josephus says that a riot would inevitably have broken out "if the sixth hour had not arrived, the hour when it is our custom on the Sabbath to take the midday meal, so that the meeting was broken off"

(279). Not a word, then, about worship. On the following days the debate on Josephus' position continues. On Monday morning, writes Josephus, "when we had started the usual (liturgy) and were engaged in prayer" (295), one of Josephus' enemies stood up to attack him again. In the end, however, everything turns out well for Josephus. So the *proseuchê*, says McKay, clearly functions here as a community centre in which all kinds of activities take place, including political ones. On three other occasions Josephus talks about *synagôgai* as buildings, namely in Caeserea, Dor, and Antioch. The passages on Caeserea (*War* II 284-292) and Dor (*Ant.* XIX 299-305) have been discussed at length above and can be omitted here. In the passage on the Jews in Syrian Antioch, also briefly mentioned, Josephus says that the bronze treasures stolen from the Temple by Antiochus IV Epiphanes were given back to the Jews by his successors, so that they could be placed in their synagogue. The Jews used these to adorn their 'sanctuary' (*hieron*)[34] and partly in this way, Josephus implies, they were able with their religious services (*tais thrêskeiais*) to attract a large group of Greeks whom they in a certain sense incorporated among themselves (*War* VII 44-45). In short, there are holy buildings, also meetings on the Sabbath in these, also liturgies and prayer on weekdays, but still no worship on the Sabbath. Worship only takes place in the Temple of Jerusalem. McKay follows S. Zeitlin in his analysis that, despite all the differences between Philo and Josephus, these authors agree that in the Hellenistic period the Jewish communities already had local centres where they gathered to discuss all kinds of matters concerning the community and also to pray at regular times, but that it was only after 70 that these centres gradually evolved into what would later become the synagogue with worship on the Sabbath.[35]

The pagan Greek and Roman authors who mention the Sabbath do not give us new information. The Sabbath is described as a day of rest, or indeed of laziness in the view of some writers, and we are also told

---

[34] It seems clear to me that the synagogue in Antioch is meant here and not the Temple in Jerusalem. For this discussion McKay 81 n. 68 refers only to Thackeray's inadequate footnote in the Loeb edition and overlooks the much more extensive and superior discussion in O. Michel & O. Bauernfeind, *Flavius Josephus. De bello judaico* II 2, Darmstadt: WBG, 1969, 228-229.

[35] See S. Zeitlin, "The Origin of the Synagogue," *Proceedings of the American Academy of Jewish Research* 2 (1930-31) 69-81, repr. in J. Gutmann (ed.), *The Synagogue. Studies in Origins, Archaeology and Architecture*, New York: Ktav, 1975, 14-26. For a brief summary of Zeitlin's views, see also his *The Rise and Fall of the Judaean State* III, Philadelphia: JPS, 1978, 169-172.

about the preparation and consumption of a Sabbath meal, but not a word is said about worship, which can only be explained if this did not exist or any case did not form a conspicuous part of Sabbath observance. However, McKay fails to report a passage by Agatharchides of Cnidos (c. 200-130 BCE), who says that on every seventh day the Jews abstain from all work, "but pray with outstretched hands in their sanctuaries until the evening" (*ap.* Josephus, *C. Ap.* I 209). Whether these 'sanctuaries' are interpreted as the Temple in Jerusalem (very improbable)[36] or as synagogues (much more likely),[37] it is clear that this pagan author is drawing attention to a special prayer service on the Sabbath.

Then the New Testament. Here the keeping of the Sabbath is described mainly in terms of abstaining from work. With some exceptions, most stories which take place on the Sabbath are set in the synagogues, but again this never involves a form of worship, though there is reading and explanation of the Torah. The stories about miraculous cures which occur in synagogues on the Sabbath contain no indications that they interrupted the normal routine (a liturgy) there. There are also references to instruction in the synagogue, but we are not told that this took place on the Sabbath; so it may have been on other days. Though the Jews in Pisidian Antioch say to Paul, who had instructed them on a Sabbath, that he must speak to them again on the next Sabbath (Acts 13:42), this need only imply that only on the Sabbath there were enough men free to listen to him. The New Testament as a whole draws a picture in which the synagogue is a place of many activities, "teaching, preaching, reading, speaking, disputing, praying, sitting, scourging, beating, and passing judgement on offenders," says McKay (154). Moreover, one can assume (with Kee) that the most detailed description of a Sabbath assembly in a synagogue, when Jesus appears in the synagogue of Nazareth and reads from the prophets (in Luke 4), reflects a later (post-70) situation. And, according to McKay, Jesus' warning against imitation of the hypocrites who like to pray in the synagogues in order to be seen by other people (Matt. 6:5) implies not so much that prayer was a

---

[36] See Hengel, "Proseuche" 163.

[37] The word *hiera* which Agatharchides uses here occurs occasionally as a term for synagogues, like *templa*; e.g. Josephus, *Bell.* VII 45; Procopius, *De aedif.* VI 2; Tacitus, *Hist.* V 5,4; Minucius Felix, *Oct.* 33,2-4. See also the discussion by S.J.D. Cohen, "Pagan and Christian Evidence on the Ancient Synagogue," in L.I. Levine, *The Synagogue in Late Antiquity*, New York-Philadelphia: JTS-ASOR, 1987, 161-162. J.M.G. Barclay, *Jews in the Mediterranean Diaspora*, Edinburgh: T.& T. Clark, 1996, 417 n. 29, suggests that also Ovid's *culta Iudaeo septima sacra* (in his *Ars amatoria* I 76) points to knowledge of sabbath services.

common activity in the synagogue as that prayer was not so usual there, which is why Jesus' criticizes it (172); moreover, we are not told that this praying took place on the Sabbath. So: "It has not been possible to find any reliable details of Sabbath worship from the time of Jesus in any of the [NT] texts surveyed," and the synagogue was "a place where Jews met to deal with *all* matters that were of concern to them as a community" (173).

This picture remains virtually unchanged in the Christian literature of the second century. The authors chiefly talk about abstinence from work as the main feature of the Jewish Sabbath. Ignatius of Antioch urges his readers to observe Sunday instead of the Sabbath, but he does not mention synagogues or religious services held there on the Sabbath. Justin Martyr describes a meeting of Christians on Sunday which is surprisingly similar to what we know about Sabbath assemblies from Jewish authors (*1 Apol.* 67:3-5):

> On the day called Sunday there is an assembly in one place of all who live in the cities and in the country, and then the memoirs of the Apostles and the writings of the prophets are read, as long as time allows. When the reader has finished, the president of the assembly verbally admonishes and urges all to imitate these good things. Then we all stand up together and offer up our prayers.

But, apart from the element of prayer, which does not occur in Jewish descriptions, "Justin does not describe these gatherings as worship" (189-190), says McKay. And as for Justin's remark that the Jews in their synagogues curse those who believe in Christ (*Dial.* 16, 93, 95, 96 etc.) – apart from the question whether this involves the *Birkat ha-minim*[38] – he does not say that this happens in the context of Sabbath worship.

Even the Mishnah confirms this picture: on the Sabbath people read from, listen to, and study Holy Scripture, but there is no mention of singing or prayer; in short, there is no worship on the Sabbath. The sanctity of the synagogue as a place, even after the building has stopped functioning as a synagogue, is strongly emphasized (see esp. *Megillah* 3:1-3); the necessity of regular prayer is underlined (*Berakhot*); but there is no text which talks about prayer as a group activity in the synagogue on the Sabbath. Rules for Torah reading on the Sabbath are also given (*Meg.* 3-4), but these obtain equally to the Sabbath and the other

---

[38] See P.W. van der Horst, "The Birkat ha-Minim in Recent Research," in his *Hellenism – Judaism – Christianity: Essays on their Interaction*, Kampen: Kok Pharos, 1994, 99-111 = *ibidem*, second enlarged edition, Leuven: Peeters, 1998, 113-124.

days of the week. Nor can McKay (207-208) be persuaded by the fact that *Meg*. 3:6 and 4:1 mention Torah reading during the Sabbath *minchah*, i.e. the afternoon 'service of sacrifice,' here in the post-biblical sense of 'prayer service in the afternoon'[39] of the Sabbath.

Finally, the non-literary data, those of archeology, epigraphy, and papyrology. These also leave the picture built up so far fully intact. The word *synagôgê* in inscriptions almost always refers to the Jewish community, not to a building, and the few cases that do relate to buildings are late inscriptions (i.e. third century and later). The Theodotus inscription from Jerusalem quoted above talks about the building of a *synagôgê* by Theodotus, but the traditional pre-70 date is very improbable, and moreover the text, when mentioning the purpose of the building, speaks only about Torah reading and instruction in the commandments (*eis anagnôsin nomou kai didachên entolôn*). And all pre-70 inscriptions and papyri which mention a community building of Jewish congregations (which is already the case from the third century BCE) call such a building a *proseuchê*, and so these do not count. But even McKay has to admit that in the inscription in Berenike (Libya) from the middle of the first century the word *synagôgê* is clearly used for both the Jewish congregation and the building of this congregation.[40] But this is the exception which confirms the rule, and furthermore this text says nothing about Sabbath worship in the building. Nor does any of the inscriptions or papyri which mention *proseuchai* make a connection with Jewish worship. There is talk about 'civic functions' (239) of these *proseuchai*, being for instance the place where slaves were released, where honorary decrees for benefactors of the congregation were drawn up, and where honorary inscriptions were placed. And since there are no undisputed archeological identifications of synagogues from the period before the third century CE, archeology cannot help us here either. Taking all the material into consideration, one must therefore conclude that we have no proof that Sabbath worship existed in the synagogues before the third century CE.

What is wrong with this argument? Let me start by saying that a minimalist interpretation of the material like that by McKay always has a

---

[39] See L. Tetzner, *Megilla* (Die Mischna II 10), Berlin: W. de Gruyter, 1968, 109 n. 10. It is certain that *minchah* in rabbinic Hebrew no longer refers to the sacrifice but to the afternoon prayer; see the relevant dictionaries *s.v.* Cf. also Acts 10:3 with 10:30 and 3:1.

[40] See the references above, note 12.

salutary effect. It opens our eyes to the fact that many scholars are too easily inclined to assume naively and as self-evident that situations which can only be attested for a much later period are also to be assumed for sources of an earlier period. It is also a good thing that from time to time long-established views and interpretations are heavily criticized, so that we are forced to examine whether the foundation of these time-honoured views is really solid. So when I ask, "What is wrong with McKay's argument?," this is not because I dispute her right to attack sacred cows. On the contrary, the more sacred cows attacked the better! My objection is of an entirely different kind. McKay's interpretation is not just minimalist, it involves 'underinterpretation,' downplaying the evidence, and even special pleading and disregard for information which points in a different direction. In my view, McKay in her fervent zeal overshoots the mark. I will now try to show this briefly.

To start with, I will confine myself to the material discussed by McKay herself. After that I will cast the net more widely, not so much to fish up new material which refutes her theory, but rather to sketch an essential feature of the Jewish faith from the period before 200 which, in my view, makes her ideas hard to maintain. Admittedly, the Jewish literature from the period between Alexander the Great and Jehuda ha-Nasi does not contain a description of Sabbath worship in a synagogue which mentions the elements of prayer and praise as well as Torah reading, nor do we find regulations enforcing such worship (except in Qumran). At first sight this is the strong point in McKay's argument and it must be said to her credit that she makes us face this fact. But, on second thoughts, we can ask the following questions.

(1) The word *proseuchê* is the oldest attested word for a building where a Jewish community gathers. The word means 'prayer' and is short for 'house of prayer.'[41] Josephus' story about the house of prayer in Tiberias (see above) also mentions an interruption of the communal prayer there, albeit on a Monday morning (*Life* 295). It is useful to note here that *proseuchê* may mean both the ordinary prose prayer and the hymn (of prayer) that was sung. It may therefore include songs of praise.[42] But if there was praying and singing in *proseuchai* on weekdays, how likely is it that this did not happen on the Sabbath? People

---

[41] It is unclear whether the 'house of prayer' (lit. 'house of prostration') in *CD* XI 22 refers to a synagogue or the Temple. On the meaning of *proseuchê*, see further J.G. Griffiths, "Egypt and the Rise of the Synagogue," in Urman & Flesher (eds.), *Ancient Synagogues* 6.

[42] Examples in Hengel, "Proseuche" 161 n. 15.

came together there on the Sabbath, read from the Torah, heard it explained, and are we to believe that precisely on the Sabbath, in contrast to other days, there was no praying and singing? This seems illogical and improbable. If one of the main functions of such a community building was the saying of prayers and the singing of hymns – which is why it was called 'house of prayer' – then it is hard to maintain that this did not take place on the Sabbath because our sources do not happen to mention it explicitly.[43] That a house of prayer, or an ancient sanctuary in general, was a place where people prayed is so obvious that there was no point in mentioning it. (Consider that the New Testament author Luke, who more than others pays attention to prayer, says nothing about the reciting of the *Shema*, the blessing of food, and the Lord's Prayer, though there is no doubt that this was common practice in Jewish and Christian circles respectively.)[44] Apparently it was only worth telling in what ways Jewish worship differed from non-Jewish: reading and explanation of Holy Scripture. Moreover, the absence of any mention of prayer in the Theodotus inscription is easily explained by the fact that Jerusalem Jews before 70 preferred to pray in the Temple (just as the earliest Christians there continued to do; see Acts 2:46; 3:1). If we also consider that, as we saw, the celebration of the Sabbath among the Qumran Essenes went naturally together with communal singing and prayer, we can assume that this was also more or less customary for other Jews.[45] The argument that "this community was far removed from mainstream Judaism, both geographically and theologically" (59) is clearly a desperate measure aimed at eliminating an awkward fact. If the Qumran Essenes were so "far removed from mainstream Judaism," it is hard to understand why Judaism in a slightly later period would have totally adopted the Sabbath customs of precisely this sect.[46] If their Sabbath worship had been so exceptional, Philo and Josephus would have mentioned this in their

---

[43] See also D.K. Falk, "Jewish Prayer Literature and the Jerusalem Church in Acts," in *The Book of Acts in its Palestinian Setting* 277-281.

[44] See B. Gerhardsson, *The Shema in the New Testament*, Lund: Novapress, 1996.

[45] Note that Philo in *In Flaccum* 122 mentions that the Jews of Alexandria left their city to sing 'hymns and odes' at the seaside because their synagogues had been destroyed. Hengel ("Proseuche" 164) suspects – not implausibly – that initially (before 70) there was no singing of hymns in the Palestinian synagogal liturgy because this was the prerogative of the temple singers in Jerusalem. *Ibid.* 177 he surmises that the fact that Isa. 56:7 calls the Temple in Jerusalem a 'house of prayer' may in Palestinian circles have impeded the rise of the term *proseuchê* as the designation of a synagogue.

[46] L.H. Schiffman points out that many liturgical texts from Qumran have exact parallels in tannaitic material: "The Dead Sea Scrolls and the Early History of Jewish Liturgy," in Levine (ed.), *The Synagogue in Late Antiquity* 35-37.

detailed descriptions of the rituals of the Essenes, certainly Josephus, who emphasizes the ways in which the Essenes were different from the rest of the Jews. As a matter of fact, "the Sabbath prayers from Qumran reveal a similarity both in detail and general character with the traditional Sabbath liturgy."[47] Moreover, as we have seen above, Pseudo-Philo's *LAB* XI 8 seems to be a clear reference to a Sabbath service.

Even if Ezra Fleischer's theory is right that the idea of prayer as a religious obligation is an innovation introduced by Gamaliel II in the last quarter of the first century,[48] this need only imply that what some people (or many?) did already before 70 subsequently became an obligation for all, or what was long customary elsewhere (in the Diaspora?) became obligatory everywhere. Furthermore, it is far-fetched to make a distinction between houses of prayer (*proseuchai*) and synagogues. These are identical institutions for which there was a different terminology in different periods and in different areas. The descriptions of what took place in *proseuchai* and *synagôgai*, no matter how summary, show that, despite the terminological difference, we are dealing with the same institutions.[49]

(2) A second factor which makes it unlikely that there were no synagogal Sabbath services up till the third century is the presence of so-called 'Godfearers' in the Sabbath gatherings in the synagogue.[50] There is no reason to doubt Luke's description in the book of Acts that such assemblies were attended by these pagan sympathizers with the Jewish faith (Acts 13:16.26.43.50; 16:14; 17:4.17). These people not only sought a social relationship with Jews, they not only desired instruction in the Torah, but they also wanted to share in the *worship* of Israel's

---

[47] E. Glickler Chazon, "On the Special Character of Sabbath Prayer" 21.

[48] See E. Fleischer, "On the Beginnings of Obligatory Jewish Prayer," *Tarbiz* 59 (1990) 397-441 [Hebr.], but also Stefan Reif's reply in "On the Earliest Development of Jewish Prayer," *ibid.* 60 (1991) 677-681.

[49] See also K. Hruby, *Aufsätze zum nachbiblischen Judentum und zum jüdischen Erbe der frühen Kirche*, Berlin: Institut Kirche und Judentum, 1996, 140-145.

[50] A Godfearer is a heathen "who is attracted enough to what he has heard of Judaism to come to the synagogue to learn more; who is, after a time, willing, as a result, to imitate the Jewish way of life in whatever way and to whatever degree he wishes (up to and including membership in community associations, where that includes legal study and prayer); who may have had held out to him various short codes of behaviour to follow, but does not seem to have been required to follow any one; who may follow the exclusive monotheism of the Jews and give up his ancestral gods, but need not do so; who can, if he wishes, take the ultimate step and convert, and is, whether he does or not, promised a share in the resurrection for his pains" (J. Reynolds and R. Tannenbaum, *Jews and Godfearers at Aphrodisias*, Cambridge: The Cambridge Philological Society, 1987, 65).

God. Their name, 'Godfearers,' both in Hebrew (*yir'e shamayim*) and in Greek (*theosebeis* or *sebomenoi [ton theon]*), indicates that these Greeks and Romans were not just concerned with knowledge, but also wanted to worship (*sebesthai*, as their Greek name says). Apparently they could experience this in the synagogue or in the house of prayer on the Sabbath.

(3) A third argument is the continuity between Judaism and Christianity in the very first phase of this new religion. Earliest Christianity was no more than a Jewish sect, which only gradually, after some time, moved away from the synagogue. Nothing could be more natural than that the Christians, when they started to organize their own assemblies for the first time, modelled these on those of the synagogue. And in fact there is a great deal of material which supports this theory. In his study of this material, *From Synagogue to Church*, Burtchaell observes that in all likelihood the hierarchical form of organization present in the synagogue (president – council of elders – assistants – congregation) was adopted by the earliest Christians.[51] We know for a fact that early on, in any case long before the year 70, the oldest Christian communities also conducted weekly religious services. It seems to me an inevitable conclusion that they adopted this, too, from their Jewish contemporaries, though for evident reasons they held these celebrations on Sunday instead of on the Sabbath. That these early Christian gatherings, besides including Torah reading and explanation, also involved worship, praise, and prayer is abundantly attested in e.g. the letters of Paul. There is nothing to indicate that this constituted a radical innovation with regard to Jewish customs.[52] So it seems virtually certain that the weekly worship in earliest Christianity was a legacy from Judaism. McKay's suggestion that early Christian worship was possibly not based on Jewish worship but that a reverse process took place seems to me utterly improbable.

(4) That the Jewish assembly building, whether it was called *proseuchê* or *synagôgê*, was more than just a community centre where people could also teach and study is furthermore shown by the synagogal manumission

---

[51] J.T. Burtchaell, *From Synagogue to Church. Public Services and Offices in the Earliest Christian Communities*, Cambridge: Cambridge University Press, 1992. Cf. also J. Ysebaert, *Die Amtsterminologie im Neuen Testament und in der Alten Kirche*, Breda: Eureka, 1994.

[52] Against W. Bauer, "Der Wortgottesdienst der ältesten Christen," in his *Aufsätze und Kleine Schriften*, Tübingen: Mohr, 1967, 155-209. See in general also W.O.E. Oesterley, *The Jewish Background of Christian Liturgy*, Oxford: Oxford University Press, 1925.

inscriptions. These inscriptions, which I have already mentioned, form a small but remarkable group of documents which have not yet received enough attention. In the Crimea, in the town of Kertsch (ancient Pantakapaion on the Cimmerian Bosporus) and in Gorgippia (also on the northern coast of the Black Sea), some Jewish inscriptions have been found from the first century CE in which Jewish owners fulfill a vow by giving freedom (manumissio) to their male or female slave in the local synagogue (proseuchê), explicitly stipulating that the regained freedom of the exslaves is unrestricted with one exception: those released must stay connected with the local Jewish community (synagôgê).[53] This is a relatively isolated phenomenon in ancient Judaism, at least as far as we know. But there is a papyrus from an entirely different region and different period, namely Egyptian Oxyrhynchus at the end of the third century CE (291), which tells us that the custom of giving back slaves their freedom in a synagogue was still common practice there and at that time (P. Oxy. 1205 = CPJ 473) and so was not geographically and chronologically confined. For our purposes it is important that many hundreds of parallels to this custom can be found in pagan Greek inscriptions from the later Hellenistic and Roman periods, in particular from Delphi. These Delphic inscriptions display a regular pattern: the slave regained his freedom owing to the fact that his or her master dedicated (or symbolically sold) him or her to the deity of the temple in which this sacred ceremony took place.[54] This, then, is a religious ritual in a cultic place, where the deity is considered to be present in a special sense (e.g. through his or her statue), so that the god(dess) could receive the votive offering or the purchase, here in the form of an (ex-)slave. This Greek religious custom was adopted by the Jews, the synagogue building or proseuchê taking the place of the Greek temple as the location where the vow was fulfilled.[55] (From the point of

---

[53] CIJ 683 (= Corpus Inscriptionum Regni Bosporani [CIRB] 70) and CIJ 690 (= CIRB 1123) from the years 80 and 41 CE are the two most important inscriptions. The local synagogue there may have been recently found; see R.S. MacLennan, "In Search of the Jewish Diaspora: A First Century Synagogue in Crimea?," BAR 22,2 (1996) 44-51. A comprehensive study of this material is presented in Leigh Gibson, The Jewish Manumission Inscriptions of the Bosporus Kingdom, Tübingen: Mohr, 1999.

[54] The best study on this subject is still that of F. Bömer, Untersuchungen über die Religion der Sklaven in Griechenland und Rom, 2nd vol.: Die sogenannte sakrale Freilassung in Griechenland und die (douloi) hieroi, Wiesbaden: Steiner, 1960; on pp. 101-106 Bömer discusses the Jewish inscriptions from the Crimea. See now also J.A. Harrill, The Manumission of Slaves in Early Christianity, Tübingen: Mohr, 1995, with pp. 172-178 on the Jewish inscriptions.

[55] See W.L. Westermann, The Slave Systems of Greek and Roman Antiquity, Philadelphia: American Philosophical Society, 1955, 124-126.

view of cultural-historical continuity we should mention that, as the main investigator of these inscriptions, Franz Bömer, has remarked, "hier die ältesten bekannten Vorstufen der späteren [christlichen] *manumissio in ecclesia* vorliegen."[56]) Of course, all this says nothing about whether the synagogue was a place of worship on the Sabbath. But it does seem important that these inscriptions show that even before 70 the synagogue (or *proseuchê*) in these Jewish Diaspora communities was pre-eminently the 'holy place,' as Philo calls the synagogue (*Omnis probus* 81) and just as many later inscriptions (from the third century and later) often call the synagogue the *hieros topos* or *'atrah qadisha* of the congregation.[57] The fact that the synagogue was the place where Jewish congregations released slaves in a sacred act seems to belie the theory that the building was no more than a secular edifice which was sometimes used for cultic purposes. It seems to me that this should be put the other way round. Rather the synagogue is a sacred place which could also be used for other, non-sacred purposes.[58] But so what made this building sacred? This brings us to our last point: the source and nature of the holiness of the synagogue as a place, and its connection with an essential feature of Jewish religion.

The increasing centrality of the Torah in Judaism in the post-exilic period, certainly after the reforms by Ezra, led to a heightened awareness of the Torah's holiness. Though in the Hebrew Bible the Torah itself is not yet adorned with the epithet 'holy', we see this starting to happen in the Hellenistic period. In the second half of the second century BCE Pseudo-Aristeas, the author of a pseudonymous work on the origin of the Septuagint, is the first to call the Torah 'holy' and 'divine' (*hagnos, theios*).[59] Thus the king of Egypt prostrates himself in adoration of the

---

[56] *Untersuchungen* II, 106. On pp. 105-6 he also talks about the religious gravity of these inscriptions.

[57] See Lifshitz, *Donateurs*, nos. 28, 32, 36, 40, 86-96; L. Roth-Gerson, *The Greek Inscriptions From the Synagogues in Eretz Israel* [Hebr.], Jerusalem: Yitzhak ben Zwi, 1987, nos. 3, 10, 17, 21, 23. Another indication of the holiness of synagogue buildings is their occasionally being granted the status of a place of asylum, as in *CIJ* 1449 (2nd cent. BCE Egypt); see W. Horbury & D. Noy, *Jewish Inscriptions of Graeco-Roman Egypt*, Cambridge: CUP, 1992, no. 125. Discussion of the motif of the synagogue as 'holy place' in J. Lightstone, *The Commerce of the Sacred. Mediation of the Divine among Jews in the Graeco-Roman Diaspora*, Chico: Scholars Press, 1984, esp. 111-123, and M. Hengel, "Die Synagogeninschrift von Stobi," in Gutmann, *The Synagogue* 110-148, esp. 138-141.

[58] On 'die Heiligkeit der Synagoge' see Hruby, *Aufsätze zum nachbiblischen Judentum* 187-194.

[59] See *Letter of Aristeas* 3, 5, 31, 45.

first Torah scroll in Greek and speaks of the oracles of God, for which he thanks God (§177).[60] In exactly the same period we see an increased use of the Torah as an oracle book (see 1 Macc. 3:48 and 2 Macc. 8:23).[61] Also such widely different writings as *Jubilees, 4 Ezra*, various documents from Qumran,[62] and authors like Philo and Josephus emphasize the holiness of the Torah on account of its divine origin. Not surprisingly, inspiration theories on the genesis of this Holy Scripture soon make their appearance.[63] Whether or not one is happy with the term 'book religion,' if this term indicates that a holy book has become the central locus of divine revelation in a religion, it certainly seems to apply to Second Temple Judaism.[64] It is probably no coincidence that the first attestations of the existence of synagogues date precisely from the period in which for the first time the Torah is called a holy and divine book. In his article on 'Buchreligion' Bernhard Lang notes that there need be no tension between 'Kultreligion' and 'Buchreligion,' for "in der Buchreligion wird der Kult (...) intellektualisiert."[65] He and others see the developing synagogal worship as "Ausdruck dieses intellektualisierten Kultverständnisses."[66] After all, if the cult focuses on the reading, explanation, and study of the Holy Book present there, because this is the place where God reveals himself, study has become a form of worship. "Study as Worship" is the title of a monograph by Benedict Viviano on the treatise *Avoth* and the New Testament.[67] He argues there that the motif of Torah study as a form of worship, formulated so frequently in *Avoth* and elsewhere in the rabbinic literature, has ancient roots in the pre-rabbinic era. A central text of the Torah itself, the *Shema*, already emphasizes learning (Deut. 6:6-7). Post-exilic texts like Ezra 7:14//25 indicate that Torah and Wisdom were identified at an

---

[60] For this and the following, see O. Wischmeyer, "Das Heilige Buch im Judentum des Zweiten Tempels," *ZNW* 86 (1995) 218-242. For the typology of the holy book in antiquity in general, see e.g. W. Speyer, "Das Buch als magisch-religiöser Kraftträger im griechischen und römischen Altertum," in his *Religionsgeschichtliche Studien*, Hildesheim: Olms, 1995, 28-55.

[61] Cf. the later *sortes biblicae*. I follow here Wischmeyer's convincing interpretation of both passages in Macc. (226-7). For other views, see the commentaries of J.A. Goldstein *ad locc.*

[62] See Wischmeyer, "Das Heilige Buch" 229-233.

[63] See e.g. H. Burkhardt, *Die Inspiration Heiliger Schriften bei Philo*, Giessen-Basel: Brunnen Verlag, 1988.

[64] See B. Lang, 'Buchreligion,' in H. Cancik *et al.* (eds.), *Handbuch religionswissenschaftlicher Grundbegriffe* II, Stuttgart: Kohlhammer, 1990, 143-165.

[65] 'Buchreligion' 144. Cf. *ibid.* 147 on the *aron* as the *sanctissimum* of the synagogue.

[66] Wischmeyer, "Heilige Buch" 240.

[67] B.T. Viviano, *Study as Worship. Avoth and the New Testament*, Leiden: Brill, 1978.

early stage (cf. later Sirach 24:23 etc.). Post-exilic priests increasingly became teachers of Torah;[68] and texts like Mal. 2:6-7 declare knowledge of the commandments to be a *religious* value of the highest order. All this, then, takes place already in the time of the Bible.[69] Subsequently this trend would only be reinforced.

Thus the saving nature of the study and knowledge of the Torah is emphasized in the *Testament of Levi* (chap. 13). The same is true of *1QS* 6:6-8 ("In a place where there are ten men, there shall not cease to be a man who studies the Torah day and night [cf. Ps. 1:2!], continually, one after another. The Many will together be on watch for a third part of all the nights of the year, reading the Book, studying the Law, and praising together"), where the ideal is clearly that everybody should be a *doresh ba-Torah*,[70] and that the study of the Torah in the community should not cease or be interrupted for even one moment (hence the 'shift work'). The combination with praise indicates how far learning ('lernen') here is experienced as a religious act, an act of worship. And it is clear that this not only applied to the Qumran Essenes. For Philo, too, as we saw above, study and instruction in the Mosaic Law was central in religious training. The fact that Josephus calls the four main religious movements in pre-70 Judaism four 'philosophies' may be partly attributed to his apologetic tendency, but (elsewhere) he, too, makes it amply clear how important the place of learning was in the life of every Jew. And, he says, there is no excuse for lack of knowledge, for ignorance (*C.Ap.* 2:176-8, *Ant.* 4:209-211).[71] So it is not a new but an old ideal which we find when we read in *Avoth*: "If you have studied much Torah, they (= God) will give you a great reward (...) but know that the reward of the just will come only in the future" (2:16); and "If there are ten together and they occupy themselves with the Torah, the Shekhina is in their midst" (3:6).[72]

---

[68] See J. Blenkinsopp's contribution to the volume *The Sage in Israel and the Ancient Near East*, Winona Lake: Eisenbrauns, 1994, 307-315.

[69] Viviano, *Study* 112-127.

[70] See I. Sonne, "Remarks on Manual of Discipline, Col. VI, 6-7," *Vetus Testamentum* 7 (1957) 405-408.

[71] Perhaps Matt. 11:25 can be explained as a protest by Jesus against the intellectualizing emphasis on knowledge of the Torah which threatened to exclude the poor of spirit.

[72] Cf. also m.*Avoth* 3:3 and m.*Qidd.* 1:10. See the discussion of these passages by F. Avemarie, *Tora und Leben. Untersuchungen zur Heilsbedeutung der Tora in der frühen rabbinischen Literatur*, Tübingen: Mohr, 1996, 247-253; cf. 399-418. Griffiths, "Egypt and the Rise of the Synagogue," who argues that the synagogue originated in the Egyptian Diaspora and under Egyptian influence, points to the close connection between worship and instruction in Egyptian sanctuaries.

The presence of the Torah made the building a sanctuary, study of the Torah thus became a cultic act. It is significant that John Chrysostom in one of his notorious sermons from 386/7 tries to impress on his herd, which, he felt, grazed too often in the synagogue on the Sabbath, that the presence of the Torah scroll does *not* make the synagogue a holy place, something which was apparently taken for granted in and outside Jewish circles.[73] And to mention an important text from the period before 70, Josephus quotes a decree by the emperor Augustus (*Ant.* XVI 164; cf. Philo, *Legatio* 311-3) benefiting the Jews in Asia Minor, in which he says that someone who is caught stealing the holy book of the Jews from a synagogue (*sabbateion*) should be treated as a desecrator (*hierosylos*).[74] It appears that even to the mind of the first emperor of the Roman Empire there was a close connection between the presence of the Torah and the holiness of the synagogue.[75]

Is it probable, in the light of these facts, that weekly gatherings in the synagogue where the Torah was read and taught did not have cultic character? The answer goes without saying. McKay's mistake is to have disregarded this typically Jewish nature of studying the Torah as a holy and cultic activity. It makes her entire theory of secular educational meetings, where people *only* read and studied, a strange anachronism. Even if she were right that there was *no* praying in the synagogue, this does not mean that no worship took place. Stefan Reif also notes: "The problem with McKay's clearcut conclusion is that her narrow definition (...) of the kind of worship and worshippers that she regards as relevant to Jewish sabbath liturgy makes it [i.e. her conclusion] virtually inevitable. Surely the reading and interpretation of specific passages of scripture, whether from a Torah scroll or in the form of the *shema'*, in some ceremonial context, have a genuine claim to be regarded as worship."[76]

---

[73] *PG* 48:850. For further references, see Cohen, "Pagan and Christian Evidence" 176 n. 17.

[74] In *Ant.* XX 115 Josephus relates a incident in the year 49 in which a Roman soldier is executed by the governor Cumanus because he took a Torah scroll from a synagogue and tore it up in public.

[75] See Cohen, "Pagan and Christian Evidence" 164-165. *Ibid.* 166 Cohen discusses a passage from *Ant.* XIV 260-1, in which the city of Sardis gives the Jewish congregation permission to build a place where they can regularly pray *and sacrifice* (!). This remains a great mystery. I leave the matter aside here.

[76] S.C. Reif, Review of McKay, *JTS* n.s. 46 (1995) 611-612. C.S. Rodd in his review also complains about McKay's "extremely narrow definition of worship" (*Exp. Times* 106 [1995/96] 163). Cf. Judith Lieu's overly mild comment: "Some will query a definition of worship in an ancient context which prioritizes singing and prayer, excluding a primary focus on study (well attested) or even preaching" (*SOTS Booklist 1995*, 156).

When we now look back and see (a) that the word *proseuchê* desig-
nates a building in which people pray, (b) that it is extremely improbable that in a building where people prayed in weekday assemblies and
listened to the Torah on the Sabbath, there was no praying on the Sabbath, (c) that the clearly attested Sabbath worship in Qumran was most
likely not a custom deviating from the rest of Judaism, (d) that at least
one pagan author from the second century BCE mentions Jewish
prayer meetings on the seventh day, (e) that in some places the Mishnah clearly presupposes a Sabbath prayer service in the afternoon
(*minchah*), (f) that the nature and development of early Christian worship is best understood as a modified adoption of Jewish liturgical
forms, and (g) that reading, explanation, and study of the Torah was
regarded as a form of worship – it seems inevitable to conclude that
the synagogue was not only a place of Sabbath worship before 200 but
even before 70.

Of course, I am not saying that *all* Jews in the *entire* Hellenistic-
Roman period *always* worshipped on the Sabbath in *all* places in Israel
and in the Diaspora. We have become too convinced of the surprising
multiformity of Judaism in the ancient world to be able to accept this
readily. Rather it is likely that the situation in practice displayed considerable variations reflecting the views and customs of countless groups in
a large number of places and periods. What seems certain is that the synagogue flourished earlier in the Diaspora than in Palestine.[77] Certainly,
too, the presence of the Temple in Jerusalem up till 70 will have strictly
confined the role of the synagogue.[78] And there can be no doubt that in
the Diaspora the synagogue building also served as a kind of Jewish
agora. There simply was no monolithic Judaism in this regard either.[79]
But it also seems certain to me that Judaism in the ancient world was not
monolithic in the sense that religious services were never held anywhere

[77] See L.L. Grabbe, "Synagogues in Pre-70 Palestine: A Reassessment", in Urman &
Flesher, *Ancient Synagogues* 17-26.
[78] On this, see now S.C. Reif, *Judaism and Hebrew Prayer*, Cambridge: CUP, 1993, 34-
47 *et aliter*.
[79] L.I. Levine, "The Second Temple Synagogue," in Levine (ed.), *The Synagogue in
Late Antiquity* 14: "It is certain that the synagogue functioned in many capacities
and served a wide range of activities within the Jewish community" (with many
examples); but on p. 15 he adds: "Despite the plethora of communal activities that
occurred in the ancient synagogue, the institution served first and foremost as a place
for religious worship" (which, in Levine's view, consisted mainly of Torah reading).
See now also L.H. Feldman, "Diaspora Synagogues: New Light from Inscriptions
and Papyri," in: idem, *Studies in Hellenistic Judaism*, Leiden: Brill, 1996, 577-602,
esp. 595-7.

and by any Jewish congregation in the synagogue on the Sabbath.[80] Though it is salutary that McKay shows that scholars often read back too much into the sources in a maximalist and anachronistic way, her minimalist interpretation, in combination with her own anachronistic view of what can be called worship, equally fails to do justice to the sources. Our conclusion can therefore be that the synagogue was a place of worship on the Sabbath not just before 200 but before the year 70.

---

[80] Though he is more sceptical than I am, Daniel K. Falk also comes to a comparable conclusion in his "Jewish Prayer Literature" 284-5.

5. THE GREEK SYNAGOGUE PRAYERS IN THE APOSTOLIC CONSTITUTIONS, BOOK VII

The so-called *Apostolic Constitutions* (henceforth *AC*) are a fourth century church order.[1] The document is a collection of materials on ecclesiastical law that is widely believed to have been compiled in Syria in the final decades of the fourth century (ca. 380), probably by the same (semi-)Arian author who also interpolated the Letters of Ignatius of Antioch and wrote the Arian commentary on Job. The work consists of eight books and deals with the following subjects: Christian behaviour (bk. I); ecclesiastical hierarchy (bk. II); widows (bk. III); orphans (bk. IV); martyrs (bk. V); schisms (bk. VI); Christian morality and initiation (bk. VII); charismata, the eucharist, ordinations, and discipline (bk. VIII). Many other important subjects are discussed as subthemes throughout the work.

Being a compilation of older material, it has incorporated 3 major sources: the *Didascalia Apostolorum*[2] (books I-VI); the *Didache*[3] (bk. VII 1-32); and the *Traditio Apostolica* (or *Diataxeis of the Holy Apostles*) by Hippolytus[4] (bk. VIII 3-45). Other, minor sources include rules pertaining to Christian initiation (bk. VII 39-45); a list of bishops (bk. VII 46); Christian prayer formularies (bk. VII 47-49); a document on charismata (bk. VIII 1-2); and the so-called *Apostolic Canons* (bk. VIII 47). As will be seen in the next paragraph, the prayers in bk. VII 33-38 are believed to have been based upon a Jewish liturgical prayerbook. The whole is pseudepigraphically presented as 'regulations' (*diatagai*)

---

[1] The best recent discussion of the *AC* is the almost 200 pages of introduction to the Sources Chrétiennes edition by M. Metzger, *Les Constitutions Apostoliques*, vol. 1, Paris 1985, 13-93; vol. 2, Paris 1986, 10-110. Vol. 3, Paris 1987, contains text and French translation of books VII and VIII into which the prayer texts under discussion here have been incorporated. See further also D. A. Fiensy, *Prayers Alleged to Be Jewish. An Examination of the Constitutiones Apostolorum*, Chico 1985, 19-41; B. Steimer, *Vertex Traditionis. Die Gattung der altchristlichen Kirchenordnungen*, Berlin 1992, 114-133; E. M. Synek, *"Dieses Gesetz ist gut, heilig, es zwingt nicht..." Zum Gesetzesbegriff der Apostolischen Konstitutionen*, Vienna 1997. Steimer and Synek have good bibliographies of the older publications on the *AC*.
[2] First half of the third century, Syria.
[3] End of the first or beginning of the second century, Syria.

addressed by 'the apostles and presbyters to all believers from among the nations' and mediated in this publication by Clement (I, *Prol.*).

Since some of his major sources are known to us (sc. the *Didache* and the *Didascalia*), we are in a position to see the compiler at work. He does not take over the text of his sources unaltered. We can observe omissions, additions, insertions, corrections etc.[5] Sometimes these are minor, at other times they are major redrafts.[6] Especially prominent are the many biblical quotations – sometimes whole chains of quotations, e.g. VII 1 – and allusions inserted by the compiler into his sources. But also otherwise he often partly but drastically rewrites and rephrases the text of his his predecessors.[7] Especially the longer interpolations are important because they enable us to get to know the compiler's own ideas and his preferred vocabulary.

Over a century ago the Jewish scholar Kaufmann Kohler was the first to draw attention to what he saw as the Jewish character of some of the prayers in books VII and VIII of the *AC*.[8] It was his intention in that contribution to demonstrate the antiquity and Essene origin (in the Persian period!) of what he called the 'Grundtypus' of the synagogal liturgy,[9] and for that reason he mentions only in passing 'die christlich-essenische Liturgie' (447) in *AC* VII 35 and VIII 12 without giving any underpinning for his reasons to regard these prayers as essentially Jew-

---

[4] Beginning of the third century, Rome.

[5] Since the *Didascalia* is by far the most extensive source used by the compiler, F. X. Funk has presented the text of both documents (the *Didascalia* in its Latin version) at facing pages in order to facilitate comparison in his monumental work, *Didascalia et Constitutiones apostolicae*, Paderborn 1905. Funk underlined the passages where the compiler deviated from his sources.

[6] For our purposes it is important to see, e.g., that the prayers in *Didache* 9-10 have been thoroughly modified in *AC* VII 25-27.

[7] II 30-41 is a good example of this procedure.

[8] In his otherwise curious article "Über die Ursprünge und Grundformen der synagogalen Liturgie," *MGWJ* 38 (1893) 441-451, 489-497. In a groundbreaking study by F. X. Funk (*Die apostolischen Konstitutionen. Eine litterarisch-historische Untersuchung*, Rottenburg 1891), which appeared only 2 years before Kohler's first contribution, there is not yet to be found the slightest suspicion of the Jewish origin of these prayers.

[9] *Ibid.* 448: "[D]er Grundtypus aller unserer Gebete [reicht] auf die vormacedonische, also persische Kulturepoche zurück." Persian influences played an important role in this process and these were mediated by the Essenes ('die essäischen Genossenschaften,' 448). Kohler assumes that Aristotle's pupil Theophrastus once attended an Essene morning-service in Jericho (451)! At p. 492 he calls the Pater Noster 'ein altessenisches Kaddischgebet' and at p. 497 he asserts that Philo 'ohne Zweifel Essäer war.' All this is typical of the view of the Essenes that was prevalent in the 19th and early 20th century.

ish. But later he would expatiate on precisely that aspect. In an article he contributed ten years later to *The Jewish Encyclopedia*[10] he set out to demonstrate that not only the two passages mentioned above, but also various others in these two books were of Jewish origin and that these prayers contain older versions of several berakhot of the Amidah in an only slightly christianized form (he refers to VII 26; 33; 34; 35; 36; 37; 38; VIII 12; 37). In particular the prayers of book VII were regarded by him as a modified form of the Seven Benedictions for Shabbat and festivals.[11] He concludes that "as all these prayers go back to pre-Christian times, they are of incalculable importance to the student of Jewish and Christian liturgy" (594).

Twenty years later Kohler again came back to this subject in a long contribution to *HUCA* in 1924.[12] After 30 years Kohler still sticks to his Essene hypothesis. He complains about the neglect his ideas about the Jewish nature of these prayers have suffered from the part of other scholars, notably Elbogen (410). He then tries to demonstrate his case *in extenso* by providing all of *AC* VII 33-38 in an English translation, adding many notes and comments intended to show the Jewish origin of these prayers and how they were christianized by various changes and additions.[13] Finally, in a posthumously published book, *The Origins of the Synagogue and the Church*,[14] he once more returns to this favourite topic of his. Pointing out several Jewish formulas such as "the God of our holy and perfect fathers, Abraham, Isaac, and Jacob" and "the Law which Thou hast planted in our souls," he stresses that chapters 33-38 of *AC* VII "contain the Seven Benedictions of the ancient Jewish Ritual turned into a new shape by Greek-speaking, probably Essene, Jews, but christianized by a few verbal changes or additions" (257).[15]

In 1915 the German protestant scholar Wilhelm Bousset published a lengthy study of the prayer texts in the *AC*, apparently without any knowledge of the contributions that Kohler made in this field in the two

---

[10] "Didascalia," *JE* 4 (1903) 593-594.
[11] VII §33 ≈ first benediction, §34 ≈ second benediction, §35 ≈ third benediction, §36 ≈ fourth benediction, §37 ≈ fifth benediction, §38 ≈ sixth benediction. VIII §37 ≈ seventh benediction. The final equation was later dropped by Kohler.
[12] "The Origin and Composition of the Eighteen Benedictions with a Translation of the Corresponding Essene Prayers in the Apostolic Constitutions," *HUCA* 1 (1924) 387-425.
[13] This translation with notes is to be found at pp. 411-425.
[14] New York 1929, 250-259, esp. 257-258.
[15] Here he also repeats his thesis that *AC* VII 26 contains an originally Jewish prayer.

preceding decades.[16] However regrettable Bousset's neglect of Kohler's work may be from a scholarly point of view, it does give us the opportunity to see that completely independently from one another a Jewish and a Christian scholar came to much the same conclusions regarding the Jewish origin and nature of these Christian prayers. Bousset begins by pointing out that *AC* VII 35 is "gar nichts anderes als die charakteristische Form der Keduscha in der jüdischen Liturgie" (436), especially in the version in the *Yotser*.[17] He points out that especially the collocation of the quotations of Is. 6:3 and Ez. 3:12 in both texts (also attested in t. *Ber.* I 9) cannot be due to coincidence. There must be some connection between the two. He then goes on to demonstrate that *AC* VII 36 is an originally Jewish prayer for Shabbat comparable with the Kiddush prayer or the Shabbat Musaph prayer and that the Christian interpolations are easily discernible because they have been so clumsily and awkwardly inserted.[18] *AC* VII 37 and 38 equally show their Jewish character by their list of exclusively Old Testament heroes of faith, into the second of which Jesus has been interpolated again in a clumsy way. *AC* VII 34 has a striking parallel in *AC* VIII 12[19] and the two prayers undoubtedly draw on a common source, namely a Jewish creation hymn that interpreted Genesis 1 in a Stoic sense. However, "wir wissen nicht, was für eine Stellung, Sinn und Zweck es [the prayer] im jüdischen Gottesdienst und liturgischem Gebrauch gehabt hat" (464). Finally Bousset discusses *AC* VII 33, an undoubtedly Jewish prayer, if only because of the formula 'God of Abraham, Isaac and Jacob,' that is so strongly reminiscent of the Amidah, and the repeated mention of these three patriarchs further on in the prayer. The use of *horamatismos* ('vision') in §4 is an indication for the composer's use of Aquila's Bible translation, again a confirmation of the Jewish provenance of the prayer.[20] Moreover, the use of

---

[16] *Eine jüdische Gebetssamlung im siebenten Buch der apostolischen Konstitutionen*, Nachrichten der königlichen Gesellschaft der Wissenschaften zu Göttingen, Philologisch-historische Klasse, Göttingen 1915; reprinted in his *Religionsgeschichtliche Studien*. ed. A.F. Verheule, Leiden 1979, 231-286

[17] References are to the pages of the original 1915 publication.

[18] Especially the line in the closing paragraph which states, after all the praise of Shabbat, that the Day of the Lord (=Sunday) is much more excellent, however.

[19] Bousset 451-454 prints the texts in parallel columns. Ibid. 455: "Es kann keinem Zweifel unterliegen, daß diese beiden Gebete im VII. und VIII. Buch der Konstitutionen Redaktionen desselben Textes sind."

[20] At p. 466 Bousset also notes the use of Σιναῖ instead of Σινᾷ (35:4) and of Φασσᾶ instead of φασεκ (37:3), both being Aquilan words. For the rest, however, the real quotations are from the LXX, which Bousset suspects come from the Christian interpolator.

Aquila's translation is also a chronological pointer: the prayer(s) must derive from a period after the first half of the second century CE.[21]

So these prayer texts are important witnesses to a form of Hellenistic Judaism of the second century and later and to its world of thought. *AC* VII 33-38 "stellt wahrscheinlich bereits eine jüdische Gebetssamlung dar, die der Bearbeiter in sehr naiver und dankenswert geringer Umarbeitung in christliche Gebete verwandelt hat" (469). Bousset suspected that the 'Sitz im Leben' of the prayer collection was the instruction of proselytes, but he admits that it is only a guess ('nur als Vermutung,' 470). Thereafter, however, Bousset proceeds beyond Kohler in suggesting that also several prayers in book VIII of the *AC* have a Jewish origin. He wants to prove that "die gesamte Gebetsliturgie des achten Buches von jüdischem Einfluß, d.h. von unserer Gebetssamlung beherrscht ist" (471-472). Since his main contention is that some 10 prayers (or parts of prayers) in book VIII are based upon the prayers of book VII or used the same source as book VII did, we can leave aside this part of his discussion for the moment.[22] Bousset concludes by saying that these Jewish prayer texts are "ein Dokument von geradezu einzig dastehender Wichtigkeit für die Geschichte des nachchristlichen griechischen Diasporajudentums" (487). The most important aspect is that the prayers demonstrate that also after 135 CE there still existed a Greek speaking Diaspora Judaism which had a Greek liturgy. "In den vorliegenden Gebeten präsentiert sich ein Judentum im Gewand griechischer Sprache, tief berührt von hellenistischem Geiste, das z.T. (...) eine Fortentwickelung über Philo hinaus zeigt und im Besitz einer griechischen Liturgie ist" (487). It should be added here that, even though Bousset goes further than Kohler in identifying Jewish prayers in *AC*, he does not identify any of them with the Seven Benedictions for Shabbat and the festival days.[23]

Erwin Ramsdell Goodenough was the first who attempted to draw a picture of the cultural and religious milieu in which these prayer texts

---

[21] At pp. 466-469 Bousset points out the relevance of the fact that in VII 33 the concept of *gnosis* plays an important role; he there speculates about a Judaism that on the basis of Gen. 15 tried to establish the relation between *gnosis* and *pistis*.

[22] The prayers he discusses are VIII 5,1-4; 6,5; 9,8-9; 12,6-27; 15,7-9; 37,1-4; 37,5-7; 38,4-5; 39,3-4; 41,4-5. A useful synoptic chart with the lists of Kohler, Bousset, and Goodenough can be found in D. A. Fiensy, *Prayers Alleged to Be Jewish. An Examination of the Constitutiones Apostolorum*, Chico 1985, 11.

[23] In 1925 W.O.E. Oesterley briefly stated in his *The Jewish Background of the Christian Liturgy*, Oxford 1925, 138, that *AC* VIII 11,5 is based on the benediction *Ahavah*, VIII 12,8 on the *Yotser*, VIII 12,24 on the *Ge'ullah*, and VIII 12,27 on the *Qedushah*. He did not deal with the prayers of book VII.

came into being. In his famous book, *By Light, Light: The Mystic Gospel of Hellenistic Judaism*,[24] he devotes a long chapter to what he calls 'The Mystic Liturgy.' He is grateful to Bousset (but does not mention Kohler!) for having brought to light a body of liturgy that is "strikingly appropriate to the thesis of this book" (306), this thesis being that in the Hellenistic and Roman period there was a strand of Judaism that was both strongly hellenized and strongly mystic.[25] He then goes on by presenting the 16 texts dealt with by Bousset in an English translation, followed by a discussion. In the translation, Christian interpolations are indicated by italics. He begins by dealing with Bousset's parade horse, *AC* VII 35, with its striking parallel to the Qedusha, and then moves on to the other fragments, the discussion being largely devoted to marking the Christian interpolations which, like Bousset, he regards as limited and easily identifiable, and to indicating the mystic character of much of what is said in these prayers. Goodenough's concept of 'Mystic Judaism' (or 'the Jewish Mystery') induces him to regard as Jewish a number of phrases that Bousset regarded as Christian interpolations[26] and even some prayer texts that Bousset had excluded as being Christian compositions.[27] Goodenough regards all these texts as "the product of specifically mystic Judaism" (336). For example, the denial of God's spatiality and temporality in *AC* VIII 15,7 is typically Philonic and has no parallel in "normative Jewish thought" or "normative Judaism" (336-338). Also the thought that God is not subject to generation and is in need of nothing whatsoever (VII 35,9; VIII 5,1; VIII 12,6; VIII 15,7) is Philonic and dubbed 'mystical' by Goodenough (337). To put it briefly, most of the Hellenistic philosophical elements in these prayers (God's unchangeability, His invisibility, His inhabiting an inaccessible light, His Logos and Sophia, etc.) are evidence for mysticism on this interpretation. We can leave aside this highly controversial way of interpreting these texts.[28] For the present purpose it suffices to see that in

---

[24] New Haven 1935, 306-358.

[25] He more or less divides Hellenistic Judaism into 'normative literalists' on the one hand and 'allegorists or mystics' on the other. At p. 345 he says that the mysticism of our prayers is of Pharisaic stamp!

[26] A glaring case can be found at pp. 328-329. At p. 351 Goodenough says that "extreme similarity to early Christian points of view" does not preclude "almost complete accord with the Jewish Mystery."

[27] These are *AC* VII 26,1-3; VIII 16,3; VIII 40,2-4.

[28] For the problematic nature of Goodenough's thesis see, e.g., Fiensy, *Prayers Alleged to Be Jewish* 4; cf. also M. Smith, "Goodenough's *Jewish Symbols* in Retrospect," *JBL* 86 (1967) 53-68.

Goodenough the history of research on these texts reaches its maximalist peak.[29] We will have to wait 50 years before the pendulum swings back to a minimalistic counterpart.

In the meantime various scholars of comparative liturgy (e.g., A. Baumstark, H. Lietzmann, E. Werner, L. Bouyer) followed Kohler, Bousset and/or Goodenough by assuming a Jewish origin for many of the prayers in *AC* VII and VIII, although sometimes with qualifications.[30] The only really dissenting voice was that of B. Botte, who denied, apparently on *a priori* grounds, the possibility that Christians could have taken over prayers from the synagogue service. His main point of criticism of Bousset was that this scholar indulged in circular reasoning: He isolated the Christian elements in these Christian prayers as interpolations in order to enable himself to declare the texts to be Jewish.[31] By and large, however, the Kohler/Bousset/Goodenough thesis was accepted, and apart from some minor corrective suggestions,[32] no real progress was made in the study of these texts.

In 1985, however, the most important monograph on our texts to date was published. David Fiensy's *Prayers Alleged to Be Jewish* originated as a Princeton dissertation directed by J.H. Charlesworth. After a survey of research from Kohler to the eighties of our century, Fiensy sets out to answer the following questions: (1) Are any of these prayers Jewish? (2) Have Kohler, Bousset, and Goodenough proven their thesis? (3) When, where, and in what circles were the prayers composed? (4) If some or all

---

[29] The reader is again referred to the convenient chart on p. 11 in David Fiensy's book *Prayers Alleged to Be Jewish*, where it can be seen that Kohler regarded 7 prayer texts in the *AC* as Jewish, Bousset 16, and Goodenough 20!

[30] See the useful survey (with bibliographical details) in Fiensy, *Prayers Alleged to Be Jewish* 5-9. Also his note 78 at p. 17 and the remark in his article "Redaction History and the Apostolic Constitutions," *JQR* 72 (19811/82) 294, to the effect that the Kohler-Bousset-Goodenough thesis has enjoyed popularity with scholars of both Jewish and Christian literature, such as J. Heinemann, A.Z. Idelsohn, A. Spanier, E. Peterson, H. Lietzmann, L. Bouyer, A. Baumstark, E. Werner, M. Simon, and J. Daniélou. In his *Jewish Liturgy and Its Development*, New York 1932 (repr. 1967), 301-308, A.Z. Idelsohn has an appendix on 'Jewish Elements in Early Christian Liturgy' in which he simply takes over Kohler's findings (esp. 305-307).

[31] B. Botte, "Liturgie chrétienne et liturgie juive," *Cahiers Sioniens* 3 (1949) 215-223. See also Botte's critical remarks in a note added to A. Baumstark's *Liturgie comparée*, 3rd ed. by B. Botte, Chevetogne – Paris 1953, 12 n.2, where he warns against Baumstark's support for Bousset.

[32] E.g., Bouyer argued that *AC* VII 33, 34, and 35 are expanded versions of the first three Benedictions of the Amidah, that VII 36 is a prayer for the sabbath, that VII 37 is a combination of Benedictions 14-17 of the Amidah, and VII 38 an expansion of Benediction 18 (see his book *Eucharist*, Notre Dame 1968, 121-122). He also regarded the long prayer in VIII 12 as a combination of the three prayers in VII 33-35.

of these prayers are Jewish, what are the implications for the history of Jewish-Christian relations?

He then first considers the nature of the *AC*. A late fourth century manual of ecclesiastical life in Syria, it is a compilation of older material (*Didache, Didascalia,* Hippolytus' *Apostolic Tradition*) some of which is still extant in its independent forms. This is of great importance since it enables us to see what the compiler of *AC* does to his sources and what his theological tendencies are. It appears that "the compiler was not a slavish collector of sources but an editor as well, and at times, it seems, an author. If there were Jewish prayers among his sources, can we now retrieve their original wording? This last question, which is so important, virtually everyone has failed to ask" (27). By way of example he then shows in a synoptic form how the compiler of the *AC* used and redrafted two chapters with prayer texts in the *Didache* in the section almost immediately preceding the prayer texts (*Did.* 9-10 in *AC* VII 25).[33]

In a long chapter (ch. III, pp. 43-127), Fiensy prints the Greek text of all 20 prayers that have been alleged to be of Jewish origin, with an English translation at facing pages and extensive notes. Here he still deals only with the final form of the prayers as we now have them, without attempting to differentiate between a Jewish and a Christian stratum. Then, in chapter IV (pp. 129-164), he analyses the arguments for originally Jewish prayers in *AC*. He states right at the outset that he will argue "that Kohler was essentially correct in saying that AC 7.33-38 is a version of the Seven Benedictions, but that Bousset – though he possessed a fine sensitivity in recognizing that AC 7.33-38 is Jewish – used an inadequate methodology in arguing for his thesis, and that this methodology led him to suggest incorrectly that other prayers in AC books seven and eight are Jewish as well" (129). This task is carried out carefully in several steps.

Even though with his Essene theory Kohler misunderstood the milieu of the prayers, his recognition of the Seven Benedictions in *AC* VII 33-38 was correct.[34] It cannot be denied that the six prayers in *AC* VII

---

[33] *Prayers* 28-35.

[34] The Seven Benedictions for Sabbaths and festival days consist of the first three (*Avoth, Gevuroth, Qedushat ha-Shem*) and last three berakhot (*Avodah, Hoda'a. Birkat Shalom*) of the Shemoneh Esreh plus a middle benediction for the sanctification of the day (*Qedushat ha-Yom*). So on Shabbath and *yamim tovim* (except *Rosh ha-Shana*) the 13 middle benedictions are replaced by one berakhah for that specific day. 'Replaced' may not be the right word since it is not impossible that the Seven Benedictions were already in existence before the Amidah got its final form.

33-38 "follow closely the contents of the first six of the Seven Benedictions (the seventh is omitted) and that in the same order" (130). The correspondences are too many to be a case of sheer coincidence. Moreover, the fact that these prayers are not scattered throughout the *AC* but grouped together corroborates the thesis that we have to do with a source here. So it seems that, as the compiler used the *Didascalia* as his source in books I-VI and the *Didache* in VII 1-32, he used a set of Jewish prayers as his source in VII 33-38. "Thus, the third source in the AC is a Jewish Greek version of the Seven Benedictions" (131). This case is further strengthened by the fact that, even though there never existed a fixed uniform formulation of these berakhoth, there are verbal Greek equivalents to phrases in the Hebrew benedictions. In a chart (at pp. 155-159) Fiensy presents the Hebrew text of the Seven Benedictions in the Babylonian version of R. Amram and the Palestinian version from the Genizah, underlining the verbal parallels to the Greek version. Every benediction turns out to have at least one verbal parallel, apart from thematic equivalents. To give just one clear instance: *AC* VII 34 ends with a clause in which God is called ὁ ζωοποιὸς τῶν νεκρῶν ('reviver of the dead') and the corresponding Hebrew benediction (*Gevuroth*) ends with God as *mehayyeh ha-metim*. Fiensy concludes: "These verbal similarities and equivalents would be striking enough if they appeared in isolated prayers. But, coming as they do in a prayer collection, and appearing for the most part in their proper order, they constitute a convincing corpus of evidence to suggest that AC 7.33-38 is a Greek version of the Hebrew Seven Benedictions" (134).

Fiensy then devotes no less than 15 pages (134-148) to Bousset's treatment of the prayers the methodology of which he thinks is deeply flawed. For instance, in his treatment of *AC* VII 35, Bousset on the one hand rightly demonstrated that the juxtaposition of Isaiah 6:3 and Ezekiel 3:12 must be the result of Jewish influence, but on the other hand he failed to consider the possibility that a Christian may have composed a prayer "using the Jewish Kedusha which he had heard recited by Jews" (134). The fact that this prayer contains a Jewish expression does not necessarily make it a Jewish prayer. "Merely finding a Jewish expression – or later on, Jewish ideas – in a prayer which is now Christian does not mean that a Jewish stratum lies underneath" (134). Moreover, in contrast to Kohler, Bousset treated each prayer individually and did not pay attention to the context so that it escaped his notice that *AC* VII 33-38 is a prayer collection of which the structure and arrangement are exactly parallelled in Jewish liturgy. Further, Bousset paid no attention to the tendency of the redactional work of the compiler. For instance, as to *AC* VII 36, the Sabbath prayer, he rightly compared it to the Jewish Qiddush prayer for Sabbath, but he failed to consider the possibility that the original prayer was Christian after all, since from several passages in the *AC* as a whole it is apparent that the compiler and his community observed the Sabbath (e.g. II 36,2: "Keep the Sabbath on account of the one who rested from his work"). Since Sabbath observance seems to have been practiced in the compiler's Christian community (a quite general practice in the early Christian East), it is equally possible that the compiler took an older Christian prayer which extolled the Sabbath, and appended a reference to the superior Sunday because he revered the Sunday even more. Still Fiensy does believe that the prayer was originally Jewish, "standing as it does exactly where the Kedushat ha-Yom stands in the Seven Benedictions" (136), but he wants to point out that by neglecting the nature of the compiler's work as a whole one excludes possibilities that are more than just imaginative. Bousset's failure to consider the theological tendencies and literary conventions of the compiler leads also to flawed results in his treatment of *AC* VII 37 and 38. Here he argues that the fact that the lists of heroes occurring in both prayers do not contain a single New Testament name (only Old Testament ones, apart from the obvious interpolation of Jesus in VII 38,3) demonstrates that the author of the original prayer was Jewish. However, even apart from the fact that such lists occur also in other early Christian writings (even in the NT itself, e.g. Hebr. 11), several of such enumerations occur elsewhere in the *AC*, mostly in redactional sections (e.g. II 55,1; V 7.12; VI 12,13; VII 5,5). "Thus it also likely that the lists in AC 7.37 and 38 are redactional" (136). To put it in other words: comparison with other passages in which the compiler "has freely edited, rearranged, recast, and interpolated his sources" makes one wonder about "the extent of redaction of any Jewish prayers which the compiler may have incorporated into his work" (137). This extent may have been much larger indeed. It is an untenable assumption that after having excised all phrases that are obviously and characteristically Christian, we can take everything else in the prayers to be Jewish.

Another of Bousset's errors is that he did not sufficiently consider the Christian liturgical tradition that was available to the compiler. This led him, e.g., to the assumption that VII 34 and VIII 12,9-20 are two different redactions of the same Hellenistic Jewish prayer in which God is thanked for his creation by listing its individual parts (with parallels in Philo). Such prayers, however, are quite common in various Eastern liturgies and other early Christian writings. So these prayers may by and large be Christian compositions. Also Bousset's argument from the occurrence of words from Aquila's Bible translation is less than convincing. The word συνθήκη turns out to occur in redactional sections of *AC* as well. As to φασσᾶ, this reading is very uncertain and it occurs in a passage that on other grounds is likely to be redactional. Also for the spelling of the word Sinai the mss. display a lot of variation and the word occurs in an otherwise LXX quotation! Only δραματισμός is from Aquila's version, but does this imply that the whole of *AC* VII 33 must have been written by a Jew? Could this word not simply have been picked up from Aquila's version by the compiler himself?

Dealing with the question of whether themes occurring in the prayers that are Jewish are found elsewhere in the *AC*, especially in its redactional sections, "often leads to the conclusion that the 'Jewish' elements are actually favorite themes or literary conventions of the compiler of AC. The emphasis upon Sabbath worship and the listing of OT heroes are examples" (143-144). So many of Bousset's argument in favour of his thesis of the Jewish character of these prayers fail to convince. To be sure, the prayers in *AC* VII 33-38 are Jewish, but not for the reasons given by Bousset, says Fiensy (144).

In a final paragraph (144-148) Fiensy criticizes Bousset's defense of the Jewish origin of the prayers other than those in *AC* VII 33-38 as being even more weak, based as it is largely upon an argument from silence. Moreover, most of these texts bristle with redactional phrases, which makes it highly likely that they are by and large creations of the compiler himself.

Understandably, Goodenough's long treatment of the material is only briefly dealt with by Fiensy (148-150). The hesitations that Bousset sometimes still voiced clearly are totally absent in Goodenough's work. He even added some more prayers to the list, with utterly weak arguments. For instance, he argued that *AC* VIII 16,3 reads perfectly as a Jewish prayer "if one supplies 'Logos' in place of 'Christ'" (335), but, as Fiensy remarks, "he did not demonstrate why one should do this" (148). This whole prayer contains the favourite themes of the compiler and should therefore be regarded as his composition. This applies in most cases to the other prayers as well. So the scholarship of the great Goodenough was not good enough in this case.

As to the four prayers contained in *AC* VIII 37-39 which both Bousset and Goodenough took to be Jewish, Fiensy admits that, as in the case of the prayer collection in *AC* VII 33-38, "these prayers contain ideas corresponding to prayers in an existing Hebrew text [sc. Ma'ariv, Ahavah, Yotser, Ahavah after Yotser], and they correspond to the order of these prayers in the Hebrew text" (151). However, unlike in the case of *AC* VII 33-38, there are no verbal parallels at all and the central themes are different, and all of these prayers betray again the hand of the compiler in containing several obvious redactional elements.

Fiensy's conclusions are as follows: "First, it is highly probable that AC 7.33-38 is a Jewish Greek version of the Hebrew Seven Benedictions. Secondly, many of the additional prayers that Bousset suggested might be Jewish, probably are the work of the compiler of AC. Goodenough's additional suggested Jewish prayers are either beyond our present scope, or probably also the work of the compiler. (...) Thirdly, the evening and morning prayers in AC 8.37-39 are curiously reminiscent of the prayers accompanying the Shema, but different enough from those prayers and edited sufficiently, that their original Jewishness is far less likely than in the case of AC 7.33-38. Even if we conclude that they were originally Jewish, we could not get at the original form of these prayers" (153).

In his chapter on the reconstruction of the original source (165-207), Fiensy operates on the basis of a minimalist approach. He assumes that the compiler faithfully represents his source only in those cases where there exist close similarities between the Greek text and the Babylonian or Palestinian versions of the Seven Benedictions. Where the resemblances are vague and there is evidence of the compiler's vocabulary, it is assumed that he has completely recast his source at that point. Editorial activity is to be found in (1) material containing explicitly Christian elements, (2) material containing words, phrases, or themes which were favoured by the compiler,[35] (3) material containing recurrent words, phrases, or themes which only appear elsewhere in books VII and VIII of *AC*, in those portions where the source is unknown,[36] (4) material discordant with the rest of the text, (5) material strongly reminiscent of Pseudo-Ignatius in expression or idea, and (6) material which has parallels in other Christian liturgies. "When we cannot show that material in

---

[35] These favourite expressions can be found by studying the way the compiler dealt with the text of the Didascalia (in books I-VI), the Didache (in VII 1-32), and the Apostolic Tradition (in parts of book VIII). Fiensy admits, however, that "it is remotely possible that the Jewish source could have furnished the compiler with a theme or expression which he favored" (166).

[36] There is an element of uncertainty here since the source is unknown, "but repeated appearance of these elements in scattered portions of books seven and eight of AC certainly suggests that the material is redactional" (166).

AC 7.33-38 meets the six criteria above, we assume that it was in the original" (167). The mistake of previous scholars is that they applied only the first criterion, with the result that they attributed much redactional material to the source.

Fiensy then analyzes the six prayers in *AC* VII 33-38 with his six criteria and in the end presents the results in a chart (pp. 198, 200). His reconstruction of the original source turns out to be less than 2 pages of Greek text. A greater contrast with the dozens of pages of text in the Bousset-Goodenough approach is hardly possible. Fiensy admits that his method inevitably implies that he may have occasionally omitted from the reconstructed source what was in the Jewish stratum (due to the compiler's recasting of an idea) and that he may have included some material which is redactional (but which fails to meet the 6 criteria). Still that would not alter the overall picture of the compiler as a person with a heavy editorial hand. Fiensy's conclusions are very sobering.

In the final chapter on literary and historical questions (209-242), Fiensy discusses the question of whether the Jewish prayers were an oral source or a written document, and he very tentatively concludes that the prayers were written down most probably by a Christian before the time of the compiler. He further discusses the original language of the prayers which he thinks must go back to Hebrew originals (there is syntactical evidence to that effect). He assumes they were composed in Hebrew in Palestine and later translated into Greek, either in Palestine or in the diaspora, for use in the Greek-speaking synagogue, where they were heard, adopted and adapted by Christians who attended synagogue services. This probably took place in Syria since most of *CA*'s sources are known to be of Syrian provenance and the *AC* themselves were compiled in Syria. Moreover, we know from a variety of other sources that there were intimate contacts between church and synagogue in second to fourth century Syria, especially in Antioch. (The compiler himself also refers several times to the 'sin' committed by Christians who attended synagogue services, e.g. II 61,1)

The date of the composition of the prayers is hard to fix. Fiensy assumes that the *terminus ad quem* should be pushed back to one or two generations before the compiler, that is circa 300 CE, since in view of his strongly anti-Jewish views he must have been unaware of the Jewish origins of the prayers. The *terminus post quem* must be the first century CE, since the parallels between other Jewish prayer texts from the second century BCE to the first century CE on the one hand and the Seven Benedictions as we know them from the Geniza fragments and

Amram's text on the other are more remote and vaguer than the parallels in *AC* VII 33-38. The older parallels consist of only a few scattered words and their order never corresponds to the Hebrew prayers. This makes it probable that *AC* reflects a later stage in the development of these prayers. Also the fact that the structure of the Qedusha as reflected in *AC* VII 35,3 is most probably a post-first century product confirms a dating to "any time between A.D. 150 and 300" (227), although the fact that Ps. 68:18 is connected with the Qedusha here, which seems to reflect a third century midrashic tradition,[37] favours the later part of this period. As to the milieu in which the prayers originated, the reconstructed text does not give the slightest clue to either Essene or 'mystical' circles, for all passages that Kohler and Goodenough used for these theories turn out to be redactional. An analysis of the reconstructed text shows that the theology of its composer(s) is "not different in thought from the Hebrew prayers" (231), with the exception of the heavy emphasis on the significance of the number seven in VII 36, which sounds more like Philo.

Fiensy summarizes his findings as follows: "The reconstructed text yields different results from the text as it stands in the AC. The compiler's source may have been oral or written, and the Greek is based upon a Hebrew source. No better suggestion for provenance than Syria can be offered. The form of the prayers is post-first century, but must have reached Christian circles by at least A.D. 300. Most significant is the different picture of milieu which the reconstruction effects. (...) The theology of the prayers is in the main that of the Hebrew benedictions and of rabbinic thought, and the prayers are probably an example of the Syrian synagogal Sabbath morning service in the late second to early fourth centuries A.D." (234).

In the same year in which Fiensy published his book (1985), there appeared also his introduction to D.R. Darnell's translation of 16 of the prayer texts in *The Old Testament Pseudepigrapha* (ed. J.H. Charlesworth, vol. 2, 671-696). Here he covers by and large the same ground as in his dissertation, so there is no need for an extensive summary of this contribution. The policy adopted in the translation is that only the passages that cannot be but Christian are indicated by underlining, but, it is added: "There is considerable difficulty in defining the perimeters of interpolation. They may begin earlier and end later than

---

[37] Here Fiensy relies on an unpublished paper by D.J. Halperin. See now Halperin's *The Faces of the Chariot. Early Jewish Responses to Ezekiel's Vision*, Tübingen 1988, 143-149, 288-289, 316-318, 501-504.

indicated, but restraint has been applied in underlining" (675). So far on the history of research.[38]

One of the intriguing aspects of the presence of these Jewish prayers in this Christian document is that on the one hand the compiler polemicizes on several occasions against the practices of judaizing Christians, while on the other hand he seems to play into their cards by adopting synagogal prayers, however modified they were by him. Is there a historical situation that can shed light on this procedure?

The clearest evidence for such a situation is the eight anti-Jewish homilies held by John Chrysostom in the year 386/7[39]. They deal exactly with the situation in Antioch in the same decade in which the compiler of the *AC* was at work. From Chrysostom's vehement invectives against Christians who go to the synagogue on sabbath, who have themselves circumcised, who celebrate Jewish Pesach, who keep Jewish food laws, who fast together with the Jews, etc., etc., – it becomes more than clear that as late as the end of the fourth century many Christians were being strongly attracted by Judaism. If the Jews are painted so black, as they are by Chrysostom, it is because to too many Christians they appear not sufficiently unattractive. "The most compelling reason for anti-Semitism was the religious vitality of Judaism."[40] How strong this vitality was in Syria and in parts of Asia Minor is also evident from several canons of the council of Laodicea (in Phrygia) which was held somewhere in the third quarter of the

---

[38] In light of Fiensy's work it is remarkable that in his new critical edition of the *AC* for the Sources Chrétiennes series Marcel Metzger (who knows Fiensy's book) states regarding the Jewish prayers in VII 33-38: "Les remaniements semblent peu importants: tantôt quelques mots, tantôt la seule mention du Christ, tantôt une phrase entière" (vol. III, 66-67). Strangely enough, even Fiensy's own supervisor, J.H. Charlesworth, wrote only a couple of years before Fiensy published his 1982 dissertation that in the 14 (!) Jewish prayers in the *AC* it is "usually (...) relatively easy to discern and remove the fabricated veneer of the Christian interpolations" (see his "Christian and Jewish Self-Definition in Light of the Christian Additions to the Apocryphal Writings," in E.P. Sanders (ed.), *Jewish and Christian Self-Definition*, Vol. 2, London 1981, 31).

[39] W.A. Meeks and R.L. Wilken, *Jews and Christians in Antioch in the First Four Centuries of the Common Era*, Missoula 1978, 83-126 *et al.* R. Brändle, "Christen und Juden in Antiochien in den Jahren 386/87. Ein Beitrag zur Geschichte altkirchlicher Judenfeindschft," *Judaica* 43 (1987) 142-160, has a very useful bibliography. See now also my article "Jews and Christians in Antioch at the End of the Fourth Century" (elsewhere in this volume).

[40] M. Simon, *Verus Israel*, Oxford 1986, 232. Cf. also E. M. Smallwood, *The Jews Under Roman Rule*, Leiden 1976, 508.

fourth century.[41] In canon 29 it is stated: "It is forbidden that Christians live like Jews (*ioudaïzein*) and rest on sabbath; they should work on that day. They should prefer the Lord's day to rest on, if possible, since they are Christians. If they turn out to be judaizers, let them be accursed (*anathema*) by Christ." Canon 38 runs as follows: "It is forbidden to take unleavened bread from the Jews or to participate in their godless acts." Canon 37 forbids any participation in the festivals of the Jews or heretics, and canon 36 warns the clergy against making *phylakteria*, which are probably *tefillin* used as magical apotropaic amulets.[42] These canons can only be explained on the assumption that keeping the sabbath, celebrating Pesach and other Jewish religious festivals, etc., were not marginal but frequently occurring and tenacious phenomena among Christians in Asia Minor in the second half of the fourth century. The same situation prevailed in Syria as the testimonies of not only John Chrysostom, but also of Aphraat and Ephrem Syrus make impressively clear.[43] Only the fact that Judaism continued to make it's presence strongly felt in the Diaspora throughout the first five centuries of our era makes it explicable that during these centuries there was a persistent tradition of judaizing in the churches of Syria and Asia Minor which defied all the anathemas of the church authorities. Marcel Simon put it well: "The anti-Jewish bias of official ecclesiastical circles was counterbalanced by equally marked pro-Jewish sentiments among the laity and among some of the clergy too. Or rather, it is the existence of the pro-Jewish sentiments among the laity that is the real explanation of Christian anti-Semitism."[44] We know from other sources that in the early centuries of the Common Era Antioch had a large and vibrant Jewish community, of which Josephus already wrote that "they were constantly attracting to their religious ceremonies multitudes of Greeks" (*Bellum* VII 45).[45] And not long after Josephus wrote

---

[41] The exact date of this synod is unknown, though most scholars incline to date this meeting to the sixties of the fourth century. The text of the canons can be found in E. J. Jonkers, *Acta et symbola conciliorum quae saeculo quarto habita sunt,* Leiden 1954, 86-96.

[42] On the great reputation of Jewish magic in antiquity see Simon, *Verus Israel* 339-368, esp. 361 on the magical use of phylacteries/tefillin. Some scholars regard also canon 35 (against *angelolatreia*) as directed against judaizing practice.

[43] On Aphraat see J. Neusner, *Judaism, Christianity, and Zoroastrianism in Talmudic Babylonia,* Lanham-New York-London 1986, 199-228; on Ephrem H.J.W. Drijvers, *Syrian Christianity and Judaism,* in his *History and Religion in Late Antique Syria,* London 1994, ch. 2, esp. 141-142.

[44] Simon, *Verus Israel* 232.

[45] See G. Downey, *A History of Antioch in Syria,* Princeton 1961, 272-316, and B.J. Brooten, "The Jews of Ancient Antioch," in Chr. Kondoleon, *Antioch: The Lost Ancient City,* Princeton 2000, 29-37.

these words, one of the first bishops of Antioch, Ignatius, at the beginning of the second century made some remarks in his letters that strongly suggest that he was upset by the fact that several Christians in his community were adopting Jewish practices, evidently under the influence of the local Jewish community (*Magn.* 8:1-2; *Phil.* 6:1). From John Chrysostom we learn that this situation persisted till centuries after Ignatius.[46] In such a situation it was a tactical move to incorporate Jewish prayers into the Christian liturgy, for 'if you can't beat them, join them.' If their existed a tenacious need among Christians in Antioch for using Jewish liturgical material, which was one of the reasons why they went to the synagogue on shabbat, then the best thing church leadership could do was to see to it that the prayers the members of his community said in the synagogue, could also be said by them in the church, albeit with some modifications, so that the need of these members was met and the danger of loosing them to the synagogue was lessened. This is the most likely *Sitz im Leben* for these prayers in the *AC*.

The implication for the dating of the prayer texts is that their composition most probably took place before 350 CE. Since m. *Rosh ha-Shana* IV 5 already mentions the Seven Benedictions by name, we may assume that they were already in existence in their Hebrew form at least by ca. 200 CE (how much earlier is impossible to determine). It stands to reason to assume that their translation into Greek for use in Greek speaking synagogues took place sometime in the third century. From j. *Sotah* VII 1, 21b we learn that in the synagogue of Caesarea around 300 CE the Shema was recited in Greek, and their are several other references to synagogue liturgies in Greek.[47] So there can be no doubt that Jewish synagogal prayer texts in Greek were in circulation in the third and fourth centuries and probably also before and after that period.[48] Fiensy opts for a dating in the third century.[49] On the one hand he rightly rejects the 'Frühdatierungen' by people like Kohler and Goodenough, on the other hand he advocates a dating of the Greek version before 300 with the unconvincing argument that in view of the compiler's anti-Jewish views he must have been unaware of the Jewish origins of the prayers.

---

[46] For a discussion of possible evidence for the period between Ignatius and Chrysostom see Fiensy, *Prayers* 218-219.

[47] S.C. Reif, *Judaism and Hebrew Prayer*, Cambridge 1993, 350 n. 47.

[48] A case in point from Egypt may be Papyrus Egerton 5, a prayer text from the late fourth century CE, on which see P. W. van der Horst, "Neglected Greek Evidence for Early Jewish Liturgical Prayers," *Journal for the Study of Judaism* 29 (1998) 278-296.

[49] *Prayers* 220-228.

As may be gathered from the previous paragraph, I think the contrary was the case. But even so, in view of other suggestive evidence for a third-century dating adduced by Fiensy (for which the reader is referred to the final paragraphs of the chapter on the history of research), it is highly probable that the Greek text of the prayers was produced at some time in the third century CE, or otherwise at any rate between 150 and 350 CE.

It is clear that after Fiensy's investigation it is no longer possible to revert to the old style maximalist approach à la Kohler, Bousset, or Goodenough. It cannot and should not be denied that Fiensy has hit on a sore spot in pointing out that none of these scholars had paid sufficient (if any) attention to the many redactional elements in the texts that are not overtly Christian in character. His minimalist position is a healthy corrective to the naïve maximalism of these earlier scholars and their followers. Does that imply now that we have to follow and swallow Fiensy's approach and results throughout? Fiensy himself will be the first to admit how many uncertainties there still are. As he points out repeatedly, "we may have occasionally omitted from our reconstructed source what was in the Jewish stratum, due to the compiler's recasting of an idea" (187). This is certainly true. Let us take as an instance his treatment of *AC* VII 34, which he sees as the equivalent of *Gevuroth*, the second berakhah of the Amidah. The endresult of his treatment (as may be seen on p. 198) is that of the 45 lines of Greek text (according to Metzger's edition) only 2 are left, namely, (part of) the opening line, εὐλόγητος εἶ, Κύριε, βασιλεῦ τῶν αἰώνων, ὁ ποιήσας τὰ ὅλα, and part of the closing line, ὁ ζωοποιὸς τῶν νεκρῶν, because these have close counterparts in *Gevuroth*. Why is everything in between left out by Fiensy? That is not just because the rest of the text does not have such obvious parallels in the second berakhah. Let us have a closer look at his arguments.[50]

The prayer is very similar to the one in *AC* VIII 12,9-20. After the opening line (with some obvious interpolations, e.g., 'through Christ') the prayer goes on with an enumeration of God's various acts of creation, roughly patterned after Genesis 1 (LXX), but with a markedly different sequence. Exactly the same is the case in the similar prayer in VIII 12,9-20,[51] and Bousset regarded both prayers as different and inde-

---

[50] Presented on pp. 172-176 (also 137-140).
[51] Both texts also mention Job 38 at the same point when speaking about the sea!

pendent redactions of one and the same Jewish text. But this common *Grundlage* was not at all a Jewish prayer text, but the Christian liturgical tradition! And it was the compiler himself who redrafted this tradition into two both similar and different prayers (the differences may have been caused by the fact that there lay several weeks or some months between his reworking of the *Grundlage* in VII 34 and in VIII 12). This Christian liturgical tradition can be traced in a variety of sources, beginning as early as *1 Clement* 20 (end of the first century), where also the various elements of creation are enumerated in praise of God. "AC 7.34 reflects the theme and language of this liturgical tradition" (140), and it was the main theme of the second berakhah (*Gevuroth* = God's powerful deeds) which led the compiler to recast this benediction using his own liturgical tradition. The fact that there are so many common themes and stock expressions in VII 34 and VIII 12 can only be explained on the assumption that the compiler himself redacted both prayers. Everything in between the opening and closing lines can be explained in terms of either the Christian liturgical tradition or the compiler's favourite themes and expressions. Only the barest framework still reminds one of the Jewish berakhah, but it does so clearly enough.

This seems to be a well argued position. On closer scrutiny, however, matters appear to be somewhat different than suggested by Fiensy. The differences between VII 34 on the one hand and VIII 12,9-20 on the other are much vaster than he suggests, if only because the second passage contains some 70 lines of Greek (in Metzger's edition) whereas the former has only 45. The verbal agreements amount to no more than a handful of turns and phrases, as can easily be gathered from Fiensy's own synoptic chart D (pp. 189-197). To explain these vast differences by the assumption that some weeks or months had lapsed between the compiler's redrafting of the source in VII 34 and in VIII 12 is not very illuminating. It would seem, therefore, that Bousset was right after all that they are different redactions of a common source by different hands, and most probably VII 34 with its shorter form was the earlier one. This would explain two things: (1) the fact that most of the parallels in the Christian liturgical tradition are parallels to VIII 12, much less to VII 34; (2) the fact that, contrary to VII 34, the prayer in VIII 12 has a eucharistic setting (the so-called *ante-sanctus*) which is also the case in the other liturgies adduced by Fiensy. In other words, what is applicable to VIII 12 is not necessarily so to VII 34, in spite of the agreements between the two texts. This re-opens up the possibility that parts of the middle section of VII 34 indeed do go back to Jewish sources.

This example was only mentioned in order to demonstrate that even Fiensy's excellent work is not necessarily the final word on the extent of the Jewish source(s) in these prayer texts.

In the case of the prayer text presented below, the first of the series of six in *AC* VII 33-38, the following procedure will be followed. A new English translation will be offered. Where important deviations from the existent translations were deemed necessary, these decisions will be argued in the Notes. A major typographical deviation from all existing translations will be that mine will use three different types: **Bold type** will be reserved for the material that certainly or almost certainly belongs to the Jewish stratum of the text (that is to say, it indicates the material the Jewish nature of which all researchers sofar agree upon *plus* material that I claim Fiensy has wrongly identified as additions by the compiler). *Italics* will be used to indicate the material that according to all scholars is demonstrably Christian. Finally, normal type will be used for the remaining material, that is, the material that some scholars claim to be Jewish whereas others claim it to be Christian. In most of the existing translations only the glaringly Christian elements (e.g. the name Jesus Christ) are indicated by underlining. After David Fiensy's investigation it turns out to be necessary to *italicize* more material as Christian. At the same time it will be argued, however, that some of the material that was dubbed Christian by Fiensy can reasonably be assumed to be Jewish, but we will set more material in **bold type** *only* in those cases where we have reached a relatively high degree of certainty as to its Jewish origin. The text will be followed by some exegetical notes.[52]

Apostolic Constutions VII 33

Translation
(2) **Our eternal Saviour, King of the Gods, the one who alone is almighty and Lord, God of all beings, and God of our** holy and blameless **fathers** who were before us, **God of Abraham, Isaac and Jacob, who is merciful and compassionate, patient and abundant in mercy, to whom every heart appears as naked and (to whom) every secret thought is revealed. To you the souls of the righteous cry out, upon**

---

[52] This is only a provisional and abridged specimen of a forthcoming commentary by the author on all the Jewish prayer texts in *AC*. The text is attested in the following mss.: **a, c, h, y**, and **z** (= fam. H); **d, e** and **s** (= fam. N); and ms. **v**.

you the devout have put their hopeful trust, you Father of the blame-less, you who listen to those who call upon you in uprightness, you who even know the supplications that are kept silent, for your foreknowledge reaches as far as the inmost parts of mankind, and by your awareness you search each person's thought, and **in every region of the inhabited world the incense that comes through prayer and words is sent up to you.**

(3) You have established the present world as a place where men should run the race of righteousness, **you have opened to all a gate of mercy, you have showed to everyone** by implanted knowledge and natural judgement as well as through the teaching of the Law, **that the possession of wealth is not eternal, that outer beauty is not everlasting, that physical power is easily dissolved,** and that all these things are nothing but vapour and vanity. Only a sincere conscience of faith, that truly ascends and traverses[53] through the midst of the heavens, receives the assurance of future bliss, and at the same time, even before the promised rebirth is realized, that soul rejoices as it is exulting in hope.

(4) For from the beginning, when our forefather Abraham laid claim to the way of truth, you have guided him by means of a vision and taught him thus what this world really is [or: what this life really is about?]. From that knowledge came forth his faith, and the covenant was the consequence of this faith [or: Faith went before his knowledge but the covenant was the follower of his faith?].[54] For you had said: "I

---

[53] All editions have διαμένει, but **c**, **h**, and fam. N read διαβαίνει. The difference in pronunciation between these two words is very small. I agree with Fiensy (53) that the following words 'through the midst of the heavens' require a verb of movement, not of remaining. Though διαμένει is *lectio difficilior*, it makes too little sense.

[54] The reading with γνώσεως ... πίστις ... πίστεως is supported by **c**, **h**, **y**(mg), **N**, **v**, whereas **a**, **y** (txt), and **z** have πίστεως ... γνῶσις ... γνώσεως. It is a complex situation in that the text with stronger mss attestation yields a much less easily understandable whole. The situation is further complicated by the fact that the same group **a**, **y**, and **z** also have instead of τῆς δὲ πίστεως ἀκόλουθος ἦν ἡ συμθήκη the following: τῆς δὲ γνώσεως ἀκόλουθος γέγονεν ἡ πίστις, τῆς δὲ πίστεως ἦν ἐπακολούθημα ἡ συν-θήκη, which yields: '(Knowledge went before his faith and) faith was the follower of his knowledge, but a consequence of his faith was the covenant.' This makes for the logical order: knowledge > faith > covenant. In the reading by the majority of mss the order seems to be: faith > knowledge, but then, illogically, covenant again as the consequence of faith. If, however, one translates προώδευσεν here with 'came forth from' (a meaning not listed in LSJ's *Greek-English Lexicon*) instead of 'went before,' the logical order is restored. Most probably, however, the majority reading is a result of an attempt by Christian copyists to give priority to Abraham's faith, influenced as they were by Paul (see Romans 4). So the most likely reading would seem to be: καὶ τῆς μὲν πίστεως αὐτοῦ προώδευσεν ἡ γνῶσις, τῆς δὲ γνώσεως ἀκόλουθος ἦν ἡ συμθήκη. This reading, however, is not to be found in any of the mss! Perhaps the best solution is to accept the well attested majority reading and to translate προώδευσεν as suggested above, however problematic that may seem. But all other solutions are at least equally problematic.

will make your seed like the stars of heaven and like the sand along the shore of the sea."

(5) Moreover, when you had given him Isaac and knew that he was going to be like him (his father) in his way of life, you called yourself also his God when you said: "I will be your God and that of your seed after you." And when our father Jacob set out for Mesopotamia, *you showed (him) Christ*, and you spoke *through him* saying: "Look, I am with you and I will increase you and multiply you exceedingly."

(6) And to Moses, your faithful and holy servant, you said in the vision of the bush: "I am the one who is. That is my eternal name and a memorial to generations after generations." (7) **Defender of the offspring of Abraham, blessed are you forever!**

Notes
(2) 'Our eternal Saviour' refers to God. Since in *AC* 'saviour' is almost always used for Jesus Christ, except here and in VII 35,1, it seems to have come from the Jewish source at both these places. 'King of the Gods' is a quote from one of the additions to Esther in the LXX, Esth. 4:17r (or add. C23). At the background are passages like Ps. 95:3: "The Lord... is a great king above all the gods." Cf. also Ps. 82:1, where God is standing "in the assembly of gods." 'The one who alone is almighty and Lord, God of all beings' is regarded by Fiensy as the compiler's addition since παντοκράτωρ is used often by him and since the compiler likes to emphasize the pre-eminence of the Father and the correlative subordination of the Son and the Holy Spirit. But it has to be objected that παντοκράτωρ is used at least as frequently by his sources (as Fiensy is forced to admit, 203 n.9),[55] and that in the instances of emphasis on the pre-eminence of the Father mentioned by Brightman[56] the use of παντοκράτωρ is missing. So it stands to reason to take this whole phrase, just as the immediately surrounding phrases, to derive from the Jewish source, though perhaps the words 'God of all beings' is a free rendering of 'our God' in the alleged counterpart of this prayer, the berakhah *Avoth* in the Amidah. 'God of our holy and blameless fathers who were before us, God of Abraham, Isaac and Jacob' is a phrase that occurs in very similar wording in *Avoth* in the Amidah: 'God of our fathers, God of Abraham, God of Isaac, God of Jacob.' The expression is from Ex. 3:16 and occurs also in the opening line of the *Prayer of Manasse*. Since, however, ἄμεμπτος is a favourite word of the compiler, that he has demonstrably inserted on various occasions into his sources, the words '(holy and) blameless' are arguably interpolations. But the formula 'God of Abraham, Isaac and Jacob' which has such a close parallel to *Avoth* that it is generally taken to be part of the original Jewish prayer, was also inserted twice into other texts by the compiler himself (VII 26,3

---

[55] Moreover, at other places in the prayer texts Fiensy himself retains παντοκράτωρ as part of the Jewish *Grundlage*, e.g. VII 36,1.

[56] F. E. Brightman, *Liturgies Eastern and Western*, Oxford 1896, xxv. Fiensy heavily relies upon Brightman's analysis of the literary and theological characteristics of the compiler at pp. xxiv-xxix.

and VIII 40,3)! It could thus be argued that this formula is from the compiler's hand as well, but in view of the parallel in *Avoth* it seems better not to do that. The matter does demonstrate in a striking way, however, how difficult it is to separate tradition from redaction.

'Who is merciful and compassionate, patient and abundant in mercy' is a quote of Joel 2:13 (cf. Ex. 34:6 and Jonah 4:2). In view of the compiler's tendency towards inserting scriptural quotes, it could be regarded as his insertion. Since, however, the only other quote from Joel in *AC* (VI 5,4) was taken over from his source, it may be part of his source here as well. The corresponding section in the berakhah *Avoth*, following upon 'God of Abraham, Isaac and Jacob,' praises God as 'great, mighty, awesome, and bestowing lovingkindness.'

'To whom every heart appears as naked and (to whom) every secret thought is revealed.' Since the Greek vocabulary of this line is completely atypical of our compiler, it most probably derives from his Jewish source. The theme of God's knowledge of even the innermost thoughts of mankind is widespread in the Bible (e.g., Ps. 139:1-2). Also the line 'to you the souls of the righteous cry out, upon you the devout have put their hopeful trust' has an atypical vocabulary and should be regarded as coming from the source. The following phrase, however, 'Father of the blameless,' is again one of the many cases in which the compiler has inserted turns with his favourite word ἄμεμπτος. 'You who listen to those who call upon you in uprightness, you who even know the supplications that are kept silent' is a phrase that recurs *verbatim* in a Christian prayer in *AC* VIII 15,2 and should therefore probably be regarded as Christian, even though it cannot be ruled out that in VIII 15,2 the compiler copied this phrase from the Jewish prayer. That God is said to hear even silent prayers has as a background the widespread ancient conviction that prayers to God or the gods should be said out loud and not in silence.[57] Since the lines 'for your foreknowledge (πρόνοια) reaches as far as the inmost parts of mankind, and by your awareness you search each person's thought' are meant to explain the previous line, they are an addition as well, the more so since πρόνοια is a favourite topic of the compiler. "In every case where the word occurs in AC, where we can compare the AC with its source, the word has come from the compiler" (Fiensy 169). Πρόνοια is usually rendered as 'providence' but that is not very fitting here. The theme is still God's knowledge of man's thoughts, so it seems that πρόνοια here has the sense of 'foreknowledge, foresight,' which is, of course, a prerequisite for providence. Most translators take συνείδησις to refer to men's conscience or consciousness, but in view of the parallelism with ἡ σὴ πρόνοια it makes better sense to have it refer to an activity of God with regard to human thoughts; hence my translation 'awareness.'

'In every region of the inhabited world the incense that comes through prayer and words is sent up to you' is a phrase that stands in some contradiction to the preceding clause. There the subject was God's knowledge of human thoughts and silent prayers, whereas here the thought seems to be that the incense is sent up to God in the form of audible prayers ('words'). This ties in with the crying

---

[57] For extensive discussion and references see P. W. van der Horst, "Silent Prayer in Antiquity," *Numen* 41 (1994) 1-25, reprinted in my *Hellenism – Judaism – Christianity: Essays on Their Interaction*, Kampen 1994, 252-281.

out of the righteous souls mentioned previously; hence we can take this phrase also to belong to the source. The vocabulary does not militate against this. On incense in a metaphorical sense (= prayer) see Ps. 141:2; G. Lampe, *Greek Patristic Lexicon, s.v.* θυμίαμα.

(3) 'You have established the present world as a place where men should run the race of righteousness.' 'World' (αἰών) may also be translated 'age' (cf. Hebrew *'olam*) or 'life.' Life in this world as a contest in a stadium is a Stoic commonplace that is also used on various occasions by Paul, e.g. 1 Cor. 9:24-27.[58] The structure of the phrase (Fiensy 169: "The whole clause is encased between an article and a participle") betrays its origin at the compiler's desk. In VIII 12,9-20 one finds a whole series of such clauses, and elsewhere as well.

'You have opened to all a gate of mercy, you have showed to everyone (...) that the possession of wealth is not eternal, that outer beauty is not everlasting, that physical power is easily dissolved.' These phrases do not show vocabulary that suggests the compiler's hand, so they can be taken to derive from the source. However, the intervening words, 'by implanted knowledge and natural judgement as well as through the teaching (?) of the Law,' reflect recurring motifs in the *AC*. The words 'implanted' (ἔμφυτος) and 'natural' (φυσικός) belong to the compiler's favourites in connection with the implanted law and natural knowledge, and his emphasis on the value of the teaching(s) of the Law (of Moses) recurs throughout the *AC*.[59] According to the compiler it is the combination of innate and revealed knowledge that makes humans aware of the passing nature of worldly affairs, but that was not a part of the original Jewish prayer. The temporary nature, and therefore the relative unimportance, of wealth, beauty, and power is a theme that one can find in various Jewish writers but also in many a Church Father. 'All these things are nothing but vapour and vanity' seems to be an addition by the compiler judging on the basis of vocabulary (Fiensy 204 n.20) and the probable reminiscence of James 4:14 (ἀτμὶς γάρ ἐστε).

'Only a sincere conscience of faith, that truly ascends and traverses through the midst of the heavens, receives the assurance of future bliss, and at the same time, even before the promised rebirth (παλιγγενεσία) is realized, that soul rejoices as it is exulting in hope.' This sentence is difficult to translate and understand, but this much is clear that it contrasts the permanent character of a blessed afterlife to the ephemeral nature of worldly affairs. It is the work of the compiler for the following reasons: (1) In a prayer that focuses on God's hearing of the prayers of mankind (strongly reminiscent also of the berakhah *Shomea' Tefillah* [=He who hears the prayer] in the Amidah!) this passage on the mystical ascent of the soul through the heavens and its vision is unfitting. (2) The central term παλιγγενεσία, though not necessarily Christian(!),[60] is a favourite word of the compiler. So it is not likely that this passage was in the source. It cannot be excluded, however, that there was something in the source here that has been recast in such a way by the compiler as to have become unrecognizable.

---

[58] See V.C. Pfitzner, *Paul and the Agon Motif*, Leiden 1976.

[59] For references see Fiensy 170 and 204 n.17.

[60] Also Philo uses the concept. Fiensy 55 n.25 has a long note on παλιγγενεσία in pagan and Christian literature.

(4-6) Here begins the long passage on the Patriarchs' and Moses' visionary experiences: Abraham's in Gen. 15, Jacob's in Gen. 38, and Moses' in Ex. 3. "He could not omit mentioning Isaac, but – since the OT does not attribute a vision to him – can only say that God found Isaac to be just like Abraham" (Fiensy 171). The whole passage seems intended to illustrate what was said in the long closing sentence of §3 and may for that reason be suspected as work of the compiler who also wrote those lines in §3. Fiensy's assertion that there is an anti-Gnostic argument in §4, since faith is elevated above knowledge, has a less than certain basis as may be clear from the text-critical remarks made in the footnote *ad locum*. It may well be that the confused textual sitation here only indicates that an (originally Jewish?) emphasis on the order 'knowledge > faith > covenant' was replaced by Christian copyists with the order 'faith > knowledge > covenant.' In that case, Abraham's (and the others') knowledge of 'what this life (or this world) really is about,' revealed to him by God, excellently fits in with what was said in §3 about God's showing mankind the ephemerity of worldly goods or outer appearance, lines we have tried to demonstrate are Jewish. So it may well be the case that the interpolator's hand is only to be found in the lines which stress the visionary nature of the way this knowledge was received ('you have guided him by means of a vision;' 'you showed him Christ;' 'you said in the vision of the bush'). When we further delete the non-necessary biblical quotations, which are so characteristic of the compiler, this yields a hypothetical Jewish *Grundlage* in more or less the following form:

"For from the beginning, when our forefather Abraham laid claim to the way of truth, you taught him what (life in) this world really is (about). From that knowledge came forth his faith, and the covenant was the consequence of this faith. When you had given him Isaac and knew that he was going to be like him (his father) in his way of life, you called yourself also his God.[61] And when our father Jacob set out for Mesopotamia, you spoke to him saying: 'Look, I am with you and I will increase you and multiply you exceedingly.'[62] And to Moses, your faithful and holy servant, you said: 'I am the one who is. That is my eternal name and a memorial to generations after generations.'"[63]

Since, however, there are too many and too great problems surrounding this proposal,[64] I refrain from printing these lines in bold type. *Non liquet.*

(7) 'Defender of the offspring of Abraham, blessed are you forever!' There is no doubt among the students of the *AC* that this line belongs to the Jewish *Grundlage*. It is perfectly parallel to the ending of the berakhah *Avoth* of the Amidah, which in all versions runs as follows: "Blessed are you, Lord, Shield of Abraham" (*barukh 'ata Adonai, magen Avraham*). 'Defender of the offspring of Abraham' is only the logical explicitation of the formula 'shield of Abraham.' The idea of God being Abraham's shield derives from Gen. 15:1: "Do

---

[61] Maybe the quote from Gen. 17:7 in the text as it stands should be left to stay there.

[62] Gen. 28:15, 48:4.

[63] Ex. 3:14-15.

[64] Maybe the final paragraph on Moses should be left out since he is clearly a favourite of the compiler (and he is not one of the Patriarchs); see E.M. Synek, *"Dieses Gesetz ist gut, heilig, es zwingt nicht..." Zum Gesetzesbegriff der Apostolischen Konstitutionen*, Vienna 1997.

not be afraid, Abraham, I am your shield." The idea is a good summary of the contents of the original berakhah in its Hebrew form, but less fitting to the Greek version as it stands in its interpolated form.

Appendix:
A hypothetical reconstruction of a Greek form of *Avoth* in English translation

Our eternal Saviour, King of the Gods, the one who alone is almighty and Lord, God of all beings, and God of our fathers, God of Abraham, Isaac and Jacob, who is merciful and compassionate, patient and abundant in mercy, to whom every heart appears as naked and to whom every secret thought is revealed. To you the souls of the righteous cry out, upon you the devout have put their hopeful trust. In every region of the inhabited world the incense that comes through prayer and words is sent up to you. You have opened to all a gate of mercy. You have showed to everyone that the possession of wealth is not eternal, that outer beauty is not everlasting, that physical power is easily dissolved. [For from the beginning, when our forefather Abraham laid claim to the way of truth, you taught him what (life in) this world really is (about). From that knowledge came forth his faith, and the covenant was the consequence of this faith. When you had given him Isaac and knew that he was going to be like him (his father) in his way of life, you called yourself also his God. And when our father Jacob set out for Mesopotamia, you spoke to him saying: 'Look, I am with you and I will increase you and multiply you exceedingly.']⁶⁵ Defender of the offspring of Abraham, blessed are you forever!

---

⁶⁵ This passage between square brackets is the most doubtful part of the reconstruction.

6. JEWS AND CHRISTIANS IN ANTIOCH AT THE END OF THE FOURTH CENTURY

In this short paper I want to focus on a brief but significant period in the history of Jewish-Christian relationships. It deals with the situation in Antioch (in Syria) in the eighties of the fourth century. It happens to be the case that from that decade we possess two documents from Antioch which each of them shed light on the relations between the large Jewish and Christian communities in that city, but in a very different way. The most interesting aspect of these documents is that they demonstrate the strong influence of Judaism upon Christianity in this city and the consequential blurring of the distinction between the two religions in the minds of a great many believers.

Clear evidence of this are firstly the 8 notorious homilies against the Jews by John Chrysostom in the year 386/7.[1] This John was a Christian scholar who lived from ca. 347-407 CE. He was ordained priest in 386 in Antioch by bishop Flavian who appointed him to devote special attention to preaching, in which his ability was so great that it earned him the nickname Chrysostom, 'the one with the golden-mouth.' His preaching was directed especially to the instruction and moral reformation of the nominally Christian society of his day. In the 8 long sermons under consideration, delivered 6 months after his ordination, we hear Chrysostom's vehement invectives against Christians who go to the synagogue on sabbath and on Jewish high holidays, who say Jewish prayers, who undergo the Jewish rite of circumcision, who celebrate Jewish Pesach, who keep Jewish food laws, who fast together with the Jews on the Day of Atonement etc. etc. These were not marginal renegades who came to

---

[1] The text can be found in J.P. Migne's *Patrologia Graeca*, vol. 48: cols. 843-942. See further R. L. Wilken, *John Chrysostom and the Jews: Rhetoric and Reality in the Late 4th Century* (Berkeley: University of California Press, 1983), still the best study of the subject in English; cf. also W. A. Meeks and R. L. Wilken, *Jews and Christians in Antioch in the First Four Centuries of the Common Era* (Missoula: Scholars Press, 1978), pp. 83-126. R. Brändle, "Christen und Juden in Antiochien in den Jahren 386/87. Ein Beitrag zur Geschichte altkirchlicher Judenfeindschft," *Judaica* 43 (1987), pp. 142-160, has a useful bibliography. See now especially R. Brändle & V. Jegher-Bucher, *Johannes Chrysostomus: Acht Reden gegen Juden* (Stuttgart: Hiersemann Verlag, 1995), which contains a German translation with an excellent introduction and commentary.

church only infrequently. "From John's comments, they appear to be regular members of his congregation who thought they could remain members of the Church while observing Jewish rites and customs."[2] In their mind that was not contradictory; Paul's distinction between Law and grace did not constitute a problem for them. But Chrysostom tries to dissuade his parishioners from keeping all these practices by a variety of rhetorical means, the most important of which is blackening the Jews and their synagogal meetings.

Let me give only a few examples of his terminology and imagery.[3] Firstly, Judaism as a dangerous disease (from *Hom.* 1):

> "Another more terrible sickness beckons and our tongue must be turned to heal a disease which is flourishing in the body of the church.... What is this sickness? The festivals of the wretched and miserable Jews which follow one after another – Trumpets, Booths, the Fasts[4] – are about to take place. And many who belong to us and say that they believe in our teaching attend their festivals and even share in their celebrations and join in their fasts. It is this evil practice that I now wish to drive from the church. (...) If those who are sick with Judaism are not healed now, when the Jewish festivals are near, I am afraid that some, out of misguided habit and gross ignorance, will share in their transgressions."

Secondly, the Jews as ravenous wolves (from *Hom.* 4):

> "Those sorry Jews, most miserable of all men, are about to hold a fast and it is necessary to protect the flock of Christ. As long as a wild beast is not causing trouble, shepherds lie down under an oak tree or a pine to play the flute, allowing the sheep to graze wherever they want. But when they realize that *wolves* are about to attack, they immediately throw down their flute, grab their sling, lay aside the shepherd's pipe, arm themselves with clubs and stones, and stand before the flock shouting with a loud and booming voice (...). So also we, in the days just past, were frolicking about in the exegesis of the Scriptures as in a meadow not touching on anything contentious because no one was troubling us. But since today the Jews, who are more troublesome than any wolves, are about to encircle our sheep, it is necessary to arm ourselves for battle so that none of our sheep become prey to wild beasts."

---

[2] Wilken, *John Chrysostom and the Jews*, pp. 75-76.

[3] The examples are taken from Wilken, *John Chrysostom and the Jews*, pp. 116-123. An English translation of all 8 homilies can be found in P. W. Harkins, *Saint John Chrysostom: Discourses Against Judaizing Christians* (The Fathers of the Church, a New Translation, Vol. 68; Washington: The Catholic University of America Press, 1979).

[4] Most probably Rosh ha-Shana (New Year), Sukkot (Feast of Tabernacles), and Yom Kippur (Day of Atonement). The three feasts were all of them celebrated within a month one after the other (usually September-October).

The venom of this rhetoric becomes all the more apparent when we realize that it suggests that the Jews were active in persuading Christians to abandon the church and join the synagogue, whereas it is most probable that in reality it was the Christians themselves who were willingly seeking contact with the synagogal community. Chrysostom's rhetoric "is intended to picture the Jews in the worst possible light to frighten Christians so that they will not attend the synagogue."[5] The same motive underlies Chrysostom's depiction of the Jewish character as concerned with "rapacity, greed, betrayal of the poor, thefts, and keeping of brothels."[6]

What all this makes abundantly clear is that as late as the final decades of the fourth century many Christians in the city of Antioch were being strongly attracted by Judaism. If the Jews were painted so black, it was because to too many Christians they appeared not sufficiently unattractive. "The most compelling reason for anti-Semitism was the religious vitality of Judaism."[7] How strong this vitality was in Asia Minor and Syria is very much evident from several canons of the council of Laodicea (Phrygia) which was held not long before Chrysostom's sermons, somewhere in the third quarter of the fourth century.[8] In canon 29 it is stated: "It is forbidden that Christians live like Jews (ioudaïzein) and rest on sabbath; they should work on that day. They should prefer the Lord's day to rest on, if possible, since they are Christians. If they turn out to be judaizers, let them be accursed (anathema) by Christ." Canon 38 runs as follows: "It is forbidden to take unleavened bread from the Jews or to participate in their godless acts." Canon 37 forbids any participation in the festivals of the Jews or heretics, and canon 36 warns the clergy against making phylakteria, which are probably tefillin, that is the small boxes containing scriptural verses bound on forehead and arm during Jewish prayers, which were used as magical apotropaic amulets.[9] These canons can only be explained on the assumption that

---

[5] Wilken, John Chrysostom and the Jews, p. 119.

[6] All quotations are from various parts of Homilies 1 and 4.

[7] M. Simon, Verus Israel. A Study of the Relations Between Christians and Jews in the Roman Empire (AD 135-425) (Oxford: Oxford University Press, 1986), p. 232. Cf. also E. M. Smallwood, The Jews Under Roman Rule (Leiden: Brill, 1976), p. 508.

[8] The exact date of this synod is unknown, though most scholars incline to date this meeting to the sixties of the fourth century. The text of the canons can be found in E. J. Jonkers, Acta et symbola conciliorum quae saeculo quarto habita sunt (Leiden: Brill, 1954), pp. 86-96.

[9] On the great reputation of Jewish magic in antiquity see Simon, Verus Israel, pp. 339-368, esp. p. 361 on the magical use of phylacteries/tefillin. Some scholars regard also canon 35 (against angelolatreia) as directed against judaizing practice.

keeping the sabbath, celebrating Pesach and other Jewish religious festivals, etc., were not marginal but frequently occurring and tenacious phenomena among Christians in Asia Minor and elsewhere in the second half of the fourth century. John Chrysostom's (and also the Syrian Churchfather Aphraat's)[10] testimonies make it highly probable that this assumption is correct. Only the fact that Judaism continued to make itself strongly felt and to be effectively influential throughout the first five centuries of our era makes it explicable that during these centuries there was a persistent tradition of judaizing in the church which defied all the anathemas of the church authorities. Marcel Simon put it well: "The anti-Jewish bias of official ecclesiastical circles was counterbalanced by equally marked pro-Jewish sentiments among the laity and among some of the clergy too. Or rather, it is the existence of the pro-Jewish sentiments among the laity that is the real explanation of Christian anti-Semitism."[11]

We can only guess at the causes or the reasons for the attraction which Judaism exercised upon both pagan and Christian minds and for the strength of its influence.[12] That Jews could present their religion as an enlightened philosophy with lofty ethics will certainly have made Judaism one of the more attractive of the Eastern cults in the Roman Empire. The rather detailed code of behaviour that Scripture and halakha contained must have been envisioned as a stabilizing factor in life by a good many people. The colourful and vivid synagogue services were to many a much more pleasant spectacle than the often lengthy and rather dull Christian services.[13] Also the Jewish charitable institutions will have been a source of attraction. For many Christians, the argument that the commandments in the Torah were after all God's words may have carried more weight than the often tortuous argumentations to the effect that God had abolished his own Law. For many pagans and Christians the antiquity of Judaism was a very important factor – we should not forget that throughout antiquity it was a never questioned axioma that

---

[10] On Aphraat see J. Neusner, *Judaism, Christianity, and Zoroastrianism in Talmudic Babylonia* (Lanham-New York-London: University Press of America, 1986), pp. 199-228.

[11] Simon, *Verus Israel*, p. 232.

[12] See for an extensive discussion of the topic of "The Attractions of the Jews" L. H. Feldman, *Jew and Gentile in the Ancient World* (Princeton: Princeton University Press, 1993), pp. 177-287. Wilken, *John Chrysostom and the Jews*, pp. 66-94, also deals with this topic.

[13] See W. Kinzig, "'Non-Separation': Closeness and Co-operation Between Jews and Christians in the Fourth Century," *Vigiliae Christianae* 45 (1991), p. 39 (pp. 27-53).

only the oldest is the best, also in religious matters.[14] Be that as it may, not only in Asia Minor and Syria but also in the rest of the Empire, Judaism and Christianity struggled with one another over the pagan soul. In the practical sphere the two religions fought over the pagan clientele that Judaism had built up for itself and whose attention the church tried to gain.

John Chrysostom's vituperative and vitriolic sermons against judaizing Christians and Jews eloquently testify to this struggle. But we have to bear in mind that they had a nefarious *Wirkungsgeschichte*: They fomented hatred against Jews and Judaism in an unprecedented manner. "They are not only a compendium of many of the themes that emerged in the Christian polemic against Judaism, but have also had an enormous influence on later Christian attitudes towards the Jews."[15]

The *Apostolic Constitutions* are another important document written shortly after 380 in Antioch and it is the nearest contemporary document to the homilies of Chrysostom we have. The *Apostolic Constitutions* are a collection of materials on ecclesiastical law that is widely believed to have been compiled in Syria in the two final decades of the fourth century, probably by the same (semi-)Arian author who also interpolated the Letters of Ignatius of Antioch and wrote the Arian commentary on Job.[16] Its potential relevance for the study of Chrysostom's homilies is hardly taken into account in the modern literature on Chrysostom's sermons. Chrysostom's main point of criticism of his own religious flock is that so many Christians attend services in the synagogues of Antioch, pray the Jewish prayers etc. and for that he threatens his co-religionists with the worst possible consequences of this behaviour. What the *Apostolic Constitutions* demonstrate is that in the same period, probably in one of

---

[14] See P. W. van der Horst, "Plato's Fear as a Topic in Early Christian Apologetics," *Journal of Early Christian Studies* 6 (1998), pp. 1-14.

[15] Wilken, *John Chrysostom and the Jews*, p. xv

[16] The best recent discussion of the *AC* is the almost 200 pages of introduction to the Sources Chrétiennes edition by M. Metzger, *Les Constitutions Apostoliques*, vol. 1 (Paris: Editions du Cerf, 1985), pp. 13-93, and vol. 2 (1986), pp. 10-110. Vol. 3 (1987) contains text and French translation of books VII and VIII into which the prayer texts under discussion have been incorporated. See further also B. Steimer, *Vertex Traditionis. Die Gattung der altchristlichen Kirchenordnungen* (Berlin: Walter de Gruyter, 1992), pp. 114-133; E. M. Synek, *"Dieses Gesetz ist gut, heilig, es zwingt nicht..."* *Zum Gesetzesbegriff der Apostolischen Konstitutionen* (Kirche und Recht 21; Vienna: Plöchl-Druck, 1997). Steimer and Synek have good bibliographies of the older publications on the *AC*.

the other churches of Antioch,[17] a very different strategy was adopted: no terrible threats, but a tactical move to obviate the needs of these so-called judaizers by incorporating elements of the synagogal liturgy into the the liturgy of the church. To be sure, the anonymous author of this writing too urged Christians to avoid Jewish festivals and dissuades even bishops and presbyters to join the Jews in their fasts and feasts (*AC* VIII 47.70!; cf. II 61, V 17). But in book VII of the *Apostolic Constitutions* we find a set of six (out of seven) originally Jewish prayers which, after having undergone some slightly christianizing editing, were taken over from the synagogal prayer book (even though the tendency of the *Apostolic Constitutions* as a whole was not at all pro-Jewish). These prayers are demonstrably Greek versions of the seven *berakhot* of the Eighteen Benedictions for the Sabbath,[18] as is now generally recognized. 'If you can't beat them, join them!' the compiler seems to have thought. The relevance of comparing Chrysostom's sermons to the *Apostolic Constitutions* may be clear: both authors have to cope with the same situation, but they do so in strikingly different ways. Whereas the rhetorically highly gifted Churchfather puts all his skills into the scales in order to scare the members of his community away from their judaizing practices, the anonymous compiler apparently takes the needs of his co-religionists much more seriously and is willing to make a compromise with them. They are allowed to continue their use of Jewish prayers, but within the Christian community and with Christian elements added. So the anonymous compiler of the *Apostolic Constitutions* can be seen to have not only a more tactical but also a more pastoral approach. What a difference there is between the slanderous language of Chrysostom and the way in which the compiler of the *Apostolic Constitutions* invites his coreligionist to pray,

> "Our eternal Saviour, King of the Gods, the one who alone is almighty and Lord, God of all beings, and God of our holy and blameless fathers who were before us, God of Abraham, Isaac and Jacob, who is merciful and compassionate, patient and abundant in mercy, to whom every heart appears as naked and (to whom) every secret thought is revealed. To you

---

[17] On the deep splits that marked the Christian community in Antioch see the remarks by W. Kinzig, "'Non-Separation,'" p. 36, and the Introduction in Harkins, *Saint John Chrysostom.*

[18] See D. Fiensy, *Prayers Alleged to Be Jewish: An Examination of the* Constitutiones Apostolorum (Chico: Scholars Press, 1985). The best edition of the text of these prayers is to be found in Metzger, *Les Constitutions Apostoliques*, vol. 3, pp. 66-95. It should be borne in mind that in the diaspora (and even sometimes in Palestine) the synagogue services were conducted in Greek.

the souls of the righteous cry out, upon you the devout have put their hope-ful trust. (…) Defender of the offspring of Abraham, blessed are you for-ever!" (*AC* VII 33).

Or from another prayer:

"Lord almighty, you created the world [*through Christ*][19] and you have instituted the sabbath in memory of this – for it was on that day that you rested from your works – for training in your laws. You have also ordained festivals for the gladdening of our souls, so that we may be reminded of the Wisdom created by you. (…) For you, o Lord, you also led our fathers out of the land of Egypt, and you saved them from an iron furnace and from clay and the making of bricks, you redeemed them from the hands of Pharaoh and his underlings, and you led them through the sea as through dry land, and in the desert you endured their manners (and presented them) with all sorts of good things. You gave them the Law of the ten words spo-ken by your voice and written by your hand, and you commanded them to keep the sabbath." (*AC* VII 36).

To be sure, at the end of this prayer the Christian interpolator has added that "the Lord's day surpasses all this!" However, even in spite of this clumsily appended correction meant to prevent the Christians from aban-doning the celebration of Sunday altogether, it is clear that the Jewish prayer for the sanctification of the shabbat in the Jewish liturgy, the *Qiddush* or *Qedushat ha-Yom*, is here an integral part of a Christian liturgy.

We know from other sources that in the early centuries of the Common Era Antioch had a very large and vibrant Jewish community, of which Josephus already wrote that "they were constantly attracting to their reli-gious ceremonies multitudes of Greeks" (*Bellum* VII 45).[20] Not long after Josephus wrote these words, one of the first bishops of Antioch, Ignatius, at the beginning of the second century made some remarks in his letters that strongly suggest that he was upset by the fact that several Christians in his community were adopting Jewish practices, evidently under the

---

[19] On these and other Christian interpolations and the question of how to distinguish the Christian redaction from the Jewish 'Grundschrift' in these texts see my forthcoming commentary in the series *Commentaries on Early Jewish Literature* (to be published by Walter de Gruyter, Berlin – New York).

[20] See on the Jews of ancient Antioch C.H. Kraeling, "The Jewish Community at Anti-och," *Journal of Biblical Literature* 51 (1932), pp. 130-160; G. Downey, *A History of Antioch in Syria from Seleucus to the Arab Conquest* (Princeton: Princeton University Press, 1961), pp. 272-316; J. Hahn, "Die jüdische Gemeinde im spätantiken Anti-ochia," in R. Jütte & A.P. Kustermann (eds.), *Jüdische Gemeinden und Organisa-tionsformen von der Antike bis zur Gegenwart* (Vienna: Böhlau, 1996), pp. 57-89; B.J. Brooten, "The Jews of Ancient Antioch," Christine Kondoleon (ed.), *Antioch: The Lost Ancient City* (Princeton: Princeton University Press, 2000), 29-37.

influence of the local Jewish community (*Magn.* 8:1-2; *Phil.* 6:1). And from John Chrysostom we learn that this situation persisted two-and-a-half centuries after Ignatius.[21] There was a thriving Jewish community that had lived there for more than six and a half centuries (twice as long as the Christians), a community of which one of the members most probably was the son of the Jewish Patriarch in Palestine, who studied in Antioch with the famous pagan orator Libanius (who had always spoken with respect of the Jews)! In this connection it is telling that in the 5 or 6 years after Chrysostom's sermons this Libanius carried on an extensive correspondence with this Jewish Patriarch (Gamaliel), with whom he was apparently befriended.[22] In these circumstances, with a powerful and selfconscious Jewish community that had good relationships with pagans[23] and a strong influence upon Christian believers – and this was not a unique situation! – it was a tactical move to incorporate Jewish prayers into the Christian liturgy. If their existed a real and tenacious need among Christians in Antioch for using Jewish liturgical material, which was one of the reasons why they went to the synagogue on sabbath, then the best thing church leadership could do was to see to it that the prayers the members of his community said in the synagogue, could also be said by them in the church – albeit with some modifications – so that the need of these members was met and the risk of loosing them to the synagogue was lessened. This may have been much more effective than John Chrysostom's aggressive policy, a policy that, as he himself indirectly admitted some 10

---

[21] For a discussion of possible evidence for the period between Ignatius and Chrysostom see Fiensy, *Prayers*, pp. 218-219. For two rich donations by the leaders of the Jewish community of Antioch to the synagogue of Apamea from the year 391 CE see the inscriptions in B. Lifshitz, *Donateurs et fondateurs dans les synagogues juives* (Paris: Gabalda, 1967), nos. 38 and 39. Also several tomb inscriptions in the famous catacombs in Beth She'arim (Galilee, third – fourth centuries CE) are of leading Antiochene Jews.

[22] See the texts and translations in M. Stern, *Greek and Latin Authors on Jews and Judaism* (3 vols.), vol. 2 (Jerusalem: The Israel Academy of Arts and Sciences, 1980), pp. 580-600.

[23] See the statement by Hahn ("Jüdische Gemeinde," p. 71) "daß die jüdische Gemeinde von Antiochia nach dem Erscheinungsbild ihrer Elite zur Zeit des Libanios eine blühende, außerordentlich wohlhabende und hellenisierte Gemeinschaft darstellte, die im Leben der Stadt und deren weiterem Umfeld ein deutliches Profil besaß, sich hierbei in ihrer sozialen Umgebung vorbehaltslos und selbstbewußt einfügte und dennoch eine unverkennbar jüdische Identität bewahrte." The relationship between Jews and Gentiles in Antioch had not always been good, however. Especially in the first century CE there was much tension with occasional outbursts of violence; see M. Hengel & A. M. Schwemer, *Paul Between Damascus and Antioch* (London: SCM Press, 1997), pp. 183-191.

years later, had been far from successful (see his *Hom. in Ep. ad Tit.* 3,2 = *PG* 62, 679).[24]

Now it could of course be argued, as indeed one of the investigators of this document has recently done, that it was not the compiler of the *AC* who incorporated these Jewish prayers into a Christian liturgical setting by christianizing them, but that this had already been done in one of its sources. We do know indeed that the *AC* is a compilation of older material, for it has incorporated 3 major sources that we know: the *Didascalia Apostolorum*[25] (books I-VI); the *Didache*[26] (bk. VII 1-32); and the *Traditio Apostolica* (or *Diataxeis of the Holy Apostles*) by Hippolytus[27] (bk. VIII 3-45). And there are some other sources too. Since some of his major sources are known to us (sc. the *Didache* and the *Didascalia*), we are in a position to see the compiler at work. He does not take over the text of his sources unaltered. We can observe omissions, additions, insertions, corrections etc. Sometimes these are minor, at other times they are major redrafts.[28] This teaches us two things. First, the anonymous author was not a slavish compiler: he made all kinds of changes in his material, as befitted his purposes, and he did so also in prayer material. That is to say that this man was perfectly capable to redraft the Jewish prayer texts himself so as to make them fit for use in a Christian setting. Secondly, the majority of the sources he used have a Syrian provenance, which is not surprising for an author who worked in Antioch. So also the set of Jewish prayer texts may well have belonged to his sources of Syrian provenance. That implies that, even if we assume for the sake of the argument that it was not the compiler himself who adopted and adapted these prayers – so that we can no longer treat it as an Antiochian document from the 380's – we still have to do with a situation in which in a Syrian context this process has taken place, albeit now at an earlier date. That would not make it a less interesting case. It still would enable us to envisage a situation in which a Christian community in Syria that was in contact with the local Jewish community took over synagogal shabbat prayers in order to use them in their weekly

---

[24] See Hahn, "Jüdische Gemeinde," p. 76. Hahn speaks of the paradoxical situation that the Jewish community of Antioch could be so influential and powerful exactly because the church was so weak and had so little inner coherence (laity and clergy were continuously at odds with each other).

[25] First half of the third century, Syria.

[26] End of the first or beginning of the second century, Syria.

[27] Beginning of the third century, Rome.

[28] For our purposes it is important to see, for instance, that the prayers in *Didache* 9-10 have been thoroughly modified in *AC* VII 25-27.

services in the church with some modifications. So what remains is the difference in approach between Chrysostom and this source, the difference between frontal attack and unbridled polemics, with all its baneful consequences, on the one hand,[29] and the more accommodating, or let me say 'ecumenical' approach of the *Apostolic Constitutions'* source, on the other. If we would look for an ancient model of Jewish-Christian encounter that is helpful in inspiring mutual respect and in building bridges, we can no doubt learn more from the *Apostolic Constitutions* than from Chrysostom, whose famous 'golden mouth' spouted so much venom.[30]

---

[29] For many other instances of this kind of literature see especially H. Schreckenberg, *Die christlichen Adversus-Judaeos-Texte und ihr literarisches und historisches Umfeld (1. – 11. Jh.)*, (2nd ed.; Frankfurt etc.: Peter Lang, 1990). At pp. 320-329 Schreckenberg discusses Chrysostom.

[30] I owe many thanks to Stanley E. Porter and Brook W.R. Pearson who were so kind to correct my English.

7. THE TOMBS OF THE PROPHETS
IN EARLY JUDAISM

Forty-two years ago, in the early summer of 1958, the famous German scholar Joachim Jeremias, gave guest lectures at the Faculty of Theology of Utrecht University, at the invitation of one of my predecessors, the late Willem C. van Unnik. His topic was: The role of tombs of holy persons in Second Temple Judaism. Later that year his book on that subject came out, the well-known *Heiligengräber in Jesu Umwelt. Eine Untersuchung zur Volksreligion der Zeit Jesu.*[1] The modest purpose of this booklet was to elucidate the background of Jesus' remark in Matthew 23:29-30 (// Luke 11:47), where he says to the scribes and the Pharisees: "You build the tombs of the prophets and decorate the graves of the righteous, and you say, 'If we had lived in the days of our ancestors, we would not have taken part with them in shedding the blood of the prophets'" (NRSV).[2] Jeremias' book is still unsurpassed as a treasure-trove of information about a fascinating aspect of Jewish religion in antiquity, the veneration of the tombs of biblical prophets and other holy persons.

He begins with a survey of the sources for our knowledge of this practice: first and foremost the enigmatic *Vitae Prophetarum*, further also *Jubilees, 4 Maccabees,* the *Testaments of the XII Patriarchs*, Josephus, and rabbinic literature. That the *Vitae Prophetarum* take pride of place is due to the fact that in this small treatise *sui generis*,[3] with its twenty-three very concise *Lives* of biblical prophets,[4] their graves unvariably

---

[1] Göttingen: Vandenhoeck & Ruprecht, 1958. For an addendum see J. Jeremias, 'Drei weitere spätjüdische Heiligengräber,' *Zeitschrift für die neutestamentliche Wissenschaft* 52 (1961) 95-101. The material discussed by Jeremias has nothing to do with the so-called 'Tomb of the Prophets' on the summit of Mt. of Olives, on which see H. Vincent, 'Le tombeau des prophètes,' *Revue Biblique* 10 (1901) 72-88.

[2] Luke has the shorter form: "You build the tomb of the prophets whom your ancestors killed" (11:47).

[3] For the unparalleled nature of the *VP* see D. Satran, *Biblical Prophets in Byzantine Palestine. Reassessing the* Lives of the Prophets, Leiden: Brill, 1995, 98-99, although I have doubts about the close connection he sees between the *VP* and the Lives of the early Desert Fathers, the more so since it does not harmonize with Satran's definition of the *VP* as "a handbook of biblical information and lore" (107).

[4] These twenty-three prophets are Isaiah, Jeremiah, Ezechiel, Daniel, the twelve Minor Prophets, and the prophets from the historical books in the Bible (except Samuel and Hulda).

and consistently receive attention; often an even somewhat dispropor-
tionate amount of attention is paid to the location of these graves,[5] so
that in the past it has sometimes been suggested that the booklet was
nothing but a pilgrim's guide to the tombs of the prophets.[6] Exaggerated
though that claim may be – the information given by the author is too
succinct to serve as a travel guide –, it is undeniable that the writer (or
the traditions he used) took pains to make as clear as possible where the
tomb of each of the twenty-three biblical prophets was to be found. For
instance, Isaiah's tomb is "next to the tomb of the kings, west of the
tombs of the priests in the southern part of the city" (*Vit. Isa.* 9). This
can hardly be regarded as sheer theoretical knowledge; it must have
served another purpose, whatever that may have been.[7]

Jeremias concedes that in the forms in which the Greek text of the
Vitae prophetarum has been handed down to us in the various recen-
sions, the writing has been christianized. Indeed, all the manuscripts we
have are from Christian hands, as is quite obvious to any reader, and we
have no textual evidence whatever that is free from Christian elements.
Over the past century, this has led scholars to assume time and again that
the whole document is of Christian origin and should be regarded as a
hagiographic work from the early Byzantine period.[8] Others, most
recently and most forcefully Anna Maria Schwemer in her impressive
and exhaustive commentary on this document,[9] emphasize that these
Vitae are much too sober to have functioned as Christian hagiography:
the prophets are not glorified;[10] unlike their Christian counterparts, the
Vitae are characterized by "Kürze und Schlichtheit;"[11] there is no
emphasis at all on their great deeds, not even on their preaching; in spite

---

[5] Note that in the superscription of the most important manuscript of these *Vitae* it says
that the treatise deals with "the names of the prophets and whence they were, where
they died and how, and *where they were buried.*"
[6] So, for instance, H.A. Fischel, "Martyr and Prophet," *JQR* 37 (1946/47) 375 (265-280,
363-386).
[7] Cf. Satran, *Biblical Prophets in Byzantine Palestine* 111: "It is the unrelenting concern
of the individual *vitae* with the manner and location of the burial of the prophets which
demands our attention."
[8] In my country this position was championed long ago by Marinus de Jonge; in Israel
more recently by David Satran. See M. de Jonge, 'Christelijke elementen in de Vitae
prophetarum,' *Nederlands Theologisch Tijdschrift* 16 (1961/62) 161-178. Satran, *Biblical Prophets in Byzantine Palestine.*
[9] A. M. Schwemer, *Studien zu den frühjüdischen Prophetenlegenden* Vitae Prophetarum,
2 vols., Tübingen: Mohr, 1995.
[10] As Schwemer rightly emphasizes (39), the early Christian hagiographic texts accord
with the rhetoric genre of the *enkomion*, but the *Vitae prophetarum* don't.
[11] Schwemer, *Studien* 40.

of the reports of violent deaths of seven prophets, there is no martyrological message whatever; and one does not find any other specifically Christian ideas and ideals being promoted in the text, apart from some blatantly Christian interpolations that can easily be detected and removed from the text. In addition to that, Schwemer says, the forms of the toponyms as well as the many details concerning local circumstances strongly suggest a first-century CE origin in Judaea, where these 'Ortstraditionen' circulated before they disappeared after the Bar Kochba war (Note that most of the tombs are located in Judaea, not in the North.)

In the framework of this short paper, I will not go into the details of this debate, which is strongly reminiscent of the old controversy surrounding the *Testaments of the XII Patriarchs* (and of the new one concerning *Joseph and Aseneth*). Suffice it to state here that I find the position of Schwemer more convincing and less forced than Satran's, although it has to be added immediately that certainty in this kind of matters is difficult – if not impossible – to attain.[12] Satran sees as the only possible context for these tomb traditions the Christian culture of Palestine in the second half of the fourth century. In this paper I will try to demonstrate, albeit tentatively, that, contrary to what Satran asserts, there *is* a context in first century Judaism for basic elements of these *Vitae*, especially as far as traditions about the tombs of the prophets are concerned.[13]

Jeremias points out that the Jewish origin of the traditions about the tombs of the prophets is confirmed by similar or identical traditions found in medieval Jewish itineraries from the 12th century onwards (Benjamin of Tudela and many others).[14] Also from the medieval period we have some Samaritan chronicles, but these too contain valuable traditional material about tombs of biblical persons, says Jeremias.

---

[12] See also the discussion by D.R.A. Hare in the *Anchor Bible Dictionary* 5 (1992) 502-503.

[13] I also tend to agree with Jeremias that most probably the text was basically composed before 70 since otherwise one would expect to find hints to the destruction of the city or the temple, but this point is not essential for my thesis. See Jeremias, *Heiligengräber* 12. If one takes *Vit. Jer.* 9 to be a reference not to the destruction of the Solomonic temple but of the Second Temple, things become different, of course.

[14] M.N. Adler, *The Itinerary of Benjamin of Tudela*, New York: Feldheim, 1907. On cultic sites in medieval Jewish itineraries see E. Reiner, 'From Joshua to Jesus: The Transformation of a Biblical Story to a Local Myth,' in A. Kofsky & G.G. Stroumsa (eds.), *Sharing the Sacred. Religious Contacts and Conflicts in the Holy Land (First – Fifteenth Centuries CE)*, Jerusalem: Yad Izhak Ben Zvi, 1998, 223-271 (I owe this reference to Prof. Joshua Schwartz).

Christian sources, such as Eusebius' *Onomasticon* from the early fourth century, contain traditions about graves of biblical persons which are almost certainly Jewish in origin. The flourishing of Christian traditions about holy tombs of biblical figures begins only after 400, as is quite clear from a comparison of the earlier and the later pilgrim-reports.[15]

Let us go back for a moment, with Jeremias, to biblical times. In early Israel veneration of the dead was denounced as one of the abhorrent practices of the Canaanites (Deut. 18:9-12), but the fact that such a practice is warned against time and again makes it quite probable that in actual practice people *did* the forbidden thing.[16] It was probably only in the exilic and early post-exilic period, when strict monotheism became dominant in Israel, that a cult of the dead wellnigh disappeared or, more probably, went underground.[17] Even so it was apparently deemed important to know exactly where the tombs of the great patriarchs and matriarchs were located: the repeated references to the burial places of Abraham, Isaac, Jacob and their wives in the cave of Machpelah (Gen. 23; 25:9-10; 49:29-32; 50:12-13) make this abundantly clear.[18]

From the second century BCE visitors were shown this cave near Hebron (see *Jubilees* 19:5-6; *Test. Ruben* 7:2; Josephus, *Bell.* 4:532),[19] on the site where it is still to be seen today. We find additional examples of this phenomenon. Thus, although the tomb of Elisha is not located in the biblical story, it is highlighted in 2 Kings 13:21, where it is said that the following happened during a raid by Moabite bands: "As a man was being buried, a marauding band was seen and the man was thrown into the grave of Elisha; as soon as the man touched the bones of Elisha, he

---

[15] P. Thomsen, 'Neue Beiträge und Funde zur Orts- und Landeskunde von Syrien und Palästina,' *Zeitschrift des Deutschen Palästina-Vereins* 65 (1942) 131 (122-143). In the pilgrim itineraries of the 4th century it is tombs of Old Testament figures that are easily in the majority, whereas in those of the 5th century and later that is definitely no longer the case. For instance, the Piacenza pilgrim (ca. 570 CE) was shown in Palestine twice as many Christian than Jewish graves. Note that this is also the period when in Christianity the veneration of non-biblical holy persons begins to spread widely. See Th. Baumeister, 'Heiligenverehrung,' *Reallexikon für Antike und Christentum* 14 (1988) 96-150.

[16] See for a recent survey H. Rouillard, 'Rephaim,' in K. van der Toorn, B. Becking & P.W. van der Horst (eds.), *Dictionary of Deities and Demons in the Bible*, 2nd ed., Leiden: Brill, 1999, 692-700. Also K. van der Toorn, *Family Religion in Babylonia, Syria and Israel*, Leiden: Brill, 1996, 206-235.

[17] In a private conversation Herbert Niehr (Tübingen) suggested to me that perhaps this cult did not even go underground but simply continued to exist without, however, leaving clear traces.

[18] Cf. Van der Toorn, *Family Religion* 216: 'In any event it is hardly likely that they are mentioned as mere topographical indications.'

[19] Jeremias, *Heiligengräber* 90-94.

came to life and stood on his feet." The story of this miracle demonstrates, as Jeremias rightly remarks, "daß wir es mit einem offenbar schon in vorexilischer Zeit hochberühmten Grab zu tun haben."[20] As in the case above, this grave too was exactly localized in postbiblical times: the *Life of Elisha* says it is in Samaria (§4) and fourth-century Christian authors know many stories about the miracles happening at that tomb.[21] Another tomb mentioned in the Bible and well-known *precisely* because it was never found is Moses' tomb. Deuteronomy explicitly states that "he was buried in a valley in the land of Moab, opposite Beth-Peor, but no one knows his burial place to this day" (34:6). But even this tomb was localized in due course, albeit much later than most others: it is only in the marginal readings of Targumim to Numbers 32:3 and in fifth-century Christian authors that we find that Moses' grave is to be found on Mt. Nebo. The emphasis on the locality of the patriarchal and matriarchal tombs and the equally emphatic remark that to this day nobody knows Moses' burial site indicate that, vaguely speaking, interest in the tombs of great personalities is not wholly absent from the Hebrew Bible,[22] although the nature of this interest is hard to pinpoint.

From the history of religions in general, it is well-known that veneration of holy persons at the site of their tombs most often has two key elements: (a) the miraculous power of the remains of the holy person that pervades the tomb; and (b) the element of intercession by the holy person with God. The first element is already discernible in the biblical legend of the dead man who is restored to life by physical contact with Elisha's dead body. The second element was developed in postbiblical Judaism, although it did not go uncontested.[23] The question now is: Did the tombs of holy biblical persons, be they patriarchs or prophets, function as places of pilgrimage where their intercession was sought and miracles were hoped for?[24] In the final chapter of his book, "Die Heiligen

---

[20] *Heiligengräber* 30.

[21] A.M. Schwemer, *Vitae Prophetarum* (JSHRZ I 7), Gütersloh: Gütersloher Verlagshaus, 1997, 649.

[22] The localization of Samson's tomb "between Zorah and Eshta'ol" (Judges 16:31) also suggests that the tomb still had a certain fame in later times.

[23] See O. Michel, 'Gebet II (Fürbitte),' *RAC* 9 (1976) 7-10, for evidence and bibliography. See also R. Fröhlich, 'Heilige, Heiligenverehrung,' *Der Neue Pauly* 5 (1998) 247-248, who singles out Philo's presentation of the patriarchs as intercessors.

[24] That the Jewish people was familiar with the phenomenon of pilgrimage since biblical times needs no demonstration; see, e.g., S. Safrai, *Die Wallfahrt im Zeitalter des Zweiten Tempels*, Neukirchen: Neukirchener Verlag, 1981; also, briefly, B. Kötting, *Peregrinatio religiosa. Wallfahrten in der Antike und das Pilgerwesen in der alten Kirche*, Münster: Stenderhoff, 1980 (=1950), 63-66.

als Thaumaturgen und Interzessoren," Jeremias tries to demonstrate that it is exactly these two functions that the tombs of the biblical holy persons had in the popular religion of pre-rabbinic Judaism. Let us weigh his arguments in order to see whether they can persevere.[25]

The position of Jeremias can be summarized as follows: It was a common popular conviction that the prophets were still active in their tombs.[26] This explains how Matthew (2:18) could say after his report on Herod's murder of the infants in Bethlehem that Jer. 31:15 ('Rachel wept for her children and she refused to be consoled') had been fulfilled. Rachel was thought to be able to witness the drama from her tomb.[27] The many rabbinic stories about the activities of biblical figures after their death demonstrate that this was a widespread idea (also in contemporary Christian sources, for that matter).[28] The God of Abraham, Isaac, and Jacob was for them not a God of the dead patriarchs, but a God of the living (cf. Mk. 12:26-27). From their graves the holy persons gave advice, made predictions, performed miracles, or took revenge for the violation of their tomb.[29]

The biblical story of Samuel and the witch of Endor in 1 Sam. 28 seemed to justify this kind of idea, as was already remarked on by Ben Sira (46:20: "Even after his death his guidance was sought; he made known to the king his fate, and from the grave he raised his voice as a

---

[25] Baumeister, 'Heiligenverehrung' 100, says that the problem with Jeremias' theory is that his main source (the *Vitae proph.*) has undergone marked Christian editing: "Da die Abgrenzung der Grundschrift von den christlichen Zusätzen nicht einfach ist und man mit den Einflüssen christlicher Heiligenverehrung rechnen muß, ist es fraglich, ob es wirklich zur Zeit Jesu schon eine explizite jüdische Heiligenverehrung mit Bitte um Vorsprache und Wundererwartung an den Gräbern gab." As will become clear, I do not agree with this point of view.

[26] Jeremias, *Heiligengräber* 129: "[S]ie alle waren für sie nicht tote Gestalten der Vergangenheit, sondern sie lebten in ihren Gräbern, nahmen teil am Ergehen des Volkes." Satran, *Biblical Prophets* 111, refers to the epitaph of St. Martin: "Here lies Martin the bishop, of holy memory, whose soul is in the hand of God, but he is fully here, present and made plain in miracles of every kind" (quoted from P. Brown, *The Cult of the Saints*, Chicago: University of Chicago Press, 1981, 4). Cf. also E. Bammel, 'Zum jüdischen Märtyrerkult,' in his *Kleine Schriften I: Judaica*, Tübingen: Mohr, 1986, 83-84.

[27] Cf. John 5:28: "All who are in the tombs will hear his voice."

[28] Jeremias, *Heiligengräber* 127-129, refers *inter alia* to *Midr. Ps.* 16:2, 10-11; *Mekh.* on Ex. 13:19; *PRE* 36; BT *BM* 58a and 85b; BT *BB* 17a; b.*Ber.* 18b; BT *Shab.* 152b; *Midr. Prov.* 9,2; *Pes. Rabb.* 21. That the holy persons from the biblical past did not decay in their graves (e.g., *Midrash Tehillim* 16:10) seems to be the background of the implied polemics in Acts 2:27-29.

[29] For the latter cf. Josephus, *Ant.* 16:179-183, where two of Herod's bodyguards are killed by a great flash of fire when they try to open David's tomb. There is a striking parallel to this story in Benjamin of Tudela, *Sefer ha-Massa'oth* 38-40.

prophet to put an end to wickedness"). But it was, understandably, especially the story of the revivification of the dead man by means of contact
with Elisha's body that sparked a good deal of expectation about the
miraculous powers of the holy persons to aid people in desparate situations. Around 400 CE, the Church Father Jerome writes in his famous
Epistula 108 about his protégée Paula's experience in Samaria/Sebaste at
the tombs of Elijah and Obadja when she had visited these (around 385):
"There she was filled with terror by the marvels she beheld; for she saw
demons screaming under different tortures before the tombs of the holy
persons, and men howling like wolves, baying like dogs, roaring like
lions, hissing like serpents and bellowing like bulls. They twisted their
heads and bent them backwards until they touched the ground. Women
too were suspended head downward but their clothes did not fall off"
(108:13).[30] And Jerome does not say it is Christians who seek remedy
for their mental suffering at Elisha's grave, it must have been people of
various religious and ethnic backgrounds, pagans, Samaritans, Jews, and
Christians (and later also Muslims). A comparable 'ecumenical' situation
is the one at the tomb of the Patriarchs in Hebron about which the Piacenza pilgrim writes (around 570) that the basilica at the spot has two
entrances, one for Jews and another for Christians who want to pray
there and offer incense (*Ant. Plac. Itin.* 30).[31] Likewise, at the beginning
of the 5th century the Church historian Sozomen writes that there were
annual celebrations and fairs (*panêgyreis*) around the oak of Mamre near
Hebron at which pagans, Jews, and Christians "conveniently exploited a
religious assembly to exchange their wares."[32] This is what Sozomen
writes: "Here the inhabitants of the country and of the region round
Palestine, the Phoenicians and the Arabs, assemble annually during the
summer season to keep a big feast; and many others, both buyers and
sellers, resort thither on account of the fair. Indeed this feast is diligently
frequented by all nations: by the Jews, because they boast of their
descent from the patriarch Abraham; by the pagans, because angels there
appeared to men; and by the Christians, because He who for the salvation of mankind was born of a virgin, afterwards manifested himself
there to a godly man. This place was moreover honoured fittingly with

---

[30] This is a description of what Jeremias calls, 'die älteste Irrenanstalt Palästinas', *Heiligengräber* 132.
[31] See H. Donner, *Pilgerfahrt ins Heilige Land. Die ältesten Berichte christlicher Palästi-
napilger (4.-7. Jhdt.)*, Tübingen: Katholisches Bibelwerk, 1979, 292.
[32] Thus E.D. Hunt, *Holy Land Pilgrimage in the Later Roman Empire AD 312-460*,
Oxford: Clarendon Press, 1982, 136.

religious exercises. Here some prayed to the God of all, some called upon the angels, poured out wine, burnt incense, offered an ox or a goat, a sheep or a cock." Among all these groups, he says, "the men abstained from approaching their wives, although during the feast these were more than ordinarily studious of their beauty and adornment" (*Eccles. Hist.* 2:4).[33] Constantine closed down the whole site and thus ended this ecumenical (or, if you wish, syncretistic) experiment, but both Sozomen's description and archaeological finds from the post-Constantinian period at the site prove that this emperor 'failed to deprive Mamre of its long-established associations.'[34] Although the description above is not of a tomb, the whole scene makes clear the blurring of religious boundaries as far as places connected with holy persons are concerned, a phenomenon that one can witness in the Near East and elsewhere till the present day.[35]

We now return to our discussion of the tombs. Jeremias tries to show that the holy persons were believed to act, from their tombs, as intercessors.[36] Especially the three great patriarchs were thought to be powerful advocates. Widely diverging works like Philo's *De praemiis et poenis* (166) and *3 Enoch* (44=§63) prove this, as do also haggadic passages in rabbinic literature, such as *Mekhilta Vayassa* on Ex. 16:14, where it is said that "God accepted the prayer of our forefathers who lay in the earth, and in return sent down the manna for Israel" (II p. 112 Lauterbach), and

---

[33] No doubt this kind of practice and the annual feasts at the tombs were in some way influenced by the heroes' tombs in the Greek and Roman world; on the latter see, e.g., E. Rohde, *Psyche. Seelencult und Unsterblichkeitsglaube der Griechen*, vol. 1, Darmstadt: Wissenschaftliche Buchgesellschaft, 1961 [=1898], 146-199, and R. Hägg (ed.), *Ancient Greek Hero Cult* (Proceedings of the Fifth International Seminar on Ancient Greek Cult, organized by the Department of Classical Archaeology and Ancient History, Göteborg University, 21-23 April 1995), Stockholm: Skrifter utgivna av Svenska Institutet i Athen, 1999.

[34] Hunt, *Holy Land Pilgrimage* 137. M. Simon, 'Les saints d'Israël dans la dévotion de l'Eglise Ancienne,' *Revue d'histoire et de philosophie religieuses* 34 (1954) 114-117. See now esp. A. Kofsky, 'Mamre: A Case of a Regional Cult?,' in Kofsky & Stroumsa (eds.), *Sharing the Sacred* 19-29.

[35] See W. Dalrymple, *From the Holy Mountain*, London: Flamingo, 1997, *passim*. It is interesting to see that at the end of the 12th century Benjamin of Tudela reports that Muslims in Iraq pray at the tombs of Ezechiel and Ezra (68 and 73). Cf. also R. Hartmann, 'Volksglaube und Volksbrauch in Palästina nach den abendländischen Pilgerschriften des ersten Jahrtausends,' *Archiv für Religionswissenschaft* 15 (1912) 137-152, esp. 138.

[36] Jeremias, *Heiligengräber* 133-138. Jeremias distinguishes here between 'Fürbitte' (intercessory prayer) and 'Fürsprache' (advocacy, mediation); it is only the latter that applies to the biblical holy persons after their death in this context, he says. On '"Life" in the Grave' see esp. S. Lieberman, 'Some Aspects of After Life in Early Rabbinic Literature,' in his *Texts and Studies*, New York: Ktav, 1974, 246-253.

BT *Sotah* 34b, where we read that "Caleb held aloof from the plan of the spies and went and prostrated himself upon the graves of the patriarchs, saying to them, 'My fathers, pray on my behalf that I may be delivered from the plan of the spies'" (Soncino translation). BT *Bava Metsia* 85b even says that Elijah daily had to wash the hands of the deceased patriarchs before they started their prayers.[37] Also Moses, Rachel, and the three great prophets, Isaiah, Jeremia and Ezechiel were regarded as influential intercessors.[38]

All this, says Jeremias, inevitably entailed pilgrimage to the tombs of the holy persons, although the evidence is far from overwhelming. Judges 11:40 already seemed to imply that, when the Israelite women went year by year to lament Jephtha's daughter, they went to her grave-site, and in the post-biblical retelling of the story by Pseudo-Philo we read more explicitly that these women even "named her tomb in accord with her name, Seila" (*LAB* 40:8). In BT *Ta'anith* 16a R. Hanina says that one visits burial sites in order that the deceased should intercede for mercy on our behalf.[39] In Roman and Byzantine Palestine the tomb of the patriarchs was probably the most important site for pilgrimage, says Jeremias. Some stories also seem to imply a beginning cult of relics of the Jewish holy persons. There are stories about the transfer of the bones of Jeremiah to Alexandria in order to protect the city from evil (*Vit. Jer.* 5). Also the rabbinic stories about the secret transfer of the bones of Rabbi Shim'on bar Yohai's son, El'azar, by the pious people of Meron to the tomb of his father is indicative of the importance of the presence of the holy person's physical remains (*Pesiqta de Rav Kahana* 11:23; cf. Ben Sira 46:12; 49:10; Hebr. 11:22). These stories definitely pre-date the second half of the 4th century CE, the period in which the cult of Christian tombs of the saints began to develop.[40] The fact that

---

[37] Cf. also the story in BT *Berakhot* 18b with the comments by Lieberman, 'Some Aspects' 250-251.

[38] For the latter three the *Vitae prophetarum* are the prime witness; e.g., *Vit. Isa.* 5.

[39] But the Talmud mentions a difference of opinion here.

[40] Of course the final redaction of *PRK* is much later. It would seem that the origins of Christian pilgrimage grew out of the practice of Jewish pilgrimage, and this seems to be a good reason why Christian pilgrims should have visited so many holy places connected with the Old Testament. Whether also the Christian cult of martyrs had Jewish roots is a moot point; see the diverging viewpoints of Th. Klauser, 'Christlicher Märtyrerkult, heidnischer Heroenkult und spätjüdische Heiligenverehrung: Neue Insichte und neue Probleme,' in his *Gesammelte Arbeiten zur Liturgiegeschichte, Kirchengeschichte und christlichen Archäologie* (Jahrbuch für Antike und Christentum, Ergänzungsband 3), Münster: Aschendorff, 1974, 221-229, and of W. Rordorf, 'Wie steht es um den jüdischen Einfluß auf den christlichen Märtyrerkult?', in J. van Amersfoort & J. van Oort (eds.), *Juden und Christen in der Antike*, Kampen: Kok, 1990, 61-71.

medieval Jewish travelogues of the Holy Land are often nothing but catalogues of the tombs that were visited indicates that the tendency to frequent and venerate tombs of biblical (and later also post-bilical) holy
persons gradually became an ever stronger force in the development of
Jewish popular religion, in spite of a generally very reserved or even
inimical attitude of the rabbis (who were aware of the idolatrous potential of this practice) and the polemic against the idea of intercession by
holy persons in pre-rabbinic authors such as Pseudo-Philo (*LAB* 33:5).[41]

This is Jeremias' position. Is it a tenable one? With due caution, I am
inclined to say yes, and I will try to demonstrate why, although our point
of departure is far from easy. Let us face the facts: There is not a single
document of undisputed Jewish origin that states clearly and unambiguously that Jews built or decorated tombs of biblical holy persons which
were to be the objects of pilgrimage and to have the function of places
where miracles could be expected and where intercession by the holy
person could be asked for. But there is a great deal of circumstantial evidence. Let me list some pieces of that evidence.

(1) Just before the beginning of the Common Era probably Herod the
Great built a mausoleum in Hebron at the site of the tombs of the patriarchs with a huge courtyard and a watersystem that by all accounts were
intended to accommodate large crowds of pilgrims, and this mausoleum
seems to replicate Herod's temple in Jerusalem. These are facts which
"invite the conclusion that the mausoleum, and in particular the tombs
therein, were considered by its pilgrims analogous in character and function to the temple cult itself."[42]

(2) There is evidence for Samaritan veneration of tombs of biblical
holy persons that is in many ways comparable to the Jewish material.[43]
For instance, the earliest Christian pilgrim who wrote an itinerarium (in

---

[41] See the commentary by Ch. Perrot & J.-M. Bogaert, *Pseudo-Philon, Les Antiquités
Bibliques*, vol. 2, Paris: Editions du Cerf, 1976, 177. As William Horbury remarks,
"Warnings that such intercession is excluded (...) seem to presuppose widespread
reliance on it" ('The Cult of Christ and the Cult of the Saints,' *New Testament Studies*
44 [1998] 459).

[42] J.N. Lightstone, *The Commerce of the Sacred. Mediation of the Divine among Jews in
the Graeco-Roman Diaspora*, Chico: Scholars Press, 1984, 71. For further bibliography see Kofsky 'Mamre' 20-22. At p. 72 Lightstone justly remarks: "Having a tomb
filled with uncleanness of the most virulent sort constitute the termination-point of a
link between heaven and earth represents a revolution of conception, at least within a
milieu defined by the Hebrew Bible." The ancient evidence for the architectural similarity of the Jerusalem temple and the Hebron mausoleum is listed by Lightstone at p.
192 note 6.

[43] See R. Pummer, *The Samaritans*, Leiden: Brill, 1987, 10-12.

333 CE), the so-called *Anonymus Burdigalensis*, tells about his visit to Joseph's tomb in Sichem (13-14), which cannot possibly be a Christian site. In 415 Theodosius I brought the bones from this tomb to Constantinople (as happened so often in other cases of Christian annexation of holy places of Jews or pagans), and on the site in Sichem he had a church built dedicated to Joseph.[44] This is a clear case of annexation of relics which we can be sure were venerated before their expropriation by Christians. According to Jewish sources the sons of Jacob were buried in Hebron, Joseph included,[45] but according to a New Testament passage, Acts 7:15-16, their tomb was in Sichem, which is also confirmed in other, later sources. Probably the site of Jacob's well in John 4:5-6, where Jesus spoke with a Samaritan woman, belonged to the same sacred area. So although we have no explicit early Jewish or Samaritan testimony to the effect that tombs of patriarchs were venerated in Sichem, the combination of the New Testament data with those from the Bordeaux pilgrim make it wellnigh certain that as early as the first century CE there were rival traditions between Jews and Samaritans as far as the tombs of the patriarchs were concerned and that these tombs attracted visitors.[46] Also, the tombs of the three Aaronites, namely Eleazar, Ithamar and Pinchas, were claimed to be in the Samaritan area, against Jewish claims, and in this case too the site was later expropriated by the Christian church.[47] A similar story could be told about the tomb of Joshua. The fact that there were Samaritan traditions about tombs of the great figures from the Pentateuch (not of the prophets, of course), traditions which were evidently directed against Jewish claims and which in some instances can be proved to be quite early (at least first century CE) makes it very probable that similar Jewish traditions existed in the same period.

(3) "According to 1 Samuel 10:2 there was a tomb of Rachel near Zelzah, a city in Benjamin to the north of Jerusalem. But Genesis 35:19 puts her tomb in the tribe of Judah, near Bethlehem, which is to the south of Jerusalem. So these had presumably once been competitive traditions between the tribes of Judah and Benjamin." This is very instructive

---

[44] Jeremias, *Heiligengräber* 33-34.

[45] Jeremias, *Heiligengräber* 36-38.

[46] J. Wilkinson, 'Jewish Holy Places and the Origins of Christian Pilgrimage,' in R. Ousterhout (ed.), *The Blessings of Pilgrimage*, Urbana-Chicago: University of Illinois Press, 1990, 41-53, esp. pp. 46-47 on the competition of traditions between Jews and Samaritans.

[47] Jeremias, *Heiligengräber* 38-40.

because "[t]he two tombs of Rachel in the Old Testament show that the idea of saints' tombs had a long tradition in Israel."[48] But it is also instructive because it shows that, apart from competing traditions between Jews and Samaritans about the location of tombs of biblical persons, such competition existed in inner-Jewish circles as well.[49]

(4) It is highly illuminating that the earliest Christian pilgrim, the Bordeaux pilgrim mentioned above, who travelled in a period (333 CE) in which the building of Christian monuments, including tombs of saints, had hardly begun, was guided along no less than seventeen tombs, only two of which (those of Jesus and Lazarus) were Christian: the fifteen others were all of them graves of holy persons from the Jewish Bible. It is highly likely that they had been built by Jews and served as monuments to be shown to pilgrims.[50] This suggests not only the existence of Jewish veneration of tombs but also of Jewish pilgrimage to these graves. Even in the pilgrim documents of half a century to seventy years later, the itinerary of Egeria and the famous *Letter* 108 of Jerome, the preponderance of Jewish graves visited by these pilgrims is still evident. Egeria mentions twelve tombs, five of which are Christian (two New Testament figures: Christ and Thomas; further Thecla, Abgar, and martyrs) but seven of Old Testament figures, although almost all of these are located outside Palestine. But Jerome mentions twenty-five graves, twenty-two of which of Old Testament figures and three of New Testament figures (or, if one counts the tomb of the twelve patriarchs as one, fourteen of which eleven OT and three NT). To emphasize the point again, it is extremely improbable that it would have been Christians who, immediately after Constantine, would have begun building tombs of Jewish instead of Christian holy persons. These tombs must have been Jewish.[51]

---

[48] Wilkinson, 'Jewish Holy Places and the Origins of Christian Pilgrimage' 46 and 48. It is also important to notice that as early as the second century BCE the book of *Jubilees* tells us that Bilha, Rachel's servant, and Jacob's daughter Dina were buried together opposite Rachel's tomb near Bethlehem (34:16). This implies that already in this early period traditions about locations of burial sites of biblical persons were circulating.

[49] See Jeremias, *Heiligengräber* 114-115, who mentions also other internal Jewish competitive traditions about the location of tombs.

[50] The Bordeaux pilgrim may have been a Jewish Christian; see Donner, *Pilgerfahrt* 41-42. That these OT monuments were indeed 'shown' is confirmed by the repeated *deiknutai* in Eusebius' *Onomasticon*; see Hunt, *Holy Land Pilgrimage* 99.

[51] J. Wilkinson, 'Visits to Jewish Tombs by Early Christians,' *Akten des XII. Internationalen Kongresses für christliche Archäologie* [= Jahrbuch für Antike und Christentum Ergänzungsband 20], 2 vols., Münster: Aschendorffsche Verlagsbuchhandlung, 1995, 1: 452-465. Cf. Simon, 'Les saints d'Israël' 98-127, esp. 106-108.

(5) From Josephus we know that in his days several tombs of biblical holy persons were not only extant but were probably also centres of religious activities. He mentions the tombs of Abraham's brother Nahor in Ur (*Ant.* 1:151), Eleazar's tomb in Gabatha (*Ant.* 5:119), Rachel's tomb near Bethlehem (*Ant.* 6:56), David's mausoleum in Jerusalem, where a miracle happened when Herod tried to open it: two of his bodyguards were killed by fire (*Ant.* 7:392-394; 13:249; 16:179-183); and of course the tombs of the patriarchs in Hebron (*Bell.* 4:532). It is also very interesting to see how often Josephus uses the expression 'at the tomb of [followed by a biblical name]' as a casual indication of where something took place.[52] This seems to point to the fact that he supposed his readers to have a certain familiarity with the location of tombs of biblical persons.

(6) It is not only the *Life of Isaiah* 8 that makes clear that a tomb of a prophet was venerated "so that through his prayers even after his death" they might enjoy benefits, it is also the polemics against the idea of intercession by the deceased in Pseudo-Philo (*LAB* 33:4) and in some other sources[53] that strongly suggest strongly that the tombs of biblical holy persons were the locus of requests for intercession.[54]

(7) The fact that Eusebius mentions a mausoleum of Joshua in the village of Thamna before 325,[55] that is, *in a period in which Christians definitely had not yet begun to build tombs for Old Testament holy persons*, indicates that it is a Jewish site. That this is indeed the case is proved by the fact that half a century later Jerome reports that at that place the heap of foreskins of Joshua's circumcision (Jos. 5:3) were still preserved.[56] No Christian would ever invent this.

(8) According to *1 Macc.* 13:25-30, Simon the Maccabee built a gigantic mausoleum for his father, his mother, and his brothers in Modiin. It was an enormous monument with seven pyramids that was to be visible from the sea. Not only Josephus (*Ant.* 13:211) but also

---

[52] One can compare here the way in which the author of the *Copper Scroll* indicates the place in which the 53rd treasure is hidden: "Underneath the south corner of the Portico, at Zadok's tomb, underneath the column of the exedra" (*3Q15* XI 2-3).

[53] See Perrot & Bogaert, *Pseudo-Philon* 177, for references. Also Wilkinson, 'Visits to Jewish Tombs' 456.

[54] Note that *Vit. Jer.* 3 says that believers still pray at Jeremiah's tomb. Also Judas' vision in *2 Macc.* 15:12-16 implies that the deceased Jeremiah is viewed as praying for Jerusalem. Cf. also *1 Enoch* 39:5.

[55] *Onomasticon* p. 70 ed. Klostermann.

[56] *Epist.* 108:12,3.

Eusebius and Jerome were still able to view it centuries later. It was apparently shown to visitors and/or pilgrims.[57]

(9) Jesus' words about the building of the tombs of the prophets (Matt. 23:29-30 and parr., discussed above) is certainly no late accretion to the tradition of *verba Domini* but is the bedrock of the tradition. There is no reason whatsoever to think that it was not spoken by Jesus. But even if the saying were a later non-dominical creation, it would still prove beyond any doubt that tombs of biblical holy persons were centres of (undoubtedly religious) activities in the first century CE. The prophets' tombs were being beautified, which implies a growth in devotion.[58]

(10) We read in Tobit 4:17, "Pour your wine [or: bread] at the graves of the righteous,"[59] and there is no denying that here a Jewish author advises his readers to engage in what was 'officially' a 'pagan' cultic act.[60] This should not come as a surprise, because there were always Jews at many times and places who simply did not observe biblical restrictions and prohibitions (cf. Deut. 26:14).[61] The views of the biblical editors often hardly represent the religious practices of the people of Israel.

(11) In BT *Sanhedrin* 47a-b we read that people visited the grave of the rabbinic holy man, Rav, in order to procure its earth for theurgic purposes.[62] Apparently it was necessary to prohibit this explicitly because there were some (or perhaps many) who continued these kinds of pagan practices 'in a hostile (or minimally ambivalent) rabbinic environment.'[63] Also, the prohibitions in the (late) treatise *Semahot* (esp. ch. 8) clearly imply that Jews of the Talmudic period continued to visit the

---

[57] See Jeremias, *Heiligengräber* 50, and for a good discussion of this complex building F.-M. Abel, *Les livres des Maccabées*, Paris: Gabalda, 1949, 239-241.

[58] See W.D. Davies & D.C. Allison, *The Gospel According to Saint Matthew*, vol. 3, Edinburgh: Clark, 1997, 304; U. Luz, *Das Evangelium nach Matthäus*, vol. 3, Neukirchen: Benziger Verlag & Neukirchener Verlag, 1997, 342-343.

[59] For the textcritical problem here ('bread' instead of 'wine' in some of the witnesses) see the discussion by C.A. Moore, *Tobit* (Anchor Bible 40A), New York etc.: Doubleday, 1996), 173.

[60] As Moore (*ibid.*) points out, there is an identical advice in the book of Ahiqar, discussed at length by J.C. Greenfield, "Two Proverbs of Ahiqar," in Tzvi Abusch et al. (edd.), *Lingering over Words. Studies in Ancient Near Eastern Literature in Honor of W.L. Moran*, Atlanta: Scholars Press, 1990, 195-201; Greenfield also thinks Jews did not shy away from pagan cultic practices if they found them useful or effective.

[61] Cf. Simon, 'Saints d'Israël' 109: "Le monothéisme islamique n'a pas empêché la vivace floraison du culte des marabouts."

[62] See Lightstone, *The Commerce of the Sacred* 75 with notes 9-11.

[63] Lightstone, *Commerce* 75-76.

tombs of their relatives well beyond the usual thirty[64] days period after the burial in order to engage there in 'heathen practices' (litt. 'ways of the Amorites,' 8:1), a nice parallel to Tobit 4:17. And in BT *Berakhot* 18b it is related that a commoner deposited some money with his land-lady, but while he was away she died. When he came back, he went to her tomb and said to her, 'Where is my money?' She replied from the grave, 'Go and take it from under the ground, in the doorpost hole, in such and such a place. But also tell my mother to send me my comb and my tube of eyepaint by the hand of So-and-so who is coming here tomorrow.'[65] We may conclude that there were Jews at many times and places who simply did not observe rabbinic restrictions and prohibitions. They simply did not care about incurring corpse impurity.[66] As Saul Lieberman aptly said, "there is no doubt that the ancient Jews engaged in these superstitious practices."[67]

(12) If the *Vitae prophetarum* were a Christian work, how then is it to be explained that there is such sustained attention to the tribal affiliation of the prophets, which was not a Christian concern at all? This seems to be much more a matter of Jewish interest.[68] And if the *Vitae prophetarum* were a Christian work, why then are no graves of Christian or New Testament personalities mentioned, not even of the

---

[64] *Varia lectio* 'three.' This variant reading is understandable because the period indicated is meant 'to inspect the dead for a sign of life' (*Semahot* 8:1). However, to justify a practice they actually frowned upon but to limit its duration the rabbis resorted to a very improbable argument. See the remarks by Lieberman, 'Some Aspects' 251 n. 32, and especially the very interesting discussion of this passage by L. Rothkrug, 'The "Odour of Sanctity," and the Hebrew Origins of Christian Relic Veneration," *Historical Reflections* 8 (1981) 95-142, at pp. 123-126. Rothkrug here remarks: 'Unable to stop ritual visits to grave sites, the rabbis simply bowed to overwhelming pressure from their flock. (...) [They] here utter no word about defilement from corpse contact, though they repeatedly warn against the offense elsewhere, throughout the tractate' (123). 'Manifestly the rabbis faced a popular practice too powerful to suppress' (124). Of course three days sufficed 'to inspect the dead for a sign of life,' but the much longer period of thirty days was the widely accepted 'way of the Amorites.'

[65] See Lieberman, 'Some Aspects of After Life' 249-251.

[66] Horbury, 'The Cult of Christ and the Cult of the Saints' 453, points out that in the rabbinic necropolis of Beth Shearim walled meeting places with stone benches were identified over two of the catacombs, which seems "to strengthen the possibility that in the third and fourth centuries Jews, not unlike Christians, assembled at tombs to honour the dead, despite Pentateuchal warnings of impurity there" (453-4; cf. 458).

[67] 'Some Aspects of After Life' 249.

[68] Satran's argument to the effect that this "is in no way foreign to the concerns of the church in Byzantine Palestine" (109) is weakly founded: preservation of tribal boundaries in the Christian onomastic tradition is not the same as attention to the tribal affiliation of the prophets!

prophet John the Baptist?[69] The most plausible explanation would seem to be that the work is a product of Jewish circles.

This final point brings us back to our main question: is there a feasible context for a writing such as the *Vitae prophetarum*, or rather: its tomb traditions, in first century Judaism? It is clear that the evidence adduced does not prove that the *Vitae Prophetarum* is a Jewish writing; it could still be Christian. However, I think that it is very likely that in these *Vitae* at least the data about the burial sites derive from Jewish traditions – which even Satran admits are present in the *Vitae* – possibly even of first century Palestinian provenance. In spite of the preponderance of tombs of Old Testament persons in the early Christian pilgrim documents of the fourth century, none of these documents mentions *only* Old Testament tombs. Always at least one but usually more than one Christian tomb is mentioned, foremost among them, of course, that of Jesus. Our *Vitae* do not fit that pattern, which suggests that it is not a Christian work. When we now take into account that the Hebrew Bible already evidences rival traditions about the location of graves; that some passages in the Old Testament seem to suggest that the dead are active in their tombs (Elisha, Samuel) and that certainly postbiblical Jewish interpreters took these passages to imply this; that there is evidence of dispute between Jews about the possibility of intercession to God via the services of the deceased; that Josephus clearly evidences that there were not only building and decorating activities as far as biblical burial sites were concerned but also that miracles took place there and that 'at the tomb of A [biblical]' was a current expression in his days, apparently because Jews used to assemble at tombs to honour the dead; that the earliest Christian pilgrims were guided to many tombs of great figures from the Hebrew Bible in a period when Christian building, decorating or veneration of tombs had not even started; that Christian sources of the fourth and fifth centuries clearly tell us that the sacred burial sites of OT worthies were crowded with sick people of Jewish, Christian and pagan conviction; that rabbinic stories imply that people went to the graves of the great biblical personalities in order to ask for their help. advice, and intercession; that the supposed early Jewish interest in 'Heiligengräber' finds its natural continuation in the reports of the medieval travelogues; that Samaritan evidence from the Imperial period and later

---

[69] For the veneration of John the Baptist's tomb, which is attested from at least the middle of the 4th century onwards, see Jeremias, 'Drei weitere spätjüdische Heiligengräber' 96-98.

strongly suggests that the Samaritans too adhered to the practices under consideration; that the relative silence of rabbinic literature about these practices can easily be explained as the natural reaction of leaders or would-be leaders about practices of their flock which they would prefer not to take place; that to argue that Judaism could not produce such a phenomenon (being against the Torah) "is begging the question of what, if anything, constitutes normative Judaism;"[70] that we see something similar happening in later times with, e.g., the tomb of Shim'on bar Yohai (who had the reputation of being a miracle worker) on Mt. Meron, to be witnessed even today;[71] that rabbinic prohibitions demonstrate that Jews – in what numbers we do not know, but there were enough of them to justify repeated warnings – visited tombs of both biblical persons and ordinary people for purposes of intercession or miracles;[72] et cetera et cetera – if all this is the case, then one can only agree with Saul Lieberman when he says in this connection: "The Torah forbade a number [of these practices], and the rabbis added their own prohibitions. However, it is easier to fight wickedness than to combat the superstitions of pious people. (...) The masses had their own ways."[73] Or, to put it in Shaye Cohen's

---

[70] Lightstone, *Commerce of the Sacred* 77.

[71] See B.-Z. Rosenfeld, 'R. Simon b.Yohai – Wonder Worker and Magician – Scholar, Saddiq and Hasid,' *Revue des Etudes Juives* 158 (1999) 349-384; and, briefly, D. Sperber. 'Shim'on bar Yohai,' in *The Oxford Dictionary of the Jewish Religion,* edd. R.J. Zwi Werblowsky & G. Wigoder, Oxford: OUP, 1997, 636.

[72] For the presence of such tombs in Jerusalem, most probably already before 70 CE, see *Avoth de-Rabbi Nathan* (rec. B) 39, where it is stated that only the tombs of David, Isaiah and Huldah were tolerated inside the walls of Jerusalem. See A.J. Saldarini, *The Fathers According to Rabbi Nathan,* Leiden: Brill, 1975, 236.

[73] 'Aspects of After Life' 252-253. Morton Smith rightly remarks that one should not create a rigid opposition between 'popular religion' on the one hand and rabbinic attitudes on the other, since "even rabbinic tradition contains some elements which show an amazing indifference to this consideration [of impurity], e.g. the story that Solomon brought the coffin of David into the Temple (Pesiq. Rab. 2, ed. Friedmann 6b, & parallels): Instead of polluting it, this produced the descent of the heavenly fire" ('The Image of God,' in his *Studies in the Cult of Yahweh,* Leiden: Brill, 1996, vol. 1:131-2 n. 73). One could also refer to *Lamentations Rabba, Proem* 25 (on 2 Chron. 32:33, 'They honoured him [Hezekiah] at his death'): "What honour did they do to him? R. Judah ben Simon said: They built a meeting place [for study] above Hezekiah's grave, and when they went there they used to say to him, 'Teach us!' R. Hanin said: They placed a Torah-scroll over Hezekiah's grave and said, 'He who lies in this coffin fulfilled what is written herein.'" (I owe this reference to Horbury, 'The Cult of Christ and the Cult of the Saints' 458.) Cf. also BT *Bava Qamma* 16b-17a. Wilkinson, 'Visits to Jewish Tombs' 463, argues that these stories imply a change in attitude towards the dead bodies of the deceased Righteous ones to the effect that these no longer underwent corruption after death.

words, for these pious people "the dead served not as sources of impurity but as intermediaries between the earthly and the heavenly
realms."[74]

Surveying this impressive array of data – which is far from being
complete![75] – we see that in the post-biblical period there is no century without evidence that suggests that there has been an uninterrupted undercurrent of religious activity related to tombs of great biblical personalities since biblical times. It is highly probable that the
Jewish visitors to the tombs 'treated the holy dead as models of religious life.'[76] That the evidence is circumstantial should not surprise
us, for people who do things that are frowned upon or even condemned by their religious authorities are not the kind of persons that
are likely to write about them; and if they write, their writings are not
the kind of texts that are likely to be preserved.[77] We can say, therefore, with some confidence that, even though there is no Jewish document from the pre-Byzantine period that states that Jews venerated
tombs of biblical holy persons as objects of pilgrimage and as places
where miracles and intercession by the holy person could be sought,
the circumstantial evidence to this effect is overwhelming. It is, therefore, an understatement to say that this evidence suggests that this is
exactly what took place. Postulating a late 4th century Christian context here creates more problems than it solves, if only because the saying of Jesus and the earliest Christian pilgrim reports about (Jewish)
tombs of biblical holy persons are then deprived of their context. Thus
we must conclude that there is indeed an early, even first century, Jewish context for the tomb traditions in the *Vitae prophetarum*.[78] No
wonder that the early Christians cherished the tradition about the exact

[74] S.J.D. Cohen, 'Pagan and Christian Evidence on the Ancient Synagogue,' in
L. I. Levine (ed.), *The Synagogue in Late Antiquity*, Philadelphia: ASOR, 1987,
169.

[75] For instance, after the Bar Kochba revolt, the emperor Hadrian forbade the Jews to
enter Jerusalem. Not long thereafter the tombs of David and Solomon, which were in
Jerusalem, were moved to Bethlehem so that Jewish pilgrims could visit them there.
This seems to imply that pilgrimage to tombs of biblical figures was a more or less current Jewish practice. But the sources are not unambiguous here; see G. Alon, *The Jews
in Their Land in the Talmudic Age*, Cambridge MA – London: Harvard University
Press, 1989, 644-645.

[76] Wilkinson, 'Visits to Jewish Tombs' 455.

[77] Gnostic literature is an illustrative case in point.

[78] This is also the conclusion of Horbury, 'The Cult of Christ and the Cult of the Saints,'
esp. 453-4, but it was already drawn by A. Schlatter, *Der Märtyrer in den Anfängen
der Kirche*, Gütersloh: Bertelsmann, 1915, 23-29.

location of Jesus' tomb from the beginning,[79] so that its location has been preserved to this day.[80]

---

[79] Cf. Horbury, 'The Cult of Christ and the Cult of the Saints' 466: "[C]oncern for the tombs of the righteous would have made Christian concern for the tomb of Christ inevitable from the first." Wilkinson, 'Visits to Jewish Tombs' 465: "[T]he disciples could hardly fail to remember the exact position of the tomb of Christ himself, and to venerate it as a place of prayer."

[80] See G. Kretschmar, 'Festkalender und Memorialstätten Jerusalems in altkirchlicher Zeit,' in H. Busse & G. Kretschmar, *Jerusalemer Heiligtumstraditionen in altkirchlicher und frühislamitischer Zeit*, Wiesbaden: Harassowitz, 1987, 29-111.

The complicated question of whether or not we have a model in this phenomenon for the later Christian cult of the saints falls outside the scope of this contribution, but there can be little doubt that there is a connection here.

8. ANTEDILUVIAN KNOWLEDGE

Graeco-Roman and Jewish Speculations
About Wisdom From Before the Flood

1. Introduction

"I studied inscriptions from before the flood." This remark can be found
in a document of Ashurbanipal, king of Assyria in the middle of the seventh century BCE, whose library included editions of creation and flood
accounts.[1] It indicates that this king claimed to have access to information
from time immemorial. This age, the antediluvian period, has fascinated
mankind ever since stories about an all-devastating flood began to circu-
late around the beginning of the second millennium BCE. In this primordial time, so it was thought, mankind certainly possessed precious knowledge now lost, great wisdom now only attainable to those who are
fortunate enough to lay hold of documents that survived that cosmic catastrophe, that is, on 'inscriptions from before the flood.'[2] No wonder that
such claims were rampant in antiquity, especially in the Hellenistic
period when claims of priority played such a large role in the cultural battle between the nations that was waged with a definite 'fondness for speculation about εὑρήματα,'[3] that is, the origins of the arts and sciences.[4]

---

[1] See R.S. Hess & D.T. Tsumura (edd.), *"I Studied Inscriptions From Before the
Flood." Ancient Near Eastern and Literary Approaches to Genesis 1-11*, Winona
Lake: Eisenbrauns, 1994, XI. For text and (German) translation of the whole passage
see M. Streck, *Assurbanipal und die letzten assyrischen Könige*, vol. 2: Texte, Leipzig:
Hinrichsche Buchhandlung, 1916, 252-259 (quote at 257); see also the Introduction and
notes in S. Parpola, *Letters from Assyrian and Babylonian Scholars* (State Archives of
Assyria 10), Helsinki: Helsinki University Press, 1993, xxxiv.

[2] On lists of antediluvian sages and kings in Babylonian documents see, e.g., W. Lambert, 'Enmeduranki and Related Matters,' *Journal of Cuneiform Studies* 21 (1967) 126-
138; and R. Borger, 'Die Beschwörungsserie BĪT MÊSERI und die Himmelfahrt
Henochs,' *Journal of Near Eastern Studies* 33 (1974) 183-196.

[3] W. Adler, *Time Immemorial. Archaic History and its Sources in Christian Chronography
from Julius Africanus to George Syncellus* (Dumbarton Oaks Studies 26), Washington:
Dumbarton Oaks, 1989, 3. Cf. also K. Thraede, 'Das Lob des Erfinders: Bemerkungen zur
Analyse der Heuremata-Kataloge,' *Rheinisches Museum für Philologie* 105 (1962) 158-186.

[4] See K. Thraede, 'Erfinder II (geistesgeschichtlich),' *RAC* 5 (1962) 1191-1278; B. L.
van der Waerden, *Die 'Ägypter' und die 'Chaldäer'* (Sitzungsberichte der Heidelberger

2. Graeco-Roman Evidence

To begin with the last-mentioned aspect, there is ample evidence that in Hellenistic and Roman times learned Babylonians and Egyptians battled over priority issues, especially as regards the invention of the then prestigious science of astronomy or astrology.[5] Let me quote some of the evidence from the first centuries BCE and CE.

In the first century BCE both the Roman orator and politician Cicero, and his contemporary, the Greek historian Diodorus Siculus, report on the respective claims of Babylonians and Egyptians as far as the great antiquity of their astronomical and astrological lore is concerned, and in the first century CE we see the same theme recurring in the writings of both the Graeco-Egyptian author Chaeremon and the Roman scholar Pliny the Elder. Apparently the topic was of some concern to authors around the turn of the era.

Since Cicero is chronologically the first, at least probably, let me start with him, even though he does not mention the flood explicitly. In *De divinatione* (I 19, 36; cf. II 46, 97), he says that we should mock the Babylonians who in their astronomical observations and calculations of the signs of heaven make the ridiculous claim that these are based upon documents which contain data that have been gathered over a period of 470.000 years.[6] No flood is mentioned here, but, as we shall presently see, it lurks at the background. Cicero's near-contemporary, the Greek historian Diodorus of Sicily devotes all of the first book of his *Bibliotheca historica* to Egypt, the country he visited himself in the early fifties of the first century BCE.[7] He calls Egypt the country where 'the earliest observations of the stars are said to have been made' (I 9, 6); it

---

Akademie der Wissenschaften: mathematisch-naturwissenschaftliche Klasse, Jahrgang 1972, 5. Abhandlung), Berlin-Heidelberg: Springer, 1972, esp. 30-31.

[5] Often no distinction between these two 'sciences' was made since many regarded astrology simply as applied astronomy (or astronomy as theoretical astrology for that matter). See W. Hübner, *Die Begriffe 'Astrologie' und 'Astronomie' in der Antike*, Mainz & Stuttgart: Steiner, 1989, and P. W. van der Horst, 'Jewish Self-Definition by Way of Contrast in *Oracula Sibyllina* III 218-247,' in my *Hellenism – Judaism – Christianity: Essays on Their Interaction*, Louvain: Peeters, 1998 (2nd ed.), 96-99. For a good general introduction in ancient astrology see T. Barton, *Ancient Astrology*, London-New York: Routledge, 1994.

[6] On the number and its variations – 400,000; 432,000; 473,000; 480,000; 490,000 – in similar traditions (deriving mostly from Berossus; see below in the text) see A.S. Pease in his commentary *M. Tulli Ciceronis de divinatione libri duo*, Darmstadt: Wissenschaftliche Buchgesellschaft, 1963 [= Urbana 1920-1923], 158.

[7] See A. Burton, *Diodorus Siculus, Book I. A Commentary*, Leiden: Brill, 1972, Introd.

is the land that 'better than any other could have been the place where mankind came into being because of the well-tempered nature of its soil' (I 10, 3); it is said, Diodorus continues, 'that if in the flood which occurred in the time of Deucalion most living beings were destroyed, it is probable that the inhabitants of southern Egypt survived rather than any others, since their country is rainless for the most part' (I 10, 4);[8] it was the Egyptian Hermes (i.e., Thoth) who 'was the first to observe the orderly arrangement of the stars' (I 16, 1); when Babylonian priests, called Chaldaeans, make observations of the stars, they only follow the example of the Egyptian priests (I 28, 1); much further on, Diodorus states that according to the Egyptians it was they who first discovered writing and the observation of the stars, and that the best proof of this is that Egypt 'for more than 4,700 years' [very probably a textual corruption for 170,000!] was ruled by kings of whom the majority were native Egyptians and that the land was the most prosperous of the whole inhabited world (I 69, 5-6); and finally he observes that the positions and arrangements of the stars as well as their motions have always been the subject of careful observation among the Egyptians: 'they have preserved to this day the records concerning each of these stars over an incredible number of years, this subject of study having been zealously preserved among them from ancient times' (I 81, 4), and according to them the Chaldaeans of Babylon enjoy the fame which they have for their astrology only because they learned that science from the priests of Egypt (I 81, 6). When in his second book Diodorus describes the Babylonians, he says on the one hand that it is reasonable to state that of all nations the Chaldaeans have the greatest knowledge of astrology. On the other hand, he says, as far as the number of years is concerned which they claim Chaldaeans have spent on the study of the heavenly bodies, it is simply not to be believed: 'for they reckon that, down to Alexander's crossing over into Asia, it has been 473,000 years since they began their observations of the stars' (II 31, 10). The rivalry between Hellenistic Egypt and Babylon as far as the origin of astrology is concerned becomes quite clear here in Diodorus' dossier, and it is to be noticed that the flood is mentioned in this connection as a catastrophe that is not likely to have occurred in Egypt.

When we turn to Pliny the Elder, we find another important element added, since, apart from a claim to an even greater antiquity, the motif

---

[8] It is notable that ancient Egypt does not seem to have known a flood legend, unlike most other civilizations in the Ancient Near East.

of inscribed stones is introduced: 'Epigenes,[9] an authority of the first rank, teaches that the Babylonians had astronomical observations for 720,000 years inscribed on baked bricks; and those who argue for a very short period, Berossus and Critodemus, make it 490,000 years' (*Naturalis historia* VII 56, 193).[10] Finally all the pieces of this puzzle are put together by our fourth witness, Pliny's contemporary Chaeremon. This Graeco-Egyptian scholar writes in his history of Egypt about the chronological quarrel between the Chaldaeans and the Egyptians as far as the invention of astrology is concerned.[11] Even though he is an Egyptian himself, he seems to concede, albeit very indirectly, that the Egyptians learned this science from the Babylonians. He writes (as summarized by Michael Psellus):

> The wisdom of the Chaldaeans is older than that practised zealously among the Egyptians, but neither people was the teacher of the other (...). The Nile once flooded the country of the Egyptians and destroyed, besides their other possessions, all the astronomical data which they had collected in books. Then, because they needed to know the eclipses and conjunctions, they collected the basic data about these from the Chaldaeans. The latter, however, being malicious in the matter of communicating these data, altered the times in their reports and gave out the movements of the planets and fixed stars contrary to their natural order. Then, when the Egyptians were in great uncertainty about the principles, they made themselves the disciples of the Chaldaeans and brought home the true knowledge of reality and inscribed these subjects on baked bricks in order that neither fire could touch them nor water could damage them in case of a flood.

This passage teaches us several things. Firstly, as already said, Chaeremon concedes that there was Chaldaean priority as far as astronomy or astrology is concerned, which is indeed correct from a historical point of view,[12] but the concession is limited: that the Chaldaeans can now claim priority is only due to an accident, namely a flood, but not a flood in Babylon or a worldwide deluge, but one restricted to Egypt, i.e. an inundation of the Nile, by which the Egyptians lost their knowledge! This

---

[9] A well-known astrologer from Byzantium who lived in the 2nd cent. BCE.

[10] For the textual uncertainty as far as the numbers are concerned, see the synopsis in the edition by R. König, *C. Plinius Secundus d. Ä.: Naturkunde, Buch VII*, Zürich: Artemis, 1996, 257.

[11] See the edition of the Greek fragments with translation and commentary by P.W. van der Horst, *Chaeremon, Egyptian Priest and Stoic Philosopher*, Leiden: Brill, 1987 (2nd ed.), 8-11, 51-52.

[12] See Van der Waerden, *Die 'Ägypter' und die 'Chaldäer'* 31, and K. von Stuckrad, *Frömmigkeit und Wissenschaft: Astrologie in Tanach, Qumran und frührabbinischer Literatur*, Frankfurt etc: Lang, 1996, 17-54.

theory seems so farfetched that it is not hard to see Egyptian patriotism
at work here,[13] although mixed with some small grains of historical
insight. Another important element in Chaeremon's account, to which
we shall return presently, is that the knowledge finally acquired by the
Egyptians is brought to safety by inscribing the data on baked bricks
because in this way it is invulnerable to both water and fire. A similar
piece of ethnic boasting as in Chaeremon, but now the other way round,
is found in Diodorus of Sicily (possibly based upon a work by Zenon of
Rhodes; see *FGH* 523 F 1)[14], where he reports a tradition that the Egyptians learned astrology from the Greeks:

> But when at a later time there came a flood among the Greeks and the
> majority of mankind perished by reason of the abundance of rain, it came
> to pass that all written documents were also destroyed in the same manner
> as mankind. This is the reason why the Egyptians, seizing this favourable
> occasion, declared the knowledge of astrology to be their own, and why,
> since the Greeks, because of their ignorance, no longer could claim to pos-
> sess any documents, the belief prevailed that the Egyptians were the first to
> make the discovery of the stars (V 57, 3-4).

Two things have to be noticed here. It is taken for granted, in contradistinction to what Chaeremon says, that the universal flood that Diodorus
speaks of, did not touch Egypt so that the Egyptians could retain their
astrological lore and wisdom. Secondly, again we find the motif of dis-
honestly claiming this knowledge to be one's own – a claim made possible by a catastrophe – whereas it had in fact been received from others.
When cultural prestige is at stake, nations are not interested in historical
truth. The desire for ethnic boasting is always stronger than the wish to
know the truth, as we know from our own times.

Now it has to be said at this point that Diodorus (or Zeno's) report is
based upon or inspired by the famous introductory passage in Plato's
Timaeus 22b-23b. There, in a story about a meeting of Solon and a very
learned and old Egyptian priest, the latter says to Solon that the Greeks
are nothing but children and that there is no such thing as an old man
among them. When Solon asks what he means by that, the Egyptian
replies:

> I mean to say that in mind you are all young; there is no old opinion
> handed down among you by ancient tradition, nor any science which is

---

[13] Adler, *Time Immemorial* 60-61, assumes that the inundation of the Nile was invented
by Chaeremon for polemical reasons.
[14] This Zeno was a local historian who lived in the early second century BCE; see *Oxford
Classical Dictionary* s.v.

hoary with age. And I will tell you why. There have been, and will be again, many destructions of mankind arising out of many causes; the greatest have been brought about by fire and water, and other lesser ones by innumerable other causes. There is a story which even you have preserved, that once upon a time Phaethon, the son of Helios, having yoked the steeds in his father's chariot, because he was not able to drive them in the path of his father, burned up all that was upon the earth and was himself destroyed by a thunderbolt. Now this has the form of a myth, but really signifies a declination of the bodies moving in the heavens around the earth, and a great conflagration of things upon the earth which recurs after long intervals; at such times those who live upon the mountains and in dry and lofty places are more liable to destruction than those who dwell by rivers or on the seashores. And from this calamity we are preserved because we have the Nile, who is our never-failing saviour. When on the other hand the gods purge the earth with a deluge of water, the survivors in your country are herdsmen and shepherds who dwell on the mountains, but those who, like you, live in cities are carried by the rivers into the sea. But in this land [Egypt] neither then nor at any other time does the water come down from above on the fields, it always has a tendency to come up from below; and it is for this reason that the traditions preserved here are the most ancient; though as a matter of fact in all regions where inordinate cold or heat does not forbid it, mankind exists, in larger or smaller numbers. Whatever great or noble achievements or otherwise exceptional events that have come to pass, either in your country or in ours or in any other region of which we are informed, they have all been written down by us of old and are preserved in our temples. Whereas when you and other nations are just beginning again to be provided with letters and the other requisites of civilized life, after the usual interval the torrents from heaven sweep down like a pestilence leaving only the rude and unlettered among you, and so you have to begin all over again like children, and you know nothing of what happened in ancient times, either among us or among yourselves.[15]

This is a very important passage. It makes clear that as early as the middle of the 4th cent. BCE in certain Greek circles it was believed that, since Egypt was safeguarded against devastating floods, only this civilization was in the privileged position of having kept records of the past in all its aspects.[16] It was this motif that induced a later Hermetic

---

[15] This translation is basically the one by B. Jowett, reprinted in *The Collected Dialogues of Plato*, ed. by E. Hamilton & H. Cairns, Princeton: Princeton University Press, 1989, 1157-1158, slightly revised after F. M. Cornford, *Plato's Cosmology*, London: Routledge & Kegan Paul, 1937, 15-16. For the contents cf. also Aristotle, *Meteor.* I 14, 352a; *De philosophia* fragm. 8 Walzer. Note the echo of this passage in Josephus, *Contra Apionem* I 7-9. It is also exploited (but now against the Jews and Christians!) by Celsus; see Origen, *Contra Celsum* I 19-20; IV 9-13.

[16] As Adler remarks, ancient Jewish and Christian chronographers agreed in their opinion of 'the poor quality of Greek records for primordial history' (*Time Immemorial* 21).

author, usually called Pseudo-Manetho, to claim that the Graeco-Egyptian priest Manetho knew stelae that were inscribed in the sacred tongue in hieroglyphic letters by Thoth, the first Hermes, and translated *after the flood* (μετὰ τὸν κατακλυσμόν) from the sacred language into Greek and deposited in books in the sanctuaries of Egyptian temples (*FGH* 609 F 25).[17] And of course these stelae contained texts with primordial, Hermetic wisdom.[18] Maybe it was in reaction to the kind of theory as set out in the *Timaeus* that in the late fourth or early third century BCE the Babylonian scholar Berossus wrote his *Babyloniaka*.[19] He was the first native Babylonian to write about Mesopotamian culture in Greek. Although, as is also the case with his Egyptian counterpart, Manetho, only small fragments of his work have been preserved, they give us some valuable glimpses into the Babylonian variant of what has been called 'apologetic historiography.'[20] The *Babyloniaka* consisted of a description of the origins of Babylonian culture and its history down to Alexander.[21] The flood figured prominently in his work as a watershed, and ten antediluvian sages or kings are mentioned. Berossus also relates Cronos' order to Xisutros (= Bel's order to Ziusudra, the Sumerian Noah) to dig a hole and to bury all writings in Sippar, the city of the sun, before the flood would destroy everything

---

[17] Quoted by Syncellus, *Ecloga chronographica* 72-73 (p. 41 ed. Mosshammer). The text is also in W.G. Waddell (ed.), *Manetho* (LCL), Cambridge MA – London: Harvard University Press – Heinemann, 1940, 208-211. See further B. Copenhaver, *Hermetica*, Cambridge: CUP, 1992, XV. Adler, *Time Immemorial* 58-59, points out the pseudepigraphic character of the text.

[18] Iamblichus tells us that Pythagoras and Plato, during their visit to Egypt, read the stelae of Hermes with the help of native priests (*Myst.* I 1,3). I owe this reference to G. Fowden, *The Egyptian Hermes: A Historical Approach to the Late Pagan Mind*, Cambridge: Cambridge University Press, 1986, 30. The complete dossier of texts about Plato's 'Egyptian connection' is collected in H. Dörrie & M. Baltes, *Der Platonismus in der Antike*, Band 2, Stuttgart – Bad Cannstatt 1990, 166-175, with commentary at 433-453.

[19] For a recent study see A. Kuhrt, 'Berossus' *Babyloniaka* and Seleucid Rule in Babylonia,' in A. Kuhrt & S. Sherwin-White (eds.), *Hellenism in the East: The Interaction of Greek and non-Greek Civilizations from Syria to Central Asia after Alexander*, London: Duckworth, 1987, 32-56. See also S.M. Burstein, *The Babyloniaca of Berossus*, Malibu: Undena Publications, 1978.

[20] G.E. Sterling, *Historiography and Self-Definition: Josephos, Luke-Acts, and Apologetic Historiography*, Leiden: Brill, 1992, 103-136 (103-117 on Berossus, 117-135 on Manetho). Sterling defines apologetic historiography as 'the story of a subgroup of people which deliberately hellenizes the traditions of the group in an effort to provide a self-definition within the context of the larger world.'

[21] Apart from being a historian, Berossus is also credited by some ancients with being an excellent astrologer (c.q. astronomer), but that is of doubtful credibility according to Kuhrt, 'Berossus' 36-44, against Burstein, *The Babyloniaca of Berossus* 31-32.

(*FGH* 680 F2-4).[22] Berossus claimed to have 'found' (these?) many ancient documents that had been preserved carefully (ἀναγραφὰς φυλασσομένας ἐπιμελῶς, *FGH* 680T1).[23] So the work may quite well have contained (perhaps implicitly) anti-Graeco-Egyptian polemics as far as the antiquity of Chaldaean lore and science is concerned, but we are not in a position to substantiate this claim fully.[24]

3. *Jewish Evidence*

It is time to turn to parallel Jewish traditions, which we will not discuss exhaustively, however, only some important aspects will be dealt with. The theme of antediluvian knowledge looms large in the Enochic literature.[25] In fact the whole of this literature is regarded as the embodiment of antediluvian wisdom since as the supposed source of all the information contained in these books, the antediluvian hero, Enoch, is deemed to

---

[22] Discussion of these fragments in W.G. Lambert & A.R. Millard, *Atra-Hasis: The Babylonian Story of the Flood*, Oxford: Clarendon Press, 1969, 134-137, and esp. Burstein, *The Babyloniaca of Besossus* 18-21. The passages are misunderstood in L. Ginzberg, *The Legends of the Jews*, vol. 5, Philadelphia: Jewish Publication Society, 1925, 203. The burying of all writings in Sippar is known from Berossus alone, not from other Mesopotamian sources, although a tradition concerning antediluvian inscriptions did exist, as Ashurbanipal's remark quoted at the beginning proves. It should be noted that the Mesopotamian counterpart of Enoch, Enmeduranki, is said to have been king of Sippar, the city of the sun, and that the 365 years that Genesis 5 claims Enoch to have lived is the number of days of the solar year; see further below in the text. See A. Jeremias, *Das Alte Testament im Lichte des Alten Orients*, Leipzig: Hinrichsche Buchhandlung, 1907, 242, but especially H.S. Kvanvig, *Roots of Apocalyptic. The Mesopotamian Background of the Enoch Figure and of the Son of Man*, Neukirchen: Neukirchener Verlag, 1988, 160-213.

[23] Syncellus adds that Berossus claims this δοξάσαι θέλων τὸ τῶν Χαλδαίων ἔθνος καὶ δεῖξαι πάντων τῶν ἐθνῶν ἀρχαιότερον (25, p. 14-15 Mosshammer). On the frequently occurring motif of the 'finding' of (heavenly) books and inscribed stelae see W. Speyer, *Bücherfunde in der Glaubenswerbung der Antike*, Göttingen: Vandenhoeck & Ruprecht, 1970; here at 114-115 a brief discussion of Berossus and some of the Jewish evidence. Adler, *Time Immemorial* 59: "The motif of stelae left for post-diluvian generations was a device commonly employed by oriental historians to explain the survival of pre-flood wisdom after the flood."

[24] Sterling, *Historiography* 116, rightly notes that in Berossus' description civilization began in Babylonia and was given to its inhabitants by means of a divine revelation (by Oannes) which was not given to the Greeks or Egyptians but only to the Babylonians. On the many traditions, especially in the Imperial period, about Chaldaeans as the teachers of humanity in general or of individual philosophers, see W.J.W. Koster, 'Chaldäer,' *Reallexikon für Antike und Christentum* 2 (1954) 1019-1020.

[25] A good survey is J. C. VanderKam, *Enoch, A Man for All Generations*, Columbia: University of South Carolina Press, 1995.

have been the only sage from before the flood who passed on his knowledge to later generations by writing it down (thus already *Jubilees* 4:17-26).[26] Although mentioned only very briefly in Genesis 5, Enoch became the central figure in several of the oldest surviving Jewish apocalypses of the pre-Christian period. As an antediluvian person who enjoyed special privileges with God (he walked with God, and he did not have to die for God took him away; Gen. 5:24), he was credited with the role of receiver of many of God's special revelations and, in a typically Greek way, with the status of 'first inventor.'[27]

One of the motifs that is prominent already in the earliest part of the Enochic Pentateuch known as *1 Enoch* (chs. 1-36, the so-called *Book of the Watchers*) is that of the activities of the Watchers, the fallen angels of Genesis 6. One of their evil deeds was that they taught humanity all kinds of magic and technology. In 7:1 we read that the angels taught women 'magical medicine, incantations, and the cutting of roots.'[28] And in 8:1-4 we read the following:

> Azazel[29] taught men to make swords, and daggers, and shields and breast-plates; and he showed them the metals of the earth and gold, how to fashion adornments and bracelets for women, and the art of making up the eyes and of beautifying the eyelids, and the most precious and choice stones, and all kinds of coloured dyes. And the world was changed by that. There arose great impiety and much fornication on the earth. They went astray, and all their ways became corrupt. (...) Baraqi'el taught them astrology, Kokavi'el the knowledge of the signs, Tami'el the observation of the stars, and Asder'el the course of the moon.[30]

In sum: the invention and teaching by the angels of metallurgy, cosmetics, magic, and astrology were the main cause of mankind's going astray.[31] Now it has to be said that in the extant versions of *1 Enoch*, the

---

[26] Cf. *Jub.* 4:21: 'He wrote down everything.' See Kvanvig, *Roots of Apocalyptic* 135-143.

[27] See G.H. Van Kooten, 'Enoch, the 'Watchers', Seth's Descendants and Abraham as Astronomers: Jewish Applications of the Greek Motif of the First Inventor (300 BCE-CE 100),' in A. Brenner & J.W. van Henten (eds.), *Recycling Biblical Figures*, Leiden: DEO Publishers, 1999, 292-316.

[28] Note that in *Jub.* 10:13-14 it is said that also Noah wrote a book with medical knowledge which he gave to his son Shem.

[29] Or: Asael, one of the leaders of the fallen angels.

[30] The text is corrupt here in many places; the Greek and Ethiopic versions (the Aramaic original is lost for the most part; see below) differ considerably, so that the translation is only an approximation, but the gist of the story is clear enough. I consulted M.A. Knibb, *The Ethiopic Book of Enoch*, 2 vols., Oxford: Clarendon Press, 1978, I 79-84; M. Black, *The Book Enoch or 1 Enoch*, Leiden: Brill, 1985, 127-128; S. Uhlig, *Das Äthiopische Henochbuch* (JSHRZ V 6), Gütersloh: Gerd Mohn, 1984, 520-522.

complete Ethiopic and the partial Greek translations, there are no references to antediluvian written documents, either on brick or on rock. But
among the Dead Sea Scrolls some Aramaic fragments with Enochic
material were found which do contain references to tablets. The fact that
these passages do not have counterparts in the versions of *1 Enoch* as we
have them has to do with the circumstance that they belong to the so-
called *Book of Giants*, a document which does belong to the Enochic
cycle, may originally even have formed part of *1 Enoch* (the Enochic
Pentateuch), but now no longer does so in the forms of the books as we
have them. Be that as it may, as the most recent editor of these fragments claims, the *Book of Giants* may have been composed during the
early 2nd century BCE in response to historiographic tendencies to
regard the giants as significant links in the spread of culture from ante-
to postdiluvian times.[32] Some of the fragments (*2Q26, 4Q203 7* B II,
4Q203 8),[33] though badly damaged, clearly refer to the washing or effac-
ing or erasing of tablets. The meaning of this is far from clear,[34] but it
suggests at least wilful destruction of information. 'If so, then it is possible that BG [= *Book of Giants*] presupposes traditions known through
Greek and Babylonian historiographical works which, from the perspectives of its author(s), are thought to espouse views about the history of
culture at the expense of an adherence to the framework of the biblical
narrative.'[35] But this remains speculative to a relatively high degree, and
we leave it therefore as it is.

In *2 Enoch* 33 we read an interesting passage about Enoch's books,
where he had written down all that God had revealed him when 'he
walked with God' (Gen. 5:24). Concerning these books God tells Enoch
that he should distribute them among his descendants and that they will

---

[31] See M.J. Davidson, *Angels at Qumran: A Comparative Study of 1 Enoch 1-36, 72-108
and Sectarian Writings from Qumran*, Sheffield: Sheffield Academic Press, 1992, 37-
53.

[32] See L.T. Stuckenbruck, *The Book of Giants from Qumran*, Tübingen: Mohr, 1997.

[33] Texts also in J.A. Fitzmyer & D.J. Harrington, *A Manual of Palestinian Aramaic Texts*,
2nd ed., Rome: Ed. Pontificio Istituto Biblico, 1994, 72-79, and F. García Martínez &
E.J.C. Tigchelaar, *The Dead Sea Scrolls Study Edition*, vol. I, Leiden: Brill, 1997, 220-
221, 399-445. Cf also J.T. Milik, *The Books of Enoch. Aramaic Fragments of Qumran
Cave IV*, Oxford: Oxford University Press, 1976, 334-335, and F. García Martínez,
Qumran and Apocalyptic, Leiden: Brill, 1992, 97-115.

[34] Even though the development of the story can be partly reconstructed with the aid of
the Manichaean Book of Giants; see J. C. Reeves, *Jewish Lore in Manichaean Cos-
mogony. Studies in the* Book of Giants *Traditions*, Cicinnati: Hebrew Union College
Press, 1992, with the many corrections by Stuckenbruck, *Book of Giants*.

[35] Stuckenbruck, *Book of Giants* 38.

not be destroyed before the end of time. 'I have commanded the seasons, so that they might preserve them so that they might not perish in the future flood that I shall bring about in your generation' (33:12). That antediluvian knowledge survives the flood is here something God himself has taken care of! The similarity with what Berossus tells us about Cronus' command to Xisutros is striking.

4. *Christian and Jewish Evidence*

The Enochic literature enjoyed a great prestige in both Jewish and Christian circles in the centuries around the turn of the era. The New Testament *Epistle of Jude* even quotes the work as Scripture (vv. 14-15).[36] And in his *De cultu feminarum* I 3, the Christian author Tertullian uses it in order to 'exploit[s] the angel story to support his belief that women's finery is to be traced back to the sinful teachings of the angels.'[37] He wants to urge Christian women to dress as modestly as possible and for that reason appeals to the book of Enoch, but he realizes that he owes his readers an explanation for that:[38]

> (1) I am aware that the Scripture of Enoch, which has assigned this role to angels, is not acceptable to some because it is not admitted in the Jewish canon. I suppose that they thought that, having been published before the flood, it could not have safely survived that world-wide calamity, which had destroyed everything. If that is their reasoning, let them bear in mind that Noah, who was the great-grandson of Enoch himself, survived the flood, and he, of course, had heard and remembered, from familial renown and hereditary tradition, about his great-grandfather's grace in the sight of God and about all his preachings, since Enoch had given no other command to Methuselah than that he should hand on the knowledge of them to posterity. There can therefore be no doubt that Noah may have succeeded in the trusteeship of his preaching; or, had it been otherwise, he would not have been silent about the plan of God, his preserver, and about the glory of his own house.

[36] The book is clearly cited here as an uncontested authority and is placed on the same level as the Old Testament prophets; see VanderKam, *Enoch* 170-171. For extensive discussion of this passage see R.J. Bauckham, *Jude, 2 Peter* (WBC 50), Waco: Word Books, 1983, 93-101; H. Paulsen, *Der zweite Petrusbrief und der Judasbrief* (KEK XII 2), Göttingen: Vandenhoeck & Ruprecht, 1992, 73-78; A. Vögtle, *Der Judasbrief, der zweite Petrusbrief* (EKK XXII), Solothurn – Neukirchen: Benziger – Neukirchener, 1994, 71-86.

[37] VanderKam, *Enoch* 174.

[38] I used the edition by M. Turcan, *Tertullien: La toilette des femmes*, Sources Chrétiennes 173, Paris: Ed. du Cerf, 1971.

(2) In case, however, that would seem less obvious, there is still another reason to warrant the authority of this Scripture: If it would have been destroyed by the violence of the flood, Noah could have restored it again by divine inspiration, just as, after the destruction of Jerusalem by the Babylonian conquest every document of the Jewish Scriptures is generally agreed to have been restored through Ezra.[39]

(3) But since in the same Scripture Enoch has also preached concerning the Lord, nothing at all must be rejected by us which pertains to us; and we read that 'every Scripture that is suitable for edification, is divinely inspired' (2 Tim. 3:16). It may later have been rejected by the Jews for exactly that reason, just like almost all other texts that speak of Christ. And it is really not surprising that they did not accept some Scriptures that have spoken of Him whom they rejected when he in person spoke in their presence. In addition to that, Enoch possesses a testimony in the apostle Jude.[40]

Some remarks are in order here. I have to leave aside the intriguing question of how at the beginning of the third century a Church Father could still regard *1 Enoch* as Holy Scripture.[41] More important for our purposes is Tertullian's argument that antediluvian literature should not necessarily be regarded as lost. This motif has older roots, of course, although the reasoning that Noah's knowledge of family traditions enabled him to restore the lost writings of his great-grandfather certainly has an air of originality (it might, however, have been based upon passages such as *1 Enoch* 68:1). Another way of solving that problem is to be found in Josephus, about a century before Tertullian. In his rendering of the book of Genesis in the *Antiquitates Judaicae*, Josephus tells us about Seth:

He strove after virtue and, being himself excellent, left descendants who imitated the same virtues. (...) They discovered the science of the heavenly bodies and their orderly arrangement. And in order that humanity might not lose their discoveries or perish before they came to be known – since Adam had predicted that there would be a destruction of the universe, at one time by a violent fire and at another time by a force with an abundance of water – they made two pillars, one of brick and the other of stones, and they described their findings on both, in order that if the brick one should be lost owing to the flood the stone one should remain and offer an opportunity to teach men what had been written on it and to

---

[39] See *4 Ezra* 14:37-50.

[40] Because Jude 14 quotes *1 Enoch*.1:9.

[41] See about that matter R. Beckwith, *The Old Testament Canon of the New Testament Church and Its Background in Early Judaism,* London: SPCK, 1985, 395-405, who points out (397) that Clement of Alexandria, a contemporary of Tertullian, also quotes *1 Enoch* as authoritative Scripture.

reveal that a pillar of brick had also been set up by them. And it remains till today in the land of Seiris (I 68-71).[42]

This is an important passage for more than one reason.[43] Discoveries pertaining to astronomy or astrology are attributed to various ante- and postdiluvian figures in early Jewish literature.[44] Especially Enoch is credited with this discovery (or rather, this knowledge is revealed to him by an angel: *1 Enoch* 72-82, *Jub.* 4:17 and Ps-Eupolemus, Fragm. 1 = Eus., *Praep. Ev.* IX 17,8-9),[45] but also Seth, Noah, Shem, and Abraham receive this honour, for instance.[46] Again it should be emphasized that, though sometimes the theoretical distinction between astronomy and astrology was indeed made, quite often the two were seen as two sides of one and the same coin, and many Jews did not feel at all embarrassed by the idea that their forefathers invented astrology, though some did

---

[42] Translation (slightly adapted) by L.H. Feldman, *Flavius Josephus. Translation and Commentary, vol. 3: Judean Antiquities 1-4*, Leiden: Brill, 2000, 24. Note that Philo too speaks about 'the constant and repeated destructions by water and fire' by reason of which the later generations did not receive from the former the memory of the order and sequence of events in the series of years (*Vit. Mos.* II 263), although this seems to be more inspired by his favourite Platonic dialogue, the *Timaeus*, than by biblical motifs.

[43] I leave aside here the topic of Adam's prediction of future events, which one finds in several other haggadic sources; see, e.g., Th. W. Franxman, *Genesis and the Jewish Antiquities of Flavius Josephus*, Rome: Biblical Institute Press, 1979, 79 with notes 33-35, where he points to b.*Avodah Zarah* 5a, *Chronicles of Jerahmeel* 24:7, and *Sefer ha-Yashar* 2:12-13.

[44] See J.H. Charlesworth, 'Jewish Interest in Astrology during the Hellenistic and Roman Period,' ANRW II 20, 2, Berlin – New York: W. de Gruyter, 1987, 926-950, and esp. K. von Stuckrad, *Frömmigkeit und Wissenschaft: Astrologie in Tanach, Qumran und frührabbinischer Literatur*, Frankfurt etc.: Peter Lang, 1996, 105-191.

[45] On the ambiguous status of astronomy/astrology in *1 Enoch* – bad when revealed to mankind by the Watchers but good when revealed by angels to Enoch – see Van Kooten, 'Enoch' 297-301.

[46] References in Charlesworth, 'Jewish Interest' and in my essay, 'Jewish Self-Definition' 97-99. Cf. also the anonymous tradition in a medieval astrological manuscript edited by F. Boll in *Catalogus Codicum Astrologorum Graecorum*, vol. VII, Brussel: Lamertin, 1980, 87: Λόγος ᾄδεται ἐξ ἀρχῆς ὅτι αἱ τῶν ἀστέρων πλοκαὶ καὶ ὀνομασίαι μηνῶν τε καὶ ἐνιαυτῶν καὶ εἴ τι ἄλλο ἐν τοῖς μετεώροις λεγόμενον Σὴθ ὁ τοῦ Ἀδὰμ υἱὸς ἐν πλαξὶ πετρίναις Ἑβραικῇ διαλέκτῳ ἐνεγράψατο παρὰ θείου ἀγγέλου διδαχθείς, εἶτα μετὰ τὴν τῶν γλωσσῶν διαίρεσιν Ἄμμων ὁ Ἕλλην ἐμήκυνε καὶ καθεξῆς ἕτεροι. λέγεται δὲ ὅτι καὶ ὁ ἕβδομος ἀπὸ Ἀδὰμ Ἐνὼχ συνέγραψε τὴν μέλλουσαν τοῦ θεοῦ ὀργὴν ἐν πλαξὶ λιθίναις Ἑβραικῇ διαλέκτῳ. καὶ μετὰ τὸν κατακλυσμὸν εὑρέθησαν ἐκ τούτων ἐν ὄρει τινὶ καὶ μετὰ καιροὺς μετεκομίσθησαν ἐν Παλαιστίνῃ. Here we see different traditions being recorded side by side. On the possible Enochic origins of the traditions about the two tablets see A.A. Orlov, 'Overshadowed by Enoch's Greatness: "Two Tablet" Traditions from the *Book of Giants* to *Palaea Historica*,' *Journal for the Study of Judaism* 32 (2001) 137-158.

(see *Orac. Sib.* III 221-229!). Be that as it may, in order to prevent their precious discoveries from getting lost for humanity, the descendants of Seth inscribed their wisdom on two pillars of different materials, one waterproof and the other fireproof, the former still preserved in a mysterious country in the Far East.[47] The two different materials are clearly related to the two possible forms of large-scale destruction, water and fire.[48] We hear here a clear echo of the passage from Plato's *Timaeus*, quoted above, where the Egyptian priest speaks about these two forms of annihilation, as does the Egyptian Manetho somewhat later.[49] But the motif of the different materials of the pillars, or stelae, is not original with Josephus either, for we also meet it in the *Life of Adam and Eve*, and there in such a different form that neither one could have borrowed it from the other.[50] In that probably first century CE document, although only in its Latin version which is widely different from the (original) Greek,[51] we read:

> Six days after Adam died, Eve, aware that she too would die, gathered all her sons and daughters, Seth with thirty brothers and thirty sisters, and Eve said to them all: 'Listen to me, my children, and I will tell you that I and your father transgressed the command of God, and the archangel Michael said to us, "Because of your transgressions, our Lord will bring over your race the wrath of his judgement, first by water and then by fire; by these two the Lord will judge the whole human race. But listen to me, my children, make now tablets of stone and other tablets of clay and write upon them all my life and your father's which you have heard and seen from us. If he [God] should judge our race by water, the tablets of earth will dissolve but the tablets of stone will remain; if, however, he should judge our race by fire, the tablets of stone will break up but those of clay will be thoroughly baked.'

---

[47] The location of Seiris is unknown, but it is probably someplace in the Far East; see G.J. Reinink, 'Das Land "Seiris" (Shir) und das Volk der Serer in jüdischen und christlichen Traditionen,' *Journal for the Study of Judaism* 6 (1975) 72-85.

[48] On these two forms of world-wide destruction see P. W. van der Horst, '"The Elements Will Be Dissolved With Fire." The Idea of Cosmic Conflagration in Hellenism, Ancient Judaism, and Early Christianity,' in my *Hellenism – Judaism – Christianity* 271-292, and the instructive note 166 in Feldman's commentary on Josephus *ad loc.*

[49] And we are also reminded of Pseudo-Manetho as quoted earlier in the text above.

[50] See M.D. Johnson, 'Life of Adam and Eve,' in J.H. Charlesworth (ed.), *The Old Testament Pseudepigrapha* II, Garden City: Doubleday, 1985, 292 n. a.

[51] All ancient versions are now easily available in G.A. Anderson & M.E. Stone (edd.), *A Synopsis of the Books of Adam and Eve*, Atlanta: Scholars Press, 1999. For valuable discussions of the many textual problems and the dating of this document see M.E. Stone, *A History of the Literature of Adam and Eve*, Atlanta: Scholars Press, 1992, and M. de Jonge & J. Tromp, *The Life of Adam and Eve*, Sheffield: Sheffield Academic Press, 1997.

After saying that Eve dies, the author ends with the remark, 'Then Seth made the tablets' (51).[52] Most striking here is the fact that the antediluvian information inscribed on the tablets is *not* about 'scientific' (astrological) lore but the story of the lives of the protoplasts, from which posterity is evidently supposed to learn a warning lesson. As we have seen, in Jewish tradition the antediluvian information is sometimes something to be evaluated negatively, since it derives from the wicked angels, or their offspring, who brought violence and idolatry into the world. We find that as early as the book of *Jubilees*.

Jubilees, a second cent. BCE retelling of Genesis and Exodus, is – perhaps apart from the *Book of Giants* – the earliest extant witness to the motif of the antediluvian stelae in Jewish literature. In *Jub.* 8:1-4 it is narrated that one of Seth's postdiluvian descendants, Arpachshad, had a son whom he named Cainan.[53] Of this Cainan the author writes:

> He went forth in order that he might seek a place where he could build a city. And he found a text which his ancestors had engraved on stone. And he read what was in it, and he transcribed it. And he sinned because of what was in it, since there was in it the teaching of the Watchers by which they used to observe the omens of the sun and moon and stars within all the signs of heaven.[54] And he copied it down, but he did not speak about it because he feared to tell Noah about it lest he be angry with him because of it.

Here there can be no doubt that the contents of the antediluvian tablets are seen as nefarious. It is highly probable that here, as elsewhere, the book of *Jubilees* draws upon the earlier parts of the Enochic Pentateuch, especially chapters 1-36, the *Book of the Watchers*.[55] It is the evil teachings of the fallen angels, described in detail in *1 Enoch* 6-11, that is referred to here. But there is a striking contrast with Josephus and the

[52] In many medieval manuscripts one finds a variety of additions, most of them to the effect that it was only Solomon who recovered the tablets inscribed by Seth. For some versions of this Latin legend see W. Meyer, 'Vita Adae et Evae,' *Abhandlungen der königlichen bayerischen Akademie der Wissenschaften, Philosophisch-philologische Klasse* 14:3 (München 1878), 244; and J.H. Mozley, 'The Vita Adae,' *Journal of Theological Studies* 30 (1929) 144-149.

[53] In the Hebrew Bible Cainan occurs only as the son of Enosh (Gen. 5:9), but the Septuagint makes him a son of Arpachshad (Gen. 11:12-13).

[54] The later rabbinic commentary on Genesis also mentions astrology/astronomy as the main activity of the antediluvian fallen angels, and the immoral behavior that was its consequence (*Bereshit Rabba* XXVI 5). Note that according to an anonymous tradition preserved in several Byzantine chronographers, Cainan found the *graphê* of the Giants hidden in a field; W. Speyer, 'Giganten,' *RAC* 10 (1978) 1263-1264.

[55] See the various contributions to the volume edited by M. Albani e.a., *Studies in the Book of Jubilees*, Tübingen: Mohr, 1997; also A.F.J. Klijn, *Seth in Jewish, Christian and Gnostic Literature*, Leiden: Brill, 1977, 13-16.

Life of Adam and Eve as far as the moral quality of the text on the pillars or stone slabs is concerned: In Josephus it is the valuable discoveries of the science of astronomy or astrology by Seth's descendants that had to be preserved for posterity; in the *Life of Adam and Eve* it is the valuable story of paradise and why the protoplasts were expelled from it; but in *Jubilees* it is the obnoxious teaching of the Watchers (i.e. astrology) that Cainan found, even though it is also explicitly stated that these teachings were inscribed by his otherwise good ancestors, Seth and Arpachshad![56] Apparently there is good and bad antediluvian knowledge, or one and the same body of antediluvian knowledge is assessed as bad by the one and as good by the other.[57] That the story of Adam and Eve in and outside paradise would be judged positively stands to reason. But that the records of the discoveries of Seth and his descendants would evoke such contrary reactions seems confusing.

Part of this confusion is caused by the biblical text itself. On the one hand the famous passage of Gen. 6:1-4 clearly implies that the behavior of the angels (there called 'sons of God') is immoral: they had sex with earthly women simply because they found them pretty, and for that reason God speaks words that can only be read as depreciative. On the other hand, at the end of the passage the offspring of these immoral unions, the giants, are called 'men of renown' (6:4), which seems to imply that they had an excellent reputation.[58] If the Bible itself seems to

---

[56] Note that in *4Q227, 2* (4QPseudo-Jubilees) it is said of Enoch that 'he wrote down everything [...] of the heavens and the paths of their armies and the months [...] so that the just would not go astray'(!). In *Jub.* 4:15 it is said that the Watchers descended upon the earth 'that they should instruct the children of men and do judgement and uprightness on the earth.' It is only after they begin to have sexual intercourse with women that the teaching of the angels changes from good to bad, at least this seems implied by *Jubilees*.

[57] Cf. Van Kooten, 'Enoch' 301 (on *Jubilees*): "There seems to have been a shift in the contents of the astronomical teachings by the Watchers after their transgression, since otherwise – if these had not differed from the astronomy they originally revealed to Enoch – their writings would not have had to be forbidden." He plausibly suggests that the difference between the two forms of astronomy is to be found in the divergences between Enochic and non-Enochic calendar systems (306, on *1 Enoch*): "Enoch is the first inventor of the 'right astronomy' whereas the angelic Watchers were the first to teach the aberrant type of astronomy, leading to eschatological destruction." See on this matter also M. Küchler, *Schweigen, Schmuck und Schleier. Drei neutestamentliche Vorschriften zur Verdrängung der Frauen auf dem Hintergrund einer frauenfeindlichen Exegese des Alten Testaments im antiken Judentum*, Göttingen: Vandenhoeck, 1986, 432-435. Also Kvanvig, *Roots of Apocalyptic* 146-147.

[58] For *shem* in the sense of 'good reputation' or 'fame' see Köhler-Baumgartner's lexicon s.v. On the merging of two traditions that has brought about this confusion in the biblical text see C. Westermann, *Genesis 1-11* (BKAT I 1), Neukirchen: Neukirchener Verlag, 1976, 491-517.

be equivocal about the ethical quality of the generations immediately preceding the flood, no wonder that the early interpreters could go either way: antediluvian documents contained either valuable or harmful information. Those who chose the latter road felt no qualms in contradicting the Bible by picturing the 'men of renown' as 'a race of tyrannical and oppressive creatures who terrorize humanity, deplete the earth's resources, and spread violence and death everywhere.'[59] But when we look at the *Sibylline Oracles*, we see that the Watchers are depicted as good and their teachings as beneficial. We read there (*Or. Sib.* I 89-96):

> They were concerned with fair deeds, noble pursuits, proud honour, and solid wisdom. They practiced skills of all kinds, discovering inventions as a result of their needs. One discovered how to till the earth by plows, another carpentry, another was concerned with sailing, another astronomy and divination by birds, another medicine, again another magic.

That they are later (in 101-103) said to end up, nevertheless, in Gehenna, – unexplained though it goes[60] – hardly detracts from the fact that the Watchers are depicted here mainly as inventors of arts that are necessary for the survival of humanity ('fair deeds and noble pursuits').[61] In the same vein the second century BCE (Samaritan?) author called Pseudo-Eupolemus (Fragm. 1 = *PE* IX 17,1-9) seems to imply that the giants were *saved* from the deluge (διασωθέντες ἐκ τοῦ κατακλυσμοῦ) and thus in a position to hand down the astrological knowledge discovered by Enoch to Abraham, who in his turn passed it on to other peoples; in the second fragment (*PE* IX 18,2) Abraham's lineage is even explicitly derived from the giants![62] These fragments link Abraham *and* the giants

---

[59] J. L. Kugel, *Traditions of the Bible. A Guide to the Bible As It Was at the Start of the Common Era*, Cambridge MA – London: Harvard University Press, 1998, 180 n. 8. At pp. 201-203 Kugel deals with traditions about the passing on of forbidden knowledge by the angels.

[60] Does it have to do with the tradition also found in Josephus, *Ant. Jud.* I 72, about the degeneration of Seth's later descendants, who are said to have 'changed from their ancestral habits for the worse'? See Feldman's valuable note *ad loc.*

[61] VanderKam, *Enoch, a Man for All Generations* 147-148. Note that according to *Jub.* 5:6 it is God himself who sent the angels to the earth, whereas *1 Enoch* 6 has the angels descend out of heaven in an act of rebellion against God. On this difference see J.T.A.G.M. van Ruiten, 'The Interpretation of the Flood Story in the Book of Jubilees,' in F. García Martínez & G.P. Luttikhuizen (edd.), *Interpretations of the Flood*, Leiden: Brill, 1999, 82.

[62] Texts in C.R. Holladay, *Fragmentrs from Hellenistic Jewish Authors,* vol. 1, Chico: Scholars Press, 1983, 157-187. On giants being saved from the flood see P.W. van der Horst 'Nimrod After the Bible,' in my *Essays on the Jewish World of Early Christianity*, Göttingen: Vandenhoeck, 1990, 220-232. On Abraham as astrologer in Ps-Eupolemus and elsewhere see M. Küchler, *Frühjüdische Weisheitstraditionen*, Göttingen:

to the transmission of Babylonian astrology. In contradistinction to the *Book of the Watchers*, this author 'does not demonstrate any effort to draw a qualitative distinction between the angels who instructed Enoch in the sciences and the giants who learned this from Enoch.'[63] Here again we see a positive depiction of the knowledge of the 'sons of God' and their offspring.[64] In order to understand this better, one has to keep in mind that, in some strands of post-biblical Jewish and Christian tradition, the 'sons of God' in Gen. 6:2 were equated with the sons of Seth. This had to do with the fact that according to some interpreters the descendants of the righteous Seth, who were of course righteous and good people, 'men of renown'(!), deserved to be called 'sons of God' (quite unlike the Cainites).[65] So there was more than one reason for differences in Jewish opinions about the moral nature of antediluvian wisdom: it depended upon the identification of the sons of God and their offspring in Gen. 6:1-4, upon the identification of the sort of knowledge that was discovered or passed on in these generations preceding the flood, upon one's assessment of astrology, and upon whether or not one was able to distinguish between astrology (which was 'officially' a sinful activity) and astronomy (which was necessary if one wanted to be strict in calendrical matters).

Though it is outside the scope of this paper to deal with the Christian 'Wirkungsgeschichte' of the motif, let me finally pay brief attention to a quite special application of the motif of the evil nature of antediluvian knowledge, which is Christian but probably of Jewish origin. We find it in a contemporary of Tertullian, this time a Greek author, the otherwise unknown Hermias, who wrote his *Irrisio gentilium philosophorum* at the

Vandenhoeck, 1979, 119-121; A.J. Droge, *Homer or Moses: Early Christian Interpretations of the History of Culture*, Tübingen: Mohr, 1989, 19-25; and P. Pilhofer, *Presbyteron Kreitton. Das Altersbeweis der jüdischen und christlichen Apologeten und seine Vorgeschichte*, Tübingen: Mohr, 1990, 149-153.

[63] Stuckenbruck, *Book of Giants* 37. On the rivalry between Enochic and Mosaic wisdom see G.W.E. Nickelsburg, 'Enochic Wisdom: An Alternative to the Mosaic Torah?,' in J. Magness & S. Gitin (edd.), *Hesed Ve-Emet. Studies in Honor of Ernest S. Frerichs*, Atlanta: Scholars Press, 1998, 123-132.

[64] Stuckenbruck, *Book of Giants* 35: 'The surviving *gigantes* become therein an important link in the introduction of culture and are not singled out for overt vilification.' Cf. M. Hengel, *Judaism and Hellenism*, London: SCM Press, 1974, 243: 'What other Jewish circles regarded as a positive wisdom tradition deriving from Seth, was rejected in the Essene movement as demonic knowledge coming from the betrayal of divine secrets by fallen angels, and it may be supposed that in fact this included all the wisdom of the pagans and the refined culture of the Hellenistic period.'

[65] See Adler, *Time Immemorial* 113-122, and Kugel, *Traditions* 209-210, for references.

beginning of the third century CE.[66] From beginning to end this short treatise is nothing but a sustained satirical attack on Greek philosophers. He accuses them of inconsistency, lack of clarity, sensationalism, boasting etc. But it is already in the opening paragraph (§1) that one short sentence reveals what is at the back of his mind: 'I think that it [this wisdom] has its origin in the apostasy of the angels' (δοκεῖ γάρ μοι τὴν ἀρχὴν εἰληφέναι ἀπὸ τῆς τῶν ἀγγέλων ἀποστασίας). This is new and unique in the history of the motif of antediluvian knowledge: it is not only astrology, the art of weapon-making and cosmetics that mankind learnt from the fallen angels, the whole of Greek philosophy has the same origin. Greek philosophy has very old roots indeed, but these are demonic![67]

5. Conclusion

We have come a long way, from the mid-7th century BCE Assyrian king Ashurbanipal to early third century CE Christian writers such as Tertullian and Hermias.[68] There seems to be no unifying thread that connects all the traditions apart from the claim to antiquity for the knowledge or wisdom one professes to have. But yet a line of development is traceable. That line begins in Mesopotamia, where after the coming into being of stories about a worldwide flood and antediluvian kings and their sages[69] in the early second millennium BCE,[70] speculations about

---

[66] The Greek title is Διασυρμὸς τῶν ἔξω φιλοσόφων = 'ridicule of the outside [= non-Christian] philosophers.' I used the Sources Chrétiennes edition by R.P.C. Hanson & D. Joussot, *Hermias: Satire des philosophes païens*, Paris: Ed. du Cerf, 1993. I published an annotated Dutch translation of this treatise in my book *Mozes – Plato – Jezus: Studies over de wereld van het vroege christendom*, Amsterdam: Prometheus, 2000, 109-119, with notes at 240-242.

[67] See R. Bauckham, 'The Fall of the Angels as the Source of Philosophy in Hermias and Clement of Alexandria,' *Vigiliae Christianae* 39 (1985) 313-330.

[68] I leave out of account not only the later history of the motif in Christian literature (for instance, in the Byzantine chronographers, on which see Adler, *Time Immemorial*), but also Gnostic literature. See, for example *The Three Stelae of Seth* = Nag Hammadi Codex VII 5 (B. Layton, *The Gnostic Scriptures*, Garden City: Doubleday, 1987, 149-158). Many more references in J.C. VanderKam, '1 Enoch, Enochic Motifs, and Enoch in Early Christian Literature,' in J.C. VanderKam & W. Adler (edd.), *The Jewish Apocalyptic Heritage in Early Christianity*, Assen: Van Gorcum – Minneapolis: Fortress, 1996, 33-101 (70-76 on Gnostic literature).

[69] Foremost among them Enmeduranki, the seventh in the king-list (cf. Jude 14!), who, together with his *apkallu* (sage) Utu'abzu, is the Sumerian equivalent of Enoch; see the informative discussion by J.C. VanderKam, *Enoch and the Growth of an Apocalyptic Tradition*, Washington: Catholic Biblical Association of America, 1984, 33-51,

the nature of their wisdom began to develop long before the Hellenistic period, as Ashurbanipal's remark demonstrates. When in Hellenistic and Roman times the meeting of cultures is more intensified and people(s) are able to exchange ideas more easily, the rivalry between Babylonia and Egypt about the antiquity of their respective civilizations begins to play a significant role. 'Egypt' had already played its trump card as a country never to be threatened by a deluge in Plato's *Timaeus*. Babylonia now claimed for that very reason to possess antediluvian inscriptions. The Jews then joined the debate, they too claiming antediluvian traditions in their wish to prove that Jewish culture is older than Greek culture,[71] but since the biblical story ties the flood to the motif of the wickedness of mankind, some of these traditions tend to be regarded as very bad and connected with idolatry and violence. Others, however, having a less negative image of the 'sons of God' in Gen. 6:1-4, or of the giants, or of their cultural achievements – *i.e.*, by and large, the Hellenistic cultural achievements! – tend to see this antediluvian knowledge as worthwhile. And in ancient Christianity, of which we have examined only two early witnesses, we saw that on the one hand even the prestigious philosophy of the Greeks was declared to be antediluvian wisdom, but of the worst possible sort, while on the other hand the wisdom of the antediluvian sage *par excellence*, Enoch, was still deemed good and authoritative enough to be used for the purpose of compelling women to dress with the greatest possible modesty.[72]

---

and Lambert, 'Enmeduranki' (see note 2 above). Lambert (126-127) also quotes a Babylonian text in which a king of the last quarter of the 12th century BCE calls himself 'distant scion of kingship, seed preserved *from before the flood*, offspring of Enmeduranki, king of Sippar, who set up the pure bowl and the cedarwood rod [divinatory activities], who sat in the presence of Shamash and Adad, the divine adjudicators.' On antediluvian kings and sages in Mesopotamian literature see esp. Kvanvig, *Roots of Apocalyptic* 160-213.

[70] See for this dating Lambert-Millard, *Atra-hasis* 139.

[71] I do not imply here that the Jews borrowed the motif of antediluvian wisdom from the Greeks (though that cannot be entirely excluded); they may well have taken it over from the Babylonians.

[72] I owe thanks to my colleagues Bob Becking and Marten Stol for some valuable suggestions.

9. *SORTES*: SACRED BOOKS AS INSTANT ORACLES IN LATE ANTIQUITY

Introduction

Divination was an important and integral element in all ancient religions. If we limit ourselves to the Greek and Roman world, the range of possibilities that the art of prognostication offered to persons who wanted to know what the gods had in store for them or demanded from them, was immense. In the official and in the private sphere there was a bewildering variety of choices. One could resort to official oracles, to interpreters of dreams, to astrologers, to augurers (who practiced divination on the basis of the flight or the sound of birds), to haruspices (interpreters of the entrails of a victim offered in sacrifice), even to persons who had mastered the details of hepatoscopy (the specialized inspection of the liver of the sacrificial animal) or of teratology (the interpretation of *monstra*), to *engastrimythoi* (channellers, or persons possessed by a divine mantic spirit that resided in their body); further there was iatromancy (obtaining medical advice via incubation), necromancy (consulting the dead), lekanomancy (looking into a dish), catoptromancy (looking into a mirror), alektryonomancy (observing the behaviour of sacred chicken), chiromancy (divination by palmistry), geomancy (divination by earth), to hydromancy (divination by water), aëromancy (divination by air), pyromancy (divination by fire), libanomancy (observing the direction of the smoke of incense), aleuromancy (divination from flour), oöscopy (divination from eggs), omoplatoscopy (observing the shoulder blades of sacrificial animals), sphondylomancy (divination from the movements of a spindle), coscinomancy (divination by means of a sieve), rhabdomancy (divination by a wand), cledonomancy (the interpretation of auditive omens, e.g. sneezing and casual remarks), and cleromancy (prognostication, or rather problem-solving, by means of the drawing of lots [*sortilegium*] or the casting of dice [astragalomancy] or other randomizing practices). And one could extend the list almost *ad libitum*.[1]

---

[1] The basic work is still A. Bouché-Leclercq, *Histoire de la divination dans l'antiquité* (4 vols., Paris 1879-1882). For a concise but convenient and up-to-date summary of the evidence with bibliography see J. N. Bremmer, "Divination," *Der Neue Pauly* 3 (1997)

In this paper I want to focus on one of the varieties of the last-mentioned form of divination, cleromancy. There were various forms of lot oracles, and because they were so simple to operate, they became one of the most important kinds of prognostication available in the ancient world. We will now discuss a specific variety, namely the art of acquiring knowledge of the will of the gods or a god by means of Sacred Books, not by reading them as texts, but by consulting them as lot oracles, either by opening at random a copy of these books and interpreting as prophetic the first line upon which the eye settled, or by randomly choosing one of several slips upon which verses from these books were written.[2]

Jewish evidence

The concept of Sacred Books was not as widespread in antiquity as one might be inclined to think. The Greeks and Romans did without them for the most part of their religious history – at least before the Hellenistic period – although there were some exceptions in some circles (Orphics);[3] the Jewish people did not have Sacred Books till far into their national history – it was only after the 6th century BCE Babylonian exile that the Pentateuch (Torah) was given its present shape and began to gain canonical status; the Christians of course had their Sacred Books from the beginning[4] in the form of the Jewish Bible (in Greek), and in the course of the first three centuries of its development the church also gradually bestowed canonical status upon the Christian New Testament. The bestowing of canonical status and the attribution

---

709-714. Though not arranged systematically, one of the most useful and learned works of our century pertinent to our subject is A.S. Pease, *M. Tulli Ciceronis de divinatione libri duo* (Darmstadt 1963 = Urbana 1923); at pp. 72-74 of this volume one finds an exposition of cleromancy [the subject of this paper] that is at the same time the most concise and one of the most informative available to date. The most recent discussion of lot oracles is D. Potter, *Prophets and Emperors. Human and Divine Authority from Augustus to Theodosius* (Cambridge, MA – London 1994) 23-29. For older treatments see e.g. P. Amandry, *La mantique apollinienne à Delphes* (Paris 1950) 25-36 and 183-187.

[2] Still one of the the the most comprehensive studies of the subject is J. Bolte, "Zur Geschichte der Losbücher," in idem (ed.), *Georg Wickrams Werke*, vol. 4 (Tübingen 1903) 276-348, esp. 278-308. See further the valuable bibliographical survey in the Appendix to T. C. Skeat, "An Early Mediaeval 'Book of Fate': The Sortes XII Patriarcharum," *Mediaeval and Renaissance Studies* 3 (1954) 41-54, at pp. 51-54.

[3] See C. Colpe, "Heilige Schriften," *RAC* 14 (1988) 197-198.

[4] Colpe, *ibid.* 208: "Das Christentum ist von Anfang an Schrift- oder Buchreligion gewesen."

of holiness mostly go hand in hand.[5] For instance, the increasing centrality of the Torah in Judaism in the post-exilic period (after 538 BCE), certainly after and due to the reforms by Ezra (5th-4th cent.), led to a heightened awareness of the Torah's holiness. In the Hebrew Bible, the Torah itself is not yet adorned with the epithet 'holy.' We see this starting to happen only in the Hellenistic period. In the second half of the second century BCE Pseudo-Aristeas, the author of a pseudonymous work on the origin of the Septuagint (the Greek translation of the Hebrew Bible), is the first to call the Torah 'holy' and 'divine' (*hagnos, theios*).[6] Thus he reports that the Ptolemaic king of Egypt prostrates himself in adoration of the first Torah scroll in Greek and speaks of the oracles of God, for which he thanks God (§177).[7] Also such widely different writings as *Jubilees*, *4 Ezra*, various documents from Qumran,[8] and authors like Philo and Josephus emphasize the holiness of the Torah on account of its divine origin. Not surprisingly, inspiration theories on the genesis of this Holy Scripture soon make their appearance.[9] Whether or not one is happy with the term 'religion of the book,' if this term indicates that a holy book has become the central locus of divine revelation in a religion, it certainly seems to apply to Second Temple Judaism.[10] It is probably no coincidence that the first attestations of the existence of synagogues date precisely from the period in which for the first time the Torah is called a holy and divine book.[11] And it is in exactly the same period that we also see the beginnings of the use of the Torah as an oracle book.

[5] Colpe, *ibid.* 205: "Die Kanonizität, wie immer sie zustande kam, ist hier (…) deshalb zu erwähnen, weil offenbar erst über sie diese Schriften 'heilige' wurden."
[6] See *Letter of Aristeas* 3, 5, 31, 45.
[7] For this and the following, see O. Wischmeyer, "Das Heilige Buch im Judentum des Zweiten Tempels," *ZNW* 86 (1995) 218-242. For the typology of the holy book in antiquity in general, see e.g. J. Leipoldt & S. Morenz, *Heilige Schriften* (Leipzig 1953) and W. Speyer, "Das Buch als magisch-religiöser Kraftträger im griechischen und römischen Altertum," in his *Religionsgeschichtliche Studien* (Hildesheim 1995) 28-55.
[8] See Wischmeyer, "Das Heilige Buch" 229-233. Cf. also Paul in *Romans* 7:12: the Law is holy.
[9] See e.g. H. Burkhardt, *Die Inspiration Heiliger Schriften bei Philo* (Giessen-Basel 1988); further the references *s.v.* 'inspiration' in the Index (p. 791) of M. Sæbø (ed.), *Hebrew Bible / Old Testament. The History of Its Interpretation*, vol. I,1 (Göttingen 1996).
[10] See the important article by B. Lang, "Buchreligion," in H. Cancik *et al.* (eds.), *Handbuch religionswissenschaftlicher Grundbegriffe* II (Stuttgart 1990) 143-165.
[11] See for the connection between synagogue and holiness of the Torah P. W. van der Horst, "Was the Synagogue a Place of Sabbath Worship Before 70?" (elsewhere in this volume).

Let me give two examples: *1 Maccabees* 3:48 and *2 Maccabees*
8:23.[12] In the first passage we read:

> And they opened (unrolled) the book of the Law to inquire into those mat-
> ters about which the gentiles consulted the likenesses of their idols (καὶ
> ἐξεπέτασαν τὸ βιβλίον τοῦ νόμου περὶ ὧν ἐξηρεύνων τὰ ἔθνη τὰ
> ὁμοιώματα τῶν εἰδώλων αὐτῶν).[13]

The context is as follows: In the middle of the sixties of the second
century BCE the Seleucid king Antiochus IV tried to enforce a hellenization of the Jewish cult in the Jerusalem temple. The Jewish opposition was organised by the priest Mattathias and his five sons, later
known as the Maccabees. They were confronted by a huge military
power and faced fearful and overwhelming odds. The Jewish army
fasted and prayed. Just before the beginning of the decisive battle they
consulted the book of the Law. In the same way in which the gentiles by
various means of divination tried to receive a verdict from their gods
about the outcome of their enterprises, the Jews opened the Torah scroll
at random in the hope that the first line their eyes hit upon would instruct
them about what God had in store for them or expected them to do.
What in former times had been the role of a prophet was now taken over

---

[12] I follow here Wischmeyer's convincing interpretation of both passages in *Maccabees*
("Das Heilige Buch" 226-7). For other views, see the commentaries of J.A. Goldstein
ad locc. (see next note).

[13] Cf. K.-D. Schunck, *1. Makkabäerbuch* (JSHRZ I 4; Gütersloh 1980) 312: "Dann roll-
ten sie das Buch des Gesetzes auf – in der gleichen Absicht, in der die Heiden die
Bilder ihrer Götzen befragen" (note a, *ad locum*: "Gemeint ist ein Öffnen des Buches
des Gesetzes aufs Geratewohl, um aus der dabei aufgeschlagenen Textstelle ein Gotte-
santwort über den Ausgang des geplanten Kampfes zu erhalten. Analog befragten die
anderen Völker ihre Götter bzw. deren Abbilder"). For the translation problems here
see the extensive discussion by F.-M. Abel, *Les Livres des Maccabées* (Paris 1949) 69-
70, who concludes: "περὶ ὧν se rapporte non à βιβλίον mais au but de l'action du
verbe susdit, étant une construction elliptique fondée sur l'omission de la préposition
répétée et de l'antecédent du relatif (KG II §451,4; §555,2) équivalente de περὶ
[τούτων περὶ] ὧν, et en vertu de la relation la formule sert à marquer également l'ob-
jet *circa quod* du verbe suivant. (…) Le livre est ouvert pour être lu (v. II Macc. 8,23)
devant les assistants. Dans l'incertitude présente on a besoin d'un conseil d'en haut. Le
rôle de médiateur est tenu non plus par un prophète mais par le livre de la Loi." The
reference "KG II" is to R. Kühner & B. Gerth, *Grammatik der griechischen Sprache
II: Satzlehre* (Hannover-Leipzig 1898; repr. Darmstadt 1966).
The interpretation by J.A. Goldstein, *1 Maccabees* (Garden City 1976) 256, who translates: "They spread open the scroll of the Torah at the passages where the gentiles
sought to find analogies to their idols," and who defends this translation by stating that
"Antiochus IV attempted to use the Torah to prove that illicit 'pagan' rites and deities
belonged in the religion of Israel" (261-262), does not make sense in this context. See
also his *II Maccabees* (Garden City 1983).

by the Law scroll.[14] Whatever the historicity of the story, at any rate it is clear that in the final quarter of the second century BCE a Jewish author presented the Torah scroll as a book that could be consulted as an oracle by opening it at random. Of course, the Jews won the battle.

In *2 Macc.* 8:23 (written somewhat later than *1 Maccabees* but using the second century BCE author Jason of Cyrene as his main source)[15] we read why they won, in a different version of the same story:

> He [*i.e.* Judas the Maccabee] cast a glance into the Holy Book and gave as watchword, 'The help of God.' Then, leading the first division himself, he joined battle with Nicanor [= the Seleucid general] (παραναγνοὺς τὴν ἱερὰν βίβλον καὶ δοὺς σύνθημα θεοῦ βοηθείας τῆς πρώτης σπείρης αὐτὸς προηγούμενος συνέβαλε τῷ Νικάνορι).[16]

Now we do not find the expression 'help of God' anywhere in the Torah, but the motif of God's help is common enough in the Hebrew Bible and, moreover, unlike *1 Macc.* 3:48, the text does not state that they read from the book of the Law (Torah) but from the Holy Book, which may also imply the Prophets or the Psalms.[17] Here again a random opening of canonical books provides the leader of the resistance army with the clue to what is going to happen: God will help them in the battle.

This is new in the history of the Jewish religion. Whereas in previous centuries, especially in the pre-exilic period, it was the prophets or some form of oracular device called the Urim and the Tummim (probably sacred dice with 'yes' and 'no' answers) that the Israelites turned to in order to consult God,[18] in the Hellenistic period it was the divinely inspired sacred book(s), which were coming more and more to be regarded as the repository of all wisdom, that they took recourse to. It was this period in which Judaism developed slowly but definitely into a

---

[14] See J.T. Nelis, *1 Makkabeeën* (Roermond 1972) 106.

[15] For discussion and extensive bibliography of this author see Martin Goodman in E. Schürer, *The History of the Jewish People in the Age of Jesus Christ*, vol. III 1 (rev. ed. by G. Vermes, F. Millar, and M. Goodman, Edinburgh 1986) 531-537.

[16] Ch. Habicht, *2. Makkabäerbuch* (JSHRZ I 3; Gütersloh 1976) 241: "Nachdem er in die Heilige Schrift Einblick genommen hatte, gab er die Parole 'Gottes Hilfe' aus und stieß, selbst an der Spitze der ersten Abteilung, mit Nikanor zusammen."

[17] Habicht, *2. Makkabäerbuch* 241 n. a *ad locum*, suggests: "Die Stelle ist Ps 3,9: τοῦ κυρίου ἡ σωτηρία. Vgl. in der 'Kriegsrolle' von Qumran 4,14 "Gottes Hilfe" als eine der Standartenaufschriften der aus der Schlacht heimkehrenden Söhnen des Lichts." In the *War Scroll* we find a whole series of short biblical expressions written on the banners of the eschatological army, among which 'help of God.'

[18] C.T. Begg, "Inquire of God," *ABD* vol. III (1992) 417-8.

'religion of the book.'[19] And it is this circumstance that made possible the development of the Torah into an oracle-book. "Überall, wo im Altertum von Heiligen Schriften (...) die Rede ist, galt das Buch als magisch-religiöser Kraftträger."[20]

We see the same phenomenon also in the rabbinic literature of the Roman and early Byzantine period, albeit there most often in the cledonomantic form of stories about biblical verses rehearsed by school-children and inquired after or overheard by rabbis. Let me quote a few examples. In the Babylonian Talmud we read in tractate *Hullin* 95b that Rav Samuel wrote letters from Babylon to Rabbi Johanan in Palestine which so impressed the latter that he decided to visit this great master there. In order to make sure that this was the right decision, he asked a child, 'What is the last biblical verse you have learned?'. The answer was from 1 Sam. 28:3: "Now Samuel was dead." Even though this was said about the biblical prophet Samuel, it was clear to Rabbi Johanan that God wanted to inform him that it no longer made sense to go to Babylon. The Talmud adds that later Rav Samuel turned out to be alive after all, but that God wanted to save him the hardships of the long and arduous trip! Another example is about the famous scholar Elisha ben Avuya, who became a notorious heretic and thus earned the nickname Aher ('the other one').[21] It is again a passage in the Babylonian Talmud, tractate *Hagigah* 15a-b (in a baraitha):

> Once Aher was riding on a horse on the Sabbath, and R. Meir was walking behind him to learn Torah from his mouth. He [Aher] said to him: 'Meir, turn back, for I have already measured by the paces of my horse that thus far extends the Sabbath limit.' He replied: 'You, too, go back!' He [Aher] answered: 'Have I not told you that I have already heard from behind the Veil, "Return, ye backsliding children" [Jer. 3:22] – except Aher?' He [R. Meir] prevailed upon him and took him to a schoolhouse. He [Aher] said to a child: 'Recite for me your verse!' He [the child] answered: "There is no peace, says the Lord, unto the wicked" [Isa. 48:22]. He then took him to another schoolhouse. He [Aher] said to a child: 'Recite for me your verse!' He answered: "For though thou wash thee with nitre, and take thee much soap, yet thine iniquity is marked before me, says the Lord God"

---

[19] B. Lang, "Buchreligion" 145: "Haben sich die heiligen Schriften einmal durchgesetzt und in einem Prozess der Kanonbildung allgemeine Anerkennung gefunden und damit zur Konsolidierung einer Religionsgemeinschaft entscheidend beigetragen, dann wirken sie als erstrangige Kulturmacht in alle Lebensbereiche hinein."

[20] W. Speyer, "Das Buch als magisch-religiöser Kraftträger" 39.

[21] On Aher see E. E. Urbach, *The Sages: Their Concepts and Beliefs* (Jerusalem 1975) 465-466, and the (uncritical) collection of material in G. Bader, *The Encyclopedia of Talmudic Sages* (Northvale-London 1988) 303-310.

[Jer. 2:22]. He [R. Meir] took him to yet another schoolhouse, and he [Aher] said to a child: 'Recite for me your verse!' He answered: "And thou, that are spoiled, what doest thou, that thou clothest thyself with scarlet, that thou deckest thee with ornaments of gold, that thou enlargest thine eyes with paint? In vain doest thou make thyself fair" [Jer. 4:30]. He took him to yet another schoolhouse until he took him to thirteen schools, and all of them quoted in similar vein.[22]

Here it is not a matter of opening the Holy Book at random, but of a random questioning of children in the expectation that the first biblical verse they will quote contains God's message for that particular situation, in this case God's condemnation and rejection of Aher as an apostate.[23] But the principle is the same: Since all that God had, has, and will have to say to mankind is contained in the Torah, and since he can be trusted to guide and control this process of consultation, the answer is incontrovertible, in fact a prophecy (*nevu'ah*).[24] As one of the early rabbis (Ben Bag-Bag) is reported to have said about the Torah: "Turn it, and turn it again [*i.e.*, study it from every angle] for *everything is in it*" (Mishna, *Avoth* V 22), not only everything of the past, but also of the present and of the future.

In again another passage in the Talmud, *Ta'anith* 9a, we even see that in a discussion of the meaning of a difficult biblical verse, the rabbis ask a young boy to quote the passage in the Bible he had learnt that day in order to elucidate their verse in the light of the one quoted by the boy. And, finally, in a rabbinic commentary on the book of Esther we read that when Mordechai heard about Haman's plan to destroy the Jews in

---

[22] Cf. b.*Hullin* 95b: "Rav used to regard [the arrival of] a ferry-boat as an omen, Samuel [a passage in] a book, and R. Johanan [a verse quoted] by a child." b.*Gittin* 58a (a baraitha): "R. Joshua ben Hananiah once happened to go to the great city of Rome, and he was told there that there was in prison a child with beautiful eyes and face and curly locks. He went and stood at the doorway of the prison and said: "Who gave Jacob for a spoil and Israel to the robbers?" [Isa. 42:24]. The child answered: "Is it not the Lord, He against whom we have sinned and in whose ways they would not walk, neither were they obedient unto his law?" [ibid.]."

[23] See also *Midrash Mishle* VI 20, where Elisha (Aher) tells: "Once I entered a synagogue and saw a student sitting in front of his teacher who was making him recite Scripture. The teacher recited first, 'And to the wicked (*we-la-rasha'*) God said, "Who are you to recite My laws?"' (Ps. 50:16). Then the student repeated it, 'And to Elisha (*u-le-Elisha'*) God said, "Who are you to recite My laws, and mouth the terms of My covenant?"' When I heard that, I said, 'The decree against me has already been sealed from above.'" Translation (slightly modified) by B. L. Visotzky, *The Midrash on Proverbs* (New Haven & London 1992) 41. Here the slip of the tongue by the student is taken by Elisha as an omen.

[24] See S. Krauss, *Talmudische Archäologie*, Vol. III (Leipzig 1912) 228-229 and esp. the notes at 352-353.

the Persian empire, he saw three children coming from school and asked them to repeat the biblical verses they had just learnt. The first one recites Prov. 3:25, "Be not afraid of sudden terror, neither of the destruction of the wicked, when it comes," and also the other two quote verses which convince him that God will see to it that Mordechai's countermeasures will be succesful (*Esther Rabba* VII 13, *ad* 3:9).[25]

The next case I want to discuss is a borderline case. It could be dealt with under the chapter 'Jewish evidence' but also under 'Christian evidence.' It is the famous passage in the Gospel of Luke in which Jesus reads two verses from the prophet Isaiah (ch. 61:1-2) in the synagogue of Nazareth (*Luke* 4:16-21) and adds that 'today this scriptural passage has been fulfilled as you are listening.'[26] Pierre Courcelle illustrates his statement, 'le découverte d'un oracle par *apertio libri* existait aussi dans le monde juif,' by referring to this passage which he interprets as follows: "Luc IV, 16-22, nous montre Jésus faisant office de lecteur à la synagogue et tirant ainsi le verset d'Isaïe LXI, 1-2, que tous considèrent comme un oracle qui le concerne.'[27] If this interpretation is correct, it depends upon the degree of historicity one is willing to ascribe to this scene whether one regards this as Jewish or as Christian evidence.[28] If

---

[25] See also b. *Gittin* 56a and 68a; *Genesis Rabba* LII 4; *Midrash Tehillim* XCIII 8. Comparable in a sense is Rabbi Johanan's dictum: "If one rises early and a Scriptural verse comes to his mouth, this is a kind of minor prophecy" (b. *Berakhoth* 55b; I owe this reference to Philip Alexander). Further instances and discussion in S. Lieberman, *Hellenism in Jewish Palestine* (New York 1962, repr. of the 1950 ed.) 194-199. L. Jacobs, *The Jewish Religion. A Companion* (Oxford 1995) 132, says that in the 19th and 20th century "Lithuanian Rabbis were in the habit of using a type of bibliomancy known as 'the Lot of Elijah, Gaon of Wilna,' although there is no evidence whatsoever that the attribution is correct. So far as one can tell, the usual method was to flip through the pages of the Hebrew Bible at random and then count seven pages from the place where a particular page opened. Seven lines from the top of this page provided the verse for the divination." M. Gaster, "Divination (Jewish)," *ERE* 4 (1911) 812, is informative about Jewish bibliomancy in the early Medieval post-Talmudic period: E.g., the Bible oracle leads to the *Shimmusha Rabba* (an oracular work with selected portions of the Bible) known in the 8th or 9th century. In the work *Shimmush Tehillim* [magical use of psalms] the Book of Psalms is used as a means of divination. The latter work "achieved the distinction of being placed on the *Index Librorum Prohibitorum* of the Catholic Church" (J. Trachtenberg, *Jewish Magic and Superstition* [New York 1939] 109). For a recent edition of Genizah fragments of the *Sefer Shimmush Tehillim* see now P. Schäfer & Sh. Shaked (eds.), *Magische Texte aus der Kairoer Geniza* III (Tübingen 1999) 202-375.

[26] In the parallel versions in Matthew 13 and Mark 6 the passage under consideration does not occur.

[27] P. Courcelle, "L'enfant et les 'sorts bibliques,'" *VC* 7 (1953) 200 n. 21.

[28] The historicity of the details under discussion is a complicated matter, partly due to the fact that the other Gospel writers do not have them. See the discussion by J. Fitzmyer, *The Gospel According to Luke*, vol. I (Garden City 1981) 526-528.

the story reflects factual circumstances, it may be regarded as Jewish (Jesus was a Jew); if it is largely a Lukan fabrication, it may be regarded as Christian (Luke was a Christian). But I am afraid Pierre Courcelle reads more into this text than is warranted. Although we do not know as much about the synagogal lectionary systems in the first century as we would like, it seems hardly imaginable that a lector in a synagogue could choose his pericope at random. If the so-called *haphtarah* system (*i.e.*, the reading of a section from the Prophets after the reading from the Torah) was already in use then – which is uncertain – it would seem to be excluded, because a fixed order was followed in that system. Since it is not unlikely that there was already a fixed reading system in first century Palestine,[29] it would seem advisable not to regard this Lucan scene as evidence for Jewish *sortilegium*. Even if there would be no reason to think of an assigned passage from Isaiah, "there is no reason either to take this phrase to mean a chance happening upon ch. 61. It sounds as if Jesus deliberately sought out the passage."[30]

Christian evidence

The first unambiguous Christian evidence for *sortilegium* dates from the third quarter of the 4th century. It is from the earliest biography of a saint we have, namely Athanasius' *Life of Anthony* (ch. 2): the young Anthony had inherited rich possessions from his deceased parents, but he also wanted to dedicate his life to God.

> Pondering over these things, he entered the church and it so happened that the Gospel was being read, and he heard the Lord saying to the rich man: 'If you want to be perfect, go and sell all your possessions and give [the money] to the poor; and come, follow me, and you will have a treasure in heaven' [*Matthew* 19:21]. Anthony, as though God had put him in mind of the saints, and the passage had been read on his account, went out immediately from the church and gave the possessions of his forefathers to the villagers.

As in the rabbinic sources, here too the *sors* is received not by drawing it literally but in a cledonomantic fashion by attributing divine

---

[29] See B. Z. Wacholder's Prolegomenon to J. Mann, *The Bible as Read and Preached in the Old Synagogue*, vol. I, New York 1971 (= 1940), esp. xiii-xx. See also L. C. Crockett, "Luke iv.16-30 and the Jewish Lectionary Cycle: A Word of Caution," *Journal of Jewish Studies* 17 (1966) 13-46.

[30] Fitzmyer, *Luke* I, 532. See also the discussion by F. Bovon, *Das Evangelium nach Lukas*, vol. I (Neukirchen 1989) 211.

significance to a biblical verse heard by chance. Conversions by chance hearing of biblical passages are also told about other saints, for instance, St. Cyprian of Antioch and St. Babylas.[31]

Athanasius' account of this incident in Anthony's life became very influential as one may see already some decades later in the famous narrative of the conversion in Milan by Augustine of Hippo.[32] Augustine tells there about his agonizing wrestling with his physical desires and about the despair that this struggle created in him. 'I felt my past to have a grip on me. It uttered wretched cries: 'How long, how long is it to be?' 'Tomorrow, tomorrow.' 'Why not now? Why not an end to my impure life in this very hour?' (*Conf.* VIII 12,28).[33] Then follows the famous *tolle lege* scene of *Confessiones* VIII 12,29, situated in a garden in Milan where Augustine is with his friend Alypius:

> As I was saying this and weeping in the bitter agony of my heart, suddenly I heard a voice from the nearby house[34] chanting as if it might be a boy or a girl (I do not know which), saying and repeating over and over again, 'Pick up and read, pick up and read (*tolle lege, tolle lege*).' At once my countenance changed, and I began to think intently whether there might be some sort of children's game in which such a chant is used. But I could not remember having heard of one. I checked the flood of my tears and stood up. I interpreted it solely as a divine command to me to open the book and read the first chapter I might find. For I had heard how Anthony happened to be present at the Gospel reading and took it as an admonition addressed to himself when the words were read: 'Go, sell all you have, give to the poor, and you shall have treasure in heaven; and come, follow me' [*Matthew* 19:21]. By such an oracle he was immediately 'converted to you' [*Psalm* 50:15]. So I hurried back to the place where Alypius was sitting. There I had put down the book of the apostle when I got up. I seized it, opened it and in silence read the first passage on which my eyes lit: 'Not in riots and drunken parties, not in eroticism and indecencies, not in strife and rivalry, but put on the Lord Jesus Christ and make no provision for the

---

[31] Texts and discussion in P. Courcelle, "L'enfant" 205-206.

[32] On the influence of the *Vita Antonii* on Augustine see Courcelle, "L'enfant" 211-217; also P. Tombeur, "'Audire' dans le thème hagiographique de la conversion," *Latomus* 24 (1965) 159-165. Add to his dossier: Theodoretus of Cyrrhus, *Life of Simeon Stylites* (= *Historia religiosa* XXVI) 2.

[33] Transl. by H. Chadwick, *Saint Augustine, Confessions* (Oxford 1991) 152.

[34] The oldest manuscript has here: 'from the house of God' (*de divina domo* instead of *de vicina domo*). See the discussion by P. Courcelle, *Recherches sur les Confessions de Saint Augustin* (Paris 1968) 195, who prefers this reading (rightly?), and his *Les Confessions de Saint Augustin dans la tradition littéraire* (Paris 1963) 165-168. For the whole debate about this question see also C. Andresen in *Gnomon* 31 (1959) 350-357, and J. J. O'Donnell, *Augustine. Confessions*, (3 vols.; Oxford 1992) III 62-63 (who refers to F. Bolgiani, *Intorno al più antico codice delle 'Confessioni' di S. Agostino* (Turin 1954; non vidi).

flesh in its lust' [*Romans* 13:13-14]. I neither wished nor needed to read further. At once, with the last words of this sentence, it was as if a light of relief from all anxiety flooded into my heart. All the shadows of doubt were dispelled.[35]

In the following chapter (30) Augustine adds that his friend Alypius happened to read the immediately following words in the same epistle of Paul: 'Receive the person who is weak in faith' (*Romans* 14:1), and also applied it to himself.

Some brief remarks are in order here.[36] First of all we have several ancient reports that "les paroles prononcées au cours d'un jeu d'enfants furent regardées comme un présage de graves événements."[37] Augustine here represents himself clearly as standing in this folkloric tradition. Furthermore the very words *tolle lege* suggest an oracular procedure. *Tollere* was one of the technical terms to designate the act of drawing a lot (*sors*) that contained the response of an oracle to the person that consulted the deity. *Legere* was the act of reading the response that was written on the *sors*, and to relate it to the problem to be solved.[38] Augustine himself confirms this interpretation by using the word *oraculum* in this very passage to refer to what had happened to Anthony according to Athanasius' *Vita Antonii*.[39]

Earlier in his *Confessiones*, Augustine had indicated that his stance towards this phenomenon was not negative. In *Conf.* IV 3, 5 he records with great sympathy how Vindicianus, a former astrologer who had now become a physician, discussed with him the use of horoscopes:

---

[35] Transl. Chadwick, 152-153 (slightly modified).

[36] I leave aside here the much debated question of the historicity of Augustine's account. Much of this paragraph relies heavily on P. Courcelle, *Les Confessions de Saint Augustin dans la tradition littéraire* (Paris 1963) 127-197. The best recent treatment is O'Donnell, *Augustine. Confessions* III 59-69. See now also R. J. O'Connell, *Images of Conversion in St. Augustine's Confessions* (New York 1996).

[37] Courcelle, *Les Confessions* 138; on the mantic role of children in many of these situations see *ibid.* 137-154 (at p. 143 he refers also to *Matthew* 21:15!, as does O'Donnell, *Augustine. Confessions* III 63); *ibid.* 137: "C'est un fait très général que les Anciens prêtaient volontiers valeur d'avertissement aux paroles ou aux sons proférés par des enfants au cours de leur jeux." In *De Iside et Osiride* 14 (356E), Plutarch states that Egyptians are of the opinion that little children possess the power of prophecy, an observation also to be found in other ancient authors.

[38] See Courcelle, *Confessions* 155. For other uses of *tolle lege* or λαβὼν ἀνάγνωθι see *ibid* 156.

[39] On the literary relationship between the *Vita Antonii* and this passage in the *Confessiones* see the analysis by B. Stock, *Augustine the Reader. Meditation, Self-Knowledge, and the Ethics of Interpretation* (Cambridge MA – London 1996) 109-110. The mantic character of the whole scene was already correctly noticed by J. Balogh, "Zu Augustins 'Konfessionen'. Doppeltes Kledon in der tolle-lege-Szene," *ZNW* 25 (1926) 265-270.

I asked him why it was that many of their forecasts turn out to be correct. He replied that the best answer he could give was the power apparent in lots, a power everywhere diffused in the nature of things. So when someone happens to consult the pages of a poet whose verses and intention are concerned with a quite different subject, in a wonderful way a verse often emerges appropriate to the decision under discussion. He used to say that it was no wonder if from the human soul, by some higher instinct that does not know what goes on within itself, some utterance emerges not by art but by 'chance' which is in sympathy with the affairs or actions of the inquirer.[40]

These lines were written sometime between 396 and 400, but only slightly later he gives expression to some concern about exactly the procedure that played such a decisive role in his own conversion to an ascetic life. In a letter written in the year 400 (*Epist.* LV 20, 37) he writes:

As to those who read the future by taking at random a text from the pages of the Gospels, although it is better that they should do this than go to consult spirits of divination, nevertheless it is in my opinion a censurable practice to try to turn those divine oracles to secular business and the vanity of this life, whereas they were intended to teach us concerning a higher life.[41]

The apparent contradiction may perhaps be solved by observing that Augustine does not condemn the practice *tout court* but only its use for worldly, *i.e.* lower, purposes.[42] "This is a backhanded concession, but it

---

[40] See on this passage P. Courcelle, "Source chrétienne et allusions paiennes de l'épisode du 'Tolle, lege'," *RHPhR* 32 (1952) 192. In his *Sermones in Ps.* XXX, 2:13 (PL 36:246) Augustine says that *sortes* are not *aliquid mali*, for in *Acts* 1:26 they are used to choose a successor to Jude; cf. *Sermo* 12.4.4 (from ca. 394): multi autem modi sunt quibus nobiscum loquitur deus.... loquitur per sortem, sicut de Matthia in locum Iudae ordinando locutus est. But Jerome, in his *Comm. in Jonam* 1 (PL 25:1126), protests that it is wrong to appeal to this exceptional case in order to legitimize such a usage in general! Augustine's more lenient attitude towards this kind of superstition is also reflected in his *Tractatus in Johannem* VII 12 (CCSL 36:73) and in *De diversis quaestionibus LXXXIII* I 45 (= PL 40:29, non arte de codicibus exit saepe versus futura praenuntians). For a Syrian example of Christian magical use of the book of *Psalms* see C. Kayser, "Gebrauch von Psalmen zur Zauberei," *ZDMG* 42 (1888) 456-462.

[41] Transl. J.G. Cunningham in vol. 1 of the First Series of the *Nicene and Post-Nicene Fathers* (Peabody 1995, repr. of the 1886 ed.).

[42] Augustine even considered it permissible in case of a headache to sleep with a copy of John's Gospel under one's pillow, *but only* because he regarded that as preferable to using amulets for that purpose, which was customary (*Tractatus in Johannem* VII 12 = CCSL vol. 36, p. 73)! I owe this reference to H. Y. Gamble, *Books and Readers in the Early Church. A History of Early Christian Texts* (New Haven – London 1995) 238. See for further references P. Courcelle, "Divinatio," *RAC* 3 (1957) 1250. Thomas Aquinas too did not condemn the practice of *sortilegium*; for him it depended upon the intention with which one practiced it (*Summa* II.II.95.8); see D. Harmening, *Superstitio. Überlieferungs- und theoriegeschichtliche Untersuchungen zur kirchlich-theologischen Aberglaubensliteratur des Mittelalters* (Berlin 1979) 191-192, 194.

is there. Such a suggestion may have done much to encourage those several unashamed early medieval Christian practitioners of the 'lottery of holy things'."[43]

It was definitely not for a worldly purpose that the Holy Scriptures were consulted in this way in the incident related by Sulpicius Severus in his *Vita Sancti Martini* (early fifth century). The people want Martin to become the bisshop of Tours, but some of the other bishops are opposed to this, especially a bishop called Defensor, who, however, was reprimanded in the following way. Martin was on his way to the church.

> (5) Then it happened that the reader, whose duty it was to read the Scriptures in public that day was blocked out by the people and failed to appear. The officials fell into confusion, while they waited for one who never showed up. Then one of those standing by laid hold of the Psalter and seized upon the first verse which presented itself to him. Now the Psalm ran thus: 'Out of the mouth of babes and sucklings thou hast perfected praise because of thine enemies, that thou mightest destroy the enemy and the avenger (*defensor*).'[44] On these words being read, a shout was raised by the people and the opposite party were confounded. It was believed that this Psalm was chosen by divine ordination, that Defensor might hear a testimony to his own work, because the praise of the Lord was perfected out of the mouth of babes and sucklings in the case of Martin, while he [Defensor] was at the same time both pointed out and destroyed as an enemy."
> (IX 5-7).[45]

So God intervened in this way to make sure that Martin would be appointed bishop of Tours.

Around the middle of the fifth century Marcus Diaconus published his biography of his teacher and hero, Porphyry, bishop of Gaza. In one of the chapters of that work the empress Eudoxia orders Porphyry and other bishops to bless her newborn son, the future emperor Theodosius II. After the ritual, she asks them whether they know which decisions she has taken. Then Porphyry says that last night he had a revelatory dream in which he was standing in front of the Marneion, the famous temple of the city-god of Gaza, Marnas, and that the empress handed him the Gospel, saying, 'Take it and read.' On opening the book his eyes struck upon the passage in which Jesus says, 'You are Peter, [the Rock,] and on

---

[43] V.I.J. Flint, *The Rise of Magic in Early Medieval Europe* (Oxford 1991) 223. Cf. O'Donnell, *Augustine. Confessions* III 66: "But these texts [sc. *Conf.* IV 3, 5 and *Ep.* LV 20,37] do leave a window through which it is possible to see the use of biblical *sortes* for strictly religious purposes, not as something sought out deliberately, but accepted when it occurs as it were spontaneously."

[44] *Psalm* 8:3. The text is that of the Vetus Latina; the Vulgate has *ultor* here.

[45] Text in J. Fontaine, *Sulpice Sévère, Vie de Saint Martin* (Paris 1967-1969).

this rock I will build my church, and the gates of Hades will never con-
quer it' (*Matthew* 16:18). Thereupon the empress said: 'Peace be with
you, be strong and act like a man.' Porphyry interprets this dream as
indicating that God will support her in her enterprises, one of which is
the destruction of the Marneion (*Vita Porphyrii* 45).[46] I will not go into
the debate about whether or not this whole scene was influenced by
Augustine's *Confessiones* VIII 12, 29.[47] The main point to notice is that
here again we have a story of a decision-making process in which the
first biblical verse found after the random opening of the Bible or a biblical book tips the balance.

Biblical *sortes* also play an important role in the so-called *Historia
Francorum* by Gregory of Tours, where they are mentioned in several
passages in this work (II 37; IV 16; V 14; V 49), written in the second
half of the sixth century.[48] For instance, just before a battle against the
Gothic king Alaric, Clovis has some of his soldiers visit the church of
St. Martin at Tours in order to ask God for a sign that would indicate the
outcome of the battle. Upon entering the church they hear the cantor
singing, "You girded me with strength for the battle, you made my
assailants sink under me. You made my enemies turn their backs to me,
and those who hated me I destroyed," which is Psalm 18:41-42. And of
course Clovis won the battle (II 37). In another story Chram, the son of
king Chlotarius, visits a church in order to find out what his fate will be.
The priests put three books on the altar, the Prophets, the Apostle (= the
letters of Paul), and the Gospels. They open the books at random and
read the first passage their eyes hit upon. These three passages make
abundantly clear that Chram will soon die in a sudden and violent way,
which indeed happened (IV 16).[49]

Biblical *sortes* in a somewhat different sense were also used when
someone who was going to devote his life to God had to choose a new
name, more fitting to his new calling. The author of the *Vita antiquior*

---

[46] Text in H. Grégoire & M.H. Kugener, *Marc le Diacre: Vie de Porphyre* (Paris 1930).
On this passage and the destruction of the Marneion by Porphyry see G. Mussies,
"Marnas God of Gaza," *ANRW* II 18, 4 (Berlin-New York 1990) 2413-2457.

[47] See e.g. Grégoire & Kugener, *Marc le Diacre* 119; J. Geffcken, "Augustins Tolle-
Lege-Erlebnis," *ARW* 31 (1934) 3-5; and P. Courcelle, "L'oracle d'Apis et l'oracle du
jardin de Milan," *RHR* 139 (1951) 216-231.

[48] Text in R. Buchner, *Gregorius Turonensis: Historiarum libri decem* (Darmstadt 1990).

[49] The three passages were *Isaiah* 5:4-5; *1 Thessalonians* 5:2-3; and *Matthew* 7:26-27.
In a very similar story in V 14 the three passages are *1 Kings* 9:9; *Psalm* 73:18-19;
and *Matthew* 26:2. On the tenacity of the practice in late antique Gaul see also W. E.
Klingshirn, *Caesarius of Arles. The Making of a Christian Community in Late Antique
Gaul* (Cambridge 1994) 219-221.

sancti Danielis stylitae (end of the 5th century) tells us that Daniel's parents wanted him to live an ascetic life in God's service and wished to choose a biblical name for him. Several biblical books were put upon the altar and the young man had to pick one out at random. The volume he drew was the book of Daniel, so that became his name (ch. 3).[50]

Again another purpose is served by this method in the well-known story of Consortia. In the *Vita sanctae Consortiae* (end of 6th century?)[51] we read that the young Consortia has a fiancee whereas in fact she wants to become a nun. In order to convince her future bridegroom that it is much better not to marry at all, she proposes to open a book of the Gospels at random and look what the first verse they see has to tell them. He agrees and she acts accordingly (*revoluto codice*) and finds Matt. 10:37 *qui amat patrem aut matrem plus quam me non est me dignus*. This was of course the end of all plans for a marriage (ch. 9).[52]

In his *Lives of the Monks of Palestine* (written between 555 and 560), Cyril of Scythopolis writes about the monk Cyriacus (who lived from the middle of the fifth till the middle of the sixth century) that early in his life – he was 18 – when meditating in the church, he overheard the following word from the Gospel of Matthew (16:24) being read: 'If anyone wishes to come after me, let him deny himself and take up his cross and follow me.' Thereupon Cyriacus left his country and sailed to Palestine, where he became an ascetic (§3).[53]

Yet we have ample evidence that the church leaders repeatedly and emphatically raised their voice against this kind of practice. Jerome complains in his *Epistula ad Paulinum Nolanum* 53:7 (CSEL LIV, 453) that many Christians consult the Bible as others do Homer and Virgil, namely for *sortilegium*. But it is especially a long series of decrees by synods and councils from the fifth century onwards[54] which demonstrate that this inveterate custom among Christians was hard to uproot. The council of Vennes (in 465, can. 16) prohibited priests from using the practice of *sortilegium* for soothsaying, and this kind of warning was repeated at the synods of Agde (in 506, can. 42), Orleans (in 511, can.

---

[50] Text in H. Delehaye, *Les saints stylites* (Brussels 1923) 3; discussion in Courcelle, *Confessions* 146.

[51] Text in *Acta Sanctorum*, June 4, 3rd ed., vol. V (1707) 215; discussion in Courcelle, *Confessions* 144.

[52] On this passage Flint, *Rise of Magic*, 300.

[53] Text in Ed. Schwartz, *Kyrillos von Skythopolis* (Leipzig 1939).

[54] See O. Rühle, "Bibel," *Handwörterbuch des deutschen Aberglaubens* I (Berlin 1927; repr. 1987], 1216; F. Boehm, "Los," *ibid.* V (1933[1987]) 1368; Flint, *Rise of Magic*, 223.

30), Auxerre (in 587, can. 4),[55] and others, although it has to be added that sometimes a distinction was made between *sortes biblicae*, which were permitted, and *sortes sanctorum*, which were not. This brings us to the question of what these *sortes sanctorum* were.

One often assumed that *sanctorum* had to be supplied with a noun like *librorum* or *bibliorum* or the like, but that has become increasingly improbable.[56] *Sortes sanctorum* are mentioned in Christian documents from the end of the 5th century onwards. What is striking in all the testimonies is that it is stressed that these *sortes* are wrongly called *sortes sanctorum*[57] and that their practitioners are liars. "Von den Büchern des Alten und Neuen Testaments hätte sicherlich niemand so gesprochen. Schon unter dieser Rücksicht hätte die stets wiederholte Gleichsetzung der Bibellose mit den 'Heiligenlosen' zu denken geben sollen."[58] As the most recent authority in this matter remarks, the sources leave little doubt that *sortes sanctorum* is a term for a form of cultic lot-casting already in use among the early German tribes (as attested by Tacitus, *Germania* 10), in which the names of the pagan gods had been replaced by those of Christian saints, a phenomenon often observed in late antiquity. "Die *sortes sanctorum* haben mit der heidnisch-christlichen Tradition des Buch- bzw. Bibelorakels nichts zu tun. [204] Unter dem christlichen Namen leben vielmehr kultische Praktiken mantischen Losens aus heidnischer Zeit weiter. Ihren Namen bekamen diese Lostechniken, weil sie, wie auch andere ältere Kultübungen, bei oder in christlichen Heiligenkirchen verrichtet worden sind."[59] "Here was a

---

[55] See J. D. Mansi, *Sacrorum conciliorum nova et amplissima collectio* (Paris & Leipzig 1901; repr. of the Florence 1762 edition), VII 955 (Vennes), VIII 332 (Agde), 356 (Orleans), IX 912 (Auxerre); cf. also XII 294. Further references in R. MacMullen, *Christianity and Paganism in the Fourth to Eighth Centuries* (New Haven-London 1997) 237-238 n. 130. Here also the critical *Epistulae* IX 65 and XI 53 (PL 77:1002 and 1171) by Gregory the Great (written ca. 600) are to be mentioned (on which see Harmening, *Superstitio* 195-196). Cf. also A. von Harnack, *Über den privaten Gebrauch der heiligen Schriften in der alten Kirche* (Beiträge zur Einleitung in das Neue Testament V; Leipzig 1912) 71: "Unter den Kanones für Mönche des Rabbulas von Edessa lautet der 19.: 'Kein Mönch suche für irgend jemanden eine Entscheidung aus Bibelstellen.'"

[56] Boehm, "Los" 1378; Harmening, *Superstitio* 197-204. I have not seen R. Ganszyniec, "Les Sortes Sanctorum," *Congrès d'histoire du christianisme. Jubilé Alfred Loisy, III, Annales d'histoire du christianisme* 3 (1928) 41-51.

[57] Sortes quas mentiuntur esse sanctorum; quas sanctorum sortes false vocant; and similar expressions in e.g. Mansi VIII 356, IX 912, XII 294. Cf. also the definition by Isidore of Sevilla, *Etymologiae* VIII 9, 28: 'qui sub nomine fictae religionis per quasdam, quas sanctorum sortes vocant, divinationis scientiam profitentur, aut quarumcunque scripturarum inspectione futura promittunt.'

[58] Harmening, *Superstitio* 200.

[59] Harmening, *Superstitio* 203-204.

device encouragingly similar to those operated by non-Christian practitioners, in the details both of the simple and of the complex forms of its
operation; yet this device was operated by differently sanctioned leaders
and (...) at a different shrine. The encouragement of such familiarities,
with these crucial distinctions made, was a most adroit and sympathetic
pastoral method of going about the transference of religious affection.
(...) Hostility is kept at bay, and conversion is often more lasting, when
custom and affection are thus respected and preserved."[60] It has to be
concluded that on this interpretation the *sortes sanctorum* fall outside the
scope of our investigation.

Graeco-Roman evidence

This matter does bring us, however, to the question of the possible pagan
origin of the phenomenon of the use of Sacred Books as *sortes* as a
whole. We have to deal now, therefore, with the so-called *sortes Homericae* and *sortes Vergilianae*.

In some circles in late antiquity little distinction was made between
the books of Homer or those of the Bible as far as their magical power
was concerned. A telling example is the fact that in one of the anonymous veterinary writings of the *Corpus hippiatricorum graecorum* (X
3.5)[61] it is said that when a horse has problems in giving birth to its
young, one should place on it a papyrus with Psalm 47[48] (up till the
words 'there were the pangs as of a woman in travail'), but when a horse
is infertile, the text on the papyrus should be *Iliad* E 749 = Θ 393 ('the
gates of heaven opened for them on their own accord').[62] We observe
here uses of Homer and of the Bible on equal footing. In his book *Les
mythes d'Homère et la pensèe grecque* (Paris 1956), Félix Buffière gives
the opening paragraphs of his first chapter the title, 'Homer, the Bible of
the Greeks.'[63] There he begins by quoting the first century CE allegorist
Heraclitus to the effect that every Greek child is given verses of Homer

---

[60] Flint, *Rise of Magic* 275. Cf. *Ibid.* 400: "They [the Sortes] were remarkably imitative,
yet could be rendered harmless, even helpful, when firmly christianized. They could
readily be adopted as bargaining counters, therefore, in return for the repudiation of
practices which were wholly unamenable to Christian use. The *Sortes* had the particular advantage, furthermore, of bringing the Bible before the eyes of those involved."
[61] On this corpus see L. Bodson in the new *OCD* (Oxford 1996³) 1592-1593.
[62] See O. Weinreich, *Religionsgeschichtliche Studien* (Darmstadt 1968) 64-65.
[63] Pp. 10-13. P. 11: "Il n'est pas étrange que (...) les écrivains grecs (...) fassent sans
cesse appel à lui, un peu comme un auteur chrétien aux saintes Ecritures."

as a spiritual nourishment from its early years onwards and that his poems accompany us in every stage of our life till our death. As soon as we stop drinking in Homer's wisdom, we immediately get thirsty and want to return to that source as soon as we can.[64] Also Marrou, in his famous work on the history of education in antiquity, emphasizes the unrivalled predominance of Homer in the entire range of educational systems in Greek antiquity.[65] "Homer beherrscht die ganze griechische Bildung, solange ihre Überlieferung dauert."[66] This can already be inferred from the fact that he, and he alone, could be referred to as 'the poet.'[67]

However, does this make the Homeric poems into 'the Bible of the Greeks'? Yes, it does, once we take into account the fact that Homer himself said that for the creation of his work he felt dependent upon a goddess, the Muse,[68] which made his readers believe that he was divinely inspired. Homer was therefore widely regarded as *theios*, "a man who had access to the higher world."[69] In later antiquity he was even regarded as a divine being, especially in Neoplatonic circles.[70] On a second century CE papyrus we find a schoolboy's remark, "Homer is a god, not a human being."[71] That this was not only a simple school-boy's sentiment is demonstrated by the fact that as early as the fifth cen-tury BCE Aristophanes makes clear that already in his days Homer was used as an authoritative oracle-book. In his comedy called *Pax*, this writer presents his audience by way of satire with an alleged oracle in the form (not of Homeric verses but) of 'a cento of Homeric tags' (1089-

---

[64] See Heraclitus, *Quaestiones Homericae* 1.

[65] Only the German version of this work was available to me: H. I. Marrou, *Geschichte der Erziehung im klassischen Altertum* (München 1977) 311: "An oberster Stelle, alles beherrschend, steht selbstverständlich Homer."

[66] Ibid. 311.

[67] See W. J. Verdenius, *Homer, the Educator of the Greeks* (Mededelingen van de Konin-klijke Nederlandse Akademie van Wetenschappen, Afdeling Letterkunde, nieuwe reeks XXXIII 5, Amsterdam-London 1970) 5. A.-M. Harmon, "The Poet κατ' ἐξοχήν," *CPh* 18 (1923) 35-47.

[68] See O. Falter, *Der Dichter und sein Gott bei den Griechen und Römern* (Würzburg 1934) 3-11, and B. Snell, *The Discovery of the Mind: The Greek Origins of European Thought* (New York 1960) 136-138.

[69] Verdenius, *Homer* 6.

[70] R. Lamberton, *Homer the Theologian. Neoplatonist Allegorical Reading and the Growth of the Epic Tradition* (Berkeley-London 1986) (esp. pp. 1-43: 'The Divine Homer and the Background of Neoplatonic Allegory'). Buffière, *Les mythes d'Homère* 25-31.

[71] Θεὸς οὐδ' ἄνθρωπος Ὅμηρος, quoted by E. Ziebarth, *Aus der antiken Schule* (Bonn 1913) nr. 26 (= *JHS* 13 [1893] 796).

1094).[72] This passage, that also refers to other oracles and to the Sibyl, clearly suggests that in his time (the late fifth century BCE)[73] verses from Homer were used in a mantic setting, and this should not surprise us, once we take into account that in this period for the Greeks Homer was already the guide for life *par excellence*. As early as the late sixth century BCE Xenophanes of Colophon says: "From the beginning all have learnt in accordance with Homer" (fragm. B 10). Homer had by that time already begun to be the 'Inbegriff' of wisdom, both practical and theoretical.

This tendency will develop strongly in the Hellenistic and Roman periods. Exercises in writing and reading were then mostly based on the text of Homer. The many hundreds of papyri with scribal exercises testify to the pervading influence of Homer, especially the first books of the *Iliad*, in the ancient educational system.[74] When in Roman Egypt a mother asked the teacher of her son how much progress he had made, the answer was: "He is learning *Zêta*," *i.e.*, the sixth book of the *Iliad*.[75] Large portions of both the *Iliad* and the *Odyssey* were learnt by heart, and there were people who knew the whole of Homer by heart,[76] as was later the case with the Bible among Christians and the Talmud among rabbinic Jews.[77] According to what Plato calls 'the encomiasts of Homer,' Homer "knows all about arts and crafts, all about human virtue and vice, and all about divine matters" (*Resp.* 598d-e), just as later the rabbis said that the Torah of Moses contains every possible sort of wisdom and knowledge.[78] "The authority of Homer was such that, just as with the Bible, passages were torn from their context and given an independent value."[79] The text of Homer was sometimes also altered in

---

[72] M. Platnauer, *Aristophanes, Peace* (Oxford 1964) 158. The text runs as follows: "What oracle can you cite to justify your sacrifice? – An excellent one, straight out of Homer: 'Thus they thrust clean away the hateful darkness of warfare, then took peace for themselves and enshrined her and gave her an altar. Then when the thighs had been burnt and the entrails been dressed for the roasting, from their cups they poured their libations, and I was their leader.' And to the oracle monger a cup was given by no-one! – That is a fake, that's not in the Sibylline collection!". Translation by Alan Sommerstein in *Aristophanes: The Knights, Peace, The Birds, The Assemblywomen, Wealth* (Penguin Classics; London 1978) 136. See also the remarks by W. Schmidt & O. Stählin, *Geschichte der griechischen Litteratur* I, 1 (München 1929) 175 n. 9.

[73] *Pax* was written in 421.

[74] See Marrou, *Geschichte* 312.

[75] *P. Oxy.* 930, 15.

[76] See Plato, *Protagoras* 325c; *Leges* 810e; Xenophon, *Symposium* III 5; Dio Chrysostom XXXVI 9. Verdenius, *Homer* 6-7.

[77] See, e.g., Palladius, *Historia Lausiaca* 18:25.

[78] See the quotation from the Mishna treatise *Avoth* V 22 above in the text.

[79] Verdenius, *Homer* 14.

order to make it suitable for supporting preconceived opinions or for political purposes, again exactly as with the Bible.[80] His epic was used not only for educational, moral, spiritual, or political guidance, but also for technical instruction, for example in the fields of housekeeping, warfare and rhetoric.[81] But most important of all for our purposes was Homer's influence in the domain of religion. "His religious authority appears from the fact that oracles were derived from his work, that his verses were used as incantations, and were inscribed on amulets."[82] In the great magical papyrus that is preserved in the Bibliothèque Nationale in Paris (Bibl. nat. suppl. gr. 574 = PGM IV), a series of three Homeric verses inscribed on an iron lamella is even assigned the function of a *parhedros*, a role usually played by demonic or divine spirits that assist the magician in achieving his goal.[83] Homer was widely regarded as a divinely inspired theologian, whose works had to be searched and analysed with all available exegetical techniques in order to retrieve the profound philosophical wisdom hidden in them, for instance by means of sophisticated allegorical methods.[84] The foundations of these methods

---

[80] Verdenius, *Homer* 14 gives instances.

[81] Abundant evidence is cited by Verdenius, *Homer* 15 n. 60.

[82] Verdenius, *Homer* 17. In his *De vita Pythagorica* 111 and 164, Iamblichus reports that Pythagoras "used selected verses of Homer and Hesiod for the improvement of the soul." See further G. J. M. Bartelink, "Homer," *RAC* 16 (1992) 117.

[83] *Iliad* X 564, 521, 572, as quoted in PGM IV 2145-2150. See L. J. Ciraolo, "Supernatural Assistants in the Greek Magical Papyri," in M. Meyer & P. Mirecki (edd.), *Ancient Magic and Ritual Power*, Leiden 1995, 279-295 (287 on our passage). The text is most easily accessible in K. Preisendanz, *Papyri Graecae Magicae* I (Leipzig 1973; repr. of the 1928 ed.) 138; English translation in H. D. Betz, *The Greek Magical Papyri in Translation* (Chicago-London 1986) 76. See the short discussion in F. Graf, *Gottesnähe und Schadenzauber. Magie in der griechisch-römischen Antike* (München 1996) 176; also K. Preisendanz, "Zum Pariser Zauberpapyrus Z. 2225," *BPhW* 38 (1918) 719-720. On *par(h)edroi* see Preisendanz, "Paredros," *RE* 18/2 (1949) 428-454. Another instance of the use of Homer in magical incantations (*P. Oxy.* 412) is discussed by R. Wünsch, "Deisidaimoniaka," *ARW* 12 (1909) 2-19. Still useful is the old collection of material in R. Heim, "Incantamenta magica graeca latina," *Jahrbücher für klassische Philologie*, Supplementband 19 (Leipzig 1893) 463-575, esp. 514-520: 'Versus Homerici et Vergiliani.' R. Helm, *Lucian und Menipp* (Leipzig-Berlin 1906; repr. Hildesheim 1967) 172 n.2, points out that Marcellus of Bordeaux, *De medicina* VIII 58, mentions healing of eye diseases by means of reciting the Homeric verse: ἠέλιος ὃς πάντ' ἐφορᾷ καὶ πάντ' ἐπακούει ('the sun who sees everything and hears everything'). This practice reminds one of what is said in a Byzantine work on agriculture *Geoponica* VII 14: If one wishes to prevent wine from becoming sour, write on the barrels: γεύσασθε καὶ ἴδετε ὅτι χρηστὸς ὁ Κύριος ('Taste and see that the Lord is good;' *Psalm* 33[34]:8)!

[84] See F. Wehrli, *Zur Geschichte der allegorischen Deutung Homers* (diss. Basel 1928); J. C. Joosen & J.H. Waszink, "Allegorese," *RAC* I (Stuttgart 1950) 283-293; J. Horn, "Allegorese außerchristlicher Texte," *TRE* II (Berlin 1977) 276-283. D. Dawson,

were laid as early as the sixth or fifth century BCE, but they came to full development only in the Hellenistic and Roman periods. We have to leave that aspect aside for the moment in order to focus now on the use of Homer's poetry as an oracular source, a use to which his work was eminently suited.

According to Cassius Dio (LXXIX 8,6 and 40,3) there was in Syrian Apamea an oracular site of Zeus Belos that delivered its oracles in the form of verses from Homer. Pseudo-Plutarch remarks at the end of his treatise on Homer that several people use Homer's poems for mantic purposes as if they are the oracles of a god.[85] That statement is well illustrated by a third century CE papyrus preserved in the British Library (Pap. gr. Brit. Mus. CXXI = PGM VII).[86] There we find a so-called *Homeromanteion*, consisting of a list of 148 oracular answers in the form of 216 verses from Homer in an apparently random order but preceded by a set of three numbers (running from 1-1-1 to 6-6-6). The system worked as follows. The petitioner who consulted the oracle or oracle monger had to roll three dice and the resulting numbers referred to the Homeric line on the papyrus at the start of which these three numbers were found. That line contained the answer or solution to the question or problem of the petitioner.[87] The papyrus also contains a small manual with instructions as to which hours of the day are the most suitable for consultation: on the first day of the month early in the morning, on the second day at noon, on the third it is not to be consulted at all, on some other days all the time, however, etc. It is hard to imagine how the whole thing could work satisfactorily. If a petitioner wanted to know whether the gods would favour an enterprise of his and he threw 1-3-3, the clear answer he got was *Iliad* XVIII 328: 'Zeus does not accomplish

---

Allegorical Readers and Cultural Revision in Ancient Alexandria (Berkeley 1992). Neoplatonists such as Proclus did not fail to find much if not all of their own metaphysics in the poetry of Homer.

[85] *De Homero* II 218, 4: καὶ χρῶνται μέν τινες πρὸς μαντείαν τοῖς ἔπεσιν αὐτοῦ, καθάπερ τοῖς χρησμοῖς τοῦ θεοῦ. Unfortunately it is not known to which poetic writings (the real) Plutarch refers when he explains the fact that the oracles in Delphi are no longer given in verse by saying that poetry has fallen in disrepute because wandering charlatan soothsayers make up oracles by taking by lot verses from certain writings (*De Pythiae oraculis* 25 [407C]).

[86] Text in Preisendanz, *Papyri Graecae Magicae* II (Leipzig 1974=1931) 1-7; English translation in Betz, *The Greek Magical Papyri* 112-119.

[87] It cannot be excluded that consultation of the Sibylline oracles in Rome went along the same or similar lines. See H.W. Parke, *Sibyls and Sibylline Oracles in Classical Antiquity* (London 1988) 191; but cf. R.M. Ogilvie, *The Romans and Their Gods* (London 1969) 62-63. See Colpe, "Heilige Schriften" 199-201, on the 'Sonderstellung' (199) of the *Oracula Sibyllina* in the religious history of Rome.

for men all their purposes' (line 15). But if a person had asked whether or not he or she should go on a specific journey and had thrown 1-5-5 with as oracular answer the famous line from *Iliad* II 204: 'The rule of the multitude is no good; let there be one ruler' (line 29), what was one to make of it?[88] Was the exact interpretation left to the ingenuity of the reader or, what would seem to be more probable, was the oracle monger supposed to provide the necessary exegesis in such a case? We do not know any details about that.[89]

What we are dealing with here is a so-called 'Würfelorakel' (*astragalomanteion*), of which we know several instances from the ancient world. The oldest known cases of divination by *sortes* obtained by throwing dice are some inscriptions from pre-Christian Asia Minor.[90] In these inscriptions we notice that each throw of the dice is named after some divinity and that each oracular answer is attached to a special throw of the dice. Pausanias describes one such oracle in Greece (*Descriptio Graeciae* VII 25, 10):

> On descending from Bura towards the sea you come to a river called Buraï-cus and to a small statue of Heracles in a cave. He too is surnamed Buraï-cus, and here one can divine by means of a tablet and dice. He who inquires of the God offers up a prayer in front of the image, and after the prayer he takes four dice, a plentiful supply of which are placed near Heracles, and throws them upon the table. For every figure made by the dice there is an explanation expressly written on the tablet.

It is important to notice that we can observe here that dice were used in the finding of oracular answers at official oracle sites in the Hellenistic and Roman periods.[91] Here we have a type of oracular device that will continue till far in the Middle Ages and even beyond.

---

[88] For the type of questions asked at oracles see G. H. R. Horsley, *New Documents Illustrating Early Christianity* 2 (Macquarie 1982) 38 and 42 (*ad* no. 8).

[89] Apuleius, *Metamorphoses* IX 8, presents us with a highly amusing picture of the ingeniuity of interpreters of fixed oracular answers. For another papyrus with a *Homeromanteion* (now in Bologna) see Y. de Kisch, "Les *Sortes Vergilianae* dans l'Histoire Auguste," *Mélanges d'archéologie et d'histoire de l'Ecole Française de Rome* 82 (1970) 343 n. 2 (lit.).

[90] F. Heinevetter, *Würfel- und Buchstabenorakel in Griechenland und Kleinasien* (Breslau 1912) is still the best treatment. See also Th. Hopfner, "Astragalomanteia," *RE* (*PW*) Supplementband 4 (1924) 51-56. M. P. Nilsson, *Geschichte der griechischen Religion* II (3rd ed., München 1961) 471-472. G. Kaibel, *Epigrammata graeca e lapidibus collecta* (Berlin 1878/Frankfurt 1879; repr. Hildesheim 1965), nos. 1038-1041, has some interesting examples. See Potter, *Prophets and Emperors* 26-27, with references to recent literature in note 66 at pp. 227-228.

[91] When Suetonius tells us that, when Vespasian "consulted the oracle of the god of Carmel in Judaea, the lots were highly encouraging" (*Vesp.* V 6), he fails to inform us about the procedure (dice, loose sheets?).

In this connection it is worthwhile to pay attention to the famous *Sortes Astrampsychi.* That is a second or third century CE oracular collection of both questions (92 in total) and answers (1030 in total) bearing the name of the legendary magician Astrampsychus.[92] It enjoyed a wide-spread popularity in the world of late antiquity. Its system worked as follows (it is explained in detail in the preface of the document but is here presented in a somewhat simplified manner).[93] The enquirer first looks in the list of 92 numbered questions to find his question or the one most like the question he wants to raise. Then he chooses by some kind of sortition or selects in his mind a number between 1 and 10 and adds it to the number of his question. The sum thus reached has now to be looked up in a list of oracular gods with a concordance following after the list of questions. The concordance indicates by means of a number after the god's name the 'decade,' i.e., the section with ten possible answers. In that decade the answer is found under the number that was chosen by lot. For example, your question is, 'Will I get the woman I want to have?' This is question no. 29. You draw by lot or select the number 7, so the total is 36. In the list of oracular gods you find under 36 Hephaestus, and after his name the concordance number 27. Decade 27 has under number 7 the following answer to your question: 'Yes, you will get the woman you want, but much to your detriment!' Since it is a god, Hephaestus, who directs the whole process, the answer cannot but be correct, for "the theory behind this method of consultation was that the god's action put the proper number in the mind [or hand, *add.* PWvdH] of the consultant."[94]

---

[92] See on this mythical person P. Tannery, "Astrampsychos," *REG* 11 (1898) 96-106; C. Harrauer, "Astrampsychos," *Der Neue Pauly* 2 (Stuttgart 1997) 121-122. The best editions of this work are G. M. Browne, *Sortes Astrampsychi. Volumen I: Ecdosis prior* (Leipzig 1983), and for the *ecdosis altera* R. Stewart, *Sortes Astrampsychi. Volumen II: Ecdosis altera* (Stuttgart-Leipzig 2001). R. Stewart's English translation of these *Sortes* is to be found in W. Hansen (ed.), *Anthology of Ancient Greek Popular Literature*, Bloomington & Indianapolis 1998, 285-324. On the date see G. M. Browne, "The Origin and Date of the Sortes Astrampsychi," *ICS* 1 (1976) 53-58, now superseded by R. Stewart, "The Textual Transmission of the *Sortes Astrampsychi*," *ICS* 20 (1995) 135-147 (I owe thanks to Prof. Stewart for providing me with a copy of his article and for valuable critical comments on this section of the paper).

[93] See J. Rendel Harris, *The Annotators of the Codex Bezae* (London 1901) 50-56; G. Björck, "Heidnische und christliche Orakel mit fertigen Antworten," *Symb. Osl.* 19 (1939) 86-98; G.M. Browne, "The Composition of the Sortes Astrampsychi," *BICS* 17 (1970) 95-100; and F. A. J. Hoogendijk & W. Clarysse, "De Sortes van Astrampsychus," *Kleio* 11 (1981) 55-99.

[94] Potter, *Prophets and Emperors* 25. Cf. Björck, "Heidnische und christliche Orakel mit fertigen Antworten" 87: "Dabei ist aber nicht zu vergessen, daß für den frommen Sinn die Losung einen Akt des göttlichen Willens bedeutete: Hom. H 175ff., N.T. Acta 1, 24ff."

Now here the answers are in simple prose, not in Homeric hexameters, but the reason for mentioning the *Sortes Astrampsychi* is that one of the most interesting things about this lot oracle is that we have it in both a pagan and a Christian version. Early papyri from the third and fourth century have the names of pagan gods in the concordance list, but in the many medieval manuscripts of the *Sortes* the names of the gods have been replaced by those of biblical persons.[95] Although the Christians had also changed a few of the questions,[96] by and large they were using the same book as the pagans did not long before them. "That the form of the oracle question and answer was assimilated to a Christian context is simply one indicator of how important it was to have links with longlived traditions."[97] It is also interesting to note that the Christian adaptors were aware of what they were doing, since the redactor of one of the medieval manuscripts of the *Sortes Astrampsychi* indicates that he is well aware of the non-Christian origin of his document.[98]

We can observe the same phenomenon in specially prepared copies of the Bible, in particular the Gospels, that Christians consulted to learn their fortunes. In one of the most famous biblical manuscripts, the *Codex Bezae* (fifth cent. CE), a later hand (between the seventh and ninth century, called M[3]) has added at the foot of the pages containing the first 10 chapters of the Gospel of Mark a list of 69 short sentences, all of them preceded by the word *proshermêneia*, which turn out to be responses to oracular questions.[99] The method of consultation is unclear, but comparison with the *Codex Sangermanensis*, a Latin biblical codex from the eighth or ninth century whose list of responses shows remarkably strong resemblances with that of *Codex Bezae*,[100] may perhaps shed some light

---

[95] See the text in Browne, *Sortes Astrampsychi* 4-5; also W. Clarysse & F. A. J. Hoogendijk, "Concordance to the Sortes Astrampsychi with list of gods," in F. A. J. Hoogendijk & P. van Minnen (eds.), *Papyri, Ostraca, Parchments and Waxed Tablets in the Leiden Papyrological Institute* (Papyrologica Lugduno-Batavia 25; Leiden 1991) 15-22.

[96] E.g., 'Will I be reconciled with my girlfriend?' had now become 'Will I become a bishop?'; see R. Lane Fox, *Pagans and Christians* (New York 1987) 677.

[97] Horsley, *New Documents* 2, 44.

[98] See Björck, "Heidnische und Christliche Orakel" 98, and Browne, "Origin and Date" 54. The scribe makes a clear distinction: οὕτω μὲν οὖν ὁ Ἀστράμψυχος, οἱ δὲ τῆς εἰς τὸν ἕνα θεὸν ... λατρείας ....

[99] Rendel Harris, *The Annotators* 45-74, is still the best study. For the dating of the 20 (!) annotators of this manuscript see *ibid.* 6. The more recent work by D. C. Parker, *Codex Bezae. An Early Christian Manuscript and its Text* (Cambridge 1992) 43-44, is disappointing as far as the annotators are concerned.

[100] Rendel Harris, *Annotators* 70, says the two systems are identical as to origin. and regards the Greek text of the Bezan *sortes* as a translation of a Latin source close to the St. Germain list.

on it. That manuscript has subdivided the text of the Gospel of John into 316 numbered sections, 185 of which contain short oracular responses written in the margin. But this codex also contains "a figure of a sort of wheel divided into eight sectors, each sector full of numbers that form a broken series from 1 to 316. Obviously the diagram is to be used in some way with the numbered sentences accompanying the sections of John's Gospel. This equipment must have been used for the purpose of divination (...) The most probable method of using the *Sortes* would be by the selection of a number (...) and then the pages of the Gospel of John were turned until the sentence was found to which that number was attached."[101] Another famous example of this genre is the *Sortes Sangallenses*, an oracular work in a Latin codex of around 600 CE in Sankt Gallen.[102] In fact the oracular responses reported here (the questions are lost) derive from the same archetype as the *Sortes Astrampsychi*.[103] But all this diverts us from our main topic: the use of sacred books as oracles.

Let us, therefore, finally turn to the *Sortes Vergilianae*.[104] There can be little doubt that the Latin Homer, Virgil, underwent the same fate as his great Greek predecessor as far as his exaltation to the status of divinely inspired author is concerned. "As with Homer, all human learning came to be seen as condensed in the *Aeneid*, a view which finds full expression in Macrobius' *Saturnalia*. The ancient biographical tradition

---

[101] B.M. Metzger, "Greek Manuscripts of John's Gospel with 'Hermeneiai'," in T. Baarda et al. (edd.), *Text and Testimony. Essays on New Testament and Apocryphal Literature in Honour of A.F.J. Klijn* (Kampen 1988) 162-169 (quote on p. 166). See also his "Sortes Biblicae," in B. M. Metzger & M. D. Coogan (eds.), *The Oxford Companion to the Bible* (New York – Oxford 1993) 713-714. Metzger demonstrates that one already finds this kind of oracular *hermêneiai* in eight early papyri of the Gospel of John dating from circa 300 to 600 CE. For *hermêneiai* in Armenian and Georgian manuscripts of the Bible see B. Outtier, "Les *prosermeneiai* du Codex Bezae," in D. C. Parker & C.-B. Amphoux, *Codex Bezae. Studies from the Lunel Colloquium June 1994* (Leiden 1996) 74-78. For Coptic *sortes* A. van Lantschoot, "Une collection sahidique de *sortes sanctorum*," *Le Muséon* 69 (1959) 35-52.

[102] H. Winnefeld, *Sortes Sangallenses ineditae* (Bonn 1887). A. Dold & R. Meister, *Die Orakelsprüche im St. Galler Palimpsestcodex 908 (die sogenannten 'Sortes Sangallenses')*, 2 vols., (Sitzungsberichte der Österreichische Akademie der Wissenschaften, Phil.-hist. Klasse, 225:4-5; Wien 1948-1951).

[103] See the discussion by Boehm, "Los" 1390; Flint, *Rise of Magic* 220-222; Rendel Harris, *The Annotators* 161-184. Meister in Dold & Meister, *Orakelsprüche* II 101-102. For a curious case of medieval *sortes* with in-built eccesiastical censure (in the form of answers denouncing fortune-telling in round terms!) see T. C. Skeat, "An Early Mediaeval "Book of Fate": The Sortes XII Patriarcharum," *Mediaeval and Renaissance Studies* 3 (1954) 41-54.

[104] H. A. Loane, "The Sortes Vergilianae," *The Classical Weekly* 21 (1928) 185-189. There is a good bibliography in Y. de Kisch, "Les *Sortes Vergilianae*" 324 n.1.

already shows a tendency to see Virgil as a *theios aner*, a divine genius, and this became pronounced in the Middle Ages."[105] The *Aeneid* had become "a sort of Bible."[106] The wish to seek divine guidance in Virgil's poetry finds its most prominent expression in the late fourth century *Historia Augusta*. Several of the *Scriptores Historiae Augustae* - or rather, the author of the *Historia Augusta*[107] – make Roman emperors have recourse to *Sortes Vergilianae*. For instance, in the *Vita Hadriani* II 8 (by 'Aelius Spartianus'),[108] we read that after the death of Nerva (emperor from 96-98) in the year 98 Trajan became emperor (98-117). The future emperor Hadrian (117-138) wanted to wind his way into Trajan's friendship, but he was uncertain about the emperor's feelings towards him. Therefore he consulted the *sortes Vergilianae*, and this was the oracle that fell to his lot (*sors excidit*):

> 'Who is yonder man, by olive wreath distinguished, who the sacred vessels bears? I see a hoary head and beard. Behold the Roman King whose laws shall stablish Rome anew, from tiny Cures' humble land called to a mighty realm'(*Aeneid* VI 808-812). Others, however, declare that this prophecy came to him from the Sibylline oracles.[109]

In the context of *Aeneid* VI, the lines refer to Numa Pompilius (traditionally 715-673), but Hadrian regards it as a prophecy of his own future reign and he marries the daughter of Trajan's sister.

In the *Vita Alexandri Severi* IV 6 (by 'Aelius Lampridius'), it is said that, when Alexander (emperor from 222-235) was plotted against by Heliogabalus, he received a lot-oracle (*sors exstitit*) in the temple of the goddess Fortuna Primigenia in Praeneste (Palestrina in Latium) that ran as follows:

> If ever you break the Fates' cruel power, you shall be a Marcellus (*Aeneid* VI 882-3).

In the temple of Fortuna in Praeneste the oracle issued its responses on *sortes*, here pieces of wood on which utterances were inscribed.

---

[105] D.P. Fowler & P.G. Fowler, "Virgil," *OCD* (Oxford 1996³) 1603b.

[106] Thus W. F. Jackson Knight, *Roman Vergil* (London 1946) 310. At p. 311 one finds a concise but good survey of the veneration of Virgil in late antiquity.

[107] It is still disputed whether or not all these authors are actually one and the same anonymous person (which seems most likely); see J.F. Matthews, "Historia Augusta," *OCD* (Oxford 1996³) 713.

[108] Extensive discussion in Kisch, "Les *Sortes Vergilianae*" 325-336.

[109] The hexametric (and therefore somewhat contorted) translation of the lines from the *Aeneid* in this and the following fragments was made by the translator of the *Historia Augusta* in the Loeb Classical Library, David Magie.

According to this source, these oracular utterances consisted of verses from Virgil, here a line that refers to Marcellus, the famous nephew of the emperor August who died so young in 23 BCE.[110] The same book reports (in XIV 5) that when Alexander Severus at his father's bidding turned his attention from philosophy and music to other pursuits, he was celebrated by the following oracle from Virgil (*Vergilii sortibus*):

> Others, indeed, shall fashion more gracefully life-breathing bronzes, well I believe it, and call from the marble faces more lifelike, others more skilfully plead in the courtroom and measure out closely pathways through heaven above and tell of the stars in their risings. Thou, o Roman, remember to rule all the nations with power. These arts ever be thine: The precepts of peace to inculcate, those that are proud to cast down from their seats, to the humbled show mercy (*parcere subiectis et debellare superbos* [*Aeneid* VI 848-854]).

In the *Life of Clodius Albinus* V 3-4 (by 'Iulius Capitolinus'; Clodius Albinus was a candidate emperor in the year 196-197),[111] it is said that

> his rule was predicted by a number of omens that occurred at the time of his birth. For instance, a snow-white bull was born, whose horns were of a deep purple hue. And he is said to have placed these, when tribune of the soldiers, in the temple of Apollo at Cumae, and when he made inquiry of the oracle there concerning his fate (*sortem de fato suo tolleret*), he received a response, it is said, in the following lines: 'He shall establish the power of Rome, though tumult beset her, riding his horse he shall smite both Poeni and Galli rebellious' (*Aeneid* VI 857-8).

Finally, in the *Vita Claudii* X 2-6 (by 'Trebellius Pollio'; M. Aurelius] Claudius [Augustus] was emperor from 268-270) we read:

> (2) When he inquired, after being made emperor, how long he was destined to rule, there came forth the following oracle (*sors talis emersit*): (3) "Thou, who dost now direct thy father's empire, who dost govern the world, the gods' vicegerent, shalt surpass men of old in thy descendants; for those children of thine shall rule as monarchs and make their children into monarchs also."[112] (4) Similarly, when once in the Apennines he asked about his future, he received the following reply: "Three times only shall

---

[110] On Fortuna's oracle in Praeneste see Cicero, *De divinatione* II 41, 85 and the commentary *ad locum* by Pease, *M. Tulli Ciceronis de divinatione libri duo* 490-492. From SHA *Ael*. IV 1 and *Gord*. XX 5 it is apparent that the quote about Marcellus from *Aen*. VI 882-3 was a favourite one with our author(s); see Kisch, "Les *Sortes*" 347-355. *Ibid*. 353 Kisch remarks that the preference for the Marcellus quote is to be seen in light of the fact that in the history of the Roman emperors 'les morts violentes sont monnaie courante.'

[111] See the discussion in Kisch, "Les *Sortes Vergilianae*" 336-340.

[112] This metrical oracle is of unknown provenance.

summer behold him a ruler in Latium" [= *Aeneid* I 265]. (5) Likewise when he asked about his descendants: "Neither a goal nor a limit of time will I set for their power" [*Aeneid* I 278]. (6) Likewise, when he asked about his brother Quintillus, whom he was planning to make his associate in the imperial power, the reply was: "Him shall Fate but display to the earth" [*Aeneid* VI 869].[113]

What is striking about these and similar passages in the *Historia Augusta* is firstly that the motif appears rather frequently, no doubt because the author himself firmly believed in this kind of divination by means of Virgil's poetry. Secondly, with only very few exceptions all oracular sentences derive from the most famous and most oracular book of the *Aeneid*, book VI, in which in the underworld Anchises reveals to his son Aeneas the distant future, a book that has had such a long and influential 'Wirkungsgeschichte' in Western Europe.[114] For the Romans, "with a speed and completeness that has few parallels in world literature, Virgil had already become a classic (...) and throughout antiquity he remained one of the fundamental school texts."[115] His verses were scratched on the walls of Pompei, and as early as the first and second centuries CE exegesis of his poems began to develop. "The ancient allegorical tradition of Virgil exegesis, already established by the time of Donatus and Servius [fourth century CE], culminated in the sixth century in the work of Fulgentius, who interpreted the twelve books of the *Aeneid* as the twelve stages of man's life from infancy to old age, while the widespread conviction that Vergil knew everything, led to the use of his verses as oracles and prophecies (*Sortes Vergilianae*)."[116] The parallel with Homer is complete.[117]

---

[113] Here again a quote from the famous passage about Marcellus. The death of Quintillus occurred just 17 days after he had ascended the throne.
[114] The classic treatment still is E. Norden, *P. Vergilius Maro Aeneis Buch VI* (Stuttgart 1916; repr. Darmstadt 1984). On Virgil's influence see now especially G. B. Conte, *Latin Literature. A History* (Baltimore-London 1994) 284-290. Cf. W.S. Teuffel – W. Kroll – F. Skutsch, *Geschichte der römischen Literatur*, vol. II, 6th ed. (Leipzig-Berlin 1910) 140.
[115] Conte, *Latin Literature* 285. Cf. also N. M. Horsfall, "Aspects of Virgilian Influence on Roman Life," *Atti del convegno mondiale scientifico di studi sul Virgilio*, vol. 2 (Milan 1984) 47-63.
[116] Conte, *Latin Literature* 286. On the persistence of this custom in later times see D. Comparetti, *Vergil in the Middle Ages* (London 1895). I have not seen the pamphlet by D. A. Slater, *Sortes Vergilianae or Vergil and Today* (Oxford 1922). Most medieval books of Fate, however, were based on Arabic models. Arabic *sortes*, based on the Quran, are discussed in Boehm, "Los" 1377, and Bolte, "Geschichte" 287-291.
[117] Other evidence for the parallellism of Virgil and Homer is to be found in Lamberton, *Homer the Theologian* 284-285.

Disturbing though it may seem that the *Historia Augusta* is our only source in which *sortes Vergilianae* are described, it would be unwise to attribute the whole motif to the fantasy of the author of these *Vitae*, even though the stories they tell may be unreliable from a historical point of view. One of the author's contemporaries, Jerome, takes the existence of both *sortes Homericae* and *sortes Vergilianae* for granted, as we saw (*Epistula ad Paulinum Nolanum* 53:7, written in 396 CE). Moreover, in most early mediaeval sources that mention this custom[118] the consultation of both *sortes Vergilianae* and *sortes biblicae* is clearly regarded as an old custom with a very long tradition, and the parallel with Homer would rather suggest that we have to do here indeed with a phenomenon of the imperial period.[119]

Conclusions

Finally we have to deal with the problem of priority and dependence. What was first, the pagan or the Jewish use of Sacred Books as oracles? And if either one can be established, is it possible to determine if one is dependent upon the other? As far as the Christian material is concerned, we have already been able to observe in the case of the *Sortes Astrampsychi* that there was a smooth transition from the pagan to the Christian form of this lot oracle. This suggests that at least in Christian circles influence of pagan practices of prognostication by means of lot oracles played an important role.[120] But as far as the Jewish and pagan material is concerned, the situation is much less clear. Part of the problem is that our earliest testimonies to this practice in both circles are somewhat problematic. The two passages in the books of the Maccabees we discussed at the beginning are interpreted in a very different way from me by some scholars,[121] and on their interpretation we have to conclude that the earliest evidence for *sortes biblicae* among Jews is to be

---

[118] They fall outside the scope of the present investigation.

[119] R. MacMullen, "Conversion: A Historian's View," *The Second Century* 5 (1985/86) 68, even assumes that Augustine was inspired by the practice of consulting Virgilian *sortes* in the *tolle lege* scene. See now also R. MacMullen, *Christianity and Paganism in the Fourth to Eighth Centuries* (New Haven-London 1997) Index s.v. *sortes* (esp. p. 139).

[120] Already in the 17th century J. le Clercq remarked on the above discussed passage in Augustinus' *Confessiones* VIII 12, 29: "Redolet hoc superstitionem ethnicam" (PL 47:210).

[121] See especially note 13 above.

found not in the books of the Maccabees but only only much later, in the rabbinic literature of the third to sixth centuries CE. And as we have seen, almost all instances found there are different from the pagan material in that the method used is not casting lots or opening books at random, but rather a more cledonomantic approach in the form of hearing children reciting the last biblical verse they have learned at school. The first pagan evidence is even more problematic. It is the passage from Aristophanes' *Pax*, where an oracle 'written by Homer' is quoted; however, it contains only Homeric phraseology but not Homeric verses. It is a parody, to be sure, but can this be regarded as hard evidence that Homer's poems were used as early as the 5th century BCE for oracular purposes? I am strongly inclined to think so, but I have to admit that there is no compelling proof.[122] Moreover, how then can we explain the large chronological gap between this passage from the fifth century BCE and the next pieces of evidence, namely the unambiguous passage from Pseudo-Plutarch about the use of Homer for oracular purposes (*De Homero* II 218, 4), the testimony of Cassius Dio (LXXIX 8,6) and the earliest papyrus with a *Homeromanteion* (PGM VII), all of them dating from the third century CE? This gap of more than 6 centuries is strange. If we leave the debatable early evidence aside for the moment, we see that the remaining material is almost all from this later period, the third through the sixth centuries CE: the just-mentioned papyrus, Dio Cassius and Pseudo-Plutarch, the papyri of the *Sortes Astrampsychi*, the passages from Athanasius and Augustine, the material about the *Sortes Vergilianae* in the *Historia Augusta*, the *Sortes Sangallenses*, the papyri of the Gospel of John with *hermêneiai*, the warnings by the Councils of the church, the Babylonian Talmud and the other rabbinic writings. There is such a concentration of the evidence in these centuries that one feels strongly inclined to assume that the whole practice originated only in that period and that the isolated passages from the books of the *Maccabees* and Aristophanes have to be explained differently. However, that would be too easy an escape. In view of the high status of Homer in the Greek world and of the Bible among the Jews in the Hellenistic period, as we have sketched it above, it was to be expected that this kind of practice would develop in a world in which other forms of cleromancy were already current. Viewed in the context of their time, the passages

---

[122] In late antiquity and the early Byzantine period, paraphrases of biblical stories in the form of Homeric *centones* were also in use among Christians; see A.-L. Rey, "*Homerocentra* et littérature apocryphe chrétienne," *Apocrypha* 7 (1996) 123-134.

from Aristophanes and the books of the *Maccabees* are no *corpora aliena*, on the contrary. One could rather say that it is strange that we do not have more evidence for this practice from the pre-Christian centuries. It may be a matter of mere chance and of the vicissitudes of the history of textual transmission that we do not have more data from an earlier period. Be that as it may, the scarcity of evidence does not permit us to determine whether or not the Jewish practice of sortilegium developed under Greek influence, as did so many post-biblical practices in Judaism, also in the sphere of manticism.[123] In view of the more or less parallel development in status of Homer and of the Bible among Greeks and Jews respectively, it is not necessary to assume such an influence. These developments probably took place independently from one another and on parallel lines.[124]

Sortes had a long life. In the Middle Ages the practice continued to flourish, and it is still current, albeit in a formalized way, among the Zinzendorfians.[125] At the beginning of this century the great British scholar James Rendel Harris, referring to the continuing use of *sortes* through the centuries, wrote: "We need not be surprised if we find that there was much vitality in the ancient superstition."[126] Taking into account that in our own days it is again possible to buy various types of modern lot oracles in New Age shops, one cannot but agree with him.[127]

---

[123] See P. W. van der Horst, "Jewish Self-Definition by Way of Contrast in *Oracula Sibyllina* III 218-247," in idem (ed.), *Aspects of Religious Contact and Conflict in the Ancient World* (Utrecht 1995) 147-166.

[124] Jewish influence on the Christian use of *sortes biblicae* would seem to be improbable, or at least improvable. The Jewish instances derive all of them from Palestinian and Babylonian sources, whereas the Christian material is mostly of Western provenance.

[125] E.g. Lang, "Buchreligion" 152: "Aus dem Bibelorakel wird das seit 1731 jährlich erscheinende Büchlein der 'Losungen', in dem die Herrnhuter Brüdergemeinde die von ihr ausgelosten alttestamentlichen Tagessprüche herausgibt."

[126] *The Annotators* 74.

[127] I owe thanks to Professors G. J. M. Bartelink, R. van den Broek, M. F. Parmentier, and R. Stewart for valuable hints.

10. CELIBACY IN EARLY JUDAISM

"Be fruitful and multiply (*peru u-revu*)" (Gen. 1:28). According to the Bible, these were the very first words that God spoke to mankind. If these first words are an imperative to the effect that mankind is obliged to produce numerous offspring, they do not create the ideal climate for the development of sexual asceticism.[1] It does not, therefore, come as a surprise that for Judaism – unlike Christianity – celibacy never came to have the status of an ideal.[2] Christianity – so we are often told – in this respect removed itself from a biblical and Jewish ideal by letting itself be influenced by Platonic philosophy with its often negative assessment of materiality and corporeality. This black-and-white picture of, on the one hand, a Judaism that remained true to its biblical roots and maintained a positive attitude towards the body and, on the other, Christianity that deviated from this path and developed a negative attitude towards the body, has come increasingly under fire of late, and rightly so.[3]

Of course it would seem advisable to present a definition of asceticism before starting to discuss our topic, but apart from the fact that there is no such definition upon which everyone agrees,[4] we have decided to restrict our discussion to only one aspect of the phenomenon of asceticism, albeit the most conspicuous one: sexual abstinence. A further restriction we make is that we will not discuss temporary but only permanent sexual abstinence. Other aspects of asceticism such as fasting, self-chastisement, voluntary poverty, anachoresis etc. fall outside the scope of this short contribution. The period under consideration is that between Alexander the Great and Muhammad.

---

[1] See on the reception history of this biblical text J. Cohen, *"Be Fertile and Increase, Fill the Earth and Master It." The Ancient and Medieval Career of a Biblical Text*, Ithaca-London 1989.

[2] Cf. H. Strathmann, *Geschichte der frühchristlichen Askese*, Leipzig 1914, 16-40 ("Der unasketische Grundzug der palästinensisch-jüdischen Frömmigkeit").

[3] See, e.g., D. Satran, 'Askese VI: Judentum,' *RGG* I[4] (1998) 839-840.

[4] S.D. Fraade, 'Ascetical Aspects of Ancient Judaism,' in A. Green (ed.), *Jewish Spirituality From the Bible Through the Middle Ages*, London 1985, 253-288, esp. 253-257. Fraade uses the following definition by Vööbus: "Asceticism, in religion, is the practice of the denial of physical or psychological desires in order to attain a spiritual ideal or goal" (A. Vööbus in *Encyclopaedia Britannica*, 15th ed., vol. 2:135).

There can be no doubt about the fact that in rabbinic literature the biblical ideal of founding a family is fully endorsed. "Nobody may abstain from keeping the law *Be fruitful and multiply*," says the Mishna (*Yebamot* 6:6). Rabbinic dicta to the effect that the unmarried state is disapproved of are found frequently.[5] To give only one example: in the Babylonian Talmud (*Qiddushin* 29b) we read that if a man is past twenty years without having married, he trespasses a divine commandment and provokes God's anger. Even though others are willing to move this age limit to 24 years, the sentiment remains the same: one has to found a family in due time, and if one does not do so, one is actually as evil as a person who sheds blood because one deprives one's potential offspring of life. Moreover, an unmarried man willy-nilly thinks of sex all the time ("he spends all his days in sinful thoughts") and is thus hindered from aspiring to higher goals. For these reasons an early marriage is strongly recommended by the Talmud, even though it never became a halakhic rule.[6]

Yet there were exceptions. Shim'on ben Azai was a well-known and much respected rabbi (of the early 2nd cent. CE) who never married.[7] His colleagues criticized him repeatedly for that, but he used to say: 'What can I do? My soul thirsts for the Torah! Let other people keep the world going' (Tosefta, *Yebamot* 8:7; Bab. Talmud, *Yebamot* 63b). By this he meant of course that humanity would not die out by his remaining unmarried. 'My soul thirsts for the Torah' implies that he was so obsessed by his Torah study, the highest ideal of rabbinic culture, that there was no room and time left for a wife. In the figure of Shim'on ben Azai we meet a rabbi who, in spite of Gen. 1:28 and in spite of the social pressure of his co-religionists, purposefully renounces marriage

---

[5] See for more references G.F. Moore, *Judaism in the First Centuries of the Christian Era, the Age of the Tannaim*, vol. 2, Cambridge 1927 (repr. 1966), 119-120, and H. McArthur, 'Celibacy in Judaism at the Time of Christian Beginnings,' *Andrews University Seminary Studies* 25 (1987) 163-181, esp. 164-168. For polemics against remaining unmarried in non-rabbinic Jewish sources see P. W. van der Horst, *The Sentences of Pseudo-Phocylides*, Leiden 1978, 225-227.

[6] See further McArthur, 'Celibacy in Judaism' 166-167. More material in D. M. Feldman, *Birth Control in Jewish Law. Marital Relations, Contraception, and Abortion as Set Forth in the Classic Texts of Jewish Law*, Westport 1980 (= New York 1968), 46-80.

[7] See Tosefta, *Yebamot* 8:7; also G. Bader, *The Encyclopedia of Talmudic Sages*, Northvale-London 1988, 295-299, for a survey of rabbinic material about Ben Azai. Some Talmudic statements to the effect that Ben Azai was married after all (b. *Ket.* 63a and b. *Sota* 4b) seem to be the product of special pleading, *pace* K.-H. Ostmeyer, 'Die Sexualethik des antiken Judentums im Licht des Babylonischen Talmuds,' *Berliner Theologische Zeitschrift* 12 (1995) 164-185, esp. 170 n. 20.

and the founding of a family in order to enable himself to pursue a higher goal with all the more determination: i.e., greater knowledge of the Torah and hence a better understanding of God's will.[8]

Let us now first go back to the pre-rabbinic period in order to see whether earlier Jewish sources, those of Second Temple Judaism, suggest that already then there were Jews who remained unmarried for the sake of pursuing a higher goal. That is indeed the case. A conspicuous ascetic figure is described by Flavius Josephus. In his autobiography, written towards the end of the first century CE, he describes his search for spiritual guidance that he started when he was 16 years of old. He 'shopped' with the Pharisees, the Sadducees, and the Essenes, but finally he remained unsatisfied by his experiences with these groups. Then he writes: 'When hearing of a man named Bannus, who dwelt in the wilderness, wearing only such clothes as trees provided, feeding on things that grew of themselves and using frequent ablutions of cold water by day and night for purity's sake, I became his devoted disciple. I lived with him for three years' (*Vita* 11).[9] From the context it is more than clear that it is a religious search that Josephus is writing about, and for that reason we have to assume, even though Josephus does not say so explicitly, that it is for religious reasons that Bannus had withdrawn into the desert (which is, by the way, a striking manifestation of what three centuries later, on a much larger scale, reappears in Christian circles when the so-called desert fathers take center stage[10]). We may safely assume that this man, clad in treebark, did not wander around in the desert with wife and children; he undoubtedly was celibate by intention. What Josephus himself actually learned from Bannus in those 3 years is a great riddle, for in his life after this training period he married no less than 3 times!

Yet it is the same Josephus who writes extensively and with apparent sympathy about the Essenes, whom he depicts as a group of celibate philosophers: "They shun pleasures as a vice and regard temperance and the control of the passions as a special virtue. They disdain marriage, but they adopt other men's children, while yet pliable and docile (…), and

---

[8] See the opening sentence of D. Boyarin's chapter 'Lusting After Learning' in his *Carnal Israel: Reading Sex in Talmudic Culture*, Berkeley 1993, 134: 'The absolute and contradictory demands of marriage and commitment to study of Torah remained one of the great unsolved tensions of rabbinic culture.' For a discussion of the possibly unmarried status of another rabbi, Hamnuna, see McArthur, 'Celibacy in Judaism' 169-170.

[9] Thackeray's LCL translation.

[10] See the introduction in P.W. van der Horst, *De Woestijnvaders. Levensverhalen van kluizenaars uit het vroege christendom*, Amsterdam 1998.

mould them according to their own principles" (*Bellum* 2:120).[11] To be sure, at the end of this long section, which shows Josephus' admiration for this group, he adds the following: "There is yet another order of the Essenes which, while at one with the rest in its way of life, differs from them in its views on marriage. They think that those who decline to marry cut off the chief function of life, the propagation of the species, and, what is more, that if all were to adopt the same view, mankind would very quickly die out" (*Bellum* 2:160). But anyway, it is clear that according to Josephus there was a considerable group of Jews who declined to marry, again for religious reasons. However, he does not go deeply into the reasons.[12]

His older contemporary Philo confirms this by stating explicitly in his description of the Essenes: "No Essene ever takes a wife" (*Hypothetica* 11:14),[13] but he adds that such is the case because women are selfish creatures, excessively jealous, and adept at corrupting the morals of their husbands and seducing them by their continued impostures, etc. Philo can hardly stop when presenting this negative picture of women, but it is questionable whether these reasons really were the motives for the Essenes not to marry. Possibly they were the reasons why Philo himself saw fit not to marry, but unfortuantely we cannot substantiate that view.

This brings us, however, to the question of whether or not the Essene movement was indeed celibate, partly or wholly. It has often been asserted that Philo and Josephus present here unhistorical descriptions, which have been heavily influenced by hellenizing ideas or hellenistic ideals.[14] But is that really the case? There can be little doubt that Philo's description of the Essenes teems with Greek philosophical terminology, which he is fond of using elsewhere as well. But that may equally well have been his way of presenting data that are in the last analysis based upon historical facts. Let us have a closer look at this matter.[15] To begin with, we can ascertain that, independently from Philo and Josephus, the Roman encyclopedic scholar, Pliny the Elder, also tells us that the

---

[11] For extensive discussion see T.S. Beall, *Josephus' Description of the Essenes Illustrated by the Dead Sea Scrolls*, Cambridge 1988, 38-41.

[12] Many years later Josephus repeats this information in his *Antiquitates Judaicae* 18:21.

[13] All this material is most easily accessible in A. Adam & Chr. Burchard, *Antike Berichte über die Essener*, Berlin 1972 (2. Aufl.); This quote from Philo at p. 7.

[14] See, e.g., W. Bauer, 'Essener,' in his *Aufsätze und Kleine Schriften*, Tübingen 1967, 1-60.

[15] See for what follows, *inter multos alios*, J.M. Baumgarten, 'Celibacy,' in L.H. Schiffman & J.C. VanderKam (eds.), *Encyclopedia of the Dead Sea Scrolls*, 2 vols., Oxford 2000, 1:122-125.

Essenes live on the North-West coast of the Dead Sea *sine ulla femina, omni venere abdicata* ('without any women because they have renounced any form of sexual activity').[16] If we assume for the moment that the Essenes were identical, be it partly or be it wholly, with the inhabitants of the Qumran settlement and the possessors of the Dead Sea Scrolls,[17] then we find here not only a striking confirmation of what Philo and Josephus state, but we also have good reasons to consult the Dead Sea Scrolls on this matter. What we find there is the following.

Even though the Qumran *Rule of the Community* (*1QS*) nowhere states that celibacy is obligatory for membership, the community that is dealt with in the document seems to be one consisting exclusively of a group of males; women and children are never mentioned. In the so-called *Damascus Document* (*CD*), however, we see that the presence of married women and children in the community is presupposed. Experts have suggested that *CD* is a document which in the course of time underwent a series of adaptations and that the references to marriages represent later strata which were added to enable married persons to become members of the Essene community, but this must remain guess-work.[18] The *Rule of the Congregation* (*1Q28a*) simply gives a set of rules for marriage. The situation is further complicated by the fact that in the graveyards around Qumran male skeletons are predominant (circa 90%).[19] Moreover, only a very limited number of the graves have been excavated. Be that as it may, at any rate it is clear that, *exactly as Josephus says*,[20] there were two groups within the Essene movement, a strictly celibate and a non-celibate one. We simply do not know whether these two groups existed simultaneously or whether there was a development from a strictly celibate movement towards a situation in which gradually married couples were also tolerated or accepted. It does remain an established fact, however, that there were members of the Qumran and/or Essene movement who remained unmarried on principle. Their awareness of a need to be in a constant state of preparedness for the eschatological war (see *Megillat Milchama* = *1QM* and *4Q491-496*)

---

[16] *Naturalis historia* 5:15, 73.

[17] This much debated question cannot be discussed here; see most recently T.S. Beall, 'Essenes,' *Encyclopedia of the Dead Sea Scrolls* 1:262-269.

[18] J.M. Baumgarten, 'Damascus Document,' *Encyclopedia of the Dead Sea Scrolls* 1:166-170.

[19] On these graveyards see H. Stegemann, *Die Essener, Qumran, Johannes der Täufer und Jesus*, Freiburg 1993, 72-74.

[20] And as Philo seems to imply when he remarks that among the Essenes "elderly men, *even if they are childless*, are treated as parents" (*Hyp.* 11:13).

can obviously have led quite easily and naturally to permanent acceptance of the rules for sexual abstinence in a war situation, as already formulated in the Bible (Deut. 23:10-15; 1 Sam. 21:5-6; 2 Sam. 11:11-13). Also the idea that the community of Qumran formed a spiritual temple, the dwelling place of God, certainly contributed to a strong conviction of the need to remain in a state of constant ritual purity.[21] If one takes into account that in Exodus 19:15 the people of Israel are required to abstain from sexual activities in preparation for the revelation on Mount Sinai, then it is not difficult to imagine that, in a group in which many were probably in constant expectation of new revelations from God, there was a strong desire to stay in the state of ritual purity required for such revelations.[22]

This brings us to an interesting motif that we can only deal with in passing, namely that of Moses' sexual abstinence ever since the revelation of the Law on Mount Sinai or since God's self-revelation at the burning bush. We find the motif for the first time in the first half of the first century CE, in Philo's *Vita Mosis* (2:68-69) where he says that Moses, in order to be able to receive God's revelations, had to be pure and therefore had to refrain from food and drink and any contact with women. Since Moses wanted to be in a continuous state of preparedness to receive these divine words, says Philo, ever since his calling he remained free from defilement by sexual intercourse. This motif recurs in rabbinic literature.[23] So we read in the rabbinic midrash *Sifre* on Num. 12:1-2 (§§99-100) that Miriam spoke to Aaron about Moses because of his Ethiopian wife, since she had noticed that this woman no longer beautified her face. When she asked her for the reason, the woman had answered that Moses was not interested in her as a woman any longer, from which Miriam drew the conclusion that Moses neglected the *peru u-revu* of Gen. 1:28. Thereupon the question is raised how it is possible that the Patriarchs, who also continuously received messages from God, did *not* back out of their marital obligations (a question that remains unanswered). In another midrash, *Exod. Rabba* 46:3, it is said that Moses thought: 'If we were told not to go near a woman at Mount Sinai,

---

[21] See F. García Martínez & J. Trebolle Barrera, *The People of the Dead Sea Scrolls. Their Writings, Beliefs and Practices*, Leiden 1993, 139-157.

[22] See O. Betz, *Offenbarung und Schriftforschung in der Qumransekte*, Tübingen 1960. According to Acts 21:9 Philippus had four daughters who were virgins and (for that reason?) had prophetic gifts.

[23] See Boyarin, *Carnal Israel* 159-165. For a contrasting view see Josephus, *Ant.* 3:212, where Moses is said to be different in no respect from ordinary people except for his caring attitude towards them.

which was sanctified only on one occasion because of the revelation of the Torah [Ex. 19:15], all the more should I, to whom He speaks all the time, keep far away from my wife.' In other passages Moses' constant celibacy is endorsed but at the same time it is emphasized that in this respect Moses is not at all a model to be followed by every Israelite, for in rabbinic circles, as we saw, the ideal of founding a family was definitely upheld.[24] Even so we encounter here an important motif: celibacy because of a person's willingness to remain in an uninterrupted state of ritual purity in order to be ready to receive a message from God at any given moment. The awareness of being a prophet, or a member of a prophetic community, called to be open towards divine communication, could have played an important role in leading many of the persons discussed here to refrain from all sexual activity.

It is not improbable that it is in this light that we have to view the lives of two important Jewish prophets from the first half of the first century CE, John the Baptist and Jesus of Nazareth. In the New Testament the Gospels present us with a description of John – his dwelling in the desert, his dress and food (Mk. 1:4-6 and parallels) – which is strongly reminiscent of the little we learn from Josephus about Bannus.[25] Although we do not know what Bannus' message was, John was clearly an eschatological prophet. His mission was one of great urgency: The axe is laid to the root of the trees (Matt. 3:10//Luk. 3:9)! One who lives in the strong conviction that the end of time is near and whose task is to send a final call to the Jewish people that they should repent and convert, certainly has other priorities than founding a family with all that it involves. Paul, too, understood this very well: in 1 Cor. 7:25-40 he gives advice on whether or not to marry, and all this is motivated by the awareness that 'the time has grown very short' (v. 29). In such a situation it is better to remain unmarried, for the only essential and necessary thing is 'undivided devotion to the Lord' (v. 35). One simply does not beget children when the last judgement is about to take place. In other words, eschatological urgency is – apart from willingness to receive revelations from God at any time – a second motive to move the first commandment in the Bible (*peru u-revu*) to second place. 'Das Gebot der Stunde' carries more weight than 'das Gebot der ersten Stunde' in Gen. 1.

---

[24] See also Targumim on Num. 12:1-2; b. *Shabbat* 87a; *Deut. Rabba* 11:10; *Avoth de-Rabbi Nathan* (rec. A) 2:3; *Mekhilta, Yithro Bachodesh* 3.

[25] Thus also J. E. Taylor, *The Immerser. John the Baptist Within Second Temple Judaism*, Grand Rapids 1997, 32-42.

It is here that we undoubtedly have to look for the background of the celibacy of Jesus of Nazareth.[26] To be sure, on the one hand, Jesus seems to draw a contrast between himself and his predecessor and teacher, John the Baptist (who fasted whereas Jesus ate and drank; Luk. 5:33-35; 7:33-35 and parallels), but, on the other hand, as far as marriage is concerned they stand very close to each other. In spite of marked differences, they ultimately have the same calling, which they have to carry out at Gods behest on behalf of his people. Total commitment to that is incompatible with marriage. It is far from impossible that Jesus' disciples, too, were men who had given up their marital life; against such a background we can make sense of Jesus' remarks about the reward for leaving one's home, parents, wife, and children for the sake of the kingdom of God in his response to what the disciples said about their having left behind everything.[27] The saying in Matt. 19:12 about those who have made themselves eunuchs for the sake of the kingdom of heaven undoubtedly pertains not only to his disciples but to Jesus himself as well. The kingdom of God can demand renunciation of sexual life.[28] Jesus' free association with women – some of them even of ill repute – should certainly not be regarded as being contradictory to that.[29]

In Jesus' case another factor comes into play here as well, namely his very reserved attitude towards sexual desire in general.[30] Passages in the Sermon on the Mount such as the one where Jesus condemns looking at a woman lustfully as being equivalent to adultery (Mt. 5:28) and the sayings that follow about plucking out one's eyes or cutting off one's hands (and in Mk. 9:45 also cutting off one's feet[31]) would seem to imply that sexual desires have to be mastered. The ideal life, in the hereafter, according to Jesus, is completely asexual (Mk. 12:25: 'For when they rise from the dead, they neither marry nor are given in marriage, but

[26] The many popular books in which Jesus is presented as having married Mary of Magdala deserve no other destination than the trash.
[27] See, e.g., Mk. 10:29//Matt. 19:29//Luke 18:29.
[28] See W.D. Davies & D.C. Allison, *A Critical and Exegetical Commentary on the Gospel according to Saint Matthew*, vol. 3, Edinburgh 1997, 21-25.
[29] It is rightly pointed out by B.J. Pitre, 'Blessing the Barren and Warning the Fecund: Jesus' Message for Women Concerning Pregnancy and Childbirth,' *Journal for the Study of the New Testament* 81 (2001) 59-80, that passages such as Luke 23:28-31 may be taken as evidence that Jesus advocated the renunciation of procreation.
[30] See for what follows D.C. Allison, *Jesus of Nazareth. Millenarian Prophet*, Minneapolis 1998, 175-182.
[31] 'Foot' may stand here euphemistically for 'genitals'; see W. Deming, 'Mark 9.42-10:12, Matthew 5:27-32, and *B. Nid.* 13b: A First Century Discussion of Male Sexuality,' *New Testament Studies* 36 (1990) 130-141, here 134.

they are like angels in heaven'). It is possible to anticipate that *bios angelikos* ('life as an angel') already now.[32]

Jesus himself probably was indifferent to sex. In this respect he was definitely not exceptional as a prophetic figure, for in prophetic movements one very often sees ascetic moods and messianic-eschatological enthusiasm going hand in hand.[33] 'To cease having sexual intercourse is one means of stopping the world.'[34] But that is not all. One should also bear in mind that in the time of Jesus, after three-and-a-half centuries exposure to Greek culture, ascetic ideals from philosophical and religious circles in that culture, had slowly but surely infiltrated Palestinian Judaism and had been appropriated by Jews.[35] This sometimes had the paradoxical consequence that, as Daniel Boyarin says in his book on Paul, 'many Jews of the first century had a sense that they were commanded by God to do that which God himself considered sinful.'[36]

Philo is a good example of this 'ascetic tension' in Judaism.[37] In his platonic-dualistic thought-world the true believer cannot but strive after one thing, namely, for the soul to liberate itself from its attachment to the material world and to try to reach a state of immaterial immortality. The greatest obstacle in this process is the body with its carnal desires. Life is, therefore, a constant battle with these desires, a struggle in which God's help (*inter alia* in the form of the commandments) is indispensable. As has already been said, Philo views his great and exemplary hero, Moses, as a celibate, but his ideal comes to the fore much more clearly in his description of the group of the Therapeutae, in a treatise with the telling title *De vita contemplativa*. There he depicts a group of Jewish men and women who lead a strictly celibate life in a monastery on a hill outside Alexandria, on the shore of Lake Mareotis. The Therapeutae devote themselves there totally to the study of Scripture, prayer, song, and contemplation, during the week each one alone in the strict

---

[32] That is also the sense of the *agraphon* that is to be found in 2 *Clement* 12 (with a parallel in *Ev. Thomae* 22), which cannot be ruled out to go back to Jesus himself; see T. Baarda, '2 Clement 12 and the Sayings of Jesus,' in his *Early Transmission of Words of Jesus*, Amsterdam 1983, 261-288.

[33] For examples see Allison, *Jesus of Nazareth* 194-196.

[34] Allison, *Jesus of Nazareth* 197.

[35] See on this process M. Hengel, *Judentum und Hellenismus. Studien zu ihrer Begegnung unter besonderer Berücksichtigung Palästinas bis zur Mitte des 2. Jh.s v. Chr.*, Tübingen 1969 (= *Judaism and Hellenism*, London 1974).

[36] D. Boyarin, *A Radical Jew. Paul and the Politics of Identity*, Berkeley 1994, 159.

[37] See, e.g., D. Winston, 'Philo and the Contemplative Life,' in Green, *Jewish Spirituality* 198-231; I. Heinemann, *Philons griechische und jüdische Bildung*, Hildesheim 1973 (= Breslau 1932), 261-273.

solitude of their own cell, but on the sabbath together in a common celebration during which men and women are separated by a partition wall
as high as a man so that they cannot see each other. They live an utterly
sober life and for that reason fasting is an essential and integral part of
their lifestyle. No one will be surprised to learn that in the past several
scholars have argued that this treatise could not have been written by
Philo but must derive from a Christian author in the fourth century.[38] No
wonder, too, that Eusebius of Caesarea calls the Therapeutae simply
Christians (*Hist. eccl.* 2:17). The similarities to what he saw happen in
his own days in the emerging movement of desert hermits and monastics
were too striking to admit of another conclusion. But nowadays we
know for sure that *De vita contemplativa* really is a text by the Jewish
philosopher, Philo, who describes here a Jewish monastic movement. To
be sure, the Therapeutae look suspiciously like personifications of
Philo's own ideals, and for that reason it has been suggested that Philo
presents us here with a description of a completely unhistorical situation
and that the Therapeutae have to be seen as an ideal model. "Philo's *De
Vita Contemplativa* as a Philosopher's Dream" is the understandable
title of a recent study of this treatise.[39] One should not forget, however,
that renunciation of marriage for the sake of study of the Holy Scriptures
played a key role in the case of Shim'on ben Azai, who is certainly a
historical person, and whose celibacy cannot be doubted. Whether one
regards Philo's presentation of the Therapeutae as an *utopia* or as an ide-
alizing description of a very special Jewish group, in any case the fact
remains that Philo felt he could present an ascetic life without marriage
as a Jewish ideal. As is to be expected, Gen. 1:28 hardly plays a role in
Philo's exegetical work, even though he nowhere states explicitly that it
is better not to marry because sex is not good for one's spiritual life. It
is possible that Philo was aware of the fact that his own Bible cherished
ideals which were not really his own, but, as is more often the case in
Philo, it is usually Plato who gains the upper hand, not Moses.

Yet it was not Philo who was to be influential in formative Judaism
but the rabbis. The latter formulated very strict rules as far as the fulfil-
ment of marital duties was concerned – and striving after lust or pleasure
was not a dominant part of that, on the contrary![40] – but they took the

---

[38] See S. Sandmel, *Philo of Alexandria*, New York – Oxford 1979, 35.

[39] T. Engberg-Pedersen in *Journal for the Study of Judaism* 30 (1999) 40-64.

[40] See, e.g., D. Boyarin, *Carnal Israel: Reading Sex in Talmudic Culture*, Berkeley 1993,
61-76 *et passim*. One should bear in mind that the rabbis saw as the driving force
behind sexuality the 'evil inclination' (*yetser ha-ra'*); see P. W. van der Horst, 'Evil

commandment of Gen. 1:28 much more seriously than their ascetic coreligionists such as Philo. One may wonder why Philo's ideals were to be influential not in Judaism but in Christianity. It is very hard to achieve any certainty in that question, but one may surmise that this form of asceticism could not become stronger in Judaism precisely because of the glorification of this ideal in Christianity. The antagonism between the two religions had become too great to make attractive for one of them what was seen as an ideal by the other.

We have seen that permanent sexual abstention did occur in early Judaism and had a variety of roots. A dualistic view of man and his world, influenced by Greek philosophy, could have been a factor of importance (Philo, perhaps the Essenes). Strong eschatological urgency definitely played a role in many cases (Qumran, John the Baptist, Jesus, perhaps Bannus). Also the awareness of being God's temple, or an army that prepares for the final holy war, may have led to sexual abstinence (Dead Sea Scrolls). Total devotion to the study of Torah, too, could bring individuals to renounce sexual activity (Ben Azai, the Therapeutae). A monocausal explanation of this phenomenon is in any case not in order. What is clear at any rate is that, when we see in the New Testament the very first impulses towards what would later expand to become the Christian ideal of (voluntary!) celibacy, earliest Christianity in this respect too, can be explained against the background of contemporary Judaism.[41] This in no way denies that Greek ideals may have already infiltrated earliest Christianity via (a hellenized) Judaism.[42] However, the traditional view that celibacy is a Christian innovation that was the result of purely Greek influence, has to be revised.[43]

Inclination,' in K. van der Toorn, B. Becking & P.W. van der Horst (edd.), *Dictionary of Deities and Demons in the Bible*, 2nd ed., Leiden-Grand Rapids 1999, 317-319. For some pagan instances of warnings against striving after pleasure in sexual intercourse see D.C. Allison, 'Divorce, Celibacy, and Joseph (Matthew 1:18-25 and 19:1-12),' *Journal for the Study of the New Testament* 49 (1993) 3-10, esp. 7-9.

[41] Thus also J.E. Goehring, 'Asceticism,' in E. Ferguson (ed.), *Encyclopedia of Early Christianity*, 2nd ed., New York – London 1998, 127-130.

[42] Even in the earliest rabbinic sources one finds typically Graeco-Roman ideals as far as sexual behaviour is concerned; see M. L. Satlow, 'Rhetoric and Assumptions: Romans and Rabbis on Sex,' in M. Goodman (ed.), *Jews in a Graeco-Roman World*, Oxford 1998, 135-144.

[43] I owe thanks to Dr. Silvia Castelli for her valuable critical comments on an earlier version of this article.

11. MARIA ALCHEMISTA, THE FIRST FEMALE JEWISH AUTHOR

It is well-known – though not undisputed – that from the beginning Jews played a not insignificant role in the development of the 'science' of alchemy.[1] It is much less well-known, however, that one of the earliest identifiable alchemist authors of whose work(s) fragments have been preserved, was a Jewish woman with the name of Maria. This long neglected author – the credit for whose rediscovery goes to the late Raphael Patai[2] – is important in more than one respect. Firstly, Maria is the first non-fictitious alchemist of the Western world (most of the 'ancient alchemists' are mythical personalities, such as Ostanes, Hermes Trismegistus, and Pibechius);[3] and secondly, she is the first Jewish woman in history we know to have written and published under her own name.[4]

Although her work(s?) – which she wrote in Greek – are lost, extensive quotations and excerpts from them have been preserved in the works of later Graeco-Roman alchemists, most notably the famous Zosimus of Panopolis (Egypt, early 4th century C.E.), who held her in the highest possible esteem.[5] It is impossible to say exactly when and where she lived, but Egypt and the period from the first till the second, perhaps third century CE are reasonable guesses.[6] We know of the existence of other Jewish alchemists in Greco-Roman Egypt, but most of them are unknown to us.[7] Only Maria rose to great fame among the

---

[1] R. Patai, *The Jewish Alchemists*, Princeton: Princeton University Press, 1994. For a critical review see R. Fontaine in *Revue d'histoire des sciences* 49 (1996) 364-5.

[2] See R. Patai, 'Maria the Jewess – Founding Mother of Alchemy,' *Ambix* 29 (1982) 177-197.

[3] R. Halleux, 'Alchemy,' *The Oxford Classical Dictionary* (3rd ed.), Oxford: Oxford University Press, 1996, 52-53.

[4] See P.W. van der Horst, 'Mary the Jewish Alchemist,' in C.E. Evans & S.E. Porter (eds.), *Dictionary of New Testament Backgrounds*, Downers Grove: Intervarsity Press, 2000, 679-680.

[5] For the texts of the fragments one can consult both M. Berthelot & Ch. E. Ruelle, *Collection des anciens alchimistes grecs*, vols. 2-3, Osnabrück: Otto Zeller, 1967 (= repr. of the Paris 1888 ed.), Index *s.v.* Maria, and M. Mertens, *Les alchimistes grecs*, vol. 4: *Zosime de Panopolis: Mémoires authentiques*, Paris: Les Belles Lettres, 1995, Index *s.v.* Maria. Patai presents most of the fragments in English translation.

[6] Patai, *The Jewish Alchemists* 60.

[7] For an anonymous alchemical treatise by a Jew see for instance A.-J. Festugière, *La révélation d'Hermès Trismégiste*, vol. 1, Paris: Gabalda, 1946, 254.

alchemists of Late Antiquity and the Middle Ages, which is primarily due to her invention of several types of ovens and boiling and distilling devices made of metal, clay, and glass, and to her extraordinary skill. As Zosimus informs us, Maria taught that "the inner, concealed nature of the metals could be discerned by a complex alchemical process that was revealed to her by God himself and that was to be transmitted only to the Jewish people."[8] Her most famous invention (or at least description) is that of what was later to become known as the *balneum Mariae*, a water bath consisting of a double vessel, of which the outer one is filled with water while the inner vessel contains the substance which must be heated to a moderate degree. The French expression *au bain Marie*, still used in every kitchen today, derives from it. One wonders how many cooks today are aware of the fact that this *Marie* was a Jewish alchemist!

Zosimus usually refers to her as 'Maria,' but sometimes as 'Maria the Hebrew (*Hebraia*),' or even 'the divine Maria' (others call her 'the Hebrew prophetess'). Her Jewishness is also apparent from the fact that she says that the Jews are the chosen people and that only they, not the gentiles, could know the deepest alchemistic secrets. She is reported to have told others not to touch the philosophers' stone with their hands, "since you are not of our nation, you are not of the nation of Abraham." Maria's claim that alchemistic procedures were revealed directly to her by God laid the foundation for a long tradition of alchemist esotericism. From the quotations by later authors Maria appears as an erudite person, well versed in the traditions and lore of her science (she is, for instance, the first to mention hydrochloric acid), for whom alchemy was more than an attempt at transmuting base metals into gold: it was a comprehensive religious worldview, that assumed an essential unity underlying all of nature, and in which the God of Israel acted as guarantor of this unity. In the alchemist traditions of subsequent centuries, Maria became identified with Miriam (= Maria), the sister of Moses.[9]

The second important aspect of her work is that we do not have any other writing from antiquity of the which we know for certain that it was authored by a Jewish woman. Whether other Jewish women did not write or whether their works were not preserved, we do not know, but in both cases the loss is a very serious one.[10] From most literary sources we

---

[8] See L.H. Feldman & M. Reinhold, *Jewish Life and Thought Among Greeks and Romans*, Minneapolis: Fortress Press, 1996, 46.

[9] On these later traditions see Patai, *The Jewish Alchemists* 74-76.

[10] Important in this resect are two essays by Ross Kraemer, 'Women's Authorship of Jewish and Christian Literature in the Greco-Roman Period,' in A.-J. Levine (ed.),

do not at all get the impression that learned women were anything of an ideal in ancient Judaism, on the contrary.[11] In real life, however, talented and intelligent women may sometimes have really got chances to develop their capacities. We know, not only from some literary sources but also from inscriptions, that there must have been highly educated Jewish women – mostly in the diaspora, hardly in Palestine[12] – whom one can imagine to have put their thoughts into writing.[13] There can be no serious doubt that there were literate Jewish women in the Hellenistic-Roman period.[14] Maria evidently was one of these happy few. It is, therefore, much to be regretted that we do not know more about her personal circumstances (was she married?), her background (did her parents encourage her activities?), her training (was she herself the first to weld this long-lasting bond between Judaism and alchemy?) et cetera. She will probably remain an elusive figure forever, but she deserves to be remembered, not only in the kitchen but also in the study! The fact that none of the existing works on the history of Jewish literature makes any mention of this first Jewish woman writer in (or known from) history is a serious defect that has to be remedied soon.[15]

"Women Like This." New Perspectives on Jewish Women in the Greco-Roman World, Atlanta: Scholars Press, 1991, 221-242, and also 'Jewish Women in the Diaspora World of Late Antiquity,' in J.R. Baskin (ed.), *Jewish Women in Historical Perspective*, Detroit: Wayne State University Press, 1991, 43-67. Unfortunately Kraemer completely overlooks our Maria. Athalya Brenner, *The Israelite Woman*, Sheffield: JSOT Press, 1985, 46-50 speculates about female authorship of the Song of Songs.

[11] See L. J. Archer, *Her Price is Beyond Rubies. The Jewish Woman in Graeco-Roman Palestine*, Sheffield: Sheffield Academic Press, 1990, 69-100; and in general T. Ilan, *Mine and Yours are Hers. Retrieving Women's History from Rabbinic Literature*, Leiden: Brill, 1997; T. Ilan, *Integrating Women into Second Temple History*, Peabody: Hendrickson, 2001.

[12] T. Ilan, *Jewish Women in Greco-Roman Palestine*, Tübingen: Mohr, 1995.

[13] On learned women in Jewish inscriptions see P.W. van der Horst, *Ancient Jewish Epitaphs. An Introductory Survey of a Millennium of Jewish Funerary Epigraphy (300 BCE – 700 CE)*, Kampen: Kok Pharos, 1991, 108-109; cf. also R.S. Kraemer, 'Hellenistic Jewish Women: The Epigraphic Evidence,' *Society of Biblical Literature Seminar Papers* 24 (1986) 183-200.

[14] See, e.g., M. Bar-Ilan, *Some Jewish Women in Antiquity*, Atlanta: Scholars Press, 1998, 31-5.

[15] Not even a specialized history of Jewish literature from antiquity such as volume 3 of the new English revision of E. Schürer (*The History of the Jewish People in the Age of Jesus Christ*, vol. 3, Edinburgh: T.&T. Clark, 1986) makes any reference to Maria the Alchemist. For the first encyclopaedia article on Mary see my contribution 'Maria the Jewish Alchemist' in the above-mentioned *Dictionary of New Testament Background* (see note 4).

12. WHO WAS APION?

Most Judaic scholars know that Apion was an anti-Jewish author against whom Flavius Josephus launched a counterattack in his *Contra Apionem*. Many Judaic scholars also know what kind of slander Apion wrote about the Jews. But very few Judaic scholars know what the nature was of Apion's other activities and writings. It is for that reason that in this paper I want to focus on Apion as the scholar and writer he was, aside from his anti-Jewish activities. I will firstly give a very brief sketch of his life and character and thereafter discuss his writings as far as we know them.[1]

Apion, whose name is theophoric (being derived from the Egyptian bull-god Apis),[2] was born the son of Posidonius in the oasis of El Kargeh in Upper Egypt sometime in the second half of the first century BCE. He studied in Alexandria under the famous polymath Didymus Chalkenteros, the author of dozens of commentaries on ancient Greek authors and of works on grammar and lexicography. Later he succeeded Theon as head of the prestigious literary school (or 'grammar school') of Alexandria. But he seems to have given up this position and moved to Rome, where he became a grammarian, *i.e.*, a professional teacher of Greek language and literature, during the reigns of Tiberius and

---

[1] For what follows I consulted (studies of *Contra Apionem* are left aside here): A. von Gutschmid, *Kleine Schriften* IV, Leipzig 1893, 356-371; L. Cohn, 'Apion,' *RE* I.2 (1894) 2803-2806; H. Willrich, *Juden und Griechen vor der makkabäischen Erhebung*, Göttingen 1895, 172-176; M. Wellmann, 'Aegyptisches,' *Hermes* 31 (1896) 221-253; W. Christ, W. Schmid & O. Stählin, *Geschichte der griechischen Litteratur* II.1, München 1920, 437-438; M. Stern, *Greek and Latin Authors on Jews and Judaism* I, Jerusalem 1974, 389-416; H. Gärtner, 'Apion,' *KP* 1 (München 1975) 432; S. Neitzel, *Apions Γλῶσσαι Ὁμηρικαί*, Sammlung griechischer und lateinischer Grammatiker 3, Berlin-New York 1977, 185-300; E. Schürer, *The History of the Jewish People in the Age of Jesus Christ* III.1, Edinburgh 1986, 604-607; F. Montanari, 'Apion,' *Der Neue Pauly* I (Stuttgart 1996) 845-847. Most of the sources are conveniently collected in F. Jacoby, *Die Fragmente der griechischen Historiker* III C, Leiden 1958, 122-145 (= Nr. 616), and in the work by Susanne Neitzel mentioned above. The work by A. Sperling, *Apion der Grammatiker und sein Verhältnis zum Judentum*, Dresden 1886, has little value; it is more an anti-Jewish pamphlet in defence of Apion than a scholarly study.

[2] For other persons with the name Apion see F. Preisigke, *Namenbuch enthaltend alle griechischen, lateinischen, ägyptischen, hebräischen, arabischen und sonstigen semitischen und nichtsemitischen Menschennamen, soweit sie in griechischen Urkunden (Papyri, Ostraka, Inschriften, Mumienschildern usw.) Ägyptens sich vorfinden*, Heidelberg 1922, 40; and D. Foraboschi, *Onomasticon alterum papyrologicum*, Milano n.d., 40.

Claudius. It was in this period that Pliny the Elder followed his lectures.[3] In between, during Caligula's reign, Apion seems to have travelled through Greece, where he lectured in a great many cities, especially on Homeric problems, which earned him the nickname Ὁμηρικός.[4] It was in this period that the city of Alexandria honoured him with its citizenship[5] and subsequently asked him to act as leader of the Alexandrian delegation to Rome in the conflict between Greeks and Jews that had divided the city after the pogrom in the year 38.[6] Probably because Apion had dealt with the Jews so harshly in his *Aegyptiaca*, he was chosen for that task in the year 39 (although it cannot be ruled out that these events took place in reverse order). Apion may also have been one of the instigators of the pogrom in 38, as Leopold Cohn surmised long ago.[7] Josephus reports not without glee and irony that Apion developed a tumor or gangrene in his genitals, which forced him to have himself circumcised (*C.Ap.* II 143). He died from this disease sometime around the middle of the first century CE.

It is not impossible, but also not provable, that a Greek inscription found on one of the colossi of Memnon in the vicinity of the Egyptian city of Thebes was incised there by Apion. The text runs as follows: Ἀπίων Πλειστον[ίκης] ἤκουσα τρίς, *i.e.*, "I, Apion, the winner of many contests, have heard it three times" (*Orientis Graecae Inscriptiones Selectae* no. 662 = *FGH* 616T2).[8] The 'hearing' most probably refers to the mysterious sounds which these colossal statues were said to produce from time to time at sunrise and which were interpreted as Memnon's greetings to the sun (e.g., Strabo XVII 816). These statues of more than 20 meters high were one of Egypt's great tourist attractions in the Imperial period, as the many grafitti indicate.[9] Many people travelled over long distances in order to see and hear these miraculous statues, among them prominent personalities. For instance, Germanicus and the

---

[3] *Naturalis historia* XXX 18.
[4] Seneca, *Epistula* LXXXVIII 34.
[5] Josephus tells that Apion congratulated the city on that occasion for having so great a man as he as a citizen (*C. Ap.* II 135). H. Jacobson, 'Apion Ciceronianus,' *Mnemosyne* 53 (2000) 592, shows that by this statement Apion surely intended 'to identify himself with no less a figure than Cicero, who similarly congratulated the city of Rome.'
[6] Josephus, *Ant.* XVIII 257.
[7] Cohn, 'Apion' 2804.
[8] The inscription is also to be found in F. Preisigke, F. Bilabel & E. Kiessling, *Sammelbuch griechischer Urkunden aus Ägypten*, vol. 5, Wiesbaden: Harassowitz, 1955, nr. 8898 (p. 353), and in A. & E. Bernand, *Les inscriptions grecques et latines du colosse de Memnon*, Paris 1960, 165.
[9] For a complete collection see Bernand, *Les inscriptions grecques et latines*.

emperor Hadrian visited them. But it should be conceded that we cannot be sure of the identity of the Apion in the inscription,[10] although it would be most remarkable if there were to have been two Apions with a nickname that began with *Pleiston-*.

Apion had a very mixed reputation. On the one hand, both as a lecturer and as a writer, he seems to have enjoyed a certain popularity, but on the other hand his behaviour seems to have irritated many people – among them the emperor Tiberius – who found him unbearably vainglorious and conceited beyond endurance.[11] His nickname Πλειστονίκης,[12] 'victor in many contests,' may well be a pun on the phonetically indistinguishable Πλειστονείκης, which means 'quarrelsome.'[13] Another nickname, Μόχθος,[14] can certainly be seen as a positive pointer to his great industry, but even in this case a meaning such as 'a pain in the ass' cannot be excluded.[15] Pliny the Elder says that the emperor Tiberius called Apion 'the world's cymbal' (*cymbalum mundi*), and he adds, 'though he might rather have been thought to be a drum, advertising his own renown,' for Apion asserted 'that persons to whom he dedicated his compositions received from him the gift of immortality.'[16] And there are several other testimonies to the man's self-importance as well.[17]

On top of that, as his own pupil Pliny testifies,[18] in order to display his great learning and unsurpassed knowledge Apion did not have any scruples

---

[10] As the editors of the 'new Schürer' (*History* III 1, 604 n. 123) remark, most of the inscriptions on the colossi are from the time after Apion's death.

[11] Neitzel, *Apions Γλῶσσαι Ὁμηρικαί* 189, speaks of 'seine unerträgliche Selbstgefälligkeit und Prahlsucht.'

[12] Pliny, *Nat. hist.* XXXVII 19; Gellius, *Noctes Atticae* V 14,1; VII 8,1; Clement of Alexandria, *Stromateis* I 21,3.

[13] See H. Jacobson, 'Apion's Nickname,' *American Journal of Philology* 98 (1977) 413-415. For the phonetic indistinguishability cf. Pliny's *Plistonices* (in *Nat. hist.* XXXVII 75). The *Suda*'s remark (*s.v.* Apion) that he was the son of Pleistonikes is an error; see L. Cohn, 'Apion,' *RE* I 2 (1894) 2803.

[14] *Suda s.v.*; Scholion on Aristophanes, *Pax* 778.

[15] Μόχθος has a semantic range from 'toil' or 'labour' to 'trouble' or 'heavy burden.'

[16] *Nat. hist.*, Praef. 25: Apion quidem grammaticus (hic quem Tiberius Caesar cymbalum mundi vocabat, quom propriae famae tympanum potius videri posset) immortalitate donari a se scripsit ad quos aliqua componebat.

[17] Gellius, *Noctes Atticae* V 14,1; Seneca, *Epistula* LXXXVIII 40; Pliny, *Nat. hist.* XXX 18. Cf. Cohn, 'Apion' 2803: "A. besass in seltenem Masse die Fähigkeit, seine eitle Person in ein günstiges Licht zu stellen, seine Reden mit einem Schwall von schönen Phrasen, Witzen und dreisten Lügen auszuschmucken und den Anschein zu erwecken, als wisse und verstehe er alles." Christ-Schmid-Stählin, *Geschichte* 437, speak of his "Eitelkeit und Sensationsbedürfnis."

[18] *Nat. hist.* XXX 6.

about inventing the most fabulous stories and telling these as events which he himself had been privy to. Thus he asserted that he had conversations with the shadow of Homer in the netherworld and had learnt from him the answer to the much-discussed questions of what was Homer's homeland and who his parents were. He also claimed to know all kinds of secret details about Penelope's suitors.[19] Seneca, who may well have known Apion personally, writes that this man impressed the Greeks by maintaining in his lectures that he knew that Homer, when he had finished his two poems, the *Iliad* and the *Odyssey*, added an opening passage to his work, in which he purposely started with two letters which contained a key to the number of his books: the letters μη in μῆνιν ἄειδε, θεά have the numerical value of 48, and Homer's *Iliad* and *Odyssee* comprised 48 books![20]

Apart from being an itinerant orator, Apion also was an author and he gained a certain "fame in many branches of literature and scholarship."[21] What kind of works did he write, as far as we know? This apparently simple question is more difficult to answer than would seem at first sight. The reason for this is that his works have not been preserved and that we can only make inferences on the basis of remarks in other authors and of quotations by them. At any rate, it is certain that his literary activity was many-sided. He wrote about subjects in fields as far apart as history, linguistics, lexicography, literature, geography, natural sciences, among which especially zoology, and cooking.

His best known work among Judaic scholars is the *Aigyptiaka* in 5 books.[22] It was a large and comprehensive but uncritical work on Egyptian history and culture, based upon older Greek works of this nature.[23] It dealt with matters of a chronological nature but also with various aspects of Egyptian religion. But apart from its anti-Jewish statements collected by Josephus, regrettably little of this work has been preserved (what little has been preserved was exhaustively collected by Felix Jacoby in his magisterial *Fragmente der griechischen Historiker*).[24] One of the many

---

[19] See Athenaeus, *Deipnosophistae* I 16f-17b.

[20] *Epistula* LXXXVIII 40. Christ-Schmid-Stählin, *Geschichte* 438, remark wryly: "Apion gab sich zwar für ein Aristarcheer aus; daß aber ein Phantast, der in den zwei ersten Buchstaben der Ilias *MH* eine Andeutung der Buchzahl (48) der beiden homerischen Epen findet, von aristarchischer Philologie weit entfernt ist, versteht sich."

[21] M. Stern, *Greek and Latin Authors on Jews and Judaism*, vol. I, Jerusalem 1974, 389. Aulus Gellius, *Noctes Atticae* V 14, speaks about Apion's *libri non incelebres*.

[22] Tatian, *Oratio ad Graecos* 38.

[23] R. Nickel, *Lexikon der antiken Literatur*, Darmstadt 1999, 33 calls it "eine weitgehend kritiklose Kompilation historischen Materials."

[24] F. Jacoby, *Fragmente der griechischen Historiker* III C, Leiden 1958, 122-144, Nr. 616 = *FGH* 616.

uncertainties about Apion's literary output is that we do not know whether or not the Ἱστορία κατ᾽ ἔθνος mentioned by the Suda was a part of this work or identical to it,[25] but that should not detain us here because we simply do not have any information about its contents. The anti-Jewish material quoted and refuted by Josephus comes from the third and fourth books of this work.[26] Some ancient sources mention a separate work by Apion with the title Κατὰ Ἰουδαίων,[27] but it is now generally – and I think rightly – agreed that this is based upon a misunderstanding of references to material 'against the Jews' (κατὰ Ἰουδαίων) as a title.[28]

In the fifth book of this work he recounts the famous story of Androclus and the lion, again with the claim of having personally witnessed this wellknown event. The story goes as follows:[29]

In the Circus Maximus in Rome a great battle with wild beasts was going on. One of the animals was a lion of enormous size. Among the slaves that had been condemned to fight with the wild beasts was a young man named Androclus. When the lion saw this man coming into the arena, he approached him slowly and quietly as if he recognized him. Androclus almost died from fright, but the huge lion gently began to lick his feet and hands. Then Androclus, regaining his courage, looked the lion into the eyes, and man and lion began to exchange greetings as if they had indeed recognized each other. The people began to shout, and the emperor called Androclus to him and asked why the lion had spared him alone. Then Androclus told him the following story: 'My master was proconsul in Africa. Because he used to flog me daily, I ran away and took refuge in lonely places and deserts. Once when the sun was scorching me, I entered a cave to protect myself against the heat. Not long afterwards this lion came into the same cave with one paw lame and bleeding, making known by groans and moans how much the pain of his wound tortured him. At first I was overwhelmed with fear, but when the lion saw me cowering at a distance in a corner of his own den,

---

[25] A. von Gutschmid, 'Vorlesungen' 361, takes it to be a separate work, for instance.

[26] Schürer, *History* III 1, 605.

[27] Clement of Alexandria, *Strom.* I 21,3; Julius Africanus *ap.* Eusebius, *Praeparatio Evangelica* X 10,16; Pseudo-Justin, *Cohortatio* 9. Gutschmid, 'Vorlesungen' 361, also lists this as a separate work by Apion.

[28] See e.g. Schürer, *History* III 1, 606-607. Schürer notes that the Pseudo-Clementine *Homilies* (V 2) assert that "Apion wrote many books against the Jews" which is, of course, nonsense. One should beare in mind the ambiguity of an expression such as ὁ λόγος κατὰ Ἰουδαίων. It can mean both 'the book *Against the Jews*' and 'the argument against the Jews.'

[29] Aulus Gellius, *Noctes Atticae* V 14.

he came to me gently and lifted up his foot to show it to me and ask for help. Then I drew out a very big splinter that was embedded in the sole of his foot and I cleaned the wound as best as I could. Relieved by my treatment, the lion put his paw in my hand, lay down and fell asleep. From that day on the lion and I lived in the same cave for three years. But later, when I was once hunting, I was caught by some soldiers and brought back to my master in Rome, who condemned me to death by being thrown to the wild beasts. This lion must also have been captured after I left him, and now he is requiting me for my kindness and my curing him.' After that story Androclus was acquitted at the request of all the people present, and the lion with him. And everyone who met the two of them anywhere exclaimed: 'This is the lion that was a man's friend, and this is the man who was physician to a lion.'

In view of several similar or identical parallel stories (*e.g.*, Pliny, *Nat. hist.* VIII 56; Aelianus, *Nat. anim.* VII 48), it is very probable that we have here a 'Wandermotiv' that the boastful Apion turned into a story about an event that he had seen happening before his own eyes.[30]

Another incredible story from Apion's *Aegyptiaka*, also quoted by Gellius (*Noct. Att.* VI 8) is about a dolphin which was in love with a boy. Again Apion claims to have been eyewitness of this remarkable event. The story deals with a dolphin swimming before the coast of Puteoli, which loved a beautiful boy, called Hyacinthus, whom he used to carry on his back. The fish came at the boy's call with passionate eagerness and drawing in his fins, so as not to wound the delicate skin of the object of his affection, he carried him as if mounted upon a horse for a distance of two hundred stadia. Rome and all Italy went out to see a fish that was under the sway of Aphrodite. Afterwards that same boy who was beloved by the dolphin fell sick and died. The lover came, as it had so often done, to the familiar shore, but the boy, who used to await its coming at the edge of the shoal water, was nowhere to be seen. The dolphin pined away from longing and died. It was found lying on the shore by those who knew the story, and was buried in the same tomb as its beloved friend.[31]

---

[30] See Jacoby, *FGH ad loc.*, 133 in app.

[31] Aulus Gellius, *Noct. Att.* X 10, also reports that in his *Aegyptiaka* Apion explains the fact that the Greeks and Romans wear their ring on the fourth finger of the left hand: "The reason for this practice is, that upon cutting into and opening human bodies, a custom in Egypt which the Greeks call *anatomai*, it was found that a very fine nerve proceeded from that finger alone of which we have spoken, and made its way to the human heart; that it therefore seemed quite reasonable that this finger in particular should be honoured with such an ornament, since it seems to be joined, and as it were united, with that supreme organ, the heart" (translation by J.C. Rolfe in the LCL).

What all this could possibly have to do with Egyptian history and culture is impossible to say.

Apion wrote several other works as well, which were, however, of a rather different nature. To begin with a strange case, there is his work Περὶ τῆς Ἀπικίου τρυφῆς, 'On Apicius' delicacies (or: dainty; or: luxury).' Marcus Gavius Apicius was one of the most famous Roman connoisseurs of luxury, especially in food, from the first half of the first century CE. He wrote on a wide variety of sauces and other gastronomic matters, and he claimed to be the creator of the *scientia popinae*, the art of the eating-house. Unfortunately his writing(s) have been lost, for the collection of recipes known by his name entitled *De re coquinaria* is almost certainly a 4th century forgery.[32] What did Apion have to write about this cook and gastronome? We don't know. The only reference to the work that has been preserved is the one by the early third century CE Athenaeus of Naucratis, which runs as follows: "The grammarian Apion, in the work *On the luxury of Apicius*, says that the fish called *elops* is this *accipesius*" (*Deipnosophistae* VII 294). The context is a discussion about the identification of a fish called *accipesius*, perhaps a kind of sturgeon, although that remains uncertain. Apion identified it as an *elops*, which is not very helpful to us since we do not know what an *elops* is. So what we can learn from this is not much, but it seems clear, in view of the wider context of the quote in Athenaeus, that Apion, probably being a gourmet himself, tried to outdo his famous contemporary Apicius in knowledge of exotic kinds of food, most likely especially of fish, since Pliny the Elder seems to imply that Apion also wrote about "remarkable qualities of fishes," *proprietates piscium mirabiles* (*Nat. hist.* I 32 = *FGH* 616T16).

A medieval source, the *Suda* (s.v. Πάσης), also mentions a work with the title Περὶ μάγου or Περὶ μάγων. Apart from the fact that Apion seems to have tried to explain there the meaning of the proverbial expression 'the half-obol [ἡμιωβόλιον] of Pases' (apparently a magician), we do not know anything of its contents. The same applies to a work mentioned by Pliny the Elder who says that Apion wrote (a book?) *de metallica medicina* (on minerals as medication; *Nat. hist.* I 35). The same Pliny mentions Apion also among authorities on medication obtained from animals (*Nat. hist.* I 30).[33] Does that imply that this grammarian also dabbled in medical or pharmaceutical science? We simply don't know, but in view of what we do know about his claims to possess extraordinary

---

[32] N. Purcell, 'Apicius,' *OCD* (1996) 121.

[33] *Ibid.* I 37 Pliny seems to imply that Apion wrote also about gems. The whole of *Nat. hist.* I 30-37 may derive largely from Apion, though certainly not solely from him.

knowledge that nobody else had, it is quite probable that he tried to advertise himself as a kind of *uomo universale*. Our sources also mention a work Περὶ Ῥωμαίων διαλέκτου, 'The Language of the Romans.' In the 15th book of his *Deipnosophistae*, Athenaeus discusses all kinds of wreaths. In that context he says that "Apion in his work *On the Latin language* says that the wreath was in times past called *chorônos* because the *choreutae* used it in the theatre, not only putting it on but also contending for it as a prize" (XV 680d). Here we should note two things: firstly, Apion here probably implies that the Latin *corona* is the equivalent of or has the same etymological root as the very rare Greek word χορωνός, meaning 'crown'; and secondly, that from an etymological point of view it has to do with χορευταί, i.e., the dancers and singers of the chorus, both derivations probably being incorrect. Be that as it may, for present purposes it suffices to draw attention to the fact that Apion is apparently fond of etymologies, and this is a feature of his interest that we will have ample opportunity to look at presently.[34] A work Περὶ στοιχείων is mentioned in a scholion on Dionysius Thrax,[35] but apart from the fact that it dealt with types of letters (not: elements), we know nothing about it.[36] Aulus Gellius mentions what may have been a work by Apion *de Alexandri regis laudibus* from which he quotes the following line: "He [Alexander] forbade the wife of his vanquished foe, a woman of surpassing loveliness, to be brought into his presence, in order that he might not touch her even with his eyes" (*Noct. Att.* VII 8 = *FGH* 616F22). We do not know, however, whether Apion wrote a *book* in praise of Alexander or whether in another work, for instance the *Aegyptiaka*, he made a *remark* in praise of Alexander. Much is bound to remain uncertain about the number and the nature of Apion's activities as an author, and it is hard to say how great the loss is, if 'loss' is the right word at all.[37]

---

[34] This feature is also noticeable in the anti-Jewish passages of Apion's *Aegyptiaka*, where he says that after the exodus from Egypt the Israelites developed tumors in the groin after a six day march, "and that is why (...) they rested on the seventh day, and called that day *sabbaton*, preserving the Egyptian terminology, for disease of the groin in Egypt is called *sabbo* (or: *sabbatosis*)" (in *C. Ap.* II 21). See M. Scheller, 'Σαββώ und σαββάτωσις,' *Glotta* 34 (1955) 298-300, on this 'Scherzbildung.'

[35] *FGH* 616F27 (Bekker's *Anecdota* II 784).

[36] Apion must have written other works than the ones mentioned here as well, as some ancient sources would seem to suggest, but we do not even know the titles. For instance, Pliny, *Nat. hist.* XXXI 22, implies that he wrote about springs and lakes, and *Nat. hist.* XXXV 88 suggests that Apion also wrote about physiognomics. Aelian, *Nat. anim.* X 29 and XI 40, suggests that he wrote about zoological matters etc.

[37] For more detailed information about the contents of Apion's writings I have to refer the reader to Jacoby's *Fragmente der griechichen Historiker*, Nr. 616.

We finally turn, therefore, to Apion's best known work among classical philologists, which is probably also his most influential work, the Γλῶσσαι Ὁμηρικαί. That is also, apart from Jacoby's edition of the historical fragments, the only work to be available in a modern critical edition.[38] This is not to imply that it has been preserved in its entirety. On the contrary, just as is the case with other works by this Alexandrian scholar, of this work, too, we have only fragments that have been preserved by later authors (some 160), especially in the valuable *Lexicon Homericum* by the late first century lexicographer Apollonius Sophistes,[39] and also in the medieval Etymologica (e.g., the *Etymologicum Magnum*, the *Etymologicum Genuinum*, and the *Etymologicum Gudianum*).[40] Because we know more about the *Glôssai Homêrikai* than about most other works of Apion, it is worthwile to pay some extra attention to it.[41]

The *Glôssai Homêrikai* deal with the explanation of Homeric vocabulary. They fall into three groups. (1) Most of Apion's explanations are of an etymological nature (note that his fondness of etymologies was already apparent in his work on the Latin language). Let me give two instances of this kind of explanation. Apion explains the Homeric hapax ἀθύρειν (playing, in *Iliad* XV 364) as ἀπὸ τοῦ πολλαχῶς θύειν, κατὰ πρόσθεσιν τοῦ ρ, ὃν τρόπον καὶ ἡ ἀιδρίη ἀιδία τις οὖσα: 'derived from raging (θύειν) in many ways, with addition of a *rho*, just as ignorance (ἀιδρίη) is also something lasting (ἀιδία)' (Nr. 10, p. 218 Neitzel). No modern etymologist would wish to take resposibility for this fanciful theory of a *rho*-infix, but it is fully within the range of possibilities in ancient etymologizing. That also applies to the second

---

[38] See the edition by Neitzel mentioned in note 1. The only previous edition was the one by H. Baumert, *Apionis quae ad Homerum pertinent fragmenta*, diss. Königsberg 1886. There is also some evidence, albeit slight, that Apion wrote either a commentary or lexicographical notes on Aristophanes; see *FGH* 616T54.

[39] On this author see F. Montanari in *Der Neue Pauly* I (1996) 883-885, but esp. H.W. Haslam, 'The Homer Lexicon of Apollonius Sophista,' *Classical Philology* 89 (1994) 1-45, 107-118.

[40] For a short but good survey see R. Tosi, 'Etymologica,' *Der Neue Pauly* IV (1998) 198-200. Still very valuable – even though it is more than a century old! – is the book by the great Richard Reitzenstein, *Geschichte der griechischen Etymologika*, Leipzig 1897.

[41] Much of what follows is based upon the Introduction in Neitzel's edition. It should be noted that the *Glôssai Homêrikai* by Apion has to be distinguished from the so-called 'Apion' Lexicon that was edited by A. Ludwich, 'Apions Homerische Glossen,' *Philologus* 74 (1917) 205-247; 75 (1918) 95-127, and reprinted in *Lexica graeca minora*, ed. K. Latte, Hildesheim 1965, 283-358. This collection was wrongly preserved under Apion's name; see Haslam, 'Homer Lexicon' 35-43.

instance, where Apion explains Homeric αἴσυλος (evil, criminal, in *Il.* V 403 etc.) as deriving from τὰ σεσυλημένα τῆς αἴσης, 'things robbed from the portion (that belongs to someone else)' (Nr. 15, p.221 Neitzel). Nonsensical though this may seem to modern eyes, one finds similar explanations of the same term in other ancient lexicographers.[42] (2) A second category consists of those instances in which we know only Apion's translation of Homeric terms without the underlying etymology being mentioned in the sources. A nice example is Apion's explanation of ἄχος (pain) as λύπη τήν σιωπὴν ἐπιφέρουσα, 'grief that induces silence' (Nr. 27, p.227 Neitzel). In view of the fact that in some medieval Etymologica the word ἄχος is explained as a combination of *alpha privans* (α στερητικόν) and χαίνειν (open one's mouth), it is clear that it is such an etymology that formed the basis of Apion's translation (not opening the mouth = silence). (3) A third category is formed by his 'clarifications' of Homer's text by means of different spellings or word divisions. For instance, in *Iliad* XXII 328 he read οὐδ᾽ ἄρ ἀπὸ σφάραγον μελίη τάμε χαλκοβάρεια (Nr. 130, p.285 Neitzel) instead of οὐδ᾽ ἄρ ἀπ᾽ ἀσφάραγον μελίη τάμε χαλκοβάρεια ('but the bronze spear did not cut his wind-pipe'). By this word-division Apion created a new word (σφάραγος) for wind-pipe, but he was criticized for this already in antiquity.[43] Also his reading ὅς φιν instead of ὅ σφιν in Iliad I 73 (Nr. 149, p.296 Neitzel) was sharply criticized, and rightly so, by Apollonius Sophistes.

Let me first make some remarks about Apion's etymologies. From the first example adduced above, his explanation of ἀθύρει, it is clear that one of his principles was the derivation of Homeric words from seemingly related or similarly sounding words (here by means of his more frequently applied principle κατὰ πρόσθεσιν, in this case the *rho*-infix). And the same example also makes clear another principle, *i.e.*, the derivation by means of *alpha privativum* (α στερητικόν) or of *alpha intensivum* (α ἐπιτατικόν); the latter being the case in his explaining the α in ἀθύρει as πολλαχῶς. Saying that this is sheer nonsense is justified from the point of view of modern etymological scholarship, but one should keep in mind that the linguistic know-how that experts in Indo-European linguistics of our days possess, was not at all available to the ancients.

At the same time it must be said that in some of the many cases in which Apion explains a Homeric word as a *compositum* of two words (a

---

[42] See Neitzel's discussion of this fragment in her *Apions Γλῶσσαι Ὁμηρικαί* 222.
[43] See Haslam, 'Homer Lexicon' 21 (with n. 47).

category in which he otherwise scores high on the scale of nonsensicality),[44] there are some cases "die noch in der modernen Sprachwissenschaft vertreten werden."[45] To give just one example, his explanation of θεσπέσιον (oracular, Nr. 42, p. 235 Neitzel) as τὸ ἐκ θεοῦ ἑπόμενον ἢ ἐκ θεοῦ λεγόμενον is still partly endorsed by modern etymologists. And more instances could be given. Even so the German-American papyrologist Albert Henrichs wrote 25 years ago about "die Auflösung der philologischen Zunft," of which he regards Apion as the main culprit.[46] Against this, however, the most recent editor of Apion's Homeric glosses, Susanne Neitzel, writes: "Eine pauschale Abwertung der philologischen Arbeit Apions, wie sie bei Henrichs anklingt, darf man sich jedenfalls erst dann erlauben, wenn man für den überwiegenden Teil der Glossen nachgewiesen hat, daß sie aus unbegründeten Spekulationen und sinnlosen Phantastereien bestehen."[47] One can hardly disagree with that, but the question is from which angle one approaches the question, that of ancient or that of modern etymological knowledge. If from the former, there can be no doubt that Apion, even with his most fantastic explanations, was still moving within the accepted limits of the 'Zunft' of ancient etymologist. The 'Abwertung' by Henrichs may be justified from a modern point of view, but it hardly needs to be said that such an approach is less then fair from an historical angle. Henrichs seems to suggest that even according to ancient standards Apion was a fraud, but that is not obvious to anyone who has read more than one page in ancient *Etymologica*.

One of the greatest Alexandrian philologists was Aristarchus of Samothrace, who wrote most of his works in the 2nd quarter of the 2nd century BCE. His most famous work was a critical edition of and a commentary on the epic poems of Homer.[48] Much of his work has come down to us via scholia on Homer. This work of Aristarchus was of some influence on Apion. What we can observe, however, is that Apion, when he uses Aristarchus, quite often does so mainly in order to propose an alternative etymology. Let me give an example (Nr. 142, p. 292 Neitzel): in *Iliad* XXII 491 Homer uses the enigmatic word

---

[44] See, for instance, his explanation of θήρ (wild animal, Nr. 43, p. 235 Neitzel) as derived from θοῶς ὀρούειν, 'running fast,' and cf. κρόταφος (Nr. 61).

[45] Thus Neitzel, *Apions Γλῶσσαι Ὁμηρικαί* 192, with the instances in note 30.

[46] A. Henrichs, 'Apollonius Sophistes' Homerlexikon,' in *Collectanea papyrologica* (FS H. Youtie), Bonn 1976, 27.

[47] Neitzel, *Apions Γλῶσσαι Ὁμηρικαί* 193.

[48] In this respect he was heavily indebted to his even more famous teacher Aristophanes of Byzantium.

ὑπεμνήμυκε,[49] which Aristarchus explained as ὑποκατανένευκε ('he has bowed his head, he is downcast'), which is probably right.[50] According to Apollonius Sophistes, Apion proposed, *on the basis of* (ὅθεν) Aristarchus' explanation: ὑπομέμυκε καὶ κλαίει (he has closed his eyes and weeps), and secondly, ἀνάμνησιν εἴληφεν (he got a memory), which can only become clear when one takes into account the context of this line. We read there that Andromache, having seen her husband Hector killed in battle, says about their only child, Astyanax: "An orphaned child is cut off from his playmates, downcast in everything, his cheeks wet with tears" (490-491). Apion's attempt to explain the difficult perfect form ὑπεμνήμυκε is twofold: Firstly he derives ὑπεμνήμυκε from ὑπομύω (to close one's eyes), and the additional remark 'and he weeps' is derived from the immediately following phrase in Homer, 'his cheeks are wet with tears.' Secondly, still unsatisfied with this explanation, Apion adds a second one, in which he derives the form from μνῶμαι (to remember, hence ἀνάμνησιν εἴληφεν), a solution that is immediately rejected by Apollonius, rightly so, of course.[51] When one examines all the cases in which Apion records the opinions of Aristarchus and other scholars, we can observe that in most cases he mentions his predecessors only to show his readers that even the most illustrious scholars of the past were wrong and that it is none other than Apion himself who has found the only right solution.

We see this again in a case where he derives the meaning of obscure words from the context in which they occur – which is in itself a respectable principle – and then thinks up an etymology that fits that meaning. For example, in *Iliad* XIII 39-41 it is said that the Trojans, after having created a breach in the defence of the Greeks, followed Hector like a fire or a storm, ἄβρομοι αὐίαχοι. Both words are *hapaxes*. Apion rejects Aristarchus' explanation of ἄβρομος that it must mean something like 'with a lot of noise' or 'joining in noise and shouting' and proposes the contrary solution (Nr. 4, p. 216 Neitzel): ἄφωνοι καὶ ἥσυχοι ὡς ἂν παρατάξεως οὐχὶ γιγνομένης (*without* noise and quietly because no battle array was formed). It is very probable that the basis of this remark is to be found in the observation that in the opening

---

[49] See W. Leaf, *The Iliad*, Amsterdam 1960 (= repr. of 1902), vol. I, 464: "The wonderful form ὑπεμνήμυκε is entirely inexplicable."

[50] See N. Richardson, *The Iliad: A Commenmtary*, vol. VI: books 21-24, Cambridge 1993, 160.

[51] For details see Neitzel, *Apions Γλῶσσαι Ὁμηρικαί* 195 and 293.

lines of book III of the *Iliad*, Homer has the Trojans make a lot of noise when they have been drawn up in battle array. Since the preceding sections in books XII and XIII make clear that at the moment they are described as ἄβρομοι the Trojan forces are in disorder,[52] Apion apparently concluded: no battle array implies no noise. Consequently, ἄβρομος must be understood as a combination of *alpha privans* and βρόμος (noise). Of course this must be wrong, if only because "it is impossible to suppose that they [the Trojans] became quiet when they were forcing the wall in their career of victory."[53] Moreover, the comparison with fire and wind makes it impossible to envisage a noiseless scene here. Again Aristarchus was right, for the *alpha* is not *privans* here but intensive.[54] Another example: Aristarchus rightly explained the Homeric νηπύτιος as a lengthened form of νήπιος, but Apion knows better: it means – again – ἄφωνος, ὡς ἐκ τοῦ νή καὶ τοῦ ἠπύειν, ὅ ἐστι φωνεῖν (Nr. 80, p.256 Neitzel). It does not fit any of the contexts at all, but Apion is here so enamoured of his own originality that one cannot but agree with Neitzel's remark that "Apion hat sich verführen lassen, um der Etymologie willen eine Wortbedeutung anzunehmen, die überhaupt nicht zum Text paßt" (256). One could multiply such instances *ad libitum*.

Let me finally make a brief remark on Apion's translations of Homeric words, which are presented without any justification. Sometimes it is impossible to find his reasons for giving specific translations, which are usually wrong. At several places it is again demonstrable that it is the context that determines the meaning defended by Apion. So, for instance, when in *Iliad* XI 165 (ἕπετο σφεδανὸν Δαναοῖσι κελεύων) he explains σφεδανόν as σκληρόν, it is clear that he took σφεδανόν to be an object to κελεύων whereas it is an adverb meaning 'vehemently' (Nr. 131, p.286 Neitzel) that is to be connected to ἕπετο.

The overall impression one gets when studying the remains of Apion's *Glossai Homerikai* is that on the one hand he sometimes follows his learned predecessors, but on the other, to quote Susanne Neitzel, "lassen sich […] sehr viel mehr Fälle aufweisen, in denen er in offenem Widerspruch zu Erklärungen und Etymologien anerkannter Philologen seine eigene Meinung verfocht," doing the latter almost invariably with inferior results. Sure, there are some cases in which Apion's explanations are better. For instance, when he explains the

---

[52] See the elaborate discussion by Neitzel, *Apions Γλῶσσαι Ὁμηρικαί* 216
[53] Leaf, *Iliad* II 6.
[54] R. Janko, *The Iliad: A Commentary*, vol. 4, Cambridge 1992, 47.

adjective κλυτόπωλος as 'having wonderful horses' (said of Hades; Nr. 51, p.240 Neitzel), this is certainly to be preferred to Aristarchus' fanciful derivation from κλυτὴ ἐπιπώλησις (famous visitation); and there are some other instances of this nature, but relatively few. It is small wonder, therefore, that Apion's successors, such as Apollonius Sophistes and later lexicographers, often severely criticized his explanations. Apollonius quotes Apion in his *Lexicon Homericum* no less than 132 times, and in several of these instances, after having mentioned Apion's view, he adds, βέλτιον δέ ... (followed by a better explanation), or he simply describes his interpretations as 'bad' (Nr. 97, κακῶς) or 'ridiculous' (Nr. 155, γελοίως), and rightly so.[55] Even so, it is clear that Apollonius felt he could not refrain from referring to Apion so often, and that is a clear sign of the fame and status of our Alexandrian, "mit dem man sich auseinanderzusetzen hatte."[56] True though it may be that the impression that is left on one's mind by the fragments of Apion's explanations is that of a pedantic personality whose main aim was to 'épater le bourgois' by means of highly 'original' (*i.e.*, far-fetched) solutions which would prove how much more clever he was than his predecessors,[57] on the other hand it is equally true what the latest editor of the fragments, Susanne Neitzel, says about this work: "Wenn wir verständnislos vor absurd anmutenden Übersetzungen stehen, groteske Mißverständnisse oder phantasievolle Spekulationen in der Etymologie belächeln, so müssen wir doch zugeben, da sie sich durchaus dem Bilde einfügen, das auch die übrige antike Etymologie bietet. Apions Deutungen homerischer Wörter sind im Vergleich mit anderen Erklärungsversuchen, wie sie in Scholien, Lexika und Etymologika im Umlauf waren, keineswegs so auffallend und ungewöhnlich, daß er eine Sonderstellung in der antiken Homererklärung verdiente" (209). And she adds that it would be extremely hard to imagine that a person who was nothing but 'ein bloßer Schwätzer und Scharlatan' could be appointed as head of the illustrious school of literary studies in Alexandria.

Summing up the results of this overview, we may say that Apion was a man of broad interests and wide reading, but that all that seems to have stood in the service of self-promotion. He strove to keep a high profile.

---

[55] Cf., however, Haslam, 'Homer lexicon' 27: "[Apollonius'] criticism of his predecessor is surprisingly muted. The majority of his reports are given neutrally."

[56] Neitzel, *Apions Γλῶσσαι Ὁμηρικαί*208.

[57] Haslam, 'Homer Lexicon' 28 n. 83: "He specialized in contriving novel etymologies for much-discussed words."

In the framework of that self-aggrandizing enterprise he developed a penchant for originality: *he* was the only or the first to have witnessed or learnt or discovered or explained things. So great was his originality that truth, facts and reality faded in the face of it. And original he was indeed: Apion is the only one to inform us that the Jews keep the sabbath because on the seventh day after the exodus they developed a tumor in the groin called *sabbo* (or *sabbatosis*) so that they could no longer walk and had to rest; and Apion is the first to inform us that the Jews had an annual cannibalistic ritual in which a fattened Greek was slaughtered and eaten by them.[58] To be the inventor of the libel of Jewish cannibalism is a form of originality that has rightly won Apion the bad reputation he has enjoyed till the present day.

---

[58] Resp. *C. Ap.* II 21 and 91-96. See E. Bickerman, 'Ritualmord und Eselskult,' in his *Studies in Jewish and Christian History*, vol. 2, Leiden 1980, 225-255.

13. THE DISTINCTIVE VOCABULARY OF JOSEPHUS' *CONTRA APIONEM*

In the Loeb Classical Library edition of Josephus' works, *Contra Apionem* takes up 112 pages of Greek text, whereas his *Vita* adds up to about 80, *Bellum* ca. 685 and *Antiquitates* ca. 1835 pages, totalling some 2600 pages for the other three works. In Niese's edition the numbers are 96 pages for *C. Ap.*, 70 for *Vita*, 626 for *Bell.*, and 1472 for *Ant*; all told, some 2170 pages for the other three works. As these numbers show, Josephus' treatise *Contra Apionem* is slightly more than 4% (almost 4.2%) of his whole œuvre. This implies that words used very often by Josephus could occur in his other works with a frequency on average 24 times as great as that in *C. Ap.* (that is to say, with almost the same frequency in *Vita*, roughly 6.5 times more frequently in *Bell.*, and ca. 16.5 times more frequently in *Ant.*). That in many cases this is indeed more or less the case, can quickly be confirmed by some browsing in Rengstorf's *Concordance*.[1]

Often enough, however, the distribution one finds turns out to be entirely different. Now it has to be admitted that it is very hard to say at which point deviations from a word distribution pattern to be expected on average begin to be statistically relevant. When words occur, for instance, 4 or 8 times as often in *Bell.*, or 10 or 20 times as often in *Ant.*, as in *C. Ap.*, there can be no doubt about the irrelevance of such data, because these minor divergences may well be due to sheer coincidence. But what can we say of cases in which a word occurs 13 times in *C. Ap.* over against only 4 times in *Bell.* and *Ant.* taken together, which is the case, e.g., with ἀρχαιότης? No one would deny that in such a case the difference from what might on average be expected is so great that it cannot fail to be significant. And, of course, as we all know, ἀρχαιότης, in the sense of the 'antiquity' of the Jewish people, is one of the main foci of Josephus' apologetic enterprise in *C. Ap.* Sometimes, words which occur *only* in *C.Ap.* and *not at all* in Josephus' other writings are equally instructive and significant. It is on these that this contribution will mainly focus: they will be listed completely hereafter. But, before

---

[1] *A Complete Concordance to Flavius Josephus*, ed. by K. H. Rengstorf in collaboration with others, 4 vols., Leiden 1973-1983.

doing so, I wish to point out, by way of example and in random order, some interesting cases of words that *do* occur in two, three or all of Josephus' writings but in a significantly different distribution than might be expected.[2]

A very obvious instance consists of the numerous terms relating to war and warfare that are extremely frequent in *Bell.* and *Ant.*, but very rare in *C. Ap.*; see for instance the concordance's long list of the many words beginning with στρατ-.[3] It is much less clear, however, why βούλη occurs 100 times in *Bell.*, *Ant.* and *Vita*, but never in *C. Ap.*, and why δῆμος occurs 275 times in *Bell.*, *Ant.* and *Vita*, but again never in *C. Ap.*[4] But the fact that δῆλος occurs 18 times in *C. Ap.*, which is relatively often when compared to some 40 cases in *Bell.* and *Ant.*, is easy to understand once it is seen that in *C. Ap.* it is most often used in the expression δῆλον ὅτι κτλ.: over against the detractors of the Jewish people Josephus time and again states emphatically that "it is clear (or: obvious to all) that" they are completely wrong. The same situation may explain why, of the 64 cases of ἐλέγχω in Josephus, no less than 16 are to be found in *C. Ap.*; why θαυμάζω is found in 21 cases over against 54 instances in the rest of Josephus' writings (N.B.: of θαυμαστόν there are 10 occurrences in *C. Ap.* against 37 in the other writings); and why λοιδορέω occurs 15 times in *C.Ap.* but only 10 times in the rest of Josephus. μῦθος, μυθεύω, μυθολογέω, and μυθολογία occur 8 times in *C.Ap.* against 9 times in the other works of Josephus, undoubtedly because of the fact that, in this work, he engages in polemics against pagan mythology and his effort to present the ideas of his opponents as nothing but myths.[5] The fact that it is at least 20 authors and their writings that Josephus is dealing with in *C. Ap.* goes far in explaining the fact that of some 76 occurrences of the words συγγράφειν, συγγραφή, συγγραφεύς and σύγγραμμα in all his works no less than 40 are found in *C. Ap.*, just as his polemics with some Greek poets may account for

---

[2] For the paucity of studies on the vocabulary of our author see the short survey by D. J. Ladouceur, "The Language of Josephus," *Journal for the Study of Judaism* 14 (1983) 18-38, esp. 19-20. Ladouceur's criticisms of the linguistic observations on Josephus' vocabulary by R. J. H. Shutt, *Studies in Josephus*, London 1961, are valid.

[3] A comparable and related example, chosen at random: σφενδονάω occurs 2 times in *Bell.* and 2 times in *Ant.*, σφενδονήτης 8 times only in *Bell.*, σφενδόνη 6 times only in *Ant.*; none of these words occurs in *C. Ap.*

[4] Is it because political history plays a much larger role in Josephus' other works than in *C. Ap.*?

[5] In the same category lie the 3 out of 7 occurrences of πλάσμα (in the sense of fiction, lie) in *C. Ap.*

the 5 occurrences out of 9 of ποιητής. The relative frequent occurrence of μάρτυς (17 times in *C. Ap.* against 36 in the rest, always in the sense of 'witness,' never of 'martyr'!) can be accounted for by Josephus' apologetic desire to adduce as many witnesses as possible to the truth of what he is saying. And Josephus' attempt to present Judaism as the best philosophy, actually as the source of the teaching of many Greek philosophers, is the explanation of the fact that no less than 20 of the 37 occurrences of φιλοσοφέω, φιλοσοφία and φιλόσοφος are found in *C.Ap.* The author's heavy emphasis on the supreme value of the Torah and on the high status of Moses explains why νόμος is probably one of the most frequently occurring words in *C.Ap.*[6]: 20 times in book 1 and 88 times in book 2; and why νομοθέτης has 25 instances in *C.Ap.* against just 26 in *Bell.* and *Ant.* together. And his stressing of the importance of learning Torah is largely responsible for the 5 occurrences of ἐκμανθάνω in *C. Ap.* against 10 elsewhere in Josephus. Although in *Bell.* Josephus does not have much positive to say about the zealots – ζηλωταί occurring 55 times in *Bell.* against 5 times in the rest of his works! – the word ζῆλος occurs 4 out of 8 times in *C. Ap.*, and that in the positive sense of admiration and imitation of the Torah.[7]

Now there are some 240 words that occur only in *C. Ap.* However, 77 (or 79) of them appear in passages quoted by Josephus from other writers. The authors cited and the numbers of these words occurring in them are as follows (in alphabetical order): Agatharchides 1; Apion 8; Apollonius Molon 1; Berossus 3; Chaeremon 3; Choerilus 5; Clearchus of Soli 3; Hecataeus of Abdera 13; Lysimachus 6; Manetho 28 [or 30][8]; Menander of Ephesus 5; Mnaseas 1. That is to say that there remain slightly over 160 words that are used by Josephus himself only in *C. Ap.* These will all be listed here with their place(s) of occurrence and the most applicable English equivalent (as listed in Rengstorf's *Concordance*, with some exceptions) added. The list contains all 240 words, *i.e.* including the terms deriving from Josephus' pagan sources, but the latter are put between square brackets [...] without a translation being

---

[6] Of course apart from pronomina, negations, words such as πᾶς etc.

[7] In Josephus' summary of the Torah in the second book of *C. Ap.* he stresses the strict sexual ethics which explains the fact that 5 out of 9 occurrences of μῖξις in Josephus occur here. It may be added here that the fact that of the 36 occurrences of ποιμήν in Josephus no less than 18 are in *C. Ap.* is due to the herdsmen's (= Hyksos') prominent role in Manetho's story that is extensively quoted by Josephus. So here the striking distribution of the word is entirely due to a source.

[8] Two words are probably glosses; but if not, they are from Manetho.

added but with a mention of the author's name. Only occasionally will short comments be added in order to highlight cases where the relation between this distinctive vocabulary and the main focus of the author is very obvious. This list is meant to be no more than a first modest step towards a study of Josephus' diction in *C. Ap.*[9]

[ἀγέννητος	2.167 unbegotten (said of God), *v.l.* for ἀγένητος]
ἀγίστεια	1.36; 2.7 ritual
ἀδόκιμος	2.236 reprobate[10]
ἆθλος	2.228 exertion
[αἰγυπτιστί	1.83 probably a gloss, otherwise from Manetho]
[ἄκ	1.83 probably a gloss, otherwise from Manetho]
ἀκολουθία	2.220 obedience
[ἄλγος	2.21; 2.27 from Apion]
ἀλληγορία	2.255 allegory
ἀμβλόω	2.202 to cause abortion (forbidden by the Law)
ἀμετάθετος	2.189 immutable[11]
[ἀμετάπειστος	2.189 *v.l.* for ἀμετάθετος]
ἄμνηστος	1.9 forgotten
ἀνάγνωσις	2.147 reading
ἀνάκαυσις	2.282 lighting
ἀνακήρυξις	2.217 public proclamation
ἀναλλοίωτος	2.167 unchangeable (said of God)
ἀναντίρρητος	1.160 not allowing contradiction[12]
[ἀναπέτομαι	1.203 conj. in a passage from Hecataeus Abderita]
ἀναπολόγητος	2.137 unanswered
[ἀναπόσβεστος	1.199 from Hecataeus of Abdera]
ἀνθρωπογονία	1.39 origin of mankind
ἀνταποστέλλω	1.111 to send to one another
[ἀντιβάλλω	2.163 *v.l.* for ἀντιπαραβάλλω]
ἀντιπαράθεσις	2.238 comparison[13]
[ἀντιπνέω	1.75 from Manetho]
ἀντίρρησις	2.1; 2.2 refutation (of Manetho and Apion)
ἀνωμαλία	2.250 inconsistency (in pagan conceptions of deity)
ἀόριστος	2.155; 2.171 undefined
ἀπαγόρευσις	2.190 prohibition[14]

[9] Also *variae lectiones* will be mentioned, but within square brackets and with *v.l.* added.
[10] Josephus says here that the anti-Jewish authors are ἀδόκιμοι σοφισταί. See on this word W. Grundmann in *TWNT* II 258f.
[11] It is with γνώμη ἀμετάθετος, unalterable determination, that the Jews keep to the rules of their Law, says Josephus.
[12] "The evidence for my assertions as to the antiquity of our people is consistent and ἀναντίρρητος."
[13] "Since our detractors expect to confute us by a comparison of the rival religions, it is impossible to remain silent."
[14] Used in combination with πρόρρησις of the positive and negative precepts of the Torah.

ἀπιθανότης	1.304 incredibility (of Lysimachus' account)[15]
ἀποτρόπαιος	2.249 to be shunned (of pagan *theoi apotropaioi*)
[ἀποτυμπανίζω	1.148 from Berossus]
ᾆσμα	1.12 song (of Homer)
ἀσόφιστος	2.292 not deceptive[16]
[ἀστεΐζομαι	2.114 from Apion]
ἄτεχνος	2.191 unfit
[ἄτμητος	1.198 from Hecataeus of Abdera]
αὐθιγενής	2.39 native
[αὐτάρ	1.173 from Choerilus]
[αὐχμαλέος	1.173 from Choerilus]
ἄφατος	2.190 ineffable (said of God)[17]
ἄφετος	2.229 free from
[ἀφηλιώτης	2.10 from Apion]
ἀφυής	2.148 untalented (?)[18]
βουβωνιάω	2.22; 2.23 to suffer from swollen inguinal glands
[βυθίζω	1.306; 1.308; 1.314 from Lysimachus]
[γεγυμνωμένως	1.191 from Hecataeus of Abdera]
[γειτνιάζω	2.33 from Apion]
γενειάω	2.242 to be bearded
γύμνασμα	1.53 exercise
[δαρτός	1.173 from Choerilus]
δεῖμος	2.248 fear (deified)[19]
[δεκαεννέα	1.97 from Manetho]
[διαβαδίζω	1.202 from Hecataeus]
διασυρμός	1.205 derision[20]
διαφωνία	1.12;19;23;37 inconsistency, contradiction[21]
διδασκαλικός	2.171; 2.214 didactic, instructive (said of the Law)
διερῶ	2.198 to prescribe

---

[15] Note that ἀπίθανος is used 6 times in *C. Ap.* as compared to 5 times in *Bell.* + *Ant.*!

[16] Here I disagree with the meaning listed in Rengstorf's *Concordance* ('not to be deceived'). The Jewish laws are ἀσόφιστοι λόγων παρασκευαῖς, "not deceptive by means of oratorical display (or: studied words)."

[17] This word occurs also as a *v.l.* for ἄβατος in *Ant.* 15.364.

[18] But this is a doubtful case since it occurs in Josephus' paraphrase of a work by Apollonius Molon. Since it is not a quotation, it may be Josephus' own diction, but it may equally well derive from Molon himself. The same problem recurs in some other instances.

[19] The synonym δεῖμα does occur in *Bell.* and *Ant.*

[20] Josephus states that derision of the Jewish people is the main purpose of the author Agatharchides.

[21] Josephus mentions this as a characteristic of pagan sources in 1.12;19;23, but stresses its absence in the Jewish Scriptures in 1.37. Note that Josephus uses διαφωνέω 5 times of which 3 are found in *C.Ap.*

διοδοιπορέω	[1.89 from Manetho] 2.157 to traverse
δοκιμαστής	2.279 tester[22]
ἐγκατασπείρω	2.239 to sow
[εἰκοσιείς	1.95 from Manetho]
ἐκπαιδεύω	2.213 to teach thoroughly (said of Moses)
[ἔκπτωσις	1.247; 1.266 from Manetho]
[ἐκτύπωμα	2.11; 2.12 from Apion]
[ἐμπερισπούδαστος	2.253 in an interpolation]
[ἐνενηκοντατρεῖς	1.231; 2.16 from Manetho]
ἐνευδοκιμέω	1.25 to gain renown in
[ἐννεακαίδεκα	1.79 from Manetho]
[ἐξασθενέω	1.211 from Agatharchides]
[ἐξοπλισία	1.79 from Manetho]
ἐξορίζω	1.257; 2.291 to banish
ἐπάγγελμα	1.24 promise[23]
ἐπεισπλέω	1.63 to make a voyage by ship to
[ἐπιβωμίτης	1.307 from Lysimachus]
ἐπιδέω	2.192 to need[24]
[ἐπιλογή	1.307 from Lysimachus]
ἐπιμίγνυμι	1.28; 2.257 to have contact with[25]
ἐπίπνοια	1.37 inspiration (of the Hebrew prophets)[26]
ἐπισεμνύνομαι	2.31 to pride oneself
[ἐπισινής	1.290 from Chaeremon]
[ἐπισύστασις	1.149 from Berossus]
ἐπιφορτίζω	2.115 to burden with a heavy load
ἐποπτεύω	2.294 to watch over[27]
ἐπόπτης	2.187 overseer
[εὕρημα	2.148 probably from Apollonius Molon]
[εὕρωστος	1.201 from Hecataeus of Abdera]
εὐχέρεια	1.57; 1.301 frivolity (of anti-Jewish writers)
ζωγράφος	2.252 painter
[ἠπιότης	1.186 from Hecataeus][28]
[θεμιστεύω	1.239 from Manetho]
θεοκρατία	2.165 theocracy (the Jewish constitution)[29]

---

[22] Time, Josephus says, has been the true tester of the Jewish Law, and it has stood the test.
[23] Here Josephus castigates pagan authors for their promises to present the readers with the truth whereas they do not do that at all.
[24] In his act of creation, Josephus says, God was not in need of any assistents.
[25] The word occurs also as a *v.l.* in *Ant.* 13.247.
[26] On the divine inspiration of the prophets in Josephus see A. Schlatter, *Die Theologie des Judentums nach dem Bericht des Josefus*, Gütersloh 1932, 58-59.
[27] See the brief discussion by W. Michaelis in *TWNT* V 374-5.
[28] Although occurring in Josephus' summary.
[29] This special word formation was undoubtedly a creative 'Neubildung,' coined by Josephus himself, for which he more or less apologizes by admitting that it is 'a forced expression'

θεολογία	[1.78 and 1.237 from Manetho] 1.225 theology[30]
[θεομαχέω	1.246; 1.263 from Manetho]
[θερεία	1.79 from Manetho]
θετέος	1.24 to be added
ἱέρεια	2.267 priestess
[ἱστοριογραφία	1.134 is a gloss]
ἰσχυρογνωμοσύνη	1.192 obstinacy (of Jews holding to the Law)
καινολογέω	1.222 to assert something new[31]
καιροπτία	2.127 seizing of a favourable opportunity
καλλιγραφέω	2.225 to write in a brilliant style (said of Plato)
[κάνθων	2.114; 2.115; 2.120 from Mnaseas][32]
κατάγελως	1.212 ridicule[33]
κατάγομος	2.115 heavily laden
καταρίθμησις	1.155 calculation[34]
κατασιωπάω	2.238 to keep silent[35]
κατάχρυσος	2.119 gold-plated
κιθαρίζω	2.242 to play the cithara
κότινος	2.217 wild olive
[κράτησις	1.248 from Manetho]
κροκόδειλος	1.254 crocodile
κυνοκέφαλος	1.254 dog-faced baboon
κωμῳδέω	2.223 to ridicule
κώνειον	2.263 hemlock
[λατομία	1.237 from Manetho]
λεπράω	1.256; 1.281; 2.15 to be a leper

(ὡς δ᾽ ἄν τις εἴποι βιασάμενος τὸν λόγον). See G. Schmid, *De Flavii Josephi elocutione observationes criticae*, Leipzig 1893, 523; E. Kautzsch, *Biblische Theologie des Alten Testaments*, Tübingen 1911, 57-9; W. Michaelis, *TWNT* III 908-909; Schlatter, *Die Theologie des Judentums nach dem Bericht des Josefus* 26.48; H. Cancik, "Theokratie und Priesterherrschaft. Die mosaische Verfassung bei Flavius Josephus, C. Ap. 2,157-198," in J. Taubes (ed.), *Religionstheorie und politische Theologie*, Band 3: Theokratie, München 1987, 65-77; Y. Amir, "THEOKRATIA as a concept of Political Philosophy: Josephus' Presentation of Moses' *Politeia*," *Studia Classica Israelica* 8/9 (1988) 83-105; and the critical discussion of Cancik's and Amir's interpretations by Chr. Gerber, "Das Judentum als Theokratie" (forthcoming; paper read at the Prague 1995 meeting of the SNTS).

[30] See Schlatter, *Die Theologie des Judentums nach dem Bericht des Josefus* 108.

[31] Josephus states that sometimes pagan authors try to assert something new, however nonsensical it may be, just in order to gain fame.

[32] But as quoted by Apion.

[33] Ridicule is what Agatharchides pours out over people who keep the sabbath, Josephus says. Note that καταγελάω occurs 3 times in *C. Ap.* against 3 times in the other works; καταγέλαστος has 2 occurrences of which 1 is in *C. Ap.*

[34] The full expression used here is καταρίθμησις τῶν χρόνων, chronology. Of 6 occurrences of καταριθμέω 3 are in *C. Ap.*

[35] See the note on ἀντιπαράθεσις, above.

λεχώ	2.198; 2.202 woman in childbed
ληρέω	1.252 to chatter foolishly (said of Manetho)
[λιθοτομία	1.235; 1.257; 1.267; 1.278; 1.296 from Manetho][36]
[λυχνίον	1.198 from Hecataeus of Abdera]
λυχνοκαῖα	2.118 feast with lighting of lamps
λυχνοφόρος	2.120 lamp-bearer
μαντεῖον	2.162 oracle (Delphi)[37]
[μαντικός	1.236 from Manetho]
μικροψυχία	1.226 narrow-mindedness (of anti-Jewish authors)
μισανθρωπία	2.291 misanthropy (which the Jews do not teach)
μισάνθρωπος	2.148 misanthropic (Apion accuses us of being so)[38]
[μολίβδινος	1.307 from Lysimachus]
[μολυσμός	1.289 from Chaeremon]
μύδρος	2.265 lump of metal[39]
μυέω	2.267 to initiate
μωρολογία	2.115 foolish talk (of Apion)
[ν' (=50)	1.123 from Menander of Ephesus]
[νδ' (=54)	1.159 from Berossus]
[νθ' (=59)	1.231 from Manetho]
νεκρόπολις	2.36 necropolis
νεοττός	2.213 young bird (from Deut. 22.6)
νή Δία	1.255; 2.263 by Zeus[40]
νομαδικός	1.91 nomadic
[ξς' (=66)	1.231 from Manetho]
ξενηλασία	2.259 expulsion of foreigners[41]
ξύρησις	1.282 shaving
οἰκοδεσπότης	2.128 domestic master[42]
οἰκοδόμησις	1.126 construction
ὁμογνωμοσύνη	2.270 agreement in opinion
ὁμωρόφιος	1.281 living under the same roof
ὀνομασία	[1.311 from Lysimachus] 2.26 designation

---

[36] Actually only §235 is a quote from Manetho but in the 4 other passages Josephus discusses Manetho's assertions to the effect that originally the Jews were a group of Egyptian lepers who were sent to work in the stone quarries (λιθοτομίαι, λατομίαι).

[37] See Schlatter, Die Theologie des Judentums nach dem Bericht des Josefus 67.

[38] On μισανθρωπία and μισάνθρωπος in Josephus see Schlatter, Die Theologie des Judentums nach dem Bericht des Josefus 29, 250; and now especially L. H. Feldman, Jew and Gentile in the Ancient World, Princeton 1993, 123-149 (142-149 on C. Ap.).

[39] This word occurs, however, in a passage in which Josephus mentions Anaxagoras' theory that the sun was nothing more than a glowing lump of metal.

[40] It is striking that in his indignation Josephus twice uses this pagan form of strong language.

[41] On this word see O. Stählin in TWNT V 4.

[42] This word is discussed by K. H. Rengstorf in TWNT II 48.

ὀνομαστός	1.36 mentioned by name
[ὀπτάνιον	1.249 from Manetho]
[ὀρκωμοτέω	1.238; 1.270 from Manetho][43]
[ὀρνιθεύω	1.202 from Hecataeus of Abdera]
οὐδοστισοῦν	2.165; 2.282 none whatsoever
ὀχλαγωγός	2.3; 2.136 hawker (= salesman, sc. Apion)
παράκουσμα	1.46 hearsay[44]
[πατάσσω	1.203 from Hecataeus of Abdera]
[πενταέτης	1.245 from Manetho]
[πεντάπλεθρος	1.198 from Hecataeus of Abdera]
[πεντηκοντατέσσαρες	1.122 from Menander of Ephesus]
περιεργία	2.12 unnecessary activity
[πέτομαι	1.203 from Hecataeus of Abdera]
πλάστης	2.252 sculptor
πολιτογραφέω	2.251 to admit to citizenship
[προδήλωσις	1.243 from Manetho]
προκαταβάλλω	1.23 to put in writing previously
προκατονομάζω	1.84 to enumerate previously[45]
προσαποδίδωμι	1.320 to add in order to complete
προσπλέκομαι	1.222 to sidle up to someone
[ρμγ´ (= 143)	1.126 from Menander of Ephesus]
[ρνε´ (= 155)	1.126 from Menander of Ephesus]
[ῥητορικός	1.178 from Clearchus]
ῥυπαίνω	1.220 to contaminate
[σαββώ	2.21; 2.26; 2.27 from Apion][46]
[σεβαστεύω	1.249 from Manetho]
σέλινον	2.217 celery
[σιτομετρέω	1.79 from Manetho]
[σκάφη	2.11 from Apion]
[σκέλλω	1.173 from Choerilus]
[σύλλεκτος	1.198 from Hecataeus of Abdera]
συμπεριλαμβάνω	2.32 to include[47]
[συμπεριπολέω	2.11 from Apion]
συμπλάσσω	1.298 to contrive (Apion is subject)

---

[43] Although the second time in Josephus' paraphrase.

[44] Hearsay not knowledge is the basis of reports about Jewish history by Greek authors. On παρακούω see G. Kittel in *TWNT* I 224.

[45] On this hapax see Schmidt, *De Flavii Josephi elocutione* 527.

[46] Apion asserts that this is an Egyptian word for a disease of the groin that the Israelites suffered from so that they could not work and that gave its name to the sabbath. M. Scheller, Σαββώ und σαββάτωσις, *Glotta* 34 [1955] 298-300, calls it a 'Scherzbildung' and says it probably is Alexandrian slang (Argot) and another attempt of Apion to poke fun at the Jews.

[47] Apion included all the rest of the Jews in his slander.

συμφιλοτιμέομαι	1.110 to share someone's zeal
συμφωνία	2.170; 2.179 harmony (effect of the Law)[48]
συναποδύρομαι	2.205 to lament together[49]
[συνατιμάζω	1.241 from Manetho]
συνεκπίπτω	1.300 to rush away together with someone
συνεξελαύνομαι	1.279; 1.299 to be expelled together (?)[50]
[συνεπιστρατεύω	1.241 from Manetho]
συνιερεύς	2.194 fellow-priest
[συνοικειόω	1.181 from Clearchus]
συνουσιαστής	1.164 follower
συντομία	1.251 brevity
συντονία	2.174 strain
σφυρήλατος	2.119 of hammered goldplates (?)[51]
[σχολαστικός	1.181 from Clearchus]
τάρταρος	2.240 underworld
τεκνοκτόνος	2.202 one who kills her/his own child[52]
[τεσσαρακοντατρεῖς	1.108; 1.121 from Menander][53]
τιμωρητικός	2.214 penal
[τριακονταοκτώ	1.291 from Chaeremon]
[τροχοκουράς	1.173 from Choerilus]
[ὕκ	1.82; 1.83 from Manetho]
ὑπεναντιότης	1.224 antagonism[54]
ὑπερπαίω	1.304 to surpass[55]
[ὑπερχαρής	1.243 from Manetho]
φιλεργός	2.283 industry[56]
φιλοχρηματέω	1.61 to strive after riches
φλυάρημα	2.116 raving (of Apion)
φλυαρία	2.22 babble (of Apion)
φράσις	2.12 statement

---

[48] Note that συμφωνέω occurs 5 out of 10 times in *C.Ap.* and σύμφωνος 6 out of 12. On both words see the useful remarks by O. Betz in *TWNT* IX 297-300 (esp. 300 on Josephus: "Er rühmt die herrliche συμφωνία in Denken und Leben des jüdischen Volkes, die in der Einheitlichkeit der Lebensführung und in der gleichen, mit dem Gesetz übereinstimmenden Auffassung von Gott begründet sei").

[49] On this hapax see again Schmidt, *De Flavii Josephi elocutione* 527.

[50] The word occurs here, however, in Josephus' summary of Manetho.

[51] The meaning of the term is far from certain.

[52] The Jewish Law regards a woman who commits abortion as one who kills her child.

[53] Josephus asserts that part of the information in 1.108 derives from a Phoenician source, but we cannot ascertain how true to the facts that is.

[54] The antagonism between Egyptians and Jews created bitter animosity. Note that 4 of the 6 occurrences of ὑπεναντίος are found in *C.Ap.*

[55] Josephus asserts that Lysimachus surpasses other authors in the incredibility of his lies.

[56] The motif of love of work is used by Josephus in a characterization of the Jewish people.

[φύτευμα	1.199 from Hecateus of Abdera]
[χάρτης	1.307 from Lysimachus]
χοίρειος	2.141 from pork
χοῖρος	2.137 pork
ψέγω	2.287 to censure[57]
[ψωρός	1.305; 1.306; 1.308; 1.312 from Lysimachus]

This brief survey highlights what are Josephus' main concerns in *C. Ap.* He wants to expose the totally unjustified character of the attacks on Jews and Judaism by Greek authors: they are full of lies, they try to ridicule and deride Judaism by slander (e.g., the charge of misanthropy) and frivolous talk, and their accounts often contain inner contradictions. In contradistinction to that, the Law of Moses is a source of harmony because it prescribes a theocratic constitution, and it is for that reason that the Jews are keeping its precepts in steadfastness.[58]

---

[57] In this work it has not been my purpose to censure the institutions of other peoples, says Josephus almost at the end of *C. Ap.*

[58] I owe thanks to Jack Levison for some useful hints.

14. THE SAMARITAN LANGUAGES IN THE PRE-ISLAMIC PERIOD*

Like the Jews – or, if one wishes, like the other Jews – the Samaritans used three languages in the near-millennium between Alexander the Great and Muhammed: Hebrew, Aramaic, and Greek. The question to be discussed in this short paper is: Who used which language(s), and when and where? Of course, the preliminary question is, as always: Does the evidence available enable us to answer these questions? And the problems begin here. Let us, therefore, begin with a review of the evidence.

Samaritan sources that are definitely from the pre-Islamic period are few and far between. As far as literature is concerned, we have very little to go by. Firstly there is the Greek fragment of the so-called Samaritan anonymous who also goes by the name of Ps-Eupolemos.[1] Theodotus, the epic author of a Greek hexametric poem on the history of Shechem, was also probably a Samaritan author.[2] Both of these authors are from the second century BCE.[3] The last piece of Greek evidence is the problematic *Samareitikon* (if it ever existed at all – although, if it did not exist, we can at least be sure of the existence of a Samaritan adaptation or revision of the Septuagint Pentateuch).[4] As to Aramaic literature, we have first and foremost the *Tibat Marqe*, at least the early parts of

---

* This paper was read at the fifth international meeting of the Société d'Etudes Samaritaines that took place in Helsinki on August 1-4, 2000.

[1] C.R. Holladay, *Fragments from Hellenistic Jewish Authors*, vol. 1, Atlanta: Scholars Press, 1983, 157-187.

[2] C.R. Holladay, *Fragments from Hellenistic Jewish Authors*, vol. 2, Atlanta: Scholars Press, 1989, 51-204.

[3] On the issue of whether or not these two authors were indeed Samaritans see the discussion in my essay 'Samaritans and Hellenism,' in my *Hellenism – Judaism – Christianity: Essays on Their Interaction*, 2nd ed., Leuven: Peeters, 1998, 49-58. For the most recent defence of Samaritan authorship of Theodotus' poem see M. Daise, 'Samaritans, Seleucids, and the Epic of Theodotus,' *Journal for the Study of the Pseudepigrapha* 17 (1998) 25-51 (with full bibliography on the question). I see no reason at all to regard other authors (such as Thallus, Cleodemus Malchus, let alone Ezekiel the Tragedian) as Samaritans, as others have done in the past, e.g. N. Schur, *History of the Samaritans*, Frankfurt etc.: P. Lang, 1989, 73.

[4] E. Tov, 'Die griechischen Bibelübersetzungen,' *Aufstieg und Niedergang der Römischen Welt* II 20,1, Berlin – New York: W. de Gruyter, 1987, 185-186; S. Noja, 'The Samareitikon,' in A.D. Crown (ed.), *The Samaritans*, Tübingen: Mohr, 1989, 408-412. But see now especially the well-balanced and authoritative study by R. Pummer, 'The Greek Bible and the Samaritans,' *Revue des études juives* 157 (1998) 269-358.

which are pre-Islamic;[5] further the liturgical poetry by Amram Dare, his son Marqe,[6] and his grandson Nanah (or Ninna), in the early portions of the *Defter*.[7] Finally we have the Samaritan Targum in its various versions.[8] The most important – and practically the only – document in Hebrew is of course the Samaritan Pentateuch.[9] We may now perhaps have to add the Masada papyrus fragment (possibly a liturgical text), which was recently claimed to be Samaritan by Sh. Talmon,[10] but this still remains uncertain.

As regards epigraphic material, we have some 70 published inscriptions (including amulets)[11] which can be dated with more or less certainty to the pre-Islamic period. Unfortunately there is as yet no *Corpus Inscriptionum Samaritanarum*. Unfortunately, too, so far there is no full publication of the numerous inscriptions found by Y. Magen in the vicinity of the Theotokos church on Mt. Garizim.[12] As a matter of fact,

---

[5] Z. Ben-Hayyim (ed.), *Tibat Marqe*, Jerusalem: The Israel Academy of Sciences and Humanities, 1988. Only the first and part of the second book are pre-Islamic.

[6] A.A. Cowley, *The Samaritan Liturgy*, 2 vols., Oxford: OUP, 1909, vol. 2, Register s.vv. See A. Tal, 'Samaritan Literature,' in A.D. Crown (ed.), *The Samaritans*, Tübingen: Mohr, 1989, 452-455. See on Marqe's poetry now also A.S. Rodrigues Pereira, *Studies in Aramaic Poetry (c. 100 BCE – 600 C.E.). Selected Jewish, Christian and Samaritan Poems*, diss. Leiden 1996, vol. 1:171-216; vol. 2:49-56.

[7] A. Tal, 'Defter,' in A.D. Crown e.a. (edd.), *A Companion to Samaritan Studies*, Tübingen: Mohr, 1993, 69, and 'Samaritan Literature' 460-462.

[8] A. Tal, *The Samaritan Targum of the Pentateuch*, 3 vols., Tel Aviv: Tel Aviv University, 1980-1983.

[9] A. von Gall, *Der hebräische Pentateuch der Samaritaner*, Giessen: Töpelmann, 1914-1918 (repr. Berlin 1966).

[10] Sh. Talmon, 'A Masada Fragment of Samaritan Origin,' *Israel Exploration Journal* 47 (1997) 220-232.

[11] Of the amulets only three contain short Greek phrases alongside biblical verses in Hebrew. The others contain only biblical verses. See R. Pummer, 'Samaritan Amulets of the Roman Byzantine Period and Their Wearers,' *Revue Biblique* 94 (1987) 251-263; also idem, 'Amulets,' *Companion* 14.

[12] The most comprehensive listing of the epigraphic material published so far is to be found in M. Baillet's lemma 'Samaritains' in *Supplément au Dictionnaire de la Bible* XI (1990) 860-874. For additions see L. Di Segni, 'The Church of Mary Theotokos on Mount Gerizim: The Inscriptions,' in G.C. Bottini et al. (edd.), *Christian Archaeology in the Holy Land. Essays in Honour of Virgilio C. Corbo*, Jerusalem: Franciscan Printing Press, 1990, 343-350; Y. Magen, 'Samaritan Synagogues,' in F. Manns & E. Alliata (eds.), *Early Christianity in Context: Monuments and Documents*, Jerusalem: Franciscan Printing Press, 1993, 193-230, esp. 200-203 and 219-220; L. Di Segni, 'The Greek Inscriptions in the Samaritan Synagogue at El-Khirbe,' *ibid.* 231-239; J. Tropper, 'Die samaritanischen Inschriften des Pergamonmuseums,' *Zeitschrift des Deutschen Palästina-Vereins* 111 (1995) 118-134. Invaluable are also F. Hüttenmeister & G. Reeg, *Die antiken Synagogen in Israel*, vol. 2: Die samaritanischen Synagogen, Wiesbaden: Reichert, 1977, and the survey in chapter 8 of J. Zangenberg, *SAMAREIA. Antike Quellen zur Geschichte und Kultur der Samaritaner in deutscher Übersetzung*, Tübingen & Basel: Francke Verlag, 1994, 314-330. On the problems of

the unpublished inscriptions far outnumber the published ones, which is a rather dramatic situation. So all I will be saying about the epigraphic sources is bound to be very provisional.[13] Many of the published inscriptions contain only quotations from the Samaritan Pentateuch (especially the Decalogue inscriptions)[14] and hence are not very instructive for our purpose. Finally, occasionally non-Samaritan sources, both literary and epigraphic, provide us with some bits and pieces of circumstantial evidence from which we can glean some information about the linguistic situation of the Samaritans.[15]

When we compare this to the amount of non-Samaritan Jewish evidence we have, the difference is vast. There we have hundreds of documents and thousands of inscriptions which provide us with abundant evidence. But even in that much more favourable situation our question remains very hard to answer, if only because the evidence itself is simply not relevant in helping us to answer our questions that arise from linguistic curiosity.[16]

Let us begin with the Hebrew evidence. Here it would seem to be even clearer than in the case of Jewish literature and epigraphy that Hebrew was no longer a spoken language but that it served mainly liturgical purposes. When we take a look at the material, we see that – unlike the situation in Judaism – there is no Samaritan literature in Hebrew other than the Pentateuch and, as far as epigraphic evidence is concerned, quotes from the Pentateuch and some liturgical formulas that have been inspired by the Samaritan Bible (for instance, *barukh sh^emo le'olam*).[17] (Maybe

dating Samaritan inscriptions by script only see R. Pummer, 'Inscriptions,' in Crown (ed.), *The Samaritans* 191. All Samaritan inscriptions from the Land of Israel will be included in the planned *Corpus Inscriptionum Iudaeae/Palestinae*, on which see H. Cotton et al., 'The Corpus Inscriptionum Iudaeae/Palestinae,' *Scripta Classica Israelica* 18 (1999) 175-176.

[13] Leah Di Segni recently announced the find of new Greek inscriptions in a Samaritan synagogue on the Carmel range (paper read at the fifth international meeting of the Société d'Etudes Samaritaines in Helsinki, August 2000).

[14] See J. Bowman & Sh. Talmon, 'Samaritan Decalogue Inscriptions,' *Bulletin of the John Rylands Library* 33 (1951) 211-236.

[15] See the evidence collected in P.W. van der Horst, 'The Samaritan Diaspora in Antiquity,' in my *Essays on the Jewish World of Early Christianity*, Fribourg-Göttingen: Universitätsverlag – Vandenhoeck & Ruprecht, 1990, 138-146.

[16] See P.W. van der Horst, 'Greek in Jewish Palestine in the Light of Epigraphy,' in J.J. Collins & G.E. Sterling (eds), *Hellenism in the Land of Israel*, Notre Dame: University of Notre Dame Press, 2001, 154-174 (repr. elsewhere in this volume).

[17] For examples from inscriptions see, for instance, the three from Amwas (Emmaus) in *Corpus Inscriptionum Judaicarum* nos. 1186-1188. See also J. Bowman, *Samaritan Documents Relating to their History, Religion and Life*, Pittsburg: The Pickwick Press, 1977, 9-15.

the above-mentioned papyrus fragment from Masada, written on both sides in palaeo-Hebrew characters, contained a hymn written by a Samaritan in Hebrew, but the piece is too minute to build any certainty upon.)[18] There is no pre-Islamic Samaritan counterpart to Jewish halakhic compilations in Hebrew such as the Mishna or the halakhic midrashim. The Samaritan halakhic sources all date from the period after Muhammed and have been written in Arabic.[19] And even if we had had pre-Islamic Samaritan halakhic documents, it is far from certain that they would have been composed in Hebrew. It would seem highly probable that Hebrew had become an extinct language by the beginning of the Hellenistic period. Scholars and priests still knew it, the common people no longer did. The Wadi Daliyeh papyri from the fourth cent. BCE are all in Aramaic, and even though it would be imprecise and anachronistic to label them as 'Samaritan' – they may be 'Samarian'[20] – they nevertheless make clear that as early as the 4th cent. BCE the vernacular in the area that was the main habitat of the people who would later become the Samaritans, was Aramaic, not Hebrew. As Rudolf Macuch remarks, Samaritan Hebrew "was similarly to Judaean Hebrew driven out from the living usage by the Aramaic vernacular in the last centuries B.C.E,"[21] although it continued to be used as a liturgical language alongside Samaritan Aramaic, both in the temple on Mount Garizim (if ever there was one) and later in the synagogues.[22]

Aramaic was without doubt the vernacular of the Samaritans for most of the pre-Islamic period, but that applies only to Palestine. When we

---

[18] Cf. Sh. Talmon, 'A Masada Fragment of Samaritan Origin,' *IEJ* 47 (1997) 220-232.

[19] See the survey in A. Tal, 'Halakhic Literature,' in *Companion* 108-111; and I.R.M. Bóid, 'The Samaritan Halacha,' in Crown (ed.), *Samaritans* 624-649

[20] 'Samarian' is the now common term for non-Samaritan inhabitants of Samaria. On the possibly Samarian character of the Wadi Daliyeh papyri see R. Pummer, 'Samaritan Material Remains and Archaeology,' in Crown (ed.), *Samaritans* 175-177, and the most recent survey by D.M. Gropp, 'Wadi ed-Daliyeh,' in L.H. Schiffman & J.C. VanderKam (eds.), *Encyclopedia of the Dead Sea Scrolls*, vol. 1, Oxford: Oxford University Press, 2000, 162-165.

[21] R. Macuch, "Samaritan Languages,' in Crown (ed.), *Samaritans* 533. I leave aside here the occasional Samarian seals with Hebrew inscriptions from the fourth century BCE – on which see J. Naveh, 'Scripts and Inscriptions from Ancient Samaria,' *Israel Exploration Journal* 48 (1998) 92-93 – and the question of the revival of Samaritan Hebrew in the 13th century CE.

[22] The fragmentary Hebrew inscriptions in the temple area on Mt. Garizim from the second century BCE seem to testify to the use of Hebrew as a sacred language in the temple. See Naveh, 'Scripts and Inscriptions' 93. (Unfortunately I have not been able to consult A. Tal, 'Languages in Contact: Hebrew and Aramaic in the Ancient Samaritan Community,' in A.D. Crown & L. Davey (eds.), *Essays in Honour of G.D. Sixdenier*, Armidale 1995, 577-586.)

look at the evidence, we can see that the sources are all of Palestinian provenance: *Tibat Marqe*, the Targum and the liturgical poems are not diaspora products. Also, the relatively few Aramaic inscriptions are all from Palestine. Does this prove that for the Samaritans who did not live in the diaspora, Aramaic, and only Aramaic, was the language of daily life? That would be a premature conclusion. In order to illustrate this point we have now to take a closer look at the Greek material.

Even though still scanty, this material is much more widespread than the Hebrew and Aramaic evidence. We have Greek inscriptions from Palestine and the diaspora, Greek literature from unknown provenance but possibly from both Palestine and the diaspora (we will come back to that), and finally there is corroborative material to be gleaned from the circumstantial evidence.

To begin with the 70 or so published inscriptions, at least some 35 are in Greek, but only 3 of these are from the diaspora, Delos and Thessaloniki, and all the rest are from Palestine![23] Let us first look at these numbers and the percentages.[24] Half of the published inscriptions are in Greek, and more than 90% of these Greek inscriptions are from Palestine, less than 10% from the diaspora. Again, the differences in relation to the Jewish evidence are vast. There we have a total of some 2,800 Jewish inscriptions, 1,800 of which are in Palestine and some 1,000 in the diaspora (of which some 600 in Rome!). Of this corpus as a whole some 70% are in Greek; in the diaspora the percentage is at least 85%, but even in Palestine well over 60% of the material is in Greek.[25] So not

---

[23] Although one of them, in Beth Shean, is Greek written in Samaritan characters; see J. Naveh, 'A Greek Dedication in Samaritan Letters,' *IEJ* 31 (1981) 220-222, and K. Beyer, *Die aramäischen Texte vom Toten Meer*, Göttingen: Vandenhoeck & Ruprecht, 1984, 400. For a Jewish parallel (Greek in square Hebrew) see *Corpus Inscriptionum Judaicarum* 595 (from Venusa in Italy), with the comments by P.W. van der Horst, *Ancient Jewish Epitaphs. An introductory survey of a millennium of Jewish funerary epigraphy (300 BCE-700 CE)*, Kampen: Kok, 1991, 33-34.

[24] Again it should be emphasized that all of the following is bound to be very provisional because the many inscriptions found recently at Mt. Garizim have not yet been fully published. Quite a number of them are in Greek; see Y. Magen, 'Gerizim, Mount,' in E. Stern (ed.), *The New Encyclopedia of Archaeological Excavations in the Holy Land*, Jerusalem: Carta, 1993, 484-492 (here, e.g., at 492: seven Samaritan dedicatory inscriptions in Greek from the fourth cent. CE); and see also Di Segni, 'The Church of Mary Theotokos,' and the summary in Zangenberg, SAMAREIA 315-318. The number of inscriptions increases at such a rapid pace that the situation sketched in the text may be outdated even at the moment of writing.

[25] For these data see my *Ancient Jewish Epitaphs* 22, and 'Greek in Jewish Palestine.' The material from Palestine will now be exhaustively collected in the new *Corpus Inscriptionum Iudaeae/Palestinae*, on which see the brief report by H. Cotton, L. Di Segni, W. Eck, and B. Isaac in *Zeitschrift für Papyrologie und Epigraphik* 127 (1999) 307-308.

only the quantity of material is different, also the percentages for Greek. But we should not let ourselves be led astray by this. The impression of vast differences is created partly by the skewed nature of the evidence. Of course, as far as the total number of inscriptions is concerned, the Jewish ones far outnumber the Samaritan ones. But even here some caution is in order, for among the many Jewish inscriptions there may be some Samaritan ones in hiding. It cannot by any means be excluded that several inscriptions which are said to be identifiably Jewish,[26] are in fact Samaritan. If an inscription is in Greek, if the names used there are typically Jewish (being Hebrew names), and if the Law of Moses is referred to, what is there for us to distinguish a Jewish from a Samaritan inscription in such a case? So there may be many more Samaritan inscriptions than we will ever be able to identify![27] In this respect it is revealing that in their book *The Greek and Latin Inscriptions of Caesarea Maritima* (Boston 2000), C.M. Lehmann and K.G. Holum state on the one hand that Samaritans are "so numerous in Caesarea and its territory in the fourth century that it took pagans and Jews together to equal the Samaritans" (19) and that they tend to lose themselves epigraphically among the Jews, while on the other hand they list all inscriptions with Jewish symbols and names under the rubric 'Jewish.' At least a number of them cannot but be Samaritan.

Further we have to take into account the rather high number of inscriptions that consist solely of biblical quotes and are therefore in Hebrew. This is a phenomenon that one finds infinitely less frequently in Jewish inscriptions. The number of Jewish inscriptions that quote biblical texts, let alone that consist solely of biblical quotes is negligible.[28] Unlike Samaritans – and unlike Christians! – the Jews apparently were much more reserved in this respect.[29] Whereas in the case of Samaritan inscriptions a majority consists of biblical quotes, in the Jewish material it is only a handful (much less than 1%). This is another explanation for the preponderance of Hebrew over Greek in the Samaritan inscriptions. Taking into account this 'distorting' factor of course does not allow us

---

[26] On the criteria for telling Jewish from non-Jewish inscriptions see my *Ancient Jewish Epitaphs* 16-18, and R.S. Kraemer, 'Jewish Tuna and Christian Fish: Identifying Religious Affiliation in Epigraphic Sources,' *Harvard Theological Review* 84 (1991) 141-162.

[27] For the same reason it is possible that some 'Jewish' synagogues are in fact Samaritan.

[28] See my *Ancient Jewish Epitaphs* 37-39.

[29] See D. Feissel, 'The Bible in Greek Inscriptions,' in P. M. Blowers (ed.), *The Bible in Greek Christian Antiquity*, Notre Dame: University of Notre Dame Press, 1997, 289-298.

in any way to gauge the extent of the use of Greek among Samaritans, if only because from a statistical point of view the evidence is so untractable. One should bear in mind that we have only some dozens of inscriptions, the majority of which are of no use for our purpose because they contain only biblical quotations; the handful of inscriptions we are then left with is so small as compared to the hundreds of thousands, if not millions, of Samaritans that must have existed in the almost 1.000 years we are dealing with, that it does not even make sense to raise the question of the representativeness of the material. To put it another way: to jump from the fact that half of the inscriptions are in Greek to the conclusion that half of the Samaritans spoke or knew Greek is obviously nonsensical. From a statistical point of view it is a completely hopeless situation.

There is, however, another source of information, that is of more weight than what we have said so far to gauge the extent of the use of Greek among Samaritans, and that is the non-Samaritan evidence for a Greek-speaking Samaritan diaspora.[30] Let us review the most important pieces of this material briefly in order to get a clearer impression. Of course we already know from the famous inscriptions in Delos and Thessalonica that the Samaritan communities there spoke Greek, as was to be expected, even though it may come as a bit of a surprise that at Delos this was already the case as early as the middle or second half of the third century BCE.[31] It may be added here that one of the interesting things about the Delos inscriptions is that one of them also makes it very probable that as early as the second century BCE Samaritans also lived in Crete (a certain Sarapion of Cnossos is honoured in one of the two inscriptions).[32] Also the fact that there was a Samaritan Bible translation in Greek – either a new one of their own or a revision of an existing

---

[30] For the following see A.D. Crown, 'The Samaritan Diaspora,' in Crown (ed.), *The Samaritans* 195-217, with the additions in my 'The Samaritan Diaspora in Antiquity' 136-147.

[31] See Ph. Bruneau, 'Les Israélites de Délos et la juiverie délienne,' *Bulletin de correspondence hellénique* 106 (1982) 465-504, which is the editio princeps. An English translation of the inscriptions is given by A. T. Kraabel, 'New Evidence of the Samaritan Diaspora Has Been Found on Delos,' *Biblical Archaeologist* 47 (1984) 44-46. For the inscription in Thessalonica see B. Lifshitz & J. Schiby, 'Une synagogue samaritaine à Thessalonique,' *Revue biblique* 75 (1968) 368-378.

[32] This interpretation is not undisputed; see P. W. van der Horst, 'The Jews of Ancient Crete,' *Journal of Jewish Studies* 39 (1988) 183-200, esp. 185-186, reprinted in my *Essays on the Jewish World of Early Christianity*, Göttingen: Vandenhoeck & Ruprecht, 1990, 148-165, here 150-151. Note that there are no Aramaic inscriptions from the diaspora.

Jewish-Greek translation – demonstrates that there was a real need for a Greek Pentateuch. But there is more material than just a few Samaritan inscriptions and Greek Pentateuch fragments. This circumstantial evidence includes the following.

(1) In *Ant.* XII 7-10 Josephus tells us that Ptolemy I Soter (end of the 4th cent. B.C.) "took many captives both from the hill country of Judaea and the district round Jerusalem and from Samaria and those on Garizim and brought them all to Egypt and settled them there"(7). Later this Ptolemy favours the Jews more than others so that "their descendants had quarrels with the Samaritans because they were determined to keep alive their fathers' way of life and customs, and so they fought with each other, those from Jerusalem saying that their temple was the holy one, and requiring that the sacrifices be sent there, while the Shechemites wanted these to go to Mount Garizim" (10). Here we clearly have to do with a conflict between two religious communities, a conflict that, also in Hellenistic Egypt, will escalate later. For in *Ant.* XIII 74-79 Josephus tells us about a violent quarrel during the reign of Ptolemy VI Philometor (180-145) between Jews and Samaritans in Alexandria over the question of whether the temple in Jerusalem or the one on Garizim was in accordance with the Law of Moses. Both parties ask the king himself to make a decision. Ptolemy follows the principle of *audi et alteram partem* and listens to speakers of both parties. But it is the champion of the Jewish cause who is able to convince the king with proof from the Torah and also on the basis of the fact that "all the kings of Asia had honoured the temple with dedicatory offerings and most splendid gifts, while none had shown any respect or regard for that on Garizim, as though it were not in existence"(78). Thereupon the Samaritan pleaders were put to death.[33] There can be little doubt that the talks and disputes between Jews and Samaritans and the king were conducted in Greek. That is also what we see happen in a Greek papyrus from Egypt that was written by a Samaritan, witness his exclamation 'by Garizim!,' in the fifth century CE.[34] This is further confirmed by what we know about the Egyptian village called Samaria. The more than 40 documentary papyri from or about that village date from the middle of the 3rd cent. BCE to the end of the 3rd cent. CE. Recent research demonstrates that at least a quarter, but possibly even more than 50%, of the inhabitants mentioned

---

[33] For an analysis of these stories see R. Egger, *Josephus Flavius und die Samaritaner*, Göttingen: Vandenhoeck & Ruprecht, 1986, 95-101, 230-237.

[34] See B. Kramer & D. Hagedorn, *Griechische Texte der Heidelberger Papyrussammlung IV*, Heidelberg 1986, no. 333.

in the documents were Jewish, which, in view of the name that the village received when it was founded, quite probably implies that most or many of them were Samaritans. The documents prove beyond doubt that the daily language in the village was Greek from the beginning (there was even a gymnasium).[35]

2) We have a divorce deed from Hermoupolis of the year 586 CE[36] in which the scribe calls the man and the woman concerned for clarity's sake *Samaritai tēn thrēskeian* (Samaritans by religion). This divorced couple show that as late as the end of the sixth century Samaritans still lived in Greek-speaking Egypt.[37] This is confirmed, moreover, by the fact that Eulogius, patriarch of Alexandria from 580 to 607, presided over a disputation between two rival groups of Samaritans (who no doubt lived in Alexandria) and afterwards promulgated a *Decree against the Samaritans*.[38] Again, there can be no doubt that all the Samaritans involved here spoke Greek.

(3) As concerns Rome, we have in Cassiodorus' *Variae* (sc. *epistulae,* a collection of deeds and letters from kings of the fifth and sixth centuries), a letter from the East-Gothic king Theodoric (early sixth cent.) in which he complains that in Rome there is a *Samareae superstitionis populus* which asserts that a building that originally was a Samaritan synagogue, had been illegally annexed by the Christian church in order to serve as a church building (*Var.* III 45).[39] Theodoric does not believe this, but a glance at the legislation of the later Roman Empire will make clear that these Samaritans most probably were not exaggerating at all. In view of what we know about the very large number of Greek-speaking Jews in Rome in the same period[40] it should be regarded as well-nigh

---

[35] For the details see C. Kuhs, *Das Dorf Samareia im griechisch-römischen Ägypten. Eine papyrologische Untersuchung,* diss. Heidelberg 1996 (published only on Internet); and O. Montevecchi, 'Samaria e Samaritani in Egitto,' *Aegyptus* 76 (1996) 81-92.

[36] *Corpus Papyrorum Judaicarum* 513. See also the new edition in B.R. Rees, *Papyri from Hermopolis,* London: Egypt Exploration Society, 1964, 55-58 (no. 29), and the translation and discussion by Zangenberg, SAMAREIA 312.

[37] Pap. Hermopolis 40 (pp. 80-1 ed. Rees) mentions a Manasseh *Samaritēs,* so there may have been a small Samaritan community in Hermopolis. *CPJ* 514, a papyrus from Nessana with an account from ca. 600 A.D., also mentions a *Samaritēs,* but there is too little context to conclude anything from it. That Samaritans still lived in Egypt, especially in Cairo, till the late Middle Ages, appears from several later sources; see E. Schürer, *The History of the Jewish People in the Age of Jesus Christ* III 1, rev. ed. by G. Vermes *et al.,* Edinburgh: T.& T. Clark, 1986, 60 n.63.

[38] See Photius' excerpt in *Bibliotheca* 230 (285a; ed. P. Henry, vol. 5, p. 60).

[39] The emendation *Samareae* for the *amarae* of the mss. has been generally accepted, rightly I think.

[40] L.V. Rutgers, *The Jews of Late Ancient Rome,* Leiden: Brill, 1995, 176-209.

certain that the Samaritans too spoke Greek there, although perhaps a few even managed to express themselves in Latin.

(4) Some relevant passages in the legislative corpora of the later Roman Empire that explicitly refer to Samaritans will now be reviewed briefly.[41] What we will be dealing with is imperial decrees from the period 390-535 CE, which are to be found in the *Codex Theodosianus* (with the *Novellae*) and the *Codex Justinianus*. In *Cod. Theod.* XIII 5, 18 (390 CE) Jews and Samaritans are exempted from the so-called *navicularia functio*, i.e. a supply of ships enforced by the state in the general public interest.[42] This first mention of Samaritans in a Roman law book protects them from unfair burdens. But things change for the worse under Theodosius II. *Cod. Theod.* XVI 8, 28 (426 CE)[43] decrees that Jews and Samaritans who have become converts to Christianity should never be disinherited by their parents or put at a disadvantage in other ways in matters of inheritance. *Novella* 3 (438 CE)[44] forbids Jews, Samaritans, pagans and heretics to exercise any judicial authority over Christians or to have any function as state dignitaries whatsoever, nor may synagogues be built any longer. *Cod. Iust.* I 5, 12 (527 CE)[45] again excludes all Jews, Samaritans, Manichaeans, and other heretics from all government services and military functions. *Cod. Iust.* I 5, 13 (527 CE)[46] decrees that orthodox Christian children from Jewish, Samaritan or heretical parents are fully entitled to be heirs, so they may not be disinherited. *Cod. Iust.* I 5, 17 (527 CE)[47] decrees that Samaritan synagogues should be destroyed and that those who rebuild them will be severely punished; Samaritans may only leave their inheritance to orthodox Christian persons. *Cod. Iust.* I 5, 18 (527 CE)[48] summarizes the prohibitions of previous laws pertaining to the Samaritans being invested with high offices. *Cod. Iust.* I 5, 19 (529 CE)[49] again forbids the disinheritance of Christian children by their Samaritan parents. *Cod. Iust.* I 5, 21

---

[41] Most of the texts are to be found in A. Linder, *The Jews in Roman Imperial Legislation*, Detroit-Jerusalem: Wayne State University Press, 1987. Another very useful tool is P. R. Coleman-Norton, *Roman State and Christian Church: A Collection of Legal Documents to A.D. 535*, 3 vols., London: SPCK, 1966, Index s.v. Samaritans.
[42] Linder no. 19. See C. Pharr, *The Theodosian Code and Novels and the Sirmondian Constitution*, Princeton: Princeton University Press, 1952, 394.
[43] Linder no. 52; Coleman-Norton no. 392 (pp. 638-639).
[44] Linder no. 54; Coleman-Norton no. 429 (pp. 711-715).
[45] Linder no. 56; Coleman-Norton no. 567 (pp.995-999).
[46] Linder no. 58; Coleman-Norton no. 570 (pp. 1003-1004).
[47] Coleman-Norton no. 574 (pp. 1007-1008).
[48] Coleman-Norton no. 575 (pp. 1008-1012).
[49] Coleman-Norton no. 599 (pp. 1047-1048).

(531 CE)[50] forbids Jews, Samaritans and heretics to act as witnesses against Christians in lawsuits, but allows them to testify against their own co-religionists. *Cod. Iust.* I 10, 2 (534 CE)[51] forbids Jews, Samaritans and pagans from holding Christian slaves.

This very concise survey of measures against Samaritans, Jews, heretics, and pagans (which is far from being complete) makes abundantly clear that the legislators definitely did not regard the Samaritans as a 'quantité négligable', as an insignificant sect that was withering away in some corner of Palestine. On the contrary, the fact that Samaritans are so often explicitly mentioned and the fact that several of these edicts were directed to the prefects of Italy, Egypt, and other areas is an indirect proof that Samaritans were present throughout the Roman Empire in late antiquity. We have no reason whatever to doubt that these diaspora Samaritans, like all – or almost all – other Jews, spoke Greek (maybe in some cases Latin).

(5) The sixth century Byzantine author Procopius, *Anecdota* 27:26-31, writes that in the reign of Justinian (527-565) there was in Constantinople a senator of high repute, Faustinus, who had become Christian in name but had in fact remained a Samaritan (a kind of Marrano Samaritano *avant la date*). This senator was accused before Justinian of hostility towards Christians and condemned to exile, but he was able to bribe Justinian so that the verdict was not carried out. This passage has given rise to the suspicion, rightly I suppose, that in the early Byzantine period there must have been more crypto-Samaritans in government service. Of course, they had to speak Greek.

(6) The pagan philosopher Damascius tells in his *Vita Isidori* (fragments 141-144, p. 196 ed. Zintzen), that Proclus' successor as head of the Platonic Academy in Athens, Marinus, was originally a Samaritan, who had become an apostate and adopted paganism under the influence of Greek philosophy. This Marinus wrote *inter alia* commentaries on Plato's *Philebus* and *Parmenides,* an introduction to Euclides' *Data*, and a *Vita Procli*.[52]

---

[50] Linder no. 60; Coleman-Norton no. 622 (pp. 1099-1100).

[51] Linder no. 59; Coleman-Norton no. 647 (p. 1162).

[52] See on this passage J. R. Masullo, *Marino di Neapoli: Vita di Proclo,* Napoli: Libreria, 1985, 17 n.15, and M. Stern, *Greek and Latin Authors on Jews and Judaism,* vol. II, Jerusalem: Israel Academy of Sciences and Humanities, 1980, 673-675. On p. 675 Stern says: "The emergence of a Samaritan philosopher in the second half of the fifth century C.E. accords well with the general impression given by the sources of the strength of the Samaritan element both in Palestine and outside it in the Byzantine period". On p. 309 Stern remarks that Galen, in his commentary on the sixth book of Hippocrates' *Epidemica* (this commentary has been preserved only in an Arabic translation), utters criticisms of Rufus of Samaria whom he calls a Jew. Stern assumes that

Of course, this Athenian Samaritan (or ex-Samaritan, if one wishes) wrote all his works in Greek.[53]

(7) That Samaritans also lived in Sicily is apparent, partly from an inscription with a biblical quote found in Syracuse,[54] but also from some letters of Gregory the Great (end of the 6th cent.) to bishops on that island, in which he says that the Samaritans there should not be allowed to circumcise their slaves (*Ep.* VI 33) and that Christian slaves of Samaritans there should be redeemed (*Ep.* VIII 21). The Samaritan community of Sicily was probably much older and may have originated around the turn of the era.[55] Since Sicily was by and large a Greek-speaking island throughout antiquity, it is reasonable to think that there, too, the Samaritans spoke Greek.

(8) Finally, we see Samaritans in the city of Kaunos in Caria (S.-W. Asia Minor), where in a Greek building inscription a number of women are mentioned as *Sikimitai*,[56] Sichem being the old name of the holy place of the Samaritan community.[57] But most other non-Samaritan inscriptions and papyri where *Samaritai*, *Samareis* or *Samaritani* outside Palestine are mentioned are uncertain cases, since we have no means to ascertain whether these are Samaritans or Samarians.[58]

---

this Rufus was probably a Samaritan because presumably Galen could not make a distinction between Jews and Samaritans and Jews did not live in Samaria in the second century. This is of course very questionable.

[53] See M. Luz, 'Marinus: An Eretz-Israel Neoplatonist at Athens,' in A. Kasher et al. (edd.), *Greece and Rome in Eretz Israel*, Jerusalem: Yad Izhak Ben-Zvi & The Israel Exploration Society, 1990, 92-104, for a description of Marinus' Platonic philosophy. Luz suggests the possibility that Marinus "may have been raised in one of the Samaritan communities now known to have existed in (...) Greece itself" (93 n.8).

[54] See for the details and bibliography R. Pummer, 'Samaritan Synagogues and Jewish Synagogues: Similarities and Differences,' in S. Fine (ed.), *Jews, Christians, and Polytheists in the Ancient Synagogue*, London – New York: Routledge, 1999, 119-120.

[55] Crown, 'Samaritan Diaspora' 202.

[56] L. Robert, 'Bulletin épigraphique,'*Revue des Etudes Grecques* 67 (1954) 169-171 (no. 229).

[57] Another proof of Samaritan presence in Asia Minor is a remark by Palladius in his *Dialogue on the Life of John Chrysostom* (PG 47:73) that there were Jewish and Samaritan synagogues in Tarsus (I owe the reference to Pummer, 'Samaritan Synagogues' 120).

[58] For the inscriptions see my 'The Samaritan Diaspora,' for the papyri M.Nagel, 'Un Samaritain dans l'Arsinoite au IIe siècle après J.C.,' *Chronique d'Egypte* 49/98 (1974) 356-365, and Kuhs, *Das Dorf Samareia* 26. See also the list in S.R.Llewelyn, *New Documents Illustrating Early Christianity*, vol. 8, Grand Rapids: Eerdmans, 1998, 150. H.G. Kippenberg, *Garizim und Synagoge. Traditionsgeschichtliche Untersuchungen zur samaritanischen Religion der aramäischen Periode*, Berlin: W. de Gruyter, 1971, 145-147, too easily overlooks the problematic nature of the papyrological and epigraphical evidence.

Nonetheless, all the evidence surveyed makes abundantly clear that members of the Samaritan religious community had settled in all parts of the ancient world from the third century B.C.E to the seventh century C.E. and we may take it for granted that for the vast majority their native language had been or became Greek. About the size of that diaspora we know very little. It would have been small, of course, in the third century B.C.E, but in the later Roman Empire it was certainly much bigger. Ancient sources report that during the great revolt of the Samaritans in Palestine against the Byzantine emperor in 529 C.E. some 100,000 Samaritans were killed.[59] Even if this number is an exaggeration, it is nevertheless indicative of a very sizeable Samaritan community in Palestine. Alan Crown once estimated the number of Palestinian Samaritans in late antiquity to have been about 300.000 and the number of Samaritans in the diaspora about 150.000.[60] This remains guesswork – it may well have been the other way round: a diaspora twice as big as the community in the homeland[61] – but anyway Crown is certainly right that we can be sure that there must have been a very considerable Samaritan diaspora, without any doubt consisting of many tens of thousands, perhaps even hundreds of thousands, of Greek-speaking Samaritans.

Greek-speaking Samaritans, however, were also to be found in their homeland. It is not only the few fragments of Samaritan writers in Greek who possibly worked in Palestine that could prove this. After all, we have no definitive proof that Theodotus and Pseudo-Eupolemus lived in Palestine, even though this is quite probable.[62] It is again the inscriptions that are our decisive evidence. Inscriptions, whether they were part of synagogues or of private homes or of other buildings or engraved on sarcophagi or amulets, were incised in Greek only if the people who frequented the buildings or tombs concerned or wore the amulets were able to read them. Reading ability of Greek is of course not the same as speaking ability, but even so we must presuppose a relatively great familiarity with the Greek language on the part of the Samaritan communities who produced these inscriptions. We may, therefore, tentatively conclude that the Samaritan community in Hellenistic, Roman and Byzantine Palestine was a largely bilingual, or, in a

---

[59] M. Avi-Yonah, *Geschichte der Juden im Zeitalter des Talmud*, Berlin: W. de Gruyter, 1962, 251-253.

[60] Crown, 'Samaritan Diaspora' 118. See also *Encycl. Jud.* XIV (1972) 736.

[61] See Kippenberg, *Garizim und Synagoge* 161 (following Avi-Yonah).

[62] Holladay, *Fragments from Hellenistic Jewish Authors* I 160, II 70-72.

sense, even trilingual, society.[63] If the bilingual Amwas inscription with both *barukh shemo le'olam* and *heis theos* is indeed from the turn of the era,[64] we may even speculate that this was already the situation in New Testament times. Alongside the vernacular Aramaic (and, to a much lesser extent, Hebrew), Greek was widely used and understood, as may also be inferred from the numerous Greek loanwords in Samaritan Aramaic.[65] But we have to add that the degree of use and understanding of the Greek language probably varied strongly according to locality and period, social status and educational background, occasion and mobility.

It is quite probable that, even though the 'Quellenlage' is dramatically different from that concerning the Jewish material, we may draw a conclusion that is markedly similar to what one might conclude about the language situation of the pre-Islamic Jewish communities. Hebrew was the holy language (*leshon ha-qodesh*); Aramaic was the vernacular of the Samaritans in the heartland, although Greek had made a heavy impact there (as it did in Jerusalem[66]) – the many Samaritan inscriptions in Greek recently discovered on Mt. Garizim make this clear again;[67] but in the sizeable diaspora most, if not all Samaritans spoke Greek, and perhaps even some of them wrote in that language.[68] If authors such as Theodotus and the so-called Samaritan anonymous were diaspora authors (and if that were the case, they were certainly not the only ones[69]), we have to establish that there were Samaritans who had mas-

---

[63] See B. Spolsky, "Jewish Multilingualism in the First Century: An Essay in Historical Sociolinguistics," J.A. Fishman (ed.), *Readings in the Sociology of Jewish Languages*, Leiden: Brill, 1985, 35-51, esp. 40-41 where trilingualism ('triglossia') is stressed. But cf. R. Schmitt, "Die Sprachverhältnisse in den östlichen Provinzen des Römischen Reiches," *Aufstieg und Niedergang der Römischen Welt* II 29, 2, Berlin – New York: W. de Gruyter, 1983, 554-586, here 576: "Man wird die Sprachgemeinschaft dieses Landes mit gutem Recht als bilingual bezeichnen dürfen."

[64] Hüttenmeister-Reeg, *Antiken Synagogen* II 603-609.

[65] See now A. Tal, *A Dictionary of Samaritan Aramaic*, Leiden: Brill, 2000.

[66] M. Hengel, 'Jerusalem als jüdische und hellenistische Stadt,' in his *Judaica, Hellenistica et Christiana (Kleine Schriften II)*, Tübingen: Mohr, 1999, 115-156.

[67] Outside the Samaritan heartland 7 synagogue inscriptions in Greek have been found in Palestine to date; see Pummer, 'The Greek Bible and the Samaritans' 312 n. 223, with the additions in the unpublished paper by L. Di Segni mentioned in note 13.

[68] Note also the fact that in much later Samaritan *ketubbot* one often finds Greek loanwords, which suggests that some standard formulas go back to a time when Greek was familiar to the Samaritans. See R. Pummer, 'Samaritan Rituals and Customs,' in Crown (ed.), *Samaritans* 662.

[69] See, for instance, the recent suggestion of Ross Kraemer to consider a Samaritan provenance for *Joseph et Aseneth* in her essay 'Could *Aseneth* Be Samaritan?' in B.G. Wright (ed.), *A Multiform Heritage: Studies on Early Judaism and Christianity in Honor of Robert A. Kraft*, Atlanta: Scholars Press, 2000, 149-165.

tered not only the Greek language but also Greek literary genres including the metrical, the stylistic and the lexicographical conventions and abilities that went with it. These authors were steeped in Greek literature, and – let us not forget it – they may well have lived and been trained in the Samaritan homeland. Of course they may have been exceptional, but they probably demonstrate that we should not underrate the impact of Greek culture on the Samaritans.[70]

---

[70] This remains true, even if I do not agree with the main thesis of A. Broadie, *A Samaritan Philosophy. A Study of the Hellenistic Cultural Ethos of the Memar Marqah*, Leiden: Brill, 1981.

15. SAMARITANS AT ROME?

In his comprehensive study *Foreigners at Rome* (London 2000), David Noy does not mention Samaritans at all. And in his equally exhaustive volume listing all the Jewish inscriptions from Rome (*Jewish Inscriptions from Western Europe*, vol. 2, Cambridge 1995), Samaritans are not mentioned even once. There is no epigraphic evidence for a Samaritan presence at Rome in antiquity. Is there then any literary evidence? No, there isn't, at least not for the first five-and-a-half centuries of the Empire. Why then waste our time with a paper about a non-topic? Let me explain why.

A high proportion of the population of Rome in the imperial period consisted of immigrants and their descendants. Of this population, which consisted by then of some 500,000 to 1,000,000 inhabitants, at least about 10% were not of Roman origin, so some 50,000 to 100,000 inhabitants were foreigners. From both epigraphical and literary data we know that these foreigners came from all parts of the world: Gaul, Spain, Germany, Raetia, Noricum, Pannonia, Moesia, Dacia, Dalmatica, Macedonia, Thrace, Greece, the various parts of Asia Minor, Syria, Palestine, Egypt, and all the countries of North Africa. We also know that inhabitants from Palestine had always been well represented among these foreigners. It was not only Pompey who took many prisoners of war. In the later wars between Jews and Romans many thousands were taken captive and brought to Rome. According to diverging estimates, between 20 and 50% of the foreign population of Rome consisted of Jews and other inhabitants of Palestine and their descendants.

We have no reason to assume that the Samaritans were exempted from this fate. Indeed, Josephus mentions a freedman from Samaria in Rome in the time of Tiberius (*Ant.* XVIII 167). One should bear in mind that the community of Samaritans worldwide was not at all a negligeable entity. Their number was much greater than one might think on the basis of our knowledge of the Bible and of the situation today. And, as far as their habitat is concerned, neither from the Bible nor from modern history have we become acquainted with a Samaritan diaspora. In the Bible we meet Samaritans only in the area of Samaria, and, if outside that area, then at least within Palestine. And also in the present day situation we

meet Samaritans only within the state of Israel: the very small Samaritan community (some 625 members) lives in Nablus and in Holon (a little town to the south of Tel Aviv). So the most important sources of
information about Samaritans for most people of our time, the Bible and
the present situation, both suggest that Samaritans lived and live only
within the borders of Israel. But it should be stressed that there is evidence for a sizeable Samaritan diaspora which, exactly like the Jewish
one, was to be found in all parts of the ancient world. Where we find
Jews, we often find Samaritans as well. Let me briefly review the most
important evidence for a Samaritan diaspora before I return to Rome.

We do not know when, why, and where the Samaritan diaspora began.
The first document that informs us about it is Josephus' *Antiquities*. In
Ant. XII 7-10 he relates that Ptolemy I Soter (end of the 4th cent. BCE)
"took many captives both from the hill country of Judaea and the district
round Jerusalem and from Samaria and those on Garizim and brought
them all to Egypt and settled them there"(7). Later this Ptolemy favours
the Jews more than others so that "their descendants had quarrels with
the Samaritans because they were determined to keep alive their fathers'
way of life and customs, and so they fought with each other, those from
Jerusalem saying that their temple was the holy one, and requiring that
the sacrifices be sent there, while the Shechemites wanted these to go to
Mount Garizim" (10). Here we clearly have to do with a conflict
between two religious communities, a conflict that will escalate later,
also in Hellenistic Egypt. For in *Ant*. XIII 74-79 Josephus tells us about
a violent quarrel during the reign of Ptolemy VI Philometor (180-145)
between Jews and Samaritans in Alexandria over the question of
whether the temple in Jerusalem or the one on Mt. Garizim was in accordance with the Law of Moses. Both parties ask the king himself to make
a decision. Ptolemy listens to speakers of both parties and it is the champion of the Jewish cause who is able to convince the king with proof
from the Torah. Thereupon the Samaritan pleaders were put to death.[1]

Now this is evidence for an early Samaritan diaspora in the third and
second cent. BCE. But when we move to the other end of the chronological spectrum, late antiquity, we find many indications that this Samaritan
diaspora had greatly expanded in the intervening (approximately) five

---

[1] In medieval Samaritan chronicles this story is told as well, but then with the outcome
reversed! That a Samaritan diaspora continued to exist in Egypt is confirmed by the
fact that Eulogius, patriarch of Alexandria from 580-607, presided over a disputation
between two rival groups of Samaritans (who no doubt lived in Alexandria) and afterwards promulgated a Decree against the Samaritans.

centuries. I am referring to the documents of the Roman imperial legisla-tion,[2] in this case decrees from the period 390-535 CE, which are to be found in the *Codex Theodosianus* (with the *Novellae*) and the *Codex Jus-tinianus*. In *Cod. Theod.* XIII 5, 18 (from 390) Jews and Samaritans are exempted from the so-called *navicularia functio*, i.e. a supply of ships enforced by the state in the general public interest. This first mention of Samaritans in a Roman law book protects them from unfair burdens. But things change to the worse under Theodosius II. *Cod. Theod.* XVI 8, 28 (from 426) decrees that Jews and Samaritans who have become converts to Christianity should never be disinherited by their parents or put at a disadvantage in other ways in matters of inheritance. *Novella* 3 (from 438) forbids Jews, Samaritans, pagans and heretics to exercise any judi-cial authority over Christians or to hold any dignitary function whatso-ever, nor are synagogues to be built any longer. *Cod Iust.* I 5, 12 (from 527) again excludes all Jews, Samaritans, Manichaeans, and other heretics from all government services and military functions. *Cod. Iust.* I 5, 13 (from 527) decrees that orthodox Christian children from Jewish, Samaritan or heretical parents are fully entitled to be heirs, so may not be disinherited. *Cod. Iust.* I 5, 17 (from 527) decrees that Samaritan syna-gogues should be destroyed and that those who rebuild them will be severely punished; Samaritans may only leave heritages to orthodox Christians. *Cod. Iust.* I 5, 18 (from 527) summarizes the prohibitions of previous laws pertaining to the Samaritans' being invested with high offices. *Cod. Iust.* I 5, 19 (from 529) again forbids the disinheritance of Christian children by their Samaritan parents. *Cod. Iust.* I 5, 21 (from 531) forbids Jews, Samaritans and heretics to act as witnesses against Christians in lawsuits, but allows them to testify against their own co-reli-gionists. *Cod. Iust.* I 10, 2 (from 534) forbids Jews, Samaritans and pagans to hold Christian slaves.

This very concise survey of measures against Samaritans, Jews, heretics, and pagans makes clear that the legislators definitely did not regard the Samaritans as a 'quantité négligeable,' as an insignificant sect that was withering away somewhere in a corner of Palestine. On the con-trary, the fact that Samaritans are so often explicitly mentioned and – what is most important! – the fact that several of these edicts were directed to prefects of Italy, Egypt, and several other areas is an indirect

---

[2] See now especially A. Linder, *The Jews in Roman Imperial Legislation,* Detroit – Jerusalem 1987, Index s.v. Samaritans. A useful tool is also P. R. Coleman-Norton, *Roman State and Christian Church,* 3 vols., London 1966, Index s.v. Samaritans.

proof that Samaritans were present throughout the Roman Empire in late antiquity.

Quite interestingly Procopius, *Anecdota* 27:26-31, writes that in the reign of Justinian (527-565) there was in Constantinople a senator of high repute, Faustinus, who had become Christian in name but had in fact remained a Samaritan (a kind of Marrano Samaritano avant la date). This senator was accused before Justinian of hostility towards Christians and condemned to exile, but he was able to bribe Justinian so that the verdict was not carried out. This passage has given rise to the suspicion, rightly I suppose, that in the early Byzantine period there must have been more crypto-Samaritans in government service.

Damascius relates in his *Vita Isidori* (fragments 141-144, p. 196 ed. Zintzen), that Proclus' successor as head of the Platonic Academy in Athens, Marinus, was originally a Samaritan, who under the influence of Greek philosophy, had become an apostate and adopted paganism. This Marinus wrote *inter alia* commentaries on Plato's *Philebus* and *Parmenides,* an introduction to Euclides' *Data,* and a *Vita Procli.*[3]

That Samaritans also lived in Sicily is apparent from some letters of Gregory the Great (end of the 6th cent.) to bishops on that island, in which he says that the Samaritans there should not be allowed to circumcise their slaves (*Ep.* VI 33) and that Christian slaves of Samaritans there should be set free (*Ep.* VIII 21).

Before we turn to inscriptional evidence, it is first time for an interlude with a note of terminological or methodological caution. It is only recently that one has become aware of the fact that when our sources speak about *Samareis, Samar(e)itai, Samaritani,* and the like, it is not always Samaritans that are referred to. For the reference can also be to 'Samarians'. Samarians is a modern term reserved for inhabitants of the city or the region of Samaria, and these are in many – perhaps even in most – cases not Samaritans; Samaritans are members of the Samaritan religious community. This terminological distinction – which was mostly not made in antiquity – is of the greatest importance for our investigation. For if this distinction is not made, the data about both categories become confused and the picture of the Samaritans is completely blurred. Recently it has convincingly been demonstrated that Josephus has always been unjustly accused of vehemently anti-Samaritan sentiments because

---

[3] See on this passage J. R. Masullo, *Marino di Neapoli: Vita di Proclo,* Napoli 1985, 17 n.15, and M. Stern, *Greek and Latin Authors on Jews andf Judaism* II, Jerusalem 1980, 673-675.

the researchers had not seen that most of the places in his works where he mentions *Samareis*, do not deal with Samaritans at all but with inhabitants of Samaria, that is Greeks and Phoenicians in many cases. That means for our present investigation that data for the study of the Samaritan diaspora are only relevant if we also have other indications (in addition to the term used) that we are dealing with a member or members of the Samaritan religious community. Unfortunately only rarely is an ancient author or scribe aware of this problem of terminological ambiguity: an exception is the papyrus (a divorce deed in 586 CE) of which the scribe unambiguously states that the two people concerned were *Samaritai tên thrêskeian*, 'Samaritans by faith' (CPJ 513), for clarity's sake.

To be sure, there are not many inscriptions that unequivocally refer to Samaritans. One can mention a Greek epitaph from Hipponion (South Italy) which records that this is the grave of *Antiochos Samaritanos*,[4] according to some a Samaritan inscription, but that is very questionable; further a tomb-inscription *Samaritôn eleutherôn* from Tyre, with the same problem;[5] inscriptions from Rhodos (*IG* [= *Inscriptiones Graecae*] XII 1, 716; XII 8, 439)[6], Sicily (*IG* XIV 336 = *JIWE* I 161), Kaunos in Caria where a building inscription mentions a number of women as *Sikimitai*,[7] and even Iran.[8] The *Corpus Inscriptionum Graecarum* 2891-2893 (= *IG* 10219-10221) contains 3 Athenian funerary inscriptions of a certain *Ammia Samareitis*, a *Theodora Samaritis*, and another Samaritan (the text is badly damaged) – or are they Samarians? In view of our criterion we have to leave open whether we are concerned with Samarians or with Samaritans in this case. The same applies to the anonymous *Samaritês* in *IG* II² 2943 (also from Athens).[9] In all these inscriptions from the Hellenistic and Roman periods the editors saw new evidence

---

[4] See *Notizie degli scavi* 1921, 485, and L. Robert, *Hellenica* III, Paris 1946, 97. Later Robert has become more cautious in this respect, see *Revue des études grecques* 82 (1969) 479.

[5] See J. P. Rey-Coquais, *Inscriptions grecques et latines découvertes dans les fouilles de Tyr (1963-1974) I: Inscriptions de la nécropole*, Paris 1977, no. 168.

[6] *IG* XII 8, 439 is mistakenly recorded there as an inscription from Thasos; see Robert in *Revue des études grecques* 82 (1969) 477-478.

[7] Robert, *Revue des études grecques* 67 (1954) 169-171 (no. 229).

[8] L. and J. Robert, *Comptes Rendus de l'Académie des Inscriptions et Belles Lettres* 1967, 281-297.

[9] See J. and L. Robert, *Revue des études grecques* 82 (1969) 478: "Il faut (...) relever que dans tous ces cas on peut se demander s'il s'agit de gens de confession samaritaine (...) ou des colons grecs de Samarie".

for a Samaritan diaspora,[10] but we have to defer our verdict. Possibly we are concerned with Samaritans here, but as long as we do not have additional criteria that guarantee such an identification, it is bound to remain uncertain, except in the case of the Carian *Sikimitai* since Sichem is the old name of the holy place of the Samaritan community.

Quite unambiguous evidence, however, has been found on the Greek island of Delos, in the mainland city of Thessalonica, and in Syracuse, Sicily. In 1980 two Samaritan inscriptions were found on Delos.[11] Both inscriptions, dating respectively from the third to second and from the second to first century BCE, do not speak about Samaritans *expressis verbis,* but they do speak about "the Israelites on Delos who pay their first offerings to the sanctuary (of) Argarizin". The mention of *Argarizin* leaves no room for doubt. These Delian Samaritans honour a certain Sarapion of Cnossos and Menippus of Heraclea for their benefactions towards the community, possibly the building of a synagogue.[12] The interesting thing about these inscriptions is not only that they are witnesses of a very early presence of Samaritans on Delos, but also that they make very probable that as early as the second century BCE Samaritans lived in Crete (Sarapion of Cnossos).[13]

Another spectacular discovery from recent times is an inscription from a Samaritan synagogue in Thessalonica of the fourth, possibly the fifth century.[14] In this inscription of 20 lines one finds first a *berakhah* in

[10] Robert, *Revue des études grecques* 67 (1954) 171.

[11] See Ph. Bruneau, "'Les Israélites de Délos' et la juiverie délienne," *Bulletin de correspondence hellénique* 106 (1982) 465-504; for an English translation A. T. Kraabel, "New Evidence of the Samaritan Diaspora Has Been Found on Delos," *Biblical Archaeologist* 47 (1984) 44-46.

[12] Bruneau extensively discusses all the problems. For *Argarizin* see now R. Pummer, "ARGARIZIN: A Criterion for Samaritan Provenance?," *Journal for the Study of Judaism* 18 (1987) 18-25.

[13] This interpretation is not undisputed; see P. W. van der Horst, "The Jews of Ancient Crete," *Journal of Jewish Studies* 39 (1988) 183-200. From which of the 10 known Heracleas Menippus came is unknown. Bruneau 479 mentions in this connection an inscription (*Inscriptions de Délos* 2616) of ca. 100 BCE in which a certain *Praylos Samareus* is mentioned who has contributed to the building of the Sarapieion of Delos. This will have been a Samarian rather than a Samaritan.

[14] This inscription was discovered at the beginning of the fifties, but only published in 1968 by B. Lifshitz and J. Schiby, "Une synagogue samaritaine à Thessalonique," *Revue Biblique* 75 (1968) 368-378. See also Lifshitz' edition and discussion in his Prolegomenon to the reprint of J. B. Frey, *Corpus Inscriptionum Iudaicarum* I, New York 1975, 70-75. Additions and corrections by E. Tov in *Rev. Bibl.* 81 (1974) 394-399, and J. D. Purvis in *Bulletin of the American School of Oriental Research* 221 (1976) 221-223.

Samaritan Hebrew, then in Greek the priestly blessing from Numbers 6:22-27, with a dozen deviations from the Septuagint that probably derive from a Samaritan revision of the Septuagint (not necessarily the *Samareitikon*), then again a *berakhah* in Samaritan Hebrew, and finally a Greek dedication to Siricius from Neapolis (Nablus), possibly the rhetorician Siricius who was a teacher of rhetoric in Athens in the fourth century, although it is not certain whether this rhetorician was a Samaritan or not.[15]

Finally we have the inscription from Syracuse (*JIWE* I 153),[16] which is unambiguously Samaritan because the inscription is a quote from Numbers 10:35 ('Rise, Lord, may your enemies be scattered') in Samaritan Hebrew. This inscription, incised on a column, is of uncertain date, but most probably from the third or fourth century. We do not know whether the column belonged to a synagogue. Most unfortunately, we also do not know whether another Sicilian inscription (*JIWE* I 161), which mentions a *Ptolemaios Samareus* and dates from the first century BCE or CE, is about a Samaritan or a Samarian.

There is still another aspect of the problem that we have to discuss because it is too often overlooked. That is the matter of hidden or unrecognizable evidence. What I mean is that "because they share iconography (e.g. the menorah) and nomenclature with Jews, Samaritans tend to lose themselves epigraphically among the Jews."[17] We have to date several thousands of Jewish inscriptions, most of them epitaphs, but some of these may be Samaritan, since titles, symbols, and names would generally have been the same. It cannot by any means be excluded that several inscriptions which are said to be identifiably Jewish,[18] are in fact

---

[15] For a discussion of other aspects of this inscription I refer the reader also to J. and L. Robert, "Bulletin épigraphique," *Revue des études grecques* 82 (1969) 476-478 and G. H. R. Horsley, *New Documents Illustrating Early Christianity* I, Macquarie 1981, 108-110. An inscription that is similar in many respects is the one from Imwas (Emmaus) in G. Reeg, *Samaritanische Synagogen*, Wiesbaden 1977, 603-609.

[16] See V. Morabito, "I samaritani e la sinagoga di Siracusa," *Archivio Storico per la Sicilia Orientale* 86 (1990) 61-87; and "The Samaritans in Sicily and the Inscription in a Probable Synagogue in Syracuse," in *New Samaritans Studies of the Société d'Etudes Samaritaines*, Proceedings of the Congresses of Oxford and Paris, edd. A. D. Crown & L. Davey, The University of Sydney, Mandelbaum Publishing, 1995, 237-258. Now also R. Pummer, "Samaritan Synagogues and Jewish Synagogues: Similarities and Differences," in S. Fine (ed.), *Jews, Christians, and Polytheists in the Ancient Synagogue*, London – New York: Routledge, 1999, 119-120.

[17] C.M. Lehmann and K.G. Holum (eds.), *The Greek and Latin Inscriptions of Caesarea Maritima*, Boston 2000, 19.

[18] On the criteria for telling Jewish from non-Jewish inscriptions see my *Ancient Jewish Epitaphs* 16-18, and R.S. Kraemer, "Jewish Tuna and Christian Fish: Identifying Religious Affiliation in Epigraphic Sources," *Harvard Theological Review* 84 (1991) 141-162.

Samaritan. If an inscription is in Greek, if the names used there are typically Jewish (being Hebrew names), and if the Law of Moses is referred to, what is there for us to distinguish a Jewish from a Samaritan inscription in such a case? So there may be many more Samaritan inscriptions than we will ever be able to identify![19] In addition to that, it must be said that most literary data about the Samaritan diaspora are late, that is from the time after Constantine. In this striking fact lurks a problem, since it has rightly been surmised that pagan authors usually made no distinction between Jews and Samaritans.[20] The consequence is that possibly much (for us unrecognizable) information about Samaritans is hidden in what they write about *Ioudaioi/Iudaei*. All the more reason to keep constantly in mind that non-evidence is not the same as non-existence.

Let us draw some conclusions. It will have become clear that much of the material that has often been adduced as evidence for a Samaritan diaspora cannot serve such a purpose. It cannot be excluded that that material deals with Samaritans, but it may equally be about Samarians. Nevertheless, there remains enough evidence: the inscriptions from Delos and Thessalonica, some papyri, passages in Josephus and several Church Fathers, and the decrees in the legislative corpora. All this evidence makes abundantly clear that, from the third century BCE to the seventh century CE, members of the Samaritan religious community had settled themselves in all parts of the ancient world. About the size of that diaspora we know very little. It will have been very small, of course, in the third century BCE, but in the later Roman Empire much bigger. Ancient sources report that during the great revolt of the Samaritans in Palestine against the Byzantine emperor in 529 some 100.000 Samaritans were killed.[21] Even if this number is exaggerated, it is nevertheless indicative of a very sizeable Samaritan community in Palestine. A prominent Samaritanologist, Alan Crown, estimates the number of Palestinian Samaritans in late antiquity to have been ca.

---

[19] In this respect it is telling that in their book *The Greek and Latin Inscriptions of Caesarea Maritima*, C.M. Lehmann and K.G. Holum state on the one hand that Samaritans are "so numerous in Caesarea and its territory in the fourth century that it took pagans and Jews together to equal the Samaritans" (19) and that they tend to lose themselves epigraphically among the Jews, while on the other hand they list all inscriptions with Jewish symbols and names under the rubric 'Jewish'.

[20] See Egger, *Josephus Flavius* 137: "Die Samaritaner können bei nichtjüdischen Autoren nämlich erst ab dem 4. Jh.n. als eine sich von den Juden unterscheidende Gruppe nachgewiesen werden, dh. erst ab dieser Zeit werden sie nicht mehr unter die Juden subsumiert."

[21] M. Avi-Yonah, *Geschichte der Juden im Zeitalter des Talmud*, Berlin 1962, 251ff.

300.000 and the number of Samaritans in the diaspora ca. 150.000.[22] This remains guesswork of course, but we can be sure that there must have been a considerable Samaritan diaspora, without any doubt consisting of many tens of thousands. In the course of the Middle Ages this diaspora disappeared, partly by a gradual process of christianization, partly by islamization, in many cases probably by a kind of 'marranization'.

Finally back to Rome. In *Antiquitates* XVIII 167, Josephus reports that Herod Agrippa I, when in financial problems in Rome, borrowed one million drachmas from a freedman of the emperor Tiberius, a *Samareus genos*. From this passage some have concluded that around the turn of our era a Samaritan community must have existed in Rome.[23] That may quite well have been the case, in view of the large numbers of Jews in Rome by that time, but it cannot be concluded from this passage directly because the man may have been a Samarian. An attempt has been made to support the view that he was a Samaritan by pointing to the fact that Justin Martyr, in *I Apol.* 26, states that Simon Magus, who created a furore in Rome during Claudius' reign, was worshipped as God by almost all Samaritans, which would indicate the presence of a great number of Samaritans in Rome in the first half of the first century. That conclusion is incorrect for two reasons. Firstly, Justin does not say that Simon was worshiped by Samaritans-in-Rome. Secondly, even if that were the case, then one need assume that he writes not about Samaritans but about Samarians, for in view of what we know about the Samaritan religion in the first century, it would seem to be ruled out that members of this religious community would have regarded someone like Simon as a god.[24] Moreover, this whole passage in Justin contains incorrect statements and does not inspire confidence as a historical source.[25] To be sure, it is definitely not improbable that there were Samaritans in Rome

---

[22] A.D. Crown, "The Samaritan Diaspora to the End of the Byzantine Era," *Australian Journal of Biblical Archaeology* 2 (1974/75) 118. See also *Encyclopaedia Judaica* XIV (1972) 736.

[23] So e.g. H. G. Kippenberg, *Garizim und Synagoge*, Berlin 1971, 146; on pp. 145-150 Kippenberg gives a useful (but incomplete) survey of the evidence for a Samaritan diaspora that was known till 1970.

[24] See B. W. Hall, *Samaritan Religion from John Hyrcanus to Baba Rabba*, Sydney 1987, who argues that Justin here undoubtedly refers to Samarians (46-47; cf. 102ff.). On pp. 262-275 Hall convincingly demonstrates that Simonianism has been from beginning to end a predominantly pagan and not a Samaritan movement.

[25] See for instance, in the same paragraph, the notorious remark about the inscription *Simoni deo sancto*. See further the discussion in Egger, *Josephus Flavius* 143-148.

in the first century, but neither Josephus nor Justin can be adduced as witnesses.[26]

There *is*, however, unambiguous evidence for a Samaritan presence at Rome, but it is of a much later date. In Cassiodorus' *Variae* (sc. *epistulae*, a collection of deeds and letters from kings of the fifth and sixth centuries) there is a letter from the Ostrogothic king Theodoric (around 500), in which it is said that in Rome there is a *Samareae superstitionis populus* which asserts that a building that was originally a Samaritan synagogue, was illegally annexed by Pope Simplicius (end of the fifth cent.) in order to serve as a church henceforth (*Var.* III 45; ed. A.J. Fridh, CCSL 96, pp. 127-8). Theodoric does not believe this, but a glance at the legislation of the later Roman Empire makes clear that these Samaritans most probably did not exaggerate.

Summing up: there are no identifiably Samaritan inscriptions in Rome, the passages from Josephus and Justin are not certain enough evidence to be taken into our service, so that leaves us only with the late quote from Cassiodorus in the first half of the sixth century. However, we now know that there was a large Samaritan diaspora of which we find traces all over the Mediterranean, ranging from the third century BCE to the sixth century CE. We also know that Rome attracted large numbers of foreigners from all over the world, among whom people from Palestine played a considerable role. We know that among the Jewish epigraphic evidence Samaritan material may be hidden. We also know that among pagan literary references to Jews evidence for Samaritans may be hidden. The Samaritans in Rome surface only in the 6th century. But it is more than stretching our imagination if we conclude that, whereas there was demonstrably a Samaritan community in Alexandria from the third cent. BCE onwards, in the equally metropolitan Rome they were to be found only 9 centuries later (the more so if we take into account that we do have evidence for a Samaritan community in Sicily much earlier). So: do we have hard evidence for Samaritan presence at Rome in the first five centuries of the empire? No. Is it probable then that Samaritans lived there in that period? Yes, highly probable, almost certain.

---

[26] I leave out of account the intriguing but unprovable suggestion by Leonard Rutgers to the effect that the 4th century Roman document called *Collatio legum Mosaicarum et Romanarum* may have had a Samaritan author; see his *The Hidden Heritage of Diaspora Judaism*, Leuven 1998, 276-277.

INDEX OF NAMES AND SUBJECTS

INDEX OF REFERENCES TO
ANCIENT SOURCES

1. J.A. Loader, *A Tale of Two Cities, Sodom and Gomorrah in the Old Testament, early Jewish and early Christian Traditions*, Kampen, 1990
2. P.W. Van der Horst, *Ancient Jewish Epitaphs. An Introductory Survey of a Millennium of Jewish Funerary Epigraphy (300 BCB-700 CE)*, Kampen, 1991
3. E. Talstra, *Solomon's Prayer. Synchrony and Diachrony in the Composition of 1 Kings 8, 14-61*, Kampen, 1993
4. R. Stahl, *Von Weltengagement zu Weltüberwindung: Theologische Positionen im Danielbuch*, Kampen, 1994
5. J.N. Bremmer, *Sacred History and Sacred Texts in early Judaism. A Symposium in Honour of A.S. van der Woude*, Kampen, 1992
6. K. Larkin, *The Eschatology of Second Zechariah: A Study of the Formation of a Mantological Wisdom Anthology*, Kampen, 1994
7. B. Aland, *New Testament Textual Criticism, Exegesis and Church History: A Discussion of Methods*, Kampen, 1994
8. P.W. Van der Horst, *Hellenism-Judaism-Christianity: Essays on their Interaction*, Kampen, Second Enlarged Edition, 1998
9. C. Houtman, *Der Pentateuch: die Geschichte seiner Erforschung neben einer Auswertung*, Kampen, 1994
10. J. Van Seters, *The Life of Moses. The Yahwist as Historian in Exodus-Numbers*, Kampen, 1994
11. Tj. Baarda, *Essays on the Diatessaron*, Kampen, 1994
12. Gert J. Steyn, *Septuagint Quotations in the Context of the Petrine and Pauline Speeches of the Acta Apostolorum*, Kampen, 1995
13. D.V. Edelman, *The Triumph of Elohim, From Yahwisms to Judaisms*, Kampen, 1995
14. J.E. Revell, *The Designation of the Individual. Expressive Usage in Biblical Narrative*, Kampen, 1996
15. M. Menken, *Old Testament Quotations in the Fourth Gospel*, Kampen, 1996
16. V. Koperski, *The Knowledge of Christ Jesus my Lord. The High Christology of Philippians 3:7-11*, Kampen, 1996
17. M.C. De Boer, *Johannine Perspectives on the Death of Jesus*, Kampen, 1996
18. R.D. Anderson, *Ancient Rhetorical Theory and Paul*, Revised edition, Leuven, 1998
19. L.C. Jonker, *Exclusivity and Variety, Perspectives on Multi-dimensional Exegesis*, Kampen, 1996
20. L.V. Rutgers, *The Hidden Heritage of Diaspora Judaism*, Leuven, 1998
21. K. van der Toorn (ed.), *The Image and the Book*, Leuven, 1998
22. L.V. Rutgers, P.W. van der Horst (eds.), *The Use of Sacred Books in the Ancient World*, Leuven, 1998
23. E.R. Ekblad Jr., *Isaiah's Servant Poems According to the Septuagint. An Exegetical and Theological Study*, Leuven, 1999
24. R.D. Anderson Jr., *Glossary of Greek Rhetorical Terms*, Leuven, 2000

25. T. Stordalen, *Echoes of Eden*, Leuven, 2000
26. H. Lalleman-de Winkel, *Jeremiah in Prophetic Tradition*, Leuven, 2000
27. J.F.M. Smit, *"About the Idol Offerings"*. *Rhetoric, Social Context and Theology of Paul's Discourse in First Corinthians 8:1-11:1*, Leuven, 2000
28. T.J. Horner, *Listening to Trypho. Justin's Martyr's Dialogue Reconsiderd*, Leuven, 2001
29. D.G. Powers, *Salvation through Participation. An Examination of the Notion of the Believers' Corporate Unity with Christ in Early Christian Soteriology*, Leuven, 2001
30. J.M. Robinson, P. Hoffmann, J.S. Kloppenborg (eds.), *The Sayings Gospel Q in Greek and English with Parallels from the Gospels of Mark and Thomas*, Leuven, 2001
31. M.K. Birge, *The Language of Belonging. A Rhetorical Analysis of Kinship Language in First Corinthians*, Leuven, 2002

PRINTED ON PERMANENT PAPER • IMPRIME SUR PAPIER PERMANENT • GEDRUKT OP DUURZAAM PAPIER - ISO 9706

N.V. PEETERS S.A., KLEIN DALENSTRAAT 42, B-3020 HERENT